Kirby

D0564555

PRINCIPLES OF RESEARCH METHODOLOGY IN PHYSIOLOGICAL PSYCHOLOGY

Harper's Physiological Psychology series
under the Editorship of H. Philip Zeigler

PRINCIPLES OF RESEARCH METHODOLOGY IN PHYSIOLOGICAL PSYCHOLOGY

William G. Webster

Carleton University
Ottawa, Canada

HARPER & ROW, PUBLISHERS
New York   Evanston   San Francisco   London

To my professors and friends,

each of whom contributed in a unique and significant way to the development of my thinking about psychology

D. O. Hebb, R. Melzack, C. Baber, P. R. Cornwell, J. M. Warren, and E. C. Webster

Sponsoring Editor: George A. Middendorf
Project Editor: Cynthia Hausdorff
Designer: Rita Naughton
Production Supervisor: Will C. Jomarrón

PRINCIPLES OF RESEARCH METHODOLOGY IN PHYSIOLOGICAL PSYCHOLOGY

Copyright © 1975 by William G. Webster

All rights reserved. Printed in the United States of America. No part of this book may be used or reproduced in any manner whatsoever without written permission except in the case of brief quotations embodied in critical articles and reviews. For information address Harper & Row, Publishers, Inc., 10 East 53rd Street, New York, N.Y. 10022.

Library of Congress Cataloging in Publication Data
Webster, William G   1944–
   Principles of research methodology in physiological
psychology.

   Includes bibliographies and index.
   1. Psychology, Physiological.   2. Psychology,
Physiological—Laboratory manuals.   I. Title.
QP360.W4   612.8   75–1085
ISBN 0–06–046972–2

contents

preface

Everything in experimental research depends upon the method, for it is the method which gives the results. (Flourens, 1842) It is this astute observation of the great nineteenth-century French physiologist Pierre Flourens that provides the underlying theme for this book, and it is appropriate that it should, for it is Pierre Flourens who has provided the theme for much of physiological psychology during this past century.

The book is directed at the undergraduate student who has completed, or who is taking concurrently, a content course in physiological psychology and who has been exposed to basic concepts of psychological research. It attempts to examine and explore principles of research methodology in that portion of physiological psychology concerned with the study of brain-behavior relations. It is important for the student to appreciate this limitation in scope and to realize that the boundaries of the book are not those that delimit physiological psychology; to have adequately explored principles of research methodology in all of physiological psychology would have required a volume of considerably greater size than this. It is also important to realize that this book is concerned with principles of research methodology rather than research methodology per se. This should be evident in the laboratory exercises, many of which involve techniques and procedures different from those used in actual contemporary research. It is also evident in certain of the other chapters, which emphasize methods of study of brain-behavior relations from the viewpoint of their history, of the questions to which they have been applied, of the logic implicit in attempting to use them to answer certain kinds of questions, and of their strengths and limitations for providing insights into the nature of brain-behavior relations.

As indicated above, the laboratory exercises were designed to illustrate principles rather than to teach techniques. The advanced undergraduate or graduate student who wants to learn sophisticated techniques and who may be disappointed with this book is referred to Myers (1971, 1972) or Thompson and Patterson (1973). An important consideration in the design of the laboratory exercises was that they involve a minimum of expensive equipment so that despite constricted educational budgets, it would be possible for psychology departments to establish (or expand) teaching laboratories with multiple sets of equipment that allow several pairs of students to work simultaneously and to learn by observing their peers as well as by doing. To equip a teaching laboratory with the facilities necessary to carry out all the laboratory exercises as written is certainly not an inexpensive proposition. Perusal of the equipment requirements for the various exercises, however, will indicate the possibility of developing a laboratory course over a number of years, with an increasing number of exercises actually done each year, to spread out the capital costs. It is also quite feasible simply to eliminate certain labs or certain parts of labs from a course, or to make them into demonstrations, which would obviate the necessity for particular pieces of expensive equipment.

Another objective of the book is to attempt to dispel certain myths and to remove some of the mystique (promulgated by the popular press and not actively dispelled by many contemporary textbooks of physiological psychology) that for many students surrounds research methods in the neurosciences. These range from the relatively harmless mystique that surrounds electronic amplifiers, oscilloscopes, and polygraphs to much more serious myths of a conceptual nature concerning the state of understanding of brain-behavior relations as made evident through methods of neural ablation and stimulation, and electrophysiological recording. Exploration of the history and the logical foundation of these methods may make evident their strengths and especially their limitations for answering questions of brain-behavior relations. It is important for the student and the instructor to be aware that in the discussion of certain of these issues, little attempt has been made to present a balanced argument in the hope that it will provoke concern and discussion which can then be developed and guided by the informed instructor.

The book is not intended to be used alone in a course on research methods, for there is little consideration of the assessment of what is usually the dependent variable of physiological psychology, that is, behavioral change. An adequate consideration of methods developed to assess behavioral change would have involved a detailed consideration of the methods of experimental psychology and would have expanded this book beyond reasonable length. Furthermore, there is presently available an excellent book entitled *Analysis of Behavioral Change* (Weiskrantz, 1967) which, although now several years old, covers this ground well for the physiological psychologist. The use of parts of it (either as assigned reading or in lectures based on it) in conjunction with this book is highly recommended and should provide the student with a reasonable introduction to problems of research methodology.

In writing any book there are many people who play critical supporting roles, and preparing the Preface gives the author the particularly enjoyable experience of acknowledging their contributions. I am most fortunate to be associated with an institution that offers as much moral, material, and technical support as Carleton University has provided me during the preparation of the manuscript. The final versions of the photographs and illustrations were prepared with great care and skill by our Graphic Arts department, and in particular by Messrs. James Wright, Ron Poling, and John Barkley; various sorts of technical advice was provided by Mr. William Ferguson of the Science Workshop; and assistance in the typing of the numerous drafts was patiently provided by Mrs. Ruth McLean, Mrs. Gladys Michie, and Miss Lana Seabrooke.

The moral support I received from my colleagues and department chairman (first, Dr. T. J. Ryan and, more recently, Dr. T. N. Tombaugh) is gratefully acknowledged, as is the financial support I received from the Publication and Research Fund of the Faculty of Arts of Carleton University and, in small part, from research grant APA–0399 from the National Research Council of Canada, which facilitated my work in the library, the development of certain laboratory procedures, and the preparation of the manuscript. I am particularly pleased to acknowledge two sources of invaluable suggestions and comments. The first source was the students who used parts of the book in manuscript form in the research methods course I have taught for several years at Carleton University and who suggested many improvements in the laboratory procedures. The second source was Dr. H. Philip Zeigler, the editor of the Harper & Row Physiological Psychology Series. From the time I first approached Harper & Row with a partial manuscript, he has provided me with numerous suggestions that I know improved immensely the organization and content of the final product.

And finally, the contribution of my wife, Ikuko, and our daughter, Reiko, cannot be underestimated; it was Ikuko's constant support and understanding that made the completion of this book a possibility. It is only now that I can fully appreciate why the Preface of so many books ends with a grateful and heartfelt acknowledgment to a spouse.

W. G. W.

part one

NEUROANATOMICAL FOUNDATIONS

1

ONTOGENETIC AND PHYLOGENETIC DEVELOPMENT OF THE MAMMALIAN NERVOUS SYSTEM

NEUROANATOMY AND PSYCHOLOGY

Neuropsychology is a discipline concerned with understanding brain-behavior relations in the broadest sense of the term, and as such can be classified as one of the neurosciences. It is therefore reasonable to expect that students of physiological psychology be acquainted with the sister neurosciences, especially neuroanatomy, which is the foundation for all the others. Without some appreciation of the basic structure of the nervous system and a familiarity with the names of the principal regions of the brain, the student will have difficulty in communicating with individuals working in other neurosciences and in working in his own discipline in attempting to understand problems of psychology from a neurological orientation.

At the outset, however, a word of caution must be extended to those who believe that if they learn the detailed structure of the brain and how all the nuclei are interconnected, they will understand complex behavior, given the assumption that complex behavior is the product of the operation of these neural circuits. Although it can reasonably be assumed that behavior is reducible to neural events, neuroanatomy is concerned principally with the *structure* of neural circuits and bears little upon those *functional* properties of neural circuits, such as inhibition, excitation, and the temporal patterning of neuronal firing, that are important in the organization of behavior. It is theoretically possible to ascertain functional relationships among neurons, but to attempt to construct behavior from neuroanatomy poses not only technical problems, but also logical ones.

Neuropsychologists, like most scientists, generally subscribe to a reductionist hypothesis about the nature of the universe. For the neuropsychologist, this hypothesis is that complex behaviors can be reduced to simpler behaviors and that these in turn can be reduced to physiological events, and so on. However, one must understand that a constructionist hypothesis is not a necessary corollary of a reductionist hypothesis—that is, the ability to reduce matter or events to constituent parts or to fundamental laws that underlie them in no way implies the ability to reconstruct matter or events given only the constituent parts or only the fundamental laws. For psychology, the ability to reduce complex behaviors to simple behaviors does not imply that complex behaviors can be reconstructed given only the understanding of simple behaviors; the complex behaviors may possess certain systemic properties not found in the simpler behaviors.

Similarly, the ability to reduce simple behaviors to neural events, to understand behavior in terms of its neural substrates, does not imply that simple behaviors can be reconstructed or can be deduced given only a knowledge of neural systems. Each increasingly molar level of organization has certain operating principles or certain systemic properties that can be understood in terms of the more molecular levels of analysis, but that cannot be deduced *a priori* from the more molecular levels. Arbib (1972) gives as an example of the emergence of systemic properties a counting device whose output at time $(t+1)$ equals $(n+1)$, when its input at time (t) equals (n). Viewing this device in isolation would suggest that its function is to add 1 to the input. However, if two copies of this device are interconnected in a closed-loop fashion so that the output of one forms the input for the second and the output of the second forms the input for the first, then an analysis of one of the two identical devices would suggest that its function was to generate even numbers, and an analysis of the other would suggest that its function was to generate odd numbers. As Arbib (1972) concludes, ". . . even if we have a complete understanding of the parts . . . we may not perceive the crucial patterns in their behavior unless we can integrate them into the right totality. . ." (p. 61).

An understanding of brain-behavior relations can be approached only by examining both the brain and behavior and attempting to integrate these different levels of analysis. The physiological psychologist must operate on at least two levels, for only by understanding the principles of behavior, by speculating on the neurological mechanisms that must underlie them (that is, developing what Hebb [1955, 1958] has called "conceptual nervous systems"), and by understanding basic neurological processes can he begin to comprehend behavior in terms of those neurological processes.

PHYLOGENETIC APPROACHES TO NEUROANATOMY

One of the easiest and most interesting ways to gain some appreciation of the structure of the brain and to understand the logic of its morphological organization is to consider mammalian neuroanatomy in terms of the evolutionary development of the nervous system from ancestral to contemporary forms and in terms of the ontogenetic development of the nervous system through embryonic stages to the adult form. Unlike the development of electronic instruments in which newer models may be totally different from earlier models, the phylogenetic development of the mammalian nervous system has involved the addition of new components and the modification of existing components, and these developments are reflected in the ontogenetic development of the brain.

To adopt an evolutionary approach necessitates an appreciation of certain assumptions and problems associated with the study of comparative neuroanatomy. The central problem is that there is no way to directly observe the changes which have occurred in brain structure and behavior during the course of evolution, since the forms from which modern species evolved are long extinct and since soft brain tissues do not fossilize and have left no fossil record of their structure. We can only make inferences about the structure of the ancestral forms by considering the variation in structure or behavior of the modern forms that are presumed to have evolved from common ancestral forms. Such inferences require knowledge of, or at least assumptions about, the evolutionary relationships that exist among species, and this is the domain of the paleontologist. Paleontologists concur that the relationship is best conceptualized not in terms of the classical Aristotelian model of a phylogenetic scale (*scala naturae*), or a continuous ladder, on which each modern species has its place, but in terms of a phylogenetic tree on which each modern species is like a leaf located at the end of a branch, sharing common ancestral forms with other modern species, but not being ancestral to other modern forms. Figures 1–1 and 1–2 show presumed evolutionary relationships among vertebrates and placental mammals, respectively, as depicted by Romer (1966). These figures are working hypotheses, or models, or even guesses, and are not necessarily facts; but if these depictions are valid, it is clear that the brains of, for example, modern teleost fish, frogs, lizards, rats, cats, monkeys, apes, and man can in no way be conceptualized as representing the course of evolutionary development of the vertebrate brain, since none of these modern forms is ancestral to another.

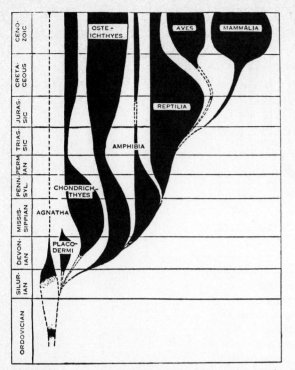

Figure 1–1. An evolutionary tree of vertebrate classes. The thickness of the various branches indicates the relative abundance of each class through time. The common names for the modern classes are: Agnatha: jawless vertebrates; Chondrichthyes: cartilaginous fishes; Osteichthyes: bony fishes; Amphibia: amphibians; Reptilia: reptiles; Aves: birds; Mammalia: mammals. (From A. S. Romer, *Vertebrate Paleontology* (3rd ed.). Chicago: University of Chicago Press, 1966, Figure 14. Copyright © 1966 by The University of Chicago.)

Figure 1–2 shows that the orders of placental mammals probably evolved from a single common ancestral form (although not the same one from which the marsupials and monotremes evolved). In no way, then, is the rat ancestral to the cat or the monkey; all have evolved quite independently from a common ancestral form. This model has enormous implications for neuropsychology. As we shall see at the end of this chapter, the ancestral form of mammals probably had very little neocortex, and the evolutionary development of the neocortex in the different mammalian orders has therefore proceeded along relatively independent lines. For neuropsychology, this means, among other things, that the cerebral cortex of species of one order may bear only the slightest functional similarity to those of other orders.

Only through a consideration of the variation found among the presumed descendants of common ancestral forms can the structure and organization of ancestral forms be inferred. One problem to be mentioned only briefly is that although much is known about the structure of the brain of certain mammals, especially primates, very little is known about the structure of the brain of most nonmammalian forms; and without as thorough a knowledge of, for example, the modern reptilian nervous system as of the modern mammalian nervous system, we end up with a biased view of the variation which is in fact found among the descendants of common ancestors, and hence in a rather poor position to infer the nature of the common ancestor.

FORMATION AND DERIVATIVES OF THE NEURAL TUBE

The central nervous system of mammals develops from the neural tube, which appears very early in the course of embryonic development. The dorsal plate of cells along the midline, called the dorsal ectoderm, thickens, and the cells along the edges of the plate divide faster than those in the middle. This results in the formation of what is called the neural groove. As this groove enlarges, the edges begin to approximate one another, and finally meet the close. The process, depicted in Figure 1–3 in a series of frontal sections through the dorsal portion of the embryo, results in the formation of the neural tube which runs along the entire length of the organism and from which the nervous system develops. As indicated in the lower portion of Figure 1–3, two plates of cells can be differentiated quite early within the neural tube: the alar plate, constituting the dorsal or upper half of the neural tube and the basal plate, constituting the ventral or lower half. These plates are separated by an indentation called the sulcus limitans. The significance of the alar and basal plates lies in the fact that it is from them that the afferent and efferent systems, respectively, develop. Hence it is no coincidence that the sensory or afferent components of the nervous system *tend* to be located dorsally, whereas the motor or efferent components *tend* to be located ventrally.

The neural tube enlarges at its anterior end, forming three expansions that are its primary derivatives. They are called, from anterior to posterior, the prosencephalon (or forebrain), the mesencephalon (or midbrain), and the rhombencephalon (or hindbrain). Two other primary neural tube derivatives are the spinal cord, which is the caudal extension of the brain, and the ventricles. The ventricles of the brain and the central canal of the spinal cord, which are derived from the central canal of the neural tube, are continuous and filled with clear cerebrospinal fluid. Figures 1–4 and 1–5 illustrate from a dorsal and a

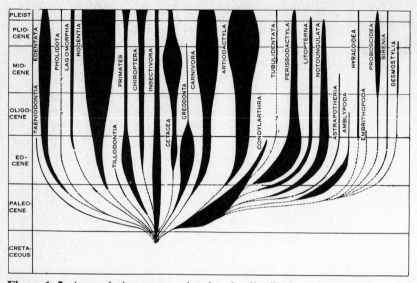

Figure 1–2. An evolutionary tree showing the distribution of placental mammals through time. Note how the various mammalian orders have evolved from a common ancestor. Examples of members of various orders include: Edentata: South American anteaters, tree sloths, armadillos; Pholidota: Old World pangolin (an anteater); Lagomorpha: hares and rabbits; Rodentia: gnawing animals (except rabbits) including rats, squirrels, guinea pigs; Primates: tree shrews, monkeys, apes, man; Chiroptera: bats; Insectivora: hedgehogs, moles; Cetacea: whales; Carnivora: racoons, cats, dogs, bears; Artiodactyla: even-toed ungulates, such as camels, deer, cows, sheep, hippopotamuses; Tubulidentata: aardvarks (an African anteater); Perissodactyla: odd-toed ungulates such as horses, zebras, rhinoceros; Hyracoidea: conies of Africa and Syria; Proboscidea: elephants, mammoths, mastodons; Sirenia: seacows. (From A. S. Romer, *Vertebrate paleontology* (3rd ed.). Chicago: University of Chicago Press, 1966, Figure 316. Copyright © 1966 by The University of Chicago.)

lateral viewpoint, respectively, the formation and further differentiation of these primary derivatives. Table 1–1 lists some of the principal structures that result from this further differentiation.

THE SPINAL CORD

Figure 1–6 shows sections of an adult human spinal cord at the sacral, lumbar, thoracic, cervical, and upper cervical spinal levels. These sections, prepared using histological techniques to be discussed in Chapter 3, have been stained so as to increase the differentiation between white and gray matter—that is, between the myelinated fibers and cell bodies. As will be clear in Laboratory Exercise I, the differentiation in unstained tissue is not very sharp. The central part of the spinal cord is made up of gray matter consisting of cell bodies and very short axons and the periphery is made up of fiber tracts. Some of the prin-

cipal sensory and motor tracts are illustrated in Figure 1–7.

The ascending fiber tracts running along the dorsal portion of the spinal cord are derived from the embryonic alar plate and are associated with afferent functions; those which constitute the ventral motor portions of the spinal cord are derived from the embryonic basal plate. A comparison of Figure 1–6 with the spinal cord section shown in Figure 1–7 makes it clear that many of the pathways cannot be differentiated in normal tissue. For example, the gracile and the cuneate pathways are virtually indistinguishable and appear as a single dorsal column pathway. Only through the use of histological degeneration techniques like those discussed in Chapter 3 can individual fiber tracts be made evident and distinct enough to study.

The central gray matter of the spinal cord has the appearance of an H-shape. Into the dorsal horns project the afferent fibers, which enter the spinal cord

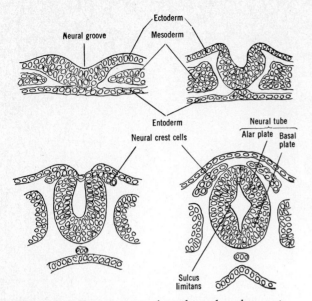

Figure 1–3. Transverse sections through embryos at increasing ages, illustrating the formation of the neural tube. (From E. Gardner, *Fundamentals of Neurology* (5th ed.). Philadelphia: Saunders, 1969, Figure 34.)

through the dorsal root portion of the segmental spinal nerves. From the ventral horns project the motor fibers that make up the ventral roots of the segmental spinal nerves. Again, these dorsal and ventral roots are derived from the embryonic alar and basal plates, respectively. A large portion of the central gray matter consists of intermediate or internuncial neurons that are neither afferent nor efferent and that do not relay information, but process it in, for example, the control of segmental and suprasegmental

reflexes and the modulation of afferent input (Melzack and Wall, 1965).

In Laboratory Exercise I, prepared slides of human spinal cord sections similar to those shown in Figure 1–6 may be available for examination, and you should note the diameter of the spinal cord and the vast amount of information transmitted through the fiber tracts and processed in the central gray matter. As would be expected, there is a great increase in the absolute size of the cord as a whole and in the size of the ascending and descending fiber tracts in particular as one ascends from the sacral through the upper cervical region. You should also note the differences among the various spinal segmental levels in the relative proportion of central gray cells to fibers, as well as in the absolute number of central gray cells.

Analogous to the 31 pairs of spinal nerves, of which there is one pair for each spinal segment, are the cranial nerves that enter and leave the brain directly rather than through the spinal cord. Generally speaking, the cranial nerves are derived from the same pattern of neural organization as are the spinal nerves; most would have been the spinal nerves of those segments of the neural tube from which the brain itself is derived.

Three general types of cranial nerves can be distinguished. First are the three special sensory cranial nerves consisting of the olfactory tract (I), the optic tract (II), and the acoustic nerve (VIII). They are not derived from embryological precursors of the spinal nerves and consequently are not analogous to spinal nerves, although they are derived from the alar plate. They are of special significance in the understanding of the phylogenetic development of the

Table 1–1 Derivatives of primary vesicles

PRIMARY VESICLE	SUBDIVISION	DERIVATIVES	LUMEN
Prosencephalon	Telencephalon	Cerebral cortex Basal nuclei Hippocampus	Lateral ventricles
	Diencephalon	Thalamus Hypothalamus	IIIrd ventricle
Mesencephalon	Mesencephalon	Tectum Tegmentum Cerebral peduncles	Cerebral aqueduct
Rhombencephalon	Metencephalon	Pons Cerebellum	IVth ventricle
	Myelencephalon	Medulla oblongata	IVth ventricle
Remainder of neural tube		Spinal cord	Central canal

From E. Gardner, *Fundamentals of neurology.* (5th ed.) Philadelphia: Saunders, 1969, Table 1.

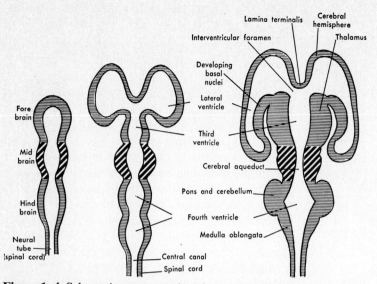

Figure 1–4. Schematic representation, from a dorsal perspective, of the embryonic development of the brain during three stages from the formation of the primary derivatives of the neural tube to the early development of the cerebral hemispheres. (From E. Gardner, *Fundamentals of neurology* (5th ed.). Philadelphia: Saunders, 1969, Figure 35.)

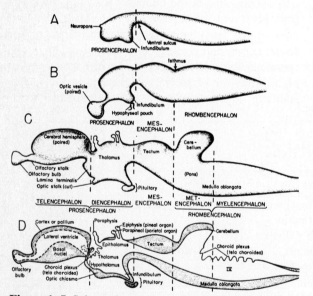

Figure 1–5. Schematic representation, from a lateral perspective, of the embryonic development of principal structures of the brain. (From A. S. Romer, *The vertebrate body* (3rd ed.). Philadelphia: Saunders, 1962, Figure 378.)

brain, for they have been associated with the forebrain, midbrain, and hindbrain regions, respectively. This suggests that in the evolutionary development of the nervous system, the forebrain has been associated with olfactory functions, the midbrain with optic or visual functions, and the hindbrain with acoustic-vestibular functions.

The cranial nerves that are analogous to dorsal root spinal nerves and that are derived from the embryonic alar plate are the terminal nerve (0), the trigeminal nerve (V), the facial nerve (VII), the glossopharyngeal nerve (IX), and the vagus nerve (X), with its accessory nerve (XI) found in mammals. The cranial nerves that are analogous to the somatic motor nerves and that are derived from the embryonic basal plate of the neural tube are the three which innervate the external muscles of the eye—the oculomotor (III), the trochlearis (IV), and the abducens (VI) nerves—and one which innervates the muscles of the tongue, the hypoglossal nerve (XII).

Despite the existence of distinct embryological precursors of sensory and motor systems and despite the apparently clear differentiation of sensory and motor systems in the nervous system, one must be cautious of too readily adopting a *sensory-motor* model, or an *input-output model,* or a *two-neuron* model of the entire nervous system, models that characterize nervous system organization in terms of telephone cables

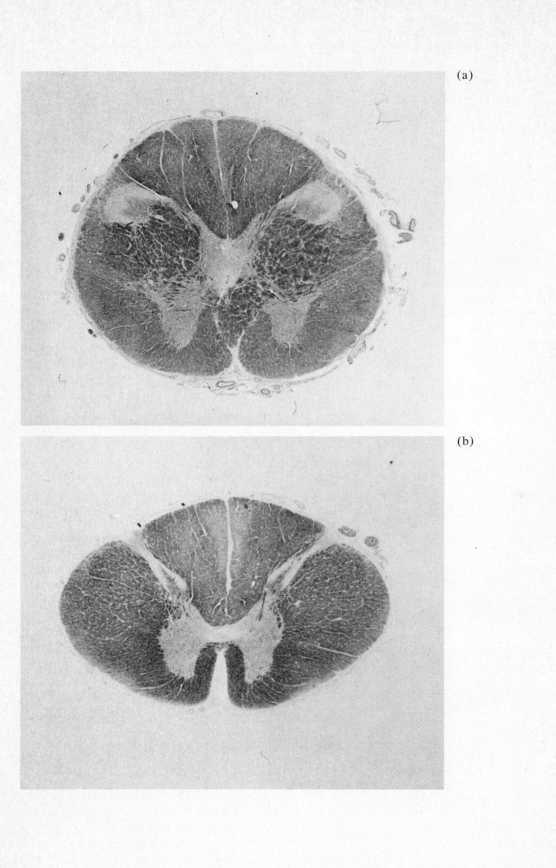

(a)

(b)

(c)

(d)

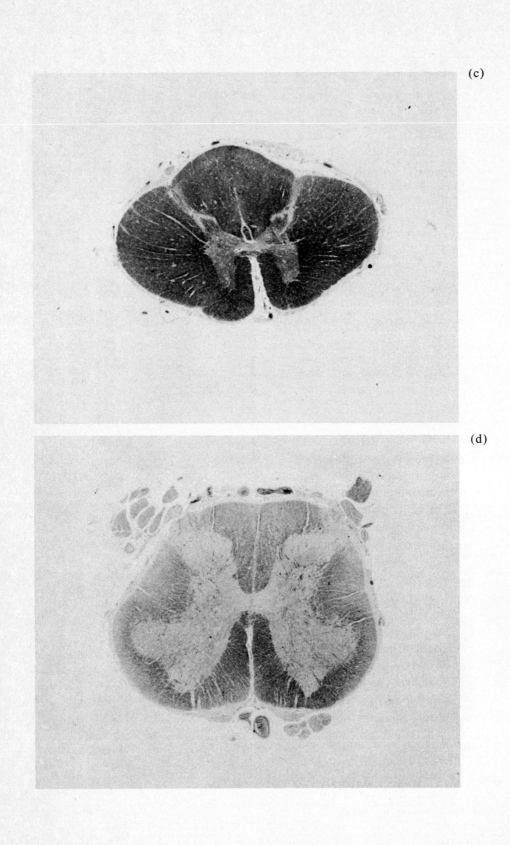

(e)

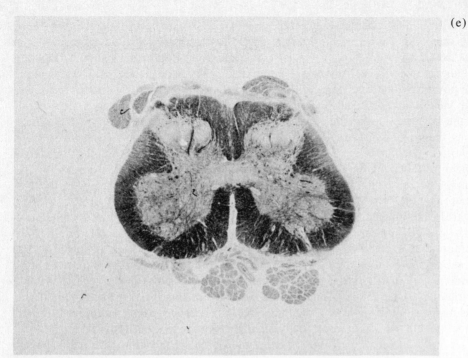

Figure 1–6. Photomicrographs of stained sections through a human spinal cord at (a) the upper cervical level, (b) the cervical level, (c) the thoracic level, (d) the lumbar level, and (e) the sacral level. The sections were prepared using a modification of the technique of Kluver and Barrera, discussed in Chapter 3, which differentially stains fiber tracts and cell bodies. In these photomicrographs, the more darkly stained portions are fiber tracts and the lightly stained portions are cell bodies.

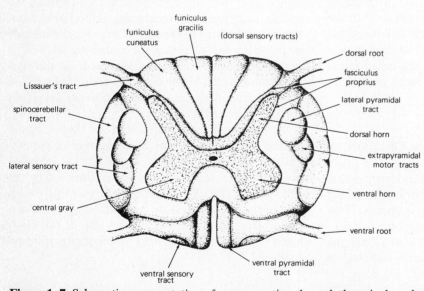

Figure 1–7. Schematic representation of a cross section through the spinal cord at the cervical level. Sensory tracts are labeled on the left and motor tracts on the right. (From *Physiological psychology* by Peter M. Milner. Copyright © 1970 by Holt, Rinehart and Winston, Inc. Reproduced by permission of Holt, Rinehart and Winston, Inc.)

transmitting information to and from higher centers. Such models have played a dominant role in the modern history of conceptualization of brain function, and these models, and the problem areas implicit in them, still have a powerful influence on contemporary thought. Such models are especially tempting when considering the organization of the spinal cord and brainstem, as there are apparently such distinct sensory and motor regions, but they ignore the existence of those neurons that synapse between the sensory and the motor neurons, the intermediate or internuncial neurons that form what Herrick (1922) called the "great intermediate net," those networks of cells that underlie events and processes of psychological interest and importance. In the nervous system of most vertebrates, the intermediate neurons certainly predominate. In fact, of the estimated 10 billion neurons found in the nervous system of advanced primates, as many as 99.95 percent may be intermediate neurons (Nauta and Karten, 1970).

To attempt to characterize the nervous system in strict sensory and motor terms, or to attempt to characterize its organization with anything less than a *three-neuron* model or a model that recognizes sensory, intermediate, and motor neurons, implicitly ignores a major segment of the nervous system. Such sensory-motor models of the nervous system also ignore feedback mechanisms that during the past twenty-five years have been shown to operate at all levels of the nervous system. These mechanisms clearly involve sensory and motor processes, but the change in emphasis from an implicit linking of the output to the input to a linking of the input to the output introduces principles of nervous organization and behavior quite different from those implicit in sensory-motor conceptualizations.

DERIVATIVES OF THE RHOMBENCEPHALON

The most posterior of the three primary neural tube derivatives is the rhombencephalon, so called because of its rhomboid shape in mammals. This becomes differentiated into the metencephalon (L, *meta,* boundary; Gk, *enkephalos,* brain) and the myelencephalon (Gk, *myelos,* marrow) shown in Figure 1–5. The former develops into the pons, the cerebellum, and the anterior portion of the medulla oblongata forming the boundary with the midbrain, and the latter develops into the posterior portion of the medulla that merges with the spinal cord, the "marrow" of the spine.

The medulla is similar in its general organization and structure to the spinal cord, and at the posterior portion appears as an enlarged spinal cord. The dorsal columns synapse in the cuneate and gracile nuclei in the medulla, and the fibers from these nuclei project anteriorly as the medial lemniscus tract, which in turn synapse in the ventrobasal complex of the thalamus. The pyramidal pathways, associated with efferent or motor functions, pass along the floor of the medulla and most fibers cross or decussate in the posterior portion. In the rostral portion of the gray matter of the medulla are nuclei associated with the cranial nerves associated with the autonomic functions of respiration, heart action, and gastrointestinal action, many of which emerge from the medulla. Also appearing here is the reticular formation, not part of either the sensory or motor horns, which extends through the entire brainstem (medulla and midbrain) to the thalamus. It is innervated by the phylogenetically older parts of the afferent systems.

Sitting on top of the medulla is the cerebellum, a major integrating center associated with motor coordination. This function is consistent with the close association of the acoustic nerve during evolutionary development, since that nerve includes a vestibular component which relays information about the direction of gravitational pull and head rotation. The cerebellum is connected with the rest of the nervous system through three pairs of cerebellar peduncles or fiber tracts, the superior or anterior pair conducting information from the cerebellum to the midbrain, the middle or lateral pair conducting information from the cerebral cortex to the cerebellum, and the inferior or posterior pair of peduncles containing afferent fibers from the midbrain and spinal cord. On the ventral surface of the hindbrain is the pons, a protrusion resulting from the great number of fibers entering and leaving the cerebellum.

As the spinal cord merges with the hindbrain, the central canal moves to the dorsal surface of the medulla and expands laterally, forming what is called the IVth ventricle, the roof of which is formed by the cerebellum. The IVth ventricle can be clearly seen in Figure 1–8, which is an exploded diagram of the brainstem. Also evident is the merging of the hindbrain with the midbrain, and the midbrain with the forebrain.

DERIVATIVES OF THE MESENCEPHALON

While the hindbrain lies around the IVth ventricle, the midbrain or mesencephalon (Gk, *mesos,*

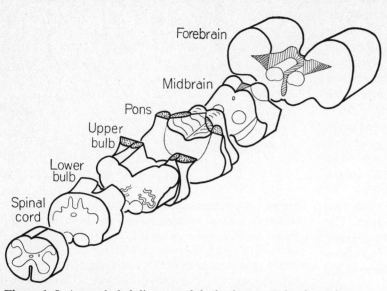

Figure 1–8. An exploded diagram of the brainstem. It has been drawn with the cerebellum removed, making the location of the IVth ventricle very evident. Note the colliculi on the dorsal surface of the midbrain. (From H. C. Elliott, *Textbook of neuroanatomy* (2nd ed.). Philadelphia: Lippincott, 1969, Figure 8–8.)

middle) can be described as the part of the brainstem through which passes the aqueduct of Sylvius, or the cerebral aqueduct, connecting the IVth with the IIIrd ventricle. The walls and floor of the midbrain consist of fiber tracts, those situated ventrally being the cerebral peduncles or pyramidal motor tracts, and those situated dorsally being ascending pathways, such as the medial lemniscus. The gray matter making up the side walls of the midbrain is the tegmentum and that making up the dorsal surface is the tectum, or corpora quadrigemina.

In ancestral forms, and in modern teleost fish and amphibians, the tectum can be regarded as the major integrating center for afferent information. During the evolution of the brain the tectum developed in association with the optic nerve (II), one of the special sensory cranial nerves, and can be legitimately regarded as a vertebrate visual center. In birds and many teleost fish the tectum developed into the very large optic lobes, but in mammals the tectum remained relatively small, sharing visual functions with certain uniquely mammalian forebrain areas to be described later. It has come to consist of four differentiated bumps on the roof of the midbrain, the anterior pair, called the superior colliculi, having visual functions, and the posterior pair, the inferior colliculi, having auditory functions.

DERIVATIVES OF THE PROSENCEPHALON— THE DIENCEPHALON

From a phylogenetic perspective, the special sensory cranial nerve associated with the forebrain is the olfactory nerve (I). While the forebrain or prosencephalon (Gk, *pro,* before, in front) has retained an olfactory function in mammals, it is the region of the nervous system that has shown the greatest differentiation, expansion, and specialization in the evolutionary development of the mammalian brain from ancestral forms. Although the organization of the mid- and hindbrain regions shows a high degree of consistency among vertebrate classes, suggesting perhaps parallel or convergent evolution or, more likely, lack of change from the common ancestral form, there are major differences with respect to forebrain development and organization among mammals.

Anterior to the midbrain, the cerebral aqueduct expands to form the IIIrd ventricle. Situated on either side of the ventricle and forming its lateral walls is the diencephalon (Gk, *dia,* through or between), one of the two divisions of the embryonic prosencephalon. This is a paired structure consisting of four "layers" or collections of cells called, from dorsal to ventral position, the epithalamus, the dorsal thalamus, the subthalamus, and the hypothalamus. The dorsal thalamus, usually referred to simply as the thalamus, and the hypothalamus are the two areas that have been of most concern to physiological psychologists.

A diagram of a primate thalamus is shown in Figure 1–9. An egg-shaped structure with the wide end situated posteriorly, it is made up of a number of nuclei that are often classified in terms of their input-output relations. The first category include the so-called sensory relay nuclei, which receive direct afferent input and which have direct projections to the cerebral cortex. One of these, the medial geniculate body, is associated with the auditory system. It is connected to the inferior colliculus by a band of fibers called the brachium of the inferior colliculus. The lateral geniculate body, associated with the visual system, receives its input through the optic tract. The ventrobasal complex is associated with the somatosensory system and receives its input principally from the medial lemniscus tract, which originates in the dorsal column nuclei. The second category includes the association nuclei, which do not receive direct sensory input but which do have direct connections with the cerebral cortex. The medialis dorsalis, for instance, projects to the dorsolateral frontal cortex, while the pulvinar and lateral posterior nuclei project to the so-called posterior cortical association areas. Some of the cortical projection areas of both sensory relay and association nuclei of the thalamus in the primate are shown in Figure 1–10. The third cate-

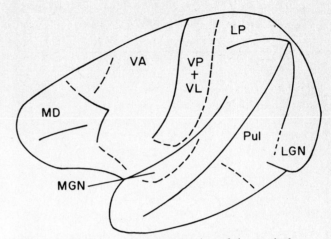

Figure 1–10. Schematic representation of the cortical projection areas of selected thalamic nuclei in the rhesus monkey. *Abbreviations:* LGN, lateral geniculate nucleus; LP, lateralis posterior; MD, medialis dorsalis; MGN, medial geniculate; PUL, pulvinar; VA, ventralis anterior; VL, ventralis lateralis; VP, ventralis posterior (VL and VP together make up the ventrobasal complex).

gory includes the intrinsic nuclei, often called the midline or intralaminar nuclei. These do not receive direct sensory input or project *directly* to the neocortex, but are part of a nonspecific afferent system that includes the reticular formation.

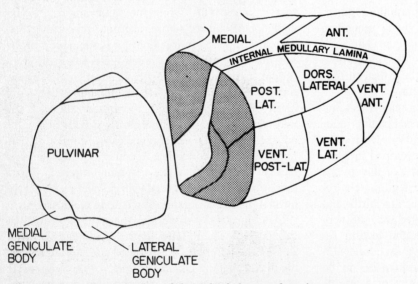

Figure 1–9. A schematic view of the right thalamus of a primate, sectioned to show the internal arrangement of nuclei. (Adapted from an original painting by Frank H. Netter, M.D., from *The CIBA collection of medical illustrations*. Copyright by CIBA Pharmaceutical Company, Division of CIBA–GEIGY Corporation. All rights reserved.)

The development of the thalamus has closely paralleled the development of the neocortex in the evolution of mammals. Modern species with poorly developed or poorly differentiated neocortices typically show a corresponding lack of differentiation among the thalamic nuclei, and the relative size and degree of differentiation of particular cortical areas corresponds to the size and differentiation of their associated thalamic nuclei.

In terms of embryonic development, the thalamus develops from the alar plate, whereas the hypothalamus, the more ventral portion of the diencephalon, develops from the embryonic basal plate. As might be expected, then, the hypothalamus is associated with efferent or motor functions, particularly those of a visceral nature. It is the major brain structure associated with the innervation of the autonomic nervous system. The highly differentiated nuclei that comprise the hypothalamus are closely associated through a portal vein system with the pituitary gland or hypophysis, a structure which regulates endocrine function. Many of the nuclei associated with internal regulation clearly operate on a negative feedback principle, detecting deviations in the internal state and initiating physiological processes to correct them. Accordingly, this "visceral motor center" is considerably different from being a simple efferent or motor center and is better conceptualized in terms of being a servomechanism than in sensory or motor terms.

DERIVATIVES OF THE PROSENCEPHALON— THE TELENCEPHALON

To acquire an understanding of the basic organization of the cerebral hemispheres in modern mammals, it is important to know the probable course of evolutionary development of the telencephalon (Gk, *telos,* end). The forebrain cerebral hemispheres developed from an anterior olfactory lobe of the brain, and in ancestral forms each hemisphere probably consisted of an undifferentiated layer of cells, called the paleopallium, with projections from the olfactory bulb passing through it to the hypothalamic and habenular (epithalamic) areas. From these areas, fibers projected to the midbrain for integration with other afferent information. This type of primitive forebrain organization, depicted in Figure 1–11, is found in the modern cyclostomes, such as the lamprey and hagfish, and forms the basis of the inference regarding the ancestral form.

In amphibians the forebrain is differentiated into three types of tissue: the paleopallium or paleocor-tex, associated with the olfactory bulb, the archipallium or archicortex located on the dorsolateral surface, and the basal nuclei situated ventrally (Figure 1–11). The further differentiation that first appeared in the early reptilian forms involved the ventral expansion of the paleocortex, pushing the basal nuclei into the hemispheres, and the dorsal expansion of the archicortex. With the evolutionary development of the advanced reptiles and the early mammals, the neocortex or isocortex made its first appearance. It is this tissue that shows the massive expansion in mammalian brain development. As the neocortex expanded, the paleocortex was pushed ventrally and was separated from the neocortex by the rhinal fissure, the one fissure common to all mammalian brains including those of lissencephalic or smooth brained species. In the "advanced" mammalian stages, as depicted in Figure 1–11, the further expansion of the neocortex resulted in an infolding of cortical tissue producing the gyri and fissures found in many mammalian brains.

The internal structure of the forebrain developed around the lateral ventricles from the archicortex and the basal nuclei. The paleocortex retained a surface position in the most ventral portion of the brain adjacent to the brainstem, and is called the pyriform cortex or hippocampal gyrus. This is not to be confused with the hippocampus, a large internal structure that developed from the archicortex. The hippocampus has close connections with the diencephalon through the fornix, which passes through the septal region from the hippocampus to the mammillary bodies of the hypothalamus. The caudate nucleus, the lenticular nuclei, the amygdaloid nuclei, and the claustrum developed from the basal nuclei. The caudate has a large head and a long tapering body and tail. The head is situated anteriorly, dorsolateral to the septum, and the body and tail surround the thalamus. The lenticular nuclei include the putamen and globus pallidus, which some anatomists argue is diencephalic. They are separated from the head and body of the caudate by the internal capsule, a massive bundle of fibers from the cerebral cortex that forms the cerebral peduncles in the midbrain. Because there are small but clearly visible bundles of white matter interconnecting the caudate and lenticular nuclei, which give it a striated appearance, these two structures together are sometimes referred to as the corpus striatum. Separated from the lenticular nuclei by the external capsule is a small band of gray matter called the claustrum. At the tip of the tail of the caudate in the ventrolateral portion of the forebrain is the amygdaloid nucleus. The corpus striatum,

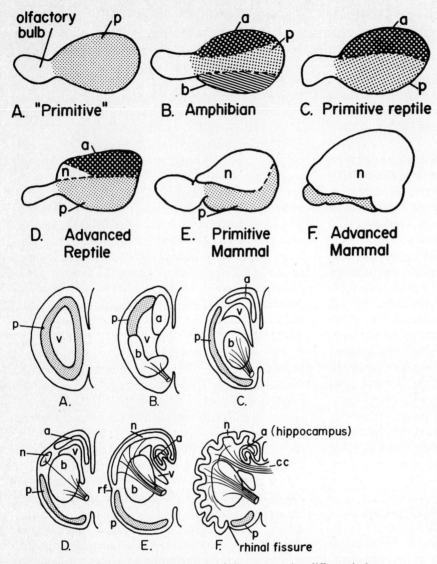

Figure 1–11. Schematic representation of the progressive differentiation of the cerebral hemispheres. Upper diagrams are lateral views of the left hemisphere and the lower diagrams are corresponding frontal sections through the left hemisphere. *Abbreviations:* a, archicortex; b, basal nuclei; cc, corpus callosum; n, neocortex; p, paleocortex; rf, rhinal fissure; v, lateral ventricle. (From A. S. Romer, *The vertebrate body* (3rd ed.). Philadelphia: Saunders, 1962, Figures 394–395.)

the claustrum, and the amygdala are referred to collectively as the basal ganglia.

Note that the paired cerebral hemispheres are not completely independent but are connected by several forebrain commissures, the principal ones being the corpus callosum, the anterior commissure, the posterior commissure, and the psalterium or hippocampal commissure.

THE NEOCORTEX

The neocortex is often referred to as the cerebral cortex, but this is not strictly correct, as the neocortex is but one of three types of cortex. The equation of terms, however, reflects the fact that in mammals the neocortex is the most predominant feature of the brain, having pushed the archicortex into the interior of the hemispheres and having displaced the paleocortex to the most ventral portion of the hemisphere surface in the course of its expansion.

Considering the relatively small amount of neocortex probably possessed by the ancestral form common to all mammals, one implication of the evolutionary relationship among mammals depicted in Figure 1–2 is that the neocortex evolved quite independently in the various orders of mammals. This makes it difficult to consider the cortex of a "generalized mammal" and necessitates a consideration of the pattern of neocortical evolution across mammalian orders.

The traditional model of neocortical evolution, based on the sensory-motor physiology and psychology of the late nineteenth century (which will be considered in Chapter 5), assumed that the cortex of the ancestral form consisted of distinct modality-specific sensory cortical areas which became differentiated from a general sensory cortex at a very early stage in development. These two presumed stages are shown in Figures 1–12 and 1–13. This model, then, implies that there should be only negligible differences among species in the organization of sensory cortex despite the independent neocortical evolution (as these areas were assumed present at the first branching and were assumed to remain unchanged). Hence, differences among species in the size or the amount of neocortex were to be interpreted in terms of the development and expansion of "association" cortex intercalated among these stable sensory cortical areas. This association cortex was assumed to form the neural substrates of intelligence, seen to be the capacity to form associations between stimuli.

I. T. Diamond has proposed a different model of neocortical evolution based on comparative neuroanatomical and behavioral considerations. In common with the traditional model, the neocortex of the ancestral form is seen as having been a highly generalized and nondifferentiated layer of cells receiving projections from an equally generalized and nondifferentiated thalamus (Figure 1–12). At this stage the tectum was the major sensory integrating center, and in particular a visual center, and probably sent projections to the generalized thalamus. Diamond and Hall (1969) have argued that the subsequent development from this early mammalian ancestral form consisted of major changes in thalamocortical organization. First, there was the differentiation of the thalamus into relatively distinct nuclei, some of which came to receive direct input from the sensory receptor systems through phylogenetically new pathways. In the case of the visual system, the retina became

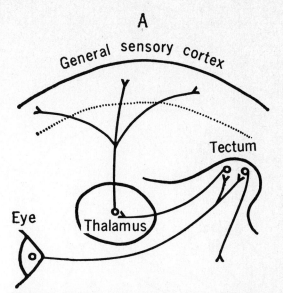

Figure 1–12. Schematic representation of the relatively undifferentiated thalamocortical neuroanatomical organization presumed to have existed in a reptilian-like ancestral form. (From I. T. Diamond and W. C. Hall, Evolution of neocortex. *Science,* 1969, **164,** 251–262, Figure 4A. Copyright © 1969 by the American Association for the Advancement of Science.)

connected directly with the lateral geniculate nucleus (LGN) of the thalamus, but did not lose its original projections to the tectum, and the retinotectal pathway formed direct connections with the part of the early thalamus that developed into the lateral posterior nucleus (LP). Hand in hand with the increased thalamic differentiation was a differentiation of the cortex into visual, auditory, somatosensory, and motor areas. Where this model departs from the traditional model, however, is in its assumption that the thalamocortical differentiation was only partial. As indicated in Figure 1–13, the visual system of the presumed ancestral form was assumed to have much overlap between the projections from LGN to the cortex and from LP to a belt of cortex between visual and auditory cortex. This early form, ancestral to all modern mammals, is seen as possessing a partially differentiated thalamocortical system that integrated the phylogenetically new with the phylogenetically older components of the sensory systems. In the subsequent independent evolution of mammalian orders, these systems showed differential expansion and differentiation in response to environmental and evolutionary pressures.

The common ancestral form to which reference has been made obviously has been long extinct and

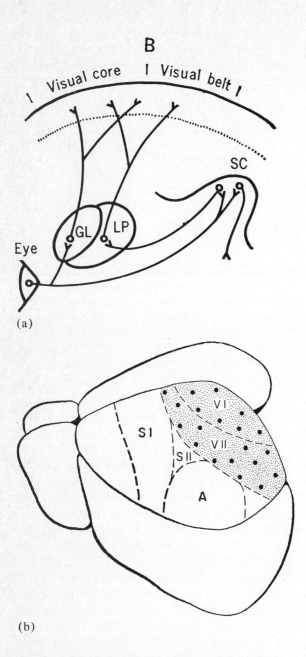

(a)

(b)

Figure 1–13. (a) Schematic representation of the neuroanatomical organization of the visual system of the modern hedgehog, presumed to resemble that of the common mammalian ancestral form.
(b) Thalamocortical projections in the hedgehog, the stippled area showing the projections from LGN and the circles the projections from LP; note the overlap. (From I. T. Diamond and W. C. Hall, Evolution of neocortex. *Science,* 1969, **164,** 251–262, Figure 4B, Figure 2. Copyright © 1969 by the American Association for the Advancement of Science.)

has left no soft tissue remains, and so it is appropriate to consider the basis of the inferences of its presumed neuroanatomical organization. On the basis of paleological data, Diamond and Hall (1969) have argued that this ancestral form was similar to the insectivores and that the neuroanatomical organization of the modern hedgehog can serve as a prototype or model of what the ancestral form was probably like. This argument is based on three considerations. First, the ratio of the amount of neocortex to paleocortex is in this species among the lowest found in any species (at least among species convenient to work with in the laboratory). The low ratio (about 0.5 as compared to about 0.9 in man) is reflected in the fact that the rhinal fissure is located along the lateral surface of the brain while in most other mammals it is found along the ventral surface, having been "pushed down" due to neocortical expansion. Second, the neocortex of the hedgehog is relatively undifferentiated, with a rather consistent cytoarchitectonic organization. The thalamus is also relatively undifferentiated, with the boundaries of the nuclei not being sharply distinct. These characteristics suggest that the neocortex of the hedgehog has changed little during evolution, although there is the possibility of retrogressive changes. The model of thalamocortical evolution proposed by Diamond and his colleagues is based then on a comparison of the neuroanatomical organization and behavior of the modern hedgehog, presumed to resemble the common mammalian ancestral form, with the neuroanatomical organization of representatives of modern mammalian orders. It is important to be very much aware that this model is just that, a model based on certain assumptions, open to test and modification.

Diamond argues that one of the features of the evolutionary line leading to primates was the great development of the visual system. Not only are the projections to the striate cortex from LGN and from the pulvinar (called LP in the hedgehog) completely non-overlapping, but LGN shows a high degree of differentiation within itself in the form of cellular layers and is totally distinct from the pulvinar nucleus.

The modern carnivores represent a highly contrasting and divergent line of evolutionary development. Their visual system bears a striking similarity to that found in the hedgehog in that there is considerable overlap in the cortical projections of LGN and LP (Figure 1–13). In contrast to this poorly developed visual system, there was a great expansion and differentiation of auditory sensory cortex, this coming to occupy the entire mid-lateral surface of the cat brain. This divergent line of specialization is reflected behaviorally in the high degree of prepotency or salience of auditory cues over visual cues as demonstrated in a compound cue discrimination study by Jane, Masterton, and Diamond (1965). Four normal cats were trained to respond in a shuttle avoidance box so that when a stimulus consisting of a low-pitched soft tone and a bright flashing light was presented, the cat had to go from the chamber it was in to the opposite chamber to avoid shock. After 90 percent performance was achieved, the animals were tested with each element of the compound CS to determine what had been attended to during training. When the tone alone was sounded, the cats continued to respond appropriately, but when the light alone was presented they did not, results which were interpreted to indicate that during the original learning the cats attended to only the auditory cue despite a rather large intensity difference.

Still another line of development is seen in the racoon. In contrast to the cat, which has an enlarged auditory cortex and associated medial geniculate thalamic nucleus, the ectosylvian auditory cortex of the racoon is relatively small but the somatic sensory cortex and its associated ventrobasal complex of the thalamus are quite enlarged, reflecting the importance of somatic sensory information in the behavior of this animal.

When these divergent patterns of neocortical evolution (as sketchy in detail as they may be) are juxtaposed, the principle of independent evolution of neocortex in mammalian orders has certain implications of rather profound significance for many of the questions which have been and are asked in physiological psychology and for the means by which attempts may be made to answer others. First, it should be clear that there is no basis for assuming *a priori* that there are homologous cortical regions among various orders of mammals nor that the Brodmann areas of the human cortex (discussed in Chapter 3) should be found in, for instance, the ruminant cortex. This independent evolution is reflected in the fact that the fissure patterns of the cortex of different orders of mammals are almost completely different, despite the use of similar names. For example, the large temporal lobes of primates associated with visual functions are unique to primates, there being no region in the brain of the cat homologous to them. Consequently, questions phrased in terms of localization of function, that is, questions concerned with assigning a function of some part of the cortex, may have to be species-specific, for there is no reason to assume *a priori* that cortical regions in different

species that are apparently homologous (for example, cats and monkeys both have a frontal cortex which in part receives thalamic projections from an apparently homologous medialis dorsalis thalamic nucleus) are in fact functionally similar. Indeed, it should not be surprising to find that ablation of apparently similar cortical regions produces quite different behavioral effects in different species. For instance, complete bilateral ablation of the striate cortex in rhesus monkeys appears to abolish pattern vision although the animal is still able to discriminate on the basis of total luminous energy or luminous flux,[1] and on the basis of the amount of edge in the stimulus display. In contrast, bilateral lesions of the striate cortex of another primate, the tree shrew, leave many aspects of pattern vision intact, as is the case with complete striate cortex lesions in the cat.

The cerebral cortex does not exist in isolation from the rest of the brain but obviously is part of functional systems involving subcortical structures. A second implication of the independent evolution of the neocortex, then, is that it cannot be assumed *a priori* that the functions of subcortical structures, especially ones having close functional relationships with the neocortex, are the same in different mammalian orders. A structure may be morphologically similar across orders and appear to have changed little during the course of evolution, but the possibly divergent evolutionary development of associated neocortex may have led to a differential and divergent functional modification of it. This certainly seems true in the case of the superior colliculus, which indeed bears a close functional relationship to the geniculostriate visual system. Considering the model of the evolutionary development of the visual system discussed earlier, it is difficult to imagine that this structure would mediate the same functions in the same way across the different mammalian orders showing divergent patterns of neocortical evolution.

---

[1] The student should remember that luminous flux is not the same as brightness, and the discrimination between stimuli differing in luminous flux could involve quite different neural mechanisms. Luminous flux refers to total light energy, and if two stimuli differ in their luminous flux, they will evoke different rates of neuronal firing in the nervous system and they could be differentiated on this basis. If two stimuli have different surface areas but have the same total energy, the one with the smaller area will appear brighter than the other. The discrimination of brightness, then, involves at least an integration of the rate of neuronal firing with an appreciation of the area of the retina from which the impulses arise. Monkeys with striate cortex lesions appear to be able to discriminate luminous flux (that is, can operate essentially as light meters) but do not have the pattern vision necessary to discriminate brightness.

The close functional relationship between much of the limbic system and the cerebral cortex also implies there could be significant species differences in limbic system functions with respect to motivational, emotional, or social behavior.

Species differences may not be as great as suggested in the preceding discussion, for although the evolutionary development of the neocortex has proceeded independently across mammalian orders, evolution does not proceed randomly but is a response to environmental demands. Given similar environments, the nervous systems of different species have probably evolved in similar ways so that many of the details of nervous system organization may indeed be common across species. However, it is not difficult to imagine similar responses to environmental pressures being handled in different ways in the evolution of mammalian orders so that similar behaviors in various species may be mediated by quite different systems.

CONCLUDING COMMENT

Mammalian neuroanatomy is often presented to the student of physiological psychology as the structure of the brain of either a "representative mammal," based largely on human neuroanatomy, or as the structure of the human brain itself. For the physiological psychologist, the fundamental problem with the approach is that it implicitly ignores species differences and the fact that the evolution of the nervous system in different species has proceeded independently and represents a response to particular ecological demands. Indeed, it is often implied in that approach that the brain of a rat is just a small cat brain, that a cat brain is just a small monkey brain, and that a monkey brain is just a small human brain. By considering neuroanatomical organization in terms of phylogenetic and ontogenetic development, however, there is an explicit recognition of the branching rather than linear nature of the course of evolution, which has implications for the neuropsychologist not only for his selection of species, but also for his choice of experimental variables in attempting to study and infer general principles of brain-behavior relations. Furthermore, the approach demonstrates that the structure of the vertebrate brain has a logic based on the differential expansion and differentiation of the derivatives of the embryonic neural tube.

2 LABORATORY EXERCISE I

DISSECTION OF A MAMMALIAN NERVOUS SYSTEM

A. CARE OF LABORATORY EQUIPMENT

Figure 2–1 shows some of the surgical instruments that will be used in this and subsequent labs. As they are quality precision instruments and can be easily damaged, they must be cared for properly. Not only are they expensive to replace (for example, the rongeurs cost about $45), but the time required for their replacement can be considerable. Many instruments, particularly the delicate ones, must be made to order and this can mean delivery times of several months

A few comments are necessary about the use and care of certain of the instruments shown in Figure 2–1.

1. The Virchow brain knife is used in this laboratory exercise to slice the brain evenly into sections, and a good cut requires that the cutting edge be smooth and free from nicks.
2. The rongeurs are used in later labs for nibbling at the cranium when exposing the brain. If chips of bone are removed from the jaws by hitting the tips on the table top rather than by dipping the tips into

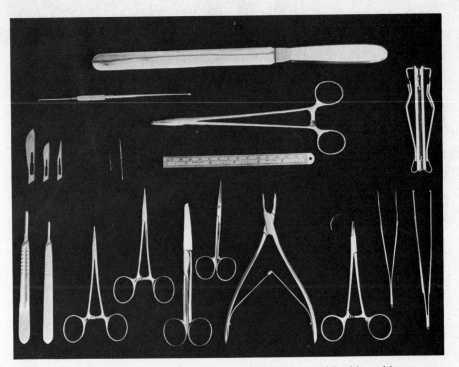

Figure 2–1. Some of the surgical instruments that will be used in this and later laboratory exercises. From the top, moving from left to right in approximate rows, the instruments are: *Top row:* Virchow brain knife; *second row:* dental probe; modified needleholder for applying bonescrews; wound clip applicator; *third row:* #22 scalpel blade; #10 scalpel blade; #11 scalpel blade; small (#½) dental bur for bonescrews; medium (#8) dental bur for drilling bone; ruler; *bottom row:* #4 scalpel handle; #3 scalpel handle; 2 mosquito forceps; large scissors; small iris scissors; Lempert rongeurs; suture needle; needleholder; Adson thumb forceps; rat-tooth forceps.

saline or wiping them with a wet gauze sponge, the jaws will quickly go out of alignment and render the instrument useless.

3. The fine-tipped iris scissors are used for cutting the dura mater. As with the rongeurs, be careful with the tips. Scissors with bent tips or with a bur on the tips will catch and rip tissue unevenly.

4. Do not ever cut string or paper with surgical scissors. Cutting string will tend to put the blades out of alignment and cutting paper will dull and ruin the cutting edges of any scissors.

5. The mosquito forceps may look similar to the needleholders but they should not be used as needleholders. The metal from which they are made may differ in temper from that used to make needleholders and the jaws may bend out of alignment if forced apart with a needle.

Overall, it is good practice to keep the instruments clean and, when working with live animals, free of blood. Periodically stop working and wipe them clean with a gauze sponge moistened with saline. Good care of the instruments includes washing and drying them carefully after use. Wash them in warm water with detergent, rinse them well in running warm water, and dry them thoroughly with a cloth towel (a cloth diaper works very well for this purpose).

Most of the equipment encountered in the labs apart from surgical instruments is quite sturdy. However, micromanipulators (used in later labs) should be operated with care and the drill (also used in later labs) should be used at high speed with light pressure rather than low speed and high pressure. Any other delicate equipment will be brought to your attention by the instructor.

B. DISSECTION OF THE BRAIN

The purpose of this laboratory exercise is to dissect the brain and spinal cord of the cow or sheep, which will allow for the identification and the localization of many of the major nuclei and fiber tracts discussed in Chapter 1. Because of the size of the ruminant brain and the rather sharp differentiation of white and gray matter, many of the principal structures of the brain can be visualized. Before the brain itself can be clearly seen, though, the dura mater which covers it must be removed. Then, following the examination of the surface gyri and sulci, the brain will be sectioned and its internal structure examined.

An excellent set of drawings of the internal structure of the cow or sheep brain is to be found in Skinner (1971). Your instructor will probably have reference copies available for use in this lab to aid in the identification of structures and for use in future labs because of the well-constructed and clear stereotaxic atlas of the rat brain. If copies of Skinner (1971) are not available, most of the internal structure of the brain can be inferred from a consideration of a stereotaxic atlas of the rat or cat brain, or from a consideration of human neuroanatomy (for example, see Grossman, 1967).

Equipment and supplies for each group

Cow or sheep brain in water-filled container
Dissection tray
Dissection instruments
    Large scissors
    Rat-tooth forceps
    Thumb forceps
    #3 scalpel handle and #11 blade
    #4 scalpel handle and #22 blade (or Virchow brain knife)
Specimen bowl with saline or water
2 pieces cheesecloth and string
Lab coats
Copy of J. E. Skinner, *Neuroscience: A laboratory manual*

Equipment and supplies to be shared by groups

10% Formalin solution
Label tape and marking pen
Disposable polyethylene gloves
Dishpans, sponges, detergent, towels

Before beginning the lab, identify the surgical instruments and put the

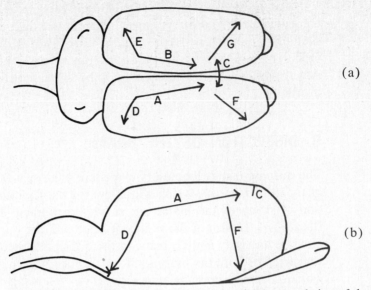

Figure 2–2. A highly schematic (a) dorsal and (b) ventral view of the brain showing those cuts to be made in order to remove the dura mater.

scalpel blade(s) into the handle(s).[1] The cow brain with which you have been supplied is preserved and has been prepared for dissection by rinsing it overnight in water. Anyone with sensitive hands may wish to use polyethylene gloves when handling it.

Removal of Dura Mater

The brain is surrounded by the meninges consisting of the innermost pia mater, the middle arachnoid mater, and the outer dura mater. In the cow, the dura mater is rather thick tissue and must be removed before the brain can be seen clearly.

Identify the anterior part of the brain by the presence of the large olfactory bulbs and the posterior part by the spinal cord and cerebellum. Along the dorsal midline between the hemispheres runs the sagittal sinus into which the venous blood of the brain drains.

Nick the dura on both hemispheres near the midline with a #11 scalpel blade. With the large scissors, cut the dura along the midline—cuts A and B in Figure 2–2(a)—and then cut through the sagittal sinus running between the hemispheres (cut C). This latter cut requires that the blades be inserted 1 or 2 cm between the hemispheres. This will allow the dorsoposterior part of the dura to be pulled loose from the brain. Then on each hemisphere cut the dura caudally and ventrally (cuts D and E). Cut the dura of the spinal cord on each side—forward to where cuts D and E terminate and then at a very

---

[1] Note how the slot in the blade can be slipped into the small grooves at the tip of the scalpel handle. To prevent cuts, or more serious damage, the blade should be held firmly in the mosquito forceps when it is inserted into the handle. To remove the blade, again clamp it with the mosquito forceps and pull while you use your thumbnail to lift up the end of the blade from the handle.

ventroposterior position, cut through the heavy cartilaginous tentorium that lies between the cerebellum and cerebrum. This cut requires that the blades be inserted some 2 to 3 cm deep between the cerebellum and cerebrum. This will allow the tentorium to be removed. It will still be attached to the dura and sagittal sinus and when removed will take with it the dorsoposterior dura loosened previously and the dura over the cerebellum. To remove the remaining dura from the anterior part of the cerebrum and from the base of the brain, make cuts F and G, use the forceps to pull the anterior part of the sagittal sinus forward and ventrally from between the hemispheres, and then slowly retract the dura, cutting the nerves holding it to the brain.

You may find some coagulated blood adhering to the cerebral cortex because of the method by which the cow or sheep was killed. The blood should be removed by scraping it off with your fingers and the brain should be rinsed in running water.

External Features

Examine the external features of the brain. Note in particular that the pattern of fissures and gyri is quite consistent from animal to animal, but the pattern is very dissimilar to that found in carnivore (Figure 3–9) and primate (Figure 3–2) brains.

Be sure you can identify the following:

1. Optic nerve, optic chiasm, and optic tract, located on the base of the brain.
2. Pons and cerebellum, if intact, located on the ventral and dorsal portions, respectively, of the brainstem.
3. Rhinal fissure, separating the neocortex from paleocortex.

Coronal and Sagittal Sections

Using either the #22 blade fastened into the #4 handle or a Virchow brain knife, cut the brain in half along the midsagittal plane. Figure 2–3 shows the principal structures that can be seen in the medial surface of the right hemisphere. Be sure you can locate and identify the structures and areas indicated.

Locate the anterior commissure and the posterior part of the optic chiasm of the left hemisphere and, cutting through them, make a coronal section through the brain. At the level of the genu of the corpus callosum, make a second cut parallel to this, and between the two, make a third cut. Then proceed to make four additional coronal sections of about the same thickness through the part of the brain posterior to the first commissure-chiasm section.

Identify the following:

1. The differentiation of white and gray matter. Note the rather highly convoluted cerebral cortex, separated from the interior of the brain by the white internal capsule.
2. The IVth, IIIrd, and lateral ventricles. Note the anterior-posterior extent of the lateral ventricles.
3. The forebrain commissures: the corpus callosum, the anterior commissure, and the posterior commissure.

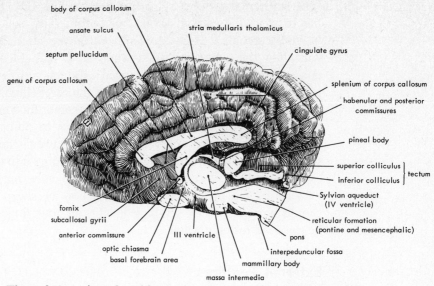

Figure 2–3. A view of a midsagittal section through a ruminant brain. (From J. E. Skinner, *Neuroscience: A laboratory manual.* Philadelphia: Saunders, 1971, Figure 2–14.)

4. The thalamus and hypothalamus, located in the coronal section that runs through the massa intermedia, just lateral to the midline.

5. The internal capsule, the white matter running through the interior of the brain, consisting of fibers projecting to and from the cerebral cortex.

6. The head, neck, and tail of the caudate nucleus, located just medial to the internal capsule, and enveloping the dorsal part of the thalamus.

7. The claustrum, lenticular nuclei (putamen and globus pallidus), and amygdala, located lateral to the internal capsule and found in the same sections as the caudate nucleus.

8. The superior and inferior colliculi of the midbrain.

9. The hippocampus, a C-shaped structure in the posterior part of the hemisphere, quite evident from its coiled appearance. Note that it projects into the fornix which can be seen in the midsagittal section.

Now, make a series of four or five sagittal sections through the intact right hemisphere, each section being about half the thickness of the coronal sections. This will enable you to see in a somewhat different perspective the structures and areas indicated above and will allow you to visualize these areas in three dimensions and to appreciate the spatial relationship that exists among some of the larger neuroanatomical areas.

When you have completed your examination of the brain, reconstruct each hemisphere, wrap the sections in cheesecloth and tie them with a piece of string (*do not cut string with surgical scissors*). Then place the sections in containers labeled with your names and cover them with 10% Formalin solution. This will keep the sections preserved. These are for your use in the future when some of the structures and areas may have more meaning for you than they do now.

C. DISSECTION OF THE SPINAL CORD

Equipment and supplies for each group

Beef spinal cord section
Magnifier
High-intensity lamp (if necessary)
Dissection instruments in tray:
#22 scalpel blade and #4 handle (or Virchow brain knife)
Dental probe
Fine-tipped iris scissors
Large surgical scissors
Rat-tooth forceps
Thumb forceps

The spinal cord will still be covered with the dura, arachnoid, and pia mater, and to examine it, especially the spinal roots, necessitates at least a partial removal of two of these three membranes. Using the large surgical scissors, slit the outermost layer, the dura mater; if this is carefully retracted, the underlying arachnoid mater, which has a weblike appearance, will be evident. You will probably not be able to see the pia mater in this preserved specimen.

If your section of spinal cord has a spinal nerve attached to it, examine beneath the dura at the point at which the spinal nerve emerges. It will be clear that each spinal nerve is made up of a relatively large number of spinal rootlets. These are small bundles of fibers that emerge from the dorsal and the ventral portions of the spinal cord and converge to form the dorsal and ventral spinal roots. As discussed in Chapter 1, the fibers making up the dorsal roots carry afferent information, while those making up the ventral roots carry efferent information. In the event that your section of spinal cord does not have a spinal nerve attached to it, the dorsal and ventral rootlets will nevertheless be evident along its sides.

Make a clean transverse section through the spinal cord and identify the white fiber bundles making up the periphery of the cord and the gray matter making up the central core. Figure 2–4 is a diagram showing some of the principal components of the spinal cord.

D. CLEANING THE WORK AREA

At the end of this and all labs, be sure to wash, rinse, and dry well all instruments, glassware, trays, etc. Clean and sponge off the work area and put away the equipment and supplies as directed by your instructor.

E. DEMONSTRATION OF STAINED SPINAL CORD SECTIONS

Equipment and supplies

X-ray viewers
Microscope slide sections of spinal cord

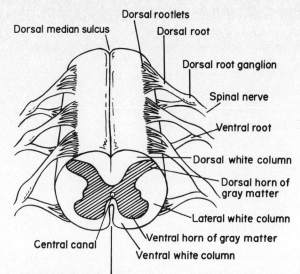

Dorsal median sulcus
Dorsal rootlets
Dorsal root
Dorsal root ganglion
Spinal nerve
Ventral root
Dorsal white column
Dorsal horn of gray matter
Lateral white column
Ventral horn of gray matter
Central canal
Ventral white column
Ventral median fissure

Figure 2–4. Diagram of the spinal cord with spinal nerves intact but with the dura mater and arachnoid mater removed. (From *Experimental neuropsychology: A laboratory manual* by Benjamin L. Hart, Figure 1–2. W. H. Freeman and Company. Copyright © 1969.)

Overhead projector
White bristol board for projecting

The stained demonstration spinal cord sections have been taken from the upper cervical, cervical, thoracic, lumbar, and sacral regions, the names of which are derived from the associated spinal vertebrae. The sections have been stained so that the fiber tracts appear bluish and the cell bodies pink. In this normal tissue preparation it is difficult to differentiate finely among the various spinal pathways.

Note first the absolute size of the diameter of the spinal cord and consider the amount of information processing occurring in it. Note the relative proportion of cells to fibers at the various levels. As discussed in Chapter 1, there is a great increase in the absolute size of the fiber pathways in ascending from the sacral through the upper cervical sections. Note how few cell bodies there are in the thoracic section.

Identify the dorsal and ventral horns of the cord and identify where the dorsal and ventral roots would emerge.

Examine the sections by placing them on the projector. Remember that the slides will be projected onto the table upside down. The focus of the projector can be adjusted with the large black knob and the magnification by rotating the three lenses.

3

THE USE OF HISTOLOGY IN PHYSIOLOGICAL PSYCHOLOGY

BASIC PRINCIPLES OF NEUROHISTOLOGY

In studying the structure of the cow brain in Laboratory Exercise I, we could see and identify many of the major fiber tracts and nuclei, since the differentiation of white and gray matter is relatively distinct. In studying the brains of small animals or in studying the structure of the nervous system in detail, for instance, in distinguishing among the various thalamic nuclei or the spinal cord fiber tracts, however, gross dissection and inspection are simply inadequate. Instead, techniques of histology (meaning the study of the minute structure of tissue) must be used. These involve slicing the neural tissue into very thin sections and subsequently staining the sections so as to increase the differentiation of white and gray matter and to make distinct those cells and/or fibers of interest.

When applied to mammalian nervous tissue, most histological procedures begin with the animal being deeply anesthetized and rapidly perfused with saline and a formaldehyde solution so as to remove all blood from the tissue and to preserve it. The brain is removed from the cranium and fixed or hardened in Formalin or alcohols. It is then further hardened by freezing or by embedding in paraffin or celloidin, and is sliced very thinly (sections 25 microns (μ) thick are quite common) on a device called a microtome (Figure 3–1). The tissue is fastened to the pedestal of the microtome, which automatically is raised some fixed amount toward the blade (for example, 25μ) after each slice is made with the microtome knife. The sections are mounted on microscope slides and stained with any one of a number of substances. The brains that will be used in Laboratory Exercise II will have been fixed in a solution of formaldehyde and saline (called Formalin) but will not have been hardened, and the difficulty encountered in cutting

29

Figure 3–1. A type of microtome used to slice tissue that has been hardened either by freezing or by embedding in celloidin. The tissue is mounted onto the circular stage and is sliced by a blade that moves back and forth. After each movement of the knife, the stage is automatically raised a specific and known amount.

thin, even slices with the hand microtome used in the lab should make clear the advantages, and indeed the necessity, of hardening tissue.

It is only during the past century, closely parallel-ing the development of the chemical dye industry, that numerous histological techniques have been de-vised. Two of the older techniques, which involve the staining of entire neurons, are the Golgi method and the Cajal method. With the Golgi method, developed in the late nineteenth century by the Italian psychia-trist Camillo Golgi (1844–1926), who discovered that metallic salts would stain neural tissue, entire neurons become covered with a black precipitate, allowing for complete fiber processes to be traced considerable distances. It was material stained with this method that formed the basis of the neuron doc-trine that holds that the nervous system is not made up of a continuous nerve net or web, but is made up of separate and distinct neurons. One peculiarity of the Golgi method is that only a small number of the neurons become stained (perhaps as few as 1 per-cent), but those which are stained are completely

stained. The Cajal method, developed by the Spanish histologist Santiago Ramon y Cajal (1852–1934), makes use of certain principles of photography. Cajal found that neural tissue has a close affinity for silver salts and when it is left for a period of time in a silver nitrate solution, entire neurons become im-pregnated with it. The tissue can then be processed in much the same manner as a photograph is devel-oped, and the impregnated neurons are easily visible with the aid of a microscope.

Other methods stain only certain portions of neu-rons rather than entire neurons. One method makes use of substances such as cresyl violet, methylene blue, and thionin, which have a close affinity for the Nissl substance (nucleoproteins) found within the cell body. Neural tissue processed with these stains will show cell bodies as blue; the fibers do not take up the stain at all as they contain no Nissl substance. The Weigert or Weil methods form the complement in that hematoxylin, the major component of the stain, has a close affinity for the fatty myelin sheaths, and so myelinated axons but not cell bodies, dendrites, or terminal boutons are selectively stained. There have also been developed quite recently techniques such as that of Kluver and Barrera (1953) that allow for differential staining of cell bodies and fiber tracts in single sections. This is the method used to stain the human spinal cord sections shown in Figure 1–6.

It is important to appreciate at the outset that the end product of histological procedures is not the same as normal living tissue and what is examined histologically is not the tissue itself but the stain. The characteristics of the tissue are only inferred from the characteristics of the stain. Anything that affects the uptake of stain by the tissue, of course, influences what can and cannot subsequently be detected in the tissue, and there are numerous points in the dehydration, staining, and differentiation phases of all procedures at which problems can arise that will produce staining artifacts. Even the manner in which the tissue is handled can produce artifacts, as in the case of the Marchi method to be mentioned later.

CYTOARCHITECTONIC MAPS OF THE BRAIN

Prior to the development of histological methods, the parts of the brain were distinguished on the basis of gross morphological characteristics. In the case of the cortex, these characteristics were the fissures and gyri. Because of the large and very pronounced lateral and central sulci, the hemispheres were seen as having four lobes which were named after the cranial bones overlying them: the frontal lobe, the temporal lobe, the occipital lobe, and the parietal lobe. Each of the lobes was further divided and those individual gyri that seemed relatively consistent from individual to individual were named, usually with reference to the lobe (for example, inferotemporal gyrus). Figure 3–2 is a sketch of the left hemisphere of the human brain on which some of the principal gyri and fissures have been indicated.

Figure 3–3 is a photomicrograph of a section of human cerebral cortex stained with a Nissl stain. This, of course, shows cell bodies and glial cells. Inspection might suggest, and indeed microscopic examination would confirm, that the distribution of stellate and pyramidal cells (Figure 3–4) through the cortex is not random but has an orderly arrangement by layers. There are, however, many differences among cortical regions in such details of fine structure as absolute cortical thickness, the number and width of the different layers, the shape and size of cells, and the density and distribution of cell types in the different layers. It is this regional variation that during the past seventy years has formed the foundation of several schemes for dividing the cortex into discrete structural units. Certainly one of the best-known schemes is that of Brodmann (1909), who divided the cortex into approximately fifty areas on the basis of such cytoarchitectonic variations in Nissl stained tissue and simply numbered each part. Underlying this work was the assumption that "the function of an organ is correlated with its histological structure" (Brodmann, 1909), and so these structurally distinct areas were regarded as being functionally distinct, an issue that will be returned to in detail in Chapters 5 and 13. A map of the structural-functional organiza-

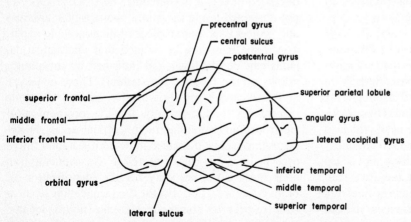

Figure 3–2. An outline sketch of the left cerebral hemisphere of man indicating some of the principal gyri and sulci named on the basis of cranial bone terminology. (Adapted from E. Gardner, *Fundamentals of neurology* (5th ed.). Philadelphia: Saunders, 1969, Figure 5.)

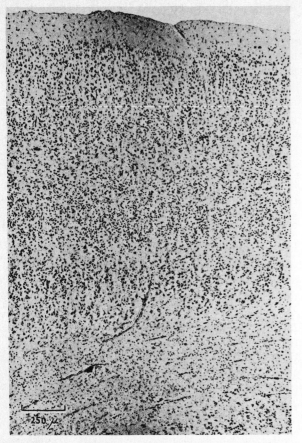

Figure 3–3. A section through human occipital cortex prepared with a Nissl stain. Shown are the perikarya of the neurons and glial elements. (From D. A. Sholl, *The organisation of the cerebral cortex.* New York: Hafner, 1956, Plate 1.)

tion of the human cortex, based on that prepared by Brodmann (1909), is shown in Figure 3–5.

Other schemes, such as that of C. and O. Vogt (1919), contain an even larger number of divisions. In the laboratory exercises, use will be made of cytoarchitectonic maps of the rat cortex based largely on the work of Krieg (1946), who used a numbering system analogous to that of Brodmann. These cytoarchitectonic maps and divisions have been criticized on the grounds of a lack of interobserver reliability (Lashley and Clark, 1946) and the absence of sharp boundaries between most areas, but they are very much in use today as a convenient means of referring to cortical areas, especially in non-primates; the old system based on four lobes and cranial bones is most frequently used in referring to the primate cortex. It is relevant to Brodmann's structural-functional assumption that many of the structurally distinct areas defined cytoarchitectonically are congruent with functionally distinct areas defined on the basis of thalamocortical connections demonstrated through retrograde degeneration (Figure 1–10) and on the basis of the sensory evoked potentials and unit recordings discussed in Part Four.

BRAIN ATLASES AND THE STEREOTAXIC METHOD

Like the cortex, the internal structure of the brain was originally divided into parts on the basis of gross morphology, and this type of division into major nuclear groups and fiber tracts (discussed in Chapter 1) is very much in use today. The development of histological procedures, however, allowed finer subdivisions than would otherwise have been possible, for the boundaries of many nuclei (for example, in the thalamus or hypothalamus) are indicated as much by a change in the distribution of cellular types as by the appearance of new features. These techniques were then widely used in preparing maps of the brain, but in contrast to cortical maps, which are usually two-dimensional (the cortex can be adequately conceptualized for most purposes as being a plane), maps of the internal features of the brain must be three-dimensional.

Such a map, called a stereotaxic atlas, consists of a series of enlarged coronal (or frontal) sections of the brain, usually taken a half millimeter apart, on which neuroanatomical structures have been identified. Sometimes these are prepared by enlarging photographs of sliced and stained brain tissue, but for reasons related to brain shrinkage (which will be discussed later), it is sometimes more satisfactory to put unstained tissue slices in a photographic enlarger and project them onto a piece of photographic paper. The tissue can then be stained and anatomical regions can be identified and indicated on the photographs on the basis of the staining. These maps are used extensively for verifying lesions and electrode placements, and especially for the positioning of electrodes and cannulae in subcortical areas, procedures that will be discussed in detail in Chapter 5 and used in later laboratory exercises. Consequently, an atlas must allow not only for the identification of brain structures, but also for the localization of them with respect to standard reference points located outside the animal.

Most atlases are constructed for use with a stereotaxic instrument like that illustrated in Figure 3–6. There is a solid base to which is attached an animal

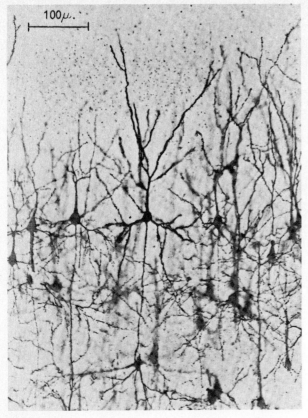

(a)

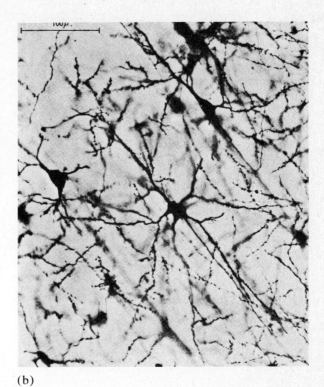

(b)

(c)

Figure 3–4. Golgi-Cox preparations (which stain axons and dendrites) showing (a) a small pyramidal neuron from the visual cortex of the cat, (b) a stellate neuron from the visual cortex of the cat, and (c) a large pyramidal neuron from human cortex. (From D. A. Sholl, *The organisation of the cerebral cortex*. New York: Hafner, 1956, Plates 4, 5, 7.)

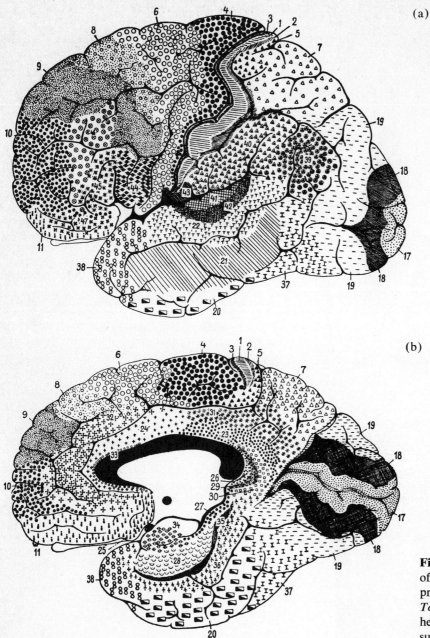

(a)

(b)

Figure 3–5. Cytoarchitectonic maps of human cerebral cortex as prepared by Brodmann (1909). *Top view:* convex surface of the hemisphere; *bottom view:* medial surface.

headholder and a movable electrode carrier. After being anesthetized, the animal's head is firmly held in the instrument by a pair of ear bars inserted into the external auditory meatus. The upper incisor teeth are placed over the incisor bar and the nose clamp tightened. Most atlases, such as those of de Groot (1959), Skinner (1971), Pelligrino and Cushman (1967), or Massopust (1961)—but not Konig and Klippel (1963)—are intended for use with stereotaxic instruments having the top of the incisor bar positioned 5 mm above the center of the ear bars.

This orients the head and brain with respect to the ear bars and incisor bar as illustrated in Figure 3–7. Note how it is the height of the incisor bar that determines the head orientation.

In the construction of an atlas, the brain is sliced in the coronal plane at right angles to the horizontal plane as shown in Figure 3–7. Most atlases include coronal sections that are a half millimeter apart and many present each section both as a photograph of the section (either stained or unstained) and as a line drawing on which the nuclei and fiber tracts are

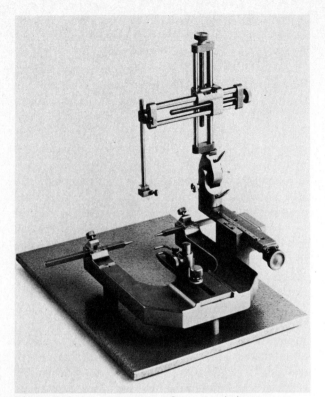

Figure 3–6. A common type of stereotaxic instrument designed for use with the rat. Note the ear bars, the upper incisor bar, and the nose clamp, all of which together hold the animal firmly in place. The electrode carrier can be moved in the three right-angled planes with respect to the base. (Courtesy David Kopf Instruments.)

identified. Since the cerebral hemispheres are symmetrical, often only one hemisphere is shown in order to conserve space. Figure 3–8 shows one coronal section taken from the atlas prepared by Skinner (1971). The section is indicated as being 8.25 mm anterior to the coronal plane running through the center of the ear bars. On the left is a photographic enlargement of the right hemisphere of the original section. On the right is a line drawing constructed after the photographed section was stained and on which are indicated the names of nuclei and fiber tracts. Note that the line drawing also contains a vertical and a lateral scale. The vertical scale is in terms of the distance, in millimeters, above and below the point at which the horizontal and coronal planes intersect (indicated by 0) and the lateral scale is in terms of the distance, in millimeters, from the midline (indicated by 0). Consequently, any brain structure can be localized with respect to the three right-angled stereotaxic planes provided that the animal's head has the same orientation as that used in the construction of the atlas. The structure can be localized in terms of its distance anterior or posterior to the coronal plane running through the center of the ear bars, its distance dorsal to the center of the ear bars (the center of the ear bars being, of course, 5 mm ventral to the 0 point on the vertical scale, as shown in Figure 3–7), and its distance from the midline. The uninsulated tip of a lesioning or recording electrode or a tip of a cannula can thus be placed into the structure using the movable electrode carrier.

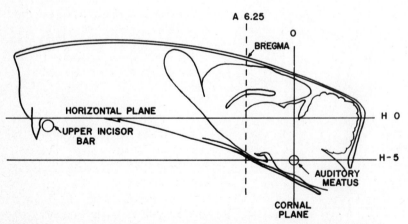

Figure 3–7. A midsagittal section through the head of the rat illustrating the orientation of the brain with respect to the horizontal and vertical planes. (Adapted from J. de Groot, *The rat forebrain in stereotaxic coordinates*. Amsterdam: North-Holland Publishing Company, 1959, Figure 1.)

A second system of reference points that uses the bone sutures of the skull will be used quite extensively in the laboratory exercises. These are the lines that can be seen on the surface of the skull at the points where the skull bones join together. The point at which the two frontal and two parietal bones meet, called bregma, bears a consistent relationship to underlying brain tissue, and so if the animal is positioned so that the coronal plane has the same angle with respect to the base of the stereotaxic instrument as that of the stereotaxic atlas, any particular brain structure again can be localized in terms of its anterior-posterior relationship to bregma, its vertical distance from the surface of the cortex, and its distance from the midline. The section illustrated in Figure 3–8 is 2.0 mm anterior to bregma. Unfortunately, some atlases (for example, de Groot, 1959) use only the ear-bar reference system, but a conversion to the bone-suture system can be made easily as bregma is 6.25 mm anterior to the ear bars when the head of the animal is oriented as in Figure 3–7.

Although in subsequent laboratory exercises the brain atlas will be used for positioning electrodes, it will be used in Laboratory Exercise II just for identifying structures present in the sections made from a rat brain. It should be evident that unless the brain is cut in the same orientation used in the preparation of the atlas, all the structures that appear in an atlas section will not be found in any one cut section. For many research purposes, this problem is handled by "blocking" the brain in a stereotaxic instrument. Following perfusion, the brain is exposed dorsally and the head is placed in a stereotaxic instrument. A vertical cut is then made through the brain which indicates how the brain should rest on the microtome stage so the slices will be in the same plane as that in the atlas.

One of the major problems of constructing a good atlas, which will become evident in the laboratory exercise, is to make the stereotaxic calibrations correspond to living tissue. When tissue is processed histologically there is invariably some shrinkage due to dehydration, and absolute distances in such tissue become meaningless for atlas construction. The problem is sometimes overcome in part by using the photographic enlarger procedure outlined earlier, since there is typically very little change in brain volume associated with frozen sections; at other times an estimate is made of the amount of shrinkage associated with a procedure by making small lesions in a living brain, measuring how far apart these are in the processed brain, and then applying a correction factor, based on the difference, to measurements on other similarly processed tissue. This, however, as-

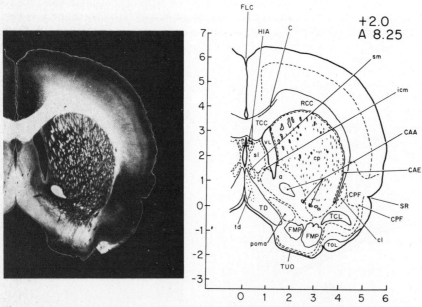

Figure 3–8. A plate from a stereotaxic atlas of the rat brain. On the left is a photographic print of a section taken with the aid of a photographic enlarger, and on the right is a reconstruction of the section with brain structures indicated with abbreviations. (From J. E. Skinner, *Neuroscience: A laboratory manual.* Philadelphia: Saunders, 1971, p. 216.)

sumes an amount of shrinkage constant throughout the brain tissue, which is sometimes questionable.

DESCRIPTIVE HISTOLOGY

One of the most common uses of histological methods in physiological psychology is to describe the state of brain tissue following some neurological manipulation such as the implantation of a stimulating electrode or the ablation of tissue. The techniques associated with making ablations or lesions are discussed in Chapter 5, but briefly, subcortical lesions are usually made by inserting into some particular tissue an electrode (a needle that is electrically insulated along its length except at the tip) and passing through it a DC current which, in effect, burns a hole in the tissue. It is usually necessary subsequently to verify that the lesion was as extensive as intended but did not invade surrounding tissue. Simply looking at the tissue will be of only limited value, but slicing the tissue and staining it with a Nissl stain such as cresyl violet allows one to clearly distinguish microscopically among neuroanatomical structures and, with the aid of a stereotaxic atlas, to determine the extent of the tissue damage.

A similar procedure might be used to verify cortical lesions, which are often made by aspiration rather than with electrolytic methods. The brain tissue is quite literally sucked away in a small-tipped pipette in a manner like that to be used in Laboratory Exercise IV. The usual issue of concern is whether all the cortical tissue in some area was in fact removed and whether the lesion was restricted to cortical tissue or invaded the underlying white matter made of fibers going to and from other parts of the cortex. Since the cortex is largely cellular, a Nissl stain gives a clear differentiation of the cortical tissue and fibers. If alternate sections are stained with the Weigert method, the extent of any undercutting can also be assessed with microscopic examination.

The placement of acute or chronic stimulating or recording electrodes can also be verified with histological procedures. Electrodes are often implanted permanently into the brain for the purpose of stimulating the brain electrically (see Part Three) or monitoring the electrical activity of the brain during various types of behavior (see Part Four). The interpretation given to the behavioral effects of stimulation or to an apparent correlation between changes in electrical activity and the manifestation of some behavior may be highly contingent upon the location of the electrode tip. This can be determined at the completion of such studies by producing a small lesion at the electrode tip, the locus of which can then be determined by staining the brain tissue for cells and for fibers. Similar procedures are sometimes used in acute electrophysiological studies, such as that of Hubel and Wiesel (1962), which determined the receptive field characteristics of single cells of the visual cortex. Several cortical cells were studied in each penetration of the cortex by the microelectrode and the distance between cells from which successive recordings were made could be determined because of the use of calibrated stereotaxic equipment. At the end of each penetration, a small lesion was made at the electrode tip; in removing the electrode small lesions were made at each site from which recordings had been made. Through tissue slicing and staining, this allowed for the subsequent identification of three recording parameters: (1) the angle of electrode penetration, which formed the basis of the finding that cells in vertical columns at right angles to the cortical surface have the same receptive field orientation, (2) the area of the cortex (that is, area 17, 18, or 19) in which each cell from which they recorded was located, which can be determined with certainty only on the basis of histological examination, and (3) the layer of cortical cells in which each cell was located.

EXPERIMENTAL AND ANALYTIC HISTOLOGY

If a cell body or its fiber processes are damaged, the entire neuron dies. The axonal degeneration that occurs, called anterograde or Wallerian degeneration, can be detected with certain histological methods, notably the Marchi technique, which exploits the fact that one of the fatty products of degenerating myelin sheaths has a close affinity for osmic acid. This allows for the selective staining of degenerating myelin sheaths. As previously pointed out, this method is highly subject to peculiar artifacts and so sometimes the much simpler Weigert method is used. These methods have been used in conjunction with experimental lesions in order to trace the terminations of axons whose cell bodies are located in the same particular nucleus, but they are limited by the fact that terminal boutons are not myelinated, so the actual point of termination of a degenerating axon cannot be detected. This is an especially severe limitation in studying thalamocortical connections, as the myelin sheath terminates before the axon enters the cortex proper. A major advance has recently occurred, however, with the development of the Nauta and the Fink-Heimer methods, which involve silver impregnation of degenerating axons and axon terminals. This makes it possible to determine the actual site of axon termination rather than the limits of axonal myelination, and so complete neuroanatomical pathways can be studied.

Damage to axons leads to analogous degenerative changes in the cell bodies referred to as retrograde degeneration or chromatolysis. The changes can be observed very clearly with a Nissl stain and have been described in some detail by Brodal (1939). A few days after the axonal damage, the Nissl substance disappears from the center of the cell body and is found only around the periphery; the cell body has also shrunk considerably in size. After two to three weeks, many of the cells have disappeared entirely and there is a proliferation of glial cells in the area. The glial cells also stain blue with Nissl stains, but they can easily be distinguished from neuron cell bodies on the basis of morphological characteristics.

The phenomena of anterograde degeneration and retrograde degeneration have been widely exploited in the study of nervous system connections. The pattern of thalamocortical connections discussed in Chapter 1 is largely an inference based on an analysis of thalamic retrograde degeneration that follows discrete cortical lesions (which damage axonal boutons) and on an analysis of the pattern of degenerating axonal boutons found in the cortex following discrete lesions in thalamic nuclei. When retrograde or anterograde degeneration occurs, one can be reasonably confident of there being direct connections between that point and the lesioned area of the brain, since transneuronal degeneration, that is, degeneration in a neuron which has not itself been damaged but which synapses with a damaged neuron, appears to be minimal. Unfortunately, the absence of degeneration does not necessarily imply the absence of direct connections. Rose and Woolsey (1958), for instance, observed that lesions of part of the auditory cortex of the cat (the region of the middle and posterior ectosylvian gyri as illustrated in Figure 3–9) resulted in retrograde degeneration in the medial geniculate nucleus (MGN) but not in the posterior nuclear group of the thalamus (Po). Similarly, ablation of the second sensory-motor area of the cortex (SM II) in the region of the anterior suprasylvian and anterior ectosylvian gyri did not lead to degeneration of Po. Hence it might appear there are no direct connections either between the auditory cortex and Po or between sensory-motor cortex and Po. However, when combined lesions were made of all ectosylvian gyri and the anterior suprasylvian gyrus, there was complete degeneration

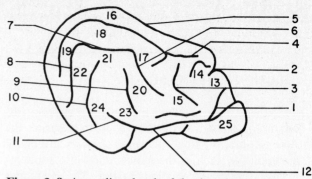

Figure 3–9. An outline sketch of the dorsolateral view of the right hemisphere of the cat brain with the principal sulci and gyri indicated. *Sulci:* (1) presylvian; (2) crutiate; (3) coronal; (4) ansate; (5) lateral; (6) anterior suprasylvian; (7) middle suprasylvian; (8) posterior suprasylvian; (9) anterior ectosylvian; (10) posterior ectosylvian; (11) sylvian; (12) rhinal fissure. *Gyri:* (13) anterior sygmoid; (14) posterior sygmoid; (15) coronal; (16) lateral or marginal; (17) anterior suprasylvian; (18) middle suprasylvian; (19) posterior suprasylvian; (20) anterior ectosylvian; (21) middle ectosylvian; (22) posterior ectosylvian; (23) anterior sylvian; (24) posterior sylvian; (25) olfactory bulb. (Adapted from J. W. Papez, *Comparative neurology.* New York: Hafner, 1929, Figure 10.)

of Po. This suggests that if there are collateral axonal branches, retrograde degeneration may occur only if there is damage to both branches. This pattern of thalamocortical projection is called *sustaining* thalamic projections and is to be contrasted with *essential* thalamic projections such as those found between the middle and posterior ectosylvian gyri and the medial geniculate thalamic nucleus.

The assessment of the extent of cortical lesions is frequently done in terms of the pattern of thalamic retrograde degeneration, for this removes some of the difficulty there can be in specifying the precise extent of cortical removal, especially in species with smooth brains. For example, given the assumption that LGN projects only to the striate cortex and that these projections are evenly distributed throughout the striate cortex, it is reasonable to characterize the extent of striate cortex lesions in terms of the amount of retrograde degeneration observed in the well-differentiated LGN. There can, however, be pitfalls resulting from questionable assumptions. For example, in studying the visual capabilities of cats with cortical lesions, Doty (1961) used as a partial criterion of complete striate cortex removal complete retrograde degeneration in LGN and rejected from his experimental group any animal not showing total degeneration. This was not unreasonable, since at that time it was informed opinion that LGN projected only to the striate cortex and that the striate cortex received thalamic projections from only LGN. Animals with complete LGN degeneration showed no evidence of pattern discrimination capabilities, whereas those with subtotal LGN degeneration were able to do so, and it was concluded that the striate cortex was a necessary substrate for pattern vision.

The basic anatomical assumption concerning thalamocortical projections, however, has proved to be incorrect. It is now clear that LGN in the cat has projections not only to the striate cortex but also to regions of the surrounding suprasylvian cortex. When Doty (1972) reanalyzed the data in the light of this new anatomical knowledge bearing on implicit assumptions that were completely reasonable at the time, it was evident that cats with complete striate cortex removal (but showing incomplete LGN degeneration) did have good visual capabilities. Those subjects showing complete LGN degeneration had lesions not only of the striate cortex but also of the suprasylvian cortex, the rest of the cortex receiving extensive projections from LP, as discussed in Chapter 1.

Given grounds for confidence concerning assumptions about thalamocortical connections, retrograde degeneration techniques are sometimes of use in estimating the possible effects of undercutting white matter when removing cortex. It will become clear in Laboratory Exercise IV that it is difficult not to inadvertently remove some of the fibers running immediately beneath the cortex when attempting restricted cortical ablations. The white matter is made up of fibers going to and from the cortex, and the interpretation given to data concerned with the effects of the intended lesion may be influenced by a consideration of the consequences of, in effect, deafferenting and de-efferenting other parts of the cortex. For example, complete removal of middle and posterior ectosylvian cortex (auditory cortex) in the cat is difficult to achieve without undercutting the optic radiations, the fibers projecting from LGN to visual cortex. But the extent of undercutting may be able to be estimated in functional terms by analyzing the retrograde degeneration in LGN. This information would be of importance in interpreting the effects of auditory cortex lesions on task performance if that task is known to be influenced by the state of the visual system. Similarly, the interpretation given to the effects of motor cortex lesions on some behavior might have to be tempered if it were found that the undercutting produced retrograde degeneration in MD, the thalamic nucleus projecting to the frontal cortex and if frontal cortex lesions themselves produced a similar kind of impairment.

RADIOACTIVE TRACING

One new and interesting histological technique that allows the tracing of the distribution and metabolism of substances in the nervous system and in the body as a whole has recently been introduced into physiological psychology. These radioactive tracer techniques, as they are called, developed along with an understanding of radioactive isotopes and exploit the fact that isotopes such as carbon-14, sulphur-35 or hydrogen-3 (tritium) can be attached to the molecules of amino acids, hormones, and drugs of interest to many physiological psychologists. After being "labeled" with a radioactive isotope, the substance is introduced into the organism, time is allowed for it to become incorporated into the system, and the animal is sacrificed. The distribution of the isotopes in the organism at the time of death can be ascertained through the use of radioactivity counters, such as Geiger counters and scintillation counters, and this should reflect the distribution of the substance in the body and in different parts of the brain. In terms of gross analysis, one of the simplest procedures is to kill the animal instantaneously by submerging it in a liquid nitrogen bath or decapitating it,[1] removing the brain, dissecting the major structures, and determining the amount of radioactivity per unit volume in each structure. Inferences can then be made as to the distribution of the substance through the brain at the time of death.

It is important to appreciate that with this particular procedure, the radioactivity also reflects the distribution of the substance in the blood supply and extracellular fluids. To determine where the substance was incorporated into cells or the actual site of action of the substance, it would be necessary to first perfuse the animal with a nonradioactive solution of the substance that removes all the labeled material from the extracellular space. A somewhat more detailed analysis can be achieved following such a perfusion by slicing the brain on a microtome, as is done in the more classical histological proce-

---

[1] Slower methods, such as administering a lethal overdose of an anesthetic, may change the distribution of the substances for any one of numerous reasons.

dures, and then, rather than staining them, coating the sections with a photographic emulsion sensitive to the emissions of the type of radioactive tracer being used. The slide is left in the dark and the radioactive emissions will then "expose" the emulsion overlying it. When the slides are developed in very much the same way as photographic film is developed, there will be small, dark grains in the tissue wherever there are sites of radioactive emissions. If a very weak beta-emitting isotope is used and if the brain tissue is sliced extremely thinly, it is at least theoretically possible to localize the radioactivity (and hence the substance) in single cells and even parts of cells. There is, however, a limit to the detail that can be achieved due to the omnipresence of general background atmospheric radiation which tends to expose the emulsion.

As part of their analysis of the neural and hor-monal determinants of female mating behavior in rats, Pfaff and his colleagues (Pfaff, 1972; Pfaff and Keiner, 1972) have used these techniques to good advantage in localizing the cellular uptake of sex hormones, specifically estrogen, in the brain. Triti-ated estradiol (that is, estradiol radioactively labeled with tritium) was injected intravenously into rats, and two hours later autoradiograms were prepared as described above. When the emulsion-coated slides were developed some months later, high concentra-tions of the radioactivity (which indicated high estra-diol uptake) were found in parts of the limbic system (amygdala, lateral septum, ventral hippocampus, diagonal band of Broca), in the preoptic area, and in various hypothalamic nuclei. The value of such find-ings with hormones or with drugs is that they can form the foundation for hypotheses as to the *possible* mediation of hormonal or drug effects on behavior.

4 LABORATORY EXERCISE II

ELEMENTS OF HISTOLOGICAL PROCEDURE

The purpose of this laboratory exercise is to study the principles involved in the preparation of neural tissue for histological study. The procedures to be followed are based on those described by Hart (1969), but are not those normally used in research in physiological psychology. First, the tissue will be sliced with a hand microtome without the aid of tissue hardening, so it will be difficult to produce slices less than ¼ mm (250μ) thick; in actual research, it is usually desirable to work with tissue slices of no more than 50μ in thickness. Second, the stained tissue prepared in this lab will be able to be kept for only a matter of hours, in contrast to usual histological procedures, which allow for permanent mounting and indefinite preservation of stained tissue. Nevertheless, the lab should illustrate some of the basic principles of neurohistology, allow for the identification of some of the larger structures in the rat brain, and also lead to a familiarity with the use of a stereotaxic atlas for the identification of brain structures.

A. SLICING AND STAINING BRAIN TISSUE

Equipment and supplies for each group

Rat brain in Formalin
Hand microtome with knife (see Figure 4–1)
Tissue capsules (15 to 20)
Magnifier
High-intensity lamp (if necessary)
Stereotaxic atlas of the rat brain
600-ml beaker
Specimen dish with saline
Petri dish
6   2″×3″ microscope slides
Small jar of 2% ferric chloride solution
Rat-tooth forceps
Thumb forceps
2   4″×4″ gauze sponges
Rubber bands
Eyedropper
Dishpan, detergent, and towels
Lab coats

Equipment and supplies to be shared by groups

Timers
Heater
Thermometer
1   1000-ml Erlenmeyer flask (for mixing phenol solution)
2   600-ml beakers for phenol
2   600-ml beakers for ice water
4 petri dishes for 2% ferric chloride solution
2 rat-tooth forceps
Ice cubes
Tubing and three-way connectors unless there are sufficient faucets and
     sinks for everyone
Chemical solutions
   Phenol solution (50 g phenol; 5 g cupric sulfate; 1.25 ml concentrated
        hydrochloric acid; 1 liter of water)
   Ferric chloride (20 g ferric chloride; 1 liter of water)
   Potassium ferrocyanide (10 g potassium ferrocyanide; 1 liter of water)
Demonstration whole and half brains
Sets of rat brain sections, cut in horizontal, sagittal, and coronal planes and
     stained with cresyl violet and with hematoxylin
X-ray viewers and microscopes if prepared demonstration slides are avail-
     able

External features

On the surface of the rat brain, identify the rhinal fissure that separates the
paleocortex (called pyriform cortex) from the neocortex. This is the only

fissure or sulcus on the cerebral hemispheres of the rat. On the ventral surface of the brain, find the olfactory tract, optic nerve, optic chiasm, optic tract, and the mammillary bodies of the hypothalamus. On the dorsal and lateral surfaces, identify the general location of the parietal, occipital, frontal, and temporal cortices. Note that these areas of cortex are so named because of the bones of the skull which overlie them.

Sectioning the brain

There are many types of microtomes that can be used to slice tissue, from the small hand microtome to be used in this lab and shown in Figure 4–1 to the large precision instruments, such as that shown in Figure 3–1, that would be used in preparing tissue for histological study in research. Basically, a microtome is a device that allows a block of tissue to be raised a known distance with respect to a knife blade so that sections of tissue can be cut with a constant and known thickness. In the case of a hand microtome, once the tissue is mounted in place, it can be raised with respect to the knife support plate by rotating the base. Each complete turn of the base raises the inside tissue well by ½ mm, and hence raises the brain ½ mm with respect to the knife support plate.

Mount the brain in the microtome with its anterior portion exposed. Be sure that the inside tissue well is as far down as it will go; this is indicated by the clamp knob being as far down in its slot as it will go. Cut off and discard the sections of the cerebral hemispheres anterior to the corpus callosum. You are now ready to slice the brain tissue and should be able to get good sections ¼ to ⅜ mm thick. Hold the blade flat on the knife support plate as indicated in Figure 4–1 and draw the knife toward you, using a slight diagonal slicing motion. Keeping both knife and brain tissue wet with saline (dropped on with the eyedropper) will greatly facilitate cutting. After each section is cut, turn the base the appropriate amount, depending on the thickness of the sections you are preparing, and you are ready for the next slice.

Keep the sections in their proper sequence by placing them in consecutively numbered tissue capsules, as indicated in Figure 4–2. Close the capsules and place them in a beaker of saline or water to prevent the tissue drying out.

It may not be possible to slice through the entire brain from the anterior to posterior extents without removing the brain, lowering the tissue well, and then reclamping the brain. This will of course mean that your first section after reclamping will not be of the same thickness as the others.

Staining procedures

Very little detail in the brain sections can be seen, but by staining them the differentiation between the white myelinated fiber tracts and the gray cell masses can be increased.

Once the sections have been placed in the numbered capsules, follow the staining procedures in the order in which they are listed below.

1. Cover the top of the beaker with an opened gauze sponge and fasten it to the beaker with a rubber band as shown in Figure 4–3. Leave the beaker under running cold tap water for about 30 minutes, and be sure

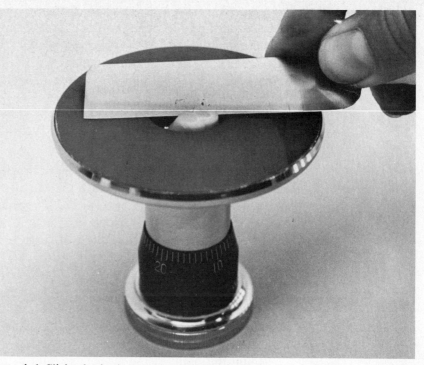

Figure 4–1. Slicing brain tissue with a hand microtome.

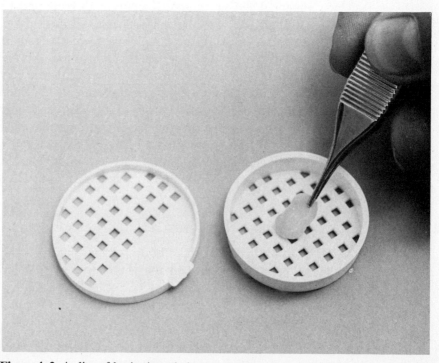

Figure 4–2. A slice of brain tissue being placed into the bottom half of a tissue capsule.

Figure 4–3. Brain slices in tissue capsules being rinsed in running water.

the sink drain is open. In the meantime, prepare a petri dish with a 1% potassium ferrocyanide solution (which will be used in step 6), and then examine any demonstration brains and slides that may be available.

2. Drain the water from the beaker and using forceps, transfer the tissue capsules to the warm solution of phenol and copper sulfate (Figure 4–4). Maintain the temperature at about 60°C and leave the capsules in it for 5 minutes. This solution applies a coating to the white matter of the tissue that will keep it from taking up the stain. Before putting the capsules in this solution, be sure that a beaker of ice water has been prepared and that the ferric chloride solution has been put into the petri dishes. *Danger:* The inhalation of a strong concentration of phenol can be very harmful; the phenol should be kept under a fume hood.

3. Using forceps, transfer the capsules into the beaker of ice water, leaving them in the water for 5 to 10 seconds.

4. Immerse the capsules for 30 to 60 seconds in the 2% solution of ferric chloride. It is suggested that 3 or 4 petri dishes of ferric chloride be used and that one lab partner look after transferring the sections from the phenol to the ice water to the ferric chloride and the other keep

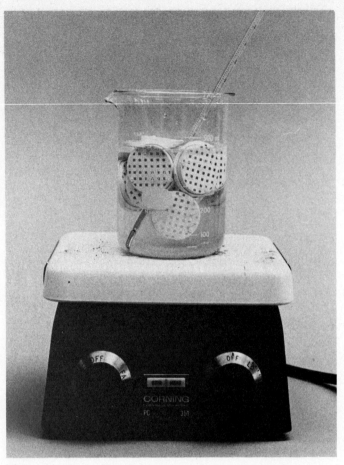

Figure 4–4. Brain slices in tissue capsules in phenol solution.

track of the sections in the ferric chloride, transferring them to the water (step 5) at the appropriate time.

5. Transfer the capsules to a beaker of water and rinse them in running water for about 2 to 3 minutes.

6. After returning to your work area, remove the bottoms of the tissue capsules so that the sections are visible (remember that it is the tops on which the tissue section numbers are written) and immerse the sections (still in the capsule tops) in a petri dish of 1% potassium ferrocyanide solution for about 5 minutes. The time is not terribly important and the sections can be removed when there seems to be a good differentiation of white and gray matter. The potassium ferrocyanide reacts with the ferric chloride to form ferric ferrocyanide. As the ferric chloride will not have been taken up by the white matter due to the treatment with phenol, the brownish-blue stain will indicate the presence of gray matter.

7. Using thumb forceps, wash the individual sections in a beaker of tap water. If the gray matter is not stained deeply, use the thumb forceps to dip the sections briefly into the 2% ferric chloride solution you prepared earlier until the gray matter turns blue.

8. The moist sections should now be placed between 2″×3″ glass microscope slides (several sections per slide) so that drying is prevented. Be sure to mount them in an orderly fashion, starting with either the anterior or the posterior section.

Examination of sections

Using your high-intensity lamp and the magnifier, examine the sections of the rat brain you have placed on the slides. Before coming to the lab, you should have identified in a stereotaxic atlas of the rat brain the structures listed below. Start with the sections at the anterior end of the brain and, proceeding posteriorly, match each section as closely as possible with the diagrams in the atlas.

> cerebral cortex
> corpus callosum
> caudate nucleus
> anterior commissure
> septal area
> amygdaloid nuclei
> stria medullaris
> fornix
> optic chiasm
> hypothalamic area
> internal capsule
> dorsal and ventral hippocampus
> columns of the fornix
> cerebral peduncle
> superior colliculus
> medial geniculate bodies

Remember when looking at your sections that they are relatively thick; some structures may be completely enclosed and not visible. For this reason, neighboring groups may wish to exchange sections so that most or all the above structures (and others that your instructor may designate) can be located. Also remember that the angle at which the brain was cut is probably not the same as the angle of cut used for the sections in making the atlas (see Chapter 3), so it will be necessary to use more than one anterior-posterior plane to identify all the structures in any particular brain section. This should illustrate the importance of the angle of cutting, an issue to which we shall return in Chapter 8.

B. EXAMINATION OF PREPARED SLIDES [1]

There may be several sets of demonstration microscope slides of the rat and cat brain prepared with Nissl and Weigert stains available for your examina-

---

[1] If emphasis is to be placed upon the examination of prepared slides, it is suggested

tion while the tissue capsules are rinsing in running water. The instructor will tell you the thickness of the particular ones you are using but they will be roughly one-twentieth of the thickness of those you prepared in this lab. Note that they are thin enough to be illuminated from below, which makes possible detailed microscopic cellular study.

The appearance of the coronal and sagittal sections should be familiar because of Laboratory Exercise I. The third type of section is the horizontal section. Try to identify some of the structures you have encountered previously; you will find the structures look very different in this orientation.

If cat brain sections are available, note the convoluted cortex; note also that because of the absolute size of the brain, individual nuclei and fiber tracts are easier to identify than in the case of the rat brain.

C. EXTERNAL FEATURES OF DEMONSTRATION BRAINS

Whole and half brains of several mammals may be available for examination. Note that the one aspect common to all is the presence of the rhinal fissure. Note the similarities in the pattern of convolutions within mammalian orders (for example, sheep and cow), as well as the differences (for example, sheep and cat and monkey).

---

that multiple sets of cat brain sections be prepared by the instructor. The brain of this species is sufficiently large that most structures can be easily identified using just an X-ray viewer (or a reasonable facsimile, which can be made by mounting milk-white Plexiglas on a wooden box containing light bulbs), obviating the necessity for either microscopes or microslide projectors.

part two

NEURAL ABLATION AND LESIONS IN PHYSIOLOGICAL PSYCHOLOGY

5

ABLATION AS A METHOD OF FUNCTIONAL ALTERATION OF THE NERVOUS SYSTEM

Part One sketched some of the neuroanatomical foundations of physiological psychology, but of more interest and concern to the physiological psychologist than brain structure is the problem of brain function from a behavioral or a psychological point of view—that is, the problem of brain-behavior relations. In the history of the empirical study of brain-behavior relations, brain ablation has been the technique most widely used in the search for the functions of the brain (or the faculties of the mind, in more classical terms) and the localization of those functions or faculties in the brain. The basic logic underlying the use of ablation, and the inferences drawn from it, is deceptively simple: If a part of the brain is removed, and if it is observed that the organism begins to do or ceases to do something, one can infer that the normal function of that part of the brain is to participate in the control of that behavior, either in an inhibitory or an excitatory way. The logic is, of course, based on certain fundamental assumptions that will be explored in detail in Chapter 13. But to appreciate these assumptions and to appreciate the strengths and the limitations of this technique and the tenuous foundation upon which the logic may rest when applied to certain types of questions concerning brain and behavior, it is necessary to have some historical perspective concerning the use of brain ablation.

A HISTORICAL OVERVIEW OF ABLATION IN PHYSIOLOGICAL PSYCHOLOGY

The history of brain ablation is intimately bound up with that of the principle of cerebral localization, the doctrine that "various parts of the brain have relatively distinct mental, behavioral and physiological functions" (Young, 1968, p. 252), so it is necessary

51

to consider briefly the development of the experimental study of the brain during the past 150 years. Because there are several very adequate accounts (Boring, 1950; Krech, 1962; Walker, 1957; and especially Young, 1968, 1970), only a general overview and a few comments need be presented here to lay the groundwork for subsequent chapters.

Although ablation had been used as early as 1809 by L. Rolando (1770–1831), it was the great French physiologist Pierre Flourens (1794–1867) who developed and advocated its use as an experimental technique and who used the findings generated with it to argue against the localizationist position of phrenology in general and Franz Joseph Gall (1758–1828) in particular. By most accounts, the modern history of brain localization starts with Gall, who by training was a neuroanatomist (and indeed an eminent one, whose accomplishments include the differentiation of white and gray matter of the brain) but whose major interest was the study of physiological correlates of individual behavioral differences. For Gall, the central problem of psychology was that which had intrigued him from early in life: understanding individual differences and accounting for why one person, for instance, could readily memorize vocabulary lists but not carry a tune while another had great musical ability but could learn vocabulary lists only with great difficulty.

The major suppositions underlying Gall's ideas were fourfold:

1. Underlying a striking or pronounced behavior, or a great talent (for example, musical ability) in an individual was a strong faculty or propensity or sentiment. Faculties were assumed by Gall to be inborn or innate, a position in marked contrast to the dominant empiricist view of the time based on the writings of the philosopher John Locke (1632–1704), which maintained that all mental processes and faculties were acquired only through experience.

2. The second supposition was that the brain is the organ of the mind and that the faculties, sentiments, and propensities of the mind can be localized in the brain. This supposition, largely unquestioned today, was not completely accepted by the scientific community in Gall's time.

3. The third supposition was that the brain is made up of a finite number of separate and distinct anatomical parts or organs, each being the seat of a distinct faculty, sentiment, or propensity. The strength of a faculty was assumed to be determined by the amount of activity of its organ; this in turn was assumed to be related to the size of the organ. Hence, variation in function was presumed to be related to variation in structure.

4. The final assumption, which was basically methodological rather than conceptual, was that the size of a particular part or organ of the brain was reflected in the size of the cranium overlying that particular organ. Consequently, the presence of a cranial prominence or bump on the skull was taken to indicate the presence of an enlarged underlying cerebral region.

Young (1970) has elegantly and succinctly sketched the series of one-to-one relationships that constituted Gall's approach to brain and behavior questions:

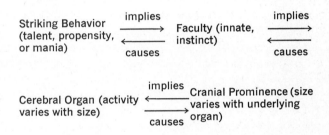

For Gall, the problem of psychology, that of understanding human behavior and individual differences in behavior, had two principal facets: First, the identification of the functions of the brain, the functions being in the form of faculties, sentiments, and propensities; and second, the localization of these functions in the brain. Gall's concern and interest were focused on the first point, and his approach was based on the conviction that the functions of the brain had to be discovered by naturalistic observation rather than by philosophical speculation. He argued that psychology was in the domain of the biologist and not the philosopher, and that the functions of the brain could be determined only by observation and empirical study in much the same way as the functions of any other part of the body. He argued that these functions were of biological significance, functions that would lead to the adaptation of the organism to its environment and to a unity of the organism with nature. It was a view that anticipated the development of evolutionary thought culminating in the writings of Charles Darwin (1809–1882). Gall specifically rejected the medieval view that the faculties of the mind were perception, attention, judgment, memory, imagination, and so on, and ultimately concluded that in man there were some 37 distinct and separate faculties, identified and localized as shown in Figure 5–1. Boring (1950), however, has pointed out that Gall's particular choice of faculties may have been based more on the writings of the Scottish philosophers Thomas Reid (1710–1796) and Dugald Stewart (1753–1828) than on any objective, unbiased, and naturalistic observations.

Gall's methodology, which was largely anecdotal, relied on establishing a correlation of cranial prominences of living individuals, skulls, and head casts with the presence of some form of striking behavior. If Gall found an individual with some striking cranial features, he would attempt to ascertain what talents or propensities the individual possessed. Conversely, if an individual was known for some striking form of behavior, some great talent or propensity, Gall would attempt to determine where on the cranium there were prominences and would infer that the part of the brain beneath the prominence was the seat of the faculty underlying that striking behavior. He also advocated the use of counterproof, showing that a lack of some skull prominence was related to a lack of some specific talent or propensity. One aspect of his methodology should be noted here, for it is relatively sophisticated by modern standards and will be returned to in Chapter 13 in the context of distinguishing between independent and hierarchical treatment effects. Given his supposition that each function of the brain is localized in a separate and distinct cerebral organ, a central problem was to determine whether different behaviors reflected different and distinct faculties or were simply different manifestations of the same faculty. His approach was to observe pathological manifestations of a particular faculty and determine which changes in behavior were independent of other behaviors and which behaviors also changed. Finally, it is of interest to note that Gall did not restrict his observations to humans but attempted a systematic study of animals, the brains of which, he maintained, shared with humans many of the same functions. In certain respects, then, it can be argued that Gall was one of the first comparative psychologists.

Gall's analysis of the functions of the brain and particularly his localization of those functions was rejected by the scientific community, in large measure because his basic methodological assumption of cranial prominences corresponding to the size of the underlying brain tissue was simply incorrect and independent attempts to directly correlate the size of the brain with cranial size, or to correlate the size of the brain with behavior or intelligence, proved unsuccessful. Also important was the fact that although Gall advocated the use of empirical methods, he used a double standard in evaluating evidence; he was highly critical of evidence not favorable to his conceptualizations and willing to accept uncritically almost any kind of supportive evidence. Certainly not unimportant for the rejection of his findings and his methodology was his popularization of his new "science" by setting up booths at fairs and giving public lectures to raise money to support himself and his work. Nevertheless, it is important to appreciate his role in the history of psychology. It was he who started the modern search for the functions of the brain, and much of the work concerned with the study of the brain during the next hundred years was in direct or indirect reference to his ideas and to the principle of cerebral localization. It was also he who insisted that psychology is in the realm of biology and not philosophy and advocated the use of empirical methods rather than philosophical arguments in the study of brain and behavior questions.

It was against Gall's advocacy of empirical, naturalistic observation, and against the emphasis on localization of brain function, that Pierre Flourens argued on the basis of findings generated with his new experimental method of brain ablation. For Flourens, cranial prominences were irrelevant and the problem of determining the functions of the brain was reduced simply to making inferences about the nature and locus of the faculties based on observed changes in behavior resulting from removal of cerebral tissue. If the organism ceased to do something following ablation of tissue, then for Flourens the function of that removed tissue in normal behavior was quite obvious. His most notable success with this approach was in the study of the functions of the cerebellum in pigeons. The removal of successive slices of cerebellar tissue led to an increasing loss of motor coordination, and from this Flourens made the quite valid inference that the cerebellum was concerned with motor coordination and not with reproduction as Gall had maintained.

Flourens' experimental method was in fact only half experimental, for he still relied on uncontrolled and naturalistic observations to assess behavioral changes, and it was upon these observations that he based his inferences about the functions of the brain. It is instructive to contrast his detailed observations of the behavioral changes that followed the removal of the cerebrum of a hen with his inferences about brain function:

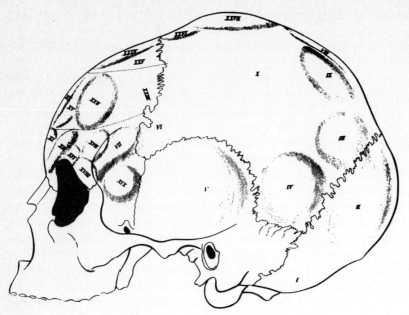

(a)

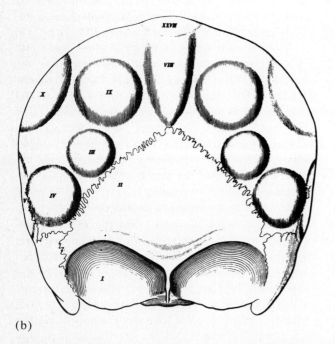

(b)

Figure 5–1. Lateral and posterior views of the skull showing the nature of and the approximate localization of moral and intellectual qualities, as depicted by Gall and Spurzheim. (I) reproduction; (II) love of offspring; (III) friendship; (IV) courage and self-defense; (V) carnivorous tendency; (VI) cunning; (VII) ownership; (VIII) pride; (IX) vanity; (X) caution; (XI) memory of things, facts; (XII) sense of place and space; (XIV) memory of words; (XV) speech and language; (XVI) sense of music; (XVIII) sense of numbers and mathematics; (XIX) sense of mechanics and architecture; (XX) wisdom; (XXII) satire, caustic retort; (XXIII) talent for poetry; (XXIV) morality, kindness; (XXV) mimicry; (XXVI) religion; (XXVII) constancy of purpose. (From F. J. Gall and G. Spurzheim, *Anatomie et physiologie du système nerveux en général, et du cerveau en particulier.* Paris: F. Schoell, 1810, Atlas Plate XCIX.)

I let this hen starve several times for as long as three days. Then I brought nourishment under her nose, I put her beak into grain, I put grain into her beak, I plunged her beak into water, I placed her on a shock of corn. She did not smell, she did not eat anything, she did not drink anything, she remained immobile on the shock of corn, and she would certainly have died of hunger if I had not returned to the old process of making her eat by myself.

Twenty times, in lieu of grain, I put sand into her beak; and she ate this as she would have eaten grain.

Finally, when this hen encounters an obstacle in her path, she throws herself against it, and this collision stops her and disturbs her, but to collide with an object is not the same as to touch it . . . she is collided with and she collides but she does not touch. (Flourens, 1842, pp. 90–91, translated by Young, 1970)

Flourens made the intuitively reasonable inference that the bird had lost its senses, but he then proceeded to infer the following:

An animal which really touches a body, judges it; an animal which does not judge anymore therefore does not touch anymore.

Animals deprived of their cerebral lobes have, therefore, neither perception, nor judgment, nor memory, nor will: because there is no volition when there is no judgment; no judgment when there is no memory; no memory when there is no perception. These cerebral lobes are therefore the exclusive seat of all the perceptions and of all the intellectual faculties. (Flourens, 1842, p. 97, translated by Young, 1970).

It is evident from this quotation that Flourens rejected not only Gall's methodology but also his ideas on the nature of the functions of the brain, and echoed the classical or medieval faculties of perception, judgment, will, volition, and memory. Furthermore, the quotation illustrates the basis of his arguments against the doctrine of localization: His ablations of the cerebrum did not result in changes in one behavior and not others, but produced graded deficits in all the behaviors he noted. It is important to recognize, however, that even if there were localization of function in the various parts of the brain as Gall had maintained, an ablation method as neuroanatomically incongruent as that used by Flourens, a method of making slices through the entire cerebrum, would almost certainly produce the results that Flourens in fact obtained—that is, an increasing loss of all functions. Gall in fact made this argument, but Flourens did not accept it for reasons that Young (1970) suggests were more philosophical than empirical. Without question Flourens had been very much influenced by René Descartes (1596–1650), and his orientation closely reflected the Cartesian distinction between mind and body and the Cartesian concepts of the divisiveness of body and unity of mind. A cerebrum that forms the substrate of a unitary mind must also be organized in a unitary fashion.

The psychological, philosophical, and neurological developments that occurred during the last sixty years of the nineteenth century and that were relevant to the issue of the principle of cerebral localization and to the use of brain ablation as an experimental method had two major themes. First was the refinement and the widespread acceptance of the experimental method of brain ablation as applied to questions of brain-behavior relations and the recognition that many problems of psychology might be better approached from a biological than from a philosophical standpoint. (It was not until the beginning of the twentieth century, however, that the approach became completely experimental with regard to both the independent and the dependent variables.) The second was the rejection of the use of faculties, which confused classification with explanation, and the acceptance of sensory-motor concepts for understanding neural organization and behavior. This shift began with the formulation of the law of dorsal and ventral roots, based on the anatomical observations of C. Bell (1774–1842) and on the physiological data of F. Magendie (1783–1855); it distinguished between sensory and motor fibers of the segmental spinal nerves and localized these in the dorsal and ventral roots, respectively.

Evolutionary concepts of biological continuity implied that since higher or phylogenetically newer parts of the nervous system should be organized according to the same principles as lower and older parts, the distinction between sensory and motor components of the spinal cord should be a general principle of neural organization, a principle that could be extended to the cerebral hemispheres and to the cortex itself. The theoretical basis for such an extension was provided by associationist psychology, which had its origins in the British empiricists and Locke in particular and which held that complex mental phenomena can be reduced to sensations and that the content of mind is built up through repetition and association of simple elements. The empirical basis for the extension was provided by the findings of Fritsch and Hitzig (1870) that unilateral motor movements could be elicited by electrical stimulation of the anterior region of the contralateral cerebral cortex but not of the posterior region. (Parts of this classic paper are reprinted in Part Three and the findings are discussed in more detail in Chapters 10 and 11.) These influences produced not only a shift toward sensory-motor conceptualizations of the brain, but a reemergence of the principle of cerebral localization.

Although it was the work of Fritsch and Hitzig that provided the direct experimental evidence for localization of function, the clinical contribution to the reemergence of this principle (and indeed to the formulation of hypotheses in all of physiological psychology, past and present) cannot be underestimated. Throughout the nineteenth century, clinical observations of aphasia combined with subsequent postmortem examination of the brain suggested localization. In 1861 Pierre Broca (1824–1880) argued on really quite inadequate data that the posterior part of the third convolution of the left frontal lobe was a center for articulate speech. John Hughlings Jackson (1835–1911), who was certainly one of the great names in the modern history of clinical neurology, made remarkable inferences and guesses about brain function from his clinical studies of epileptics. In addition to providing evidence for localization, he proposed the general concept of hierarchical levels of nervous control, which implied that brain lesions produce their effects not only from the loss of function of the damaged tissue, but from a release from inhibition of lower centers normally inhibited by the higher centers. Until today, systematic clinical studies of patients with brain tumors and cerebrovascular disorders, with gunshot wounds of the head (Teuber, Battersby, and Bender, 1960), with surgically removed brain tissue (Milner, 1958), and with surgically separated hemispheres (Gazzaniga, Bogen, and Sperry, 1962, 1963, 1965) have continued to make an important contribution to questions concerned with localization of brain function (Milner, 1971).

The work of David Ferrier (1843–1928) followed from that of Fritsch and Hitzig and combined the use of the new method of electrical stimulation of the brain with the older method of brain ablation to map out motor regions of the cortex in various species and to identify localized sensory regions as well. Those other regions of the cortex that when ablated did not appear to produce sensory loss and that when stimulated did not evoke motor movements came to be referred to vaguely as "association" regions, reflecting the influence of associationist psychology and implying that sensations and movements were associated in these regions.

During the fifty years from the publication of Gall's major work, *The functions of the brain,* to the publication of Ferrier's work of the same title, there was an interesting shift in emphasis in the approach to the question of cerebral localization of function. Gall's emphasis had been on determining the functions of the brain at a behavioral or a psychological level; despite his being a neuroanatomist and despite his phrenological maps, very little of his work was actually concerned with physiological questions. In contrast, most of Ferrier's work was concerned with physiological questions that he reduced to sensory-motor terms, with only a small part of his work concerned with what he called the "subjective aspects of the functions of the brain," in other words, with categories of experience. As Young (1970) has pointed out, Gall and Ferrier can be seen as two extremes on a continuum of approaches to research on brain function and behavior.

With the emphasis on physiology, ablation techniques had become relatively sophisticated by the beginning of the twentieth century, but the analysis of behavioral change remained as anecdotal and subjective as it had been at the time of Flourens. This was in part due to the pervasiveness of sensory-motor physiology and associationism, which implied that only changes in sensory and motor processes need to be studied following neurological manipulation, since all complex mental phenomena are reducible to those terms. With the twentieth century came the explicit recognition that the localization of sensory and motor regions of the cortex was simply inadequate to form the neural substrate of complex behavior and mental processes of psychological interest, processes like problem solving, learning, memory, and intelligence.

With the twentieth century as well came the development of animal learning techniques and objective testing methods providing quantifiable measures of behavior. This work was initiated by Edward L. Thorndike (1874–1949) in 1898 and first applied to brain-behavior research questions by S. I. Franz (1874–1933) in 1902 in the study of frontal lobe function. The work of Karl Lashley (1890–1958) produced refinements in these techniques, such as the use of a sufficient number of subjects for an analysis of the reliability of data and the use of appropriate histological verification of brain damage. Most important, his work produced a reappearance of the basic psychological questions to which Gall had addressed himself. It should be clear from Lashley's paper (reprinted in Chapter 9) that ablation continued to play a major role in the development of physiological psychology during the twentieth century and, as indicated by the comment of Birch, Cotman, and Thompson (1969) in a recent review of techniques and instrumentation in physiological psychology, today "among physiological procedures the lesion approach still appears to be the sine qua non of physiological psychology" (p. 264).

METHODS OF ABLATION AND LESIONING [1]

The experimental study of brain-behavior relations began with an examination of the effects on behavior of altering the functions of the nervous system, and for the first fifty years of that study, the only method of functional alteration was ablation. Virtually every conceivable means of ablation has been attempted. Flourens, who was not concerned with removing what now must be regarded as anatomically distinct parts, simply sliced through and removed cerebral tissue as a whole. However, during the latter part of the nineteenth century, when there developed a concern for identifying the functions of specific brain regions and when the anatomy and vascular distribution of nonhuman brains became better known, the common method of tissue removal was careful cutting and spooning, using the fissures and large blood vessels as guides. As will be clear from Laboratory Exercise IV, cortical tissue has a consistency not dissimilar to vanilla pudding and it can easily be scooped, but the major problem with scooping is hemorrhage. To obviate this problem, methods using heat were developed. Sometimes the cortical tissue was cauterized or burned with hot wires inserted through small trephine holes drilled in the skull, but in the case of small animals such as rats, which have thin crania, the cautery method involved simply placing a hot soldering iron against the cranium which then burned the cortical tissue beneath. The obvious disadvantage with any such method involving heat is that it produces brain damage having a highly unpredictable extent. A second disadvantage is that it leaves epileptogenic scar tissue, that is, scar tissue than can trigger seizure activity.

The method generally used today in making cortical lesions was developed in the 1930s by Wilder

Penfield, a Canadian neurosurgeon, for use in removing epileptogenic scar tissue and diseased brain tissue in humans without itself leaving new scar tissue. This is done with suction applied through a fine-tipped glass or metal pipette, similar to that shown in Figure 5–2. Using the gyri and large blood vessels as landmarks on the cortex, well-defined lesions can be made by simply sucking out the cortical tissue, as well as any blood from ruptured vessels. This is the method that will be used to make the cortical lesions in Laboratory Exericse IV. Of course the brain of the rat does not have fissures (except the rhinal fissure), so the ablation will be made in reference to bregma.

Because aspiration (or indeed even tissue scooping) requires visualization, it is not a method appropriate for making well-defined lesions in subcortical or nonsuperficial areas. Such lesions require the use of stereotaxic procedures, the principles of which, first formulated in 1908 by V. Horsley and R. H. Clarke, did not become at all widely used until the late 1930s. The basic principles of introducing subcortical lesions with stereotaxic procedures were outlined in Chapter 3 in the context of describing the construction and use of stereotaxic atlases. Using a stereotaxic atlas, and assuming that the animal's head is held in the same orientation with respect to the instrument as that used in constructing the atlas, the tip of an electrode can be placed quite accurately into any specific region of the brain on the basis of the horizontal, vertical, and coronal relationship of that region to the center of the ear bars or to the cranial suture landmarks. The electrode is usually just a piece of wire or an insect pin insulated along its length except at the tip (see Appendix B–5), and the usual method of making a lesion involves passing a DC current between the electrode tip and some large surface electrode, often attached to a muscle or inserted into the rectum. The flow of current, which is very concentrated at the small electrode tip but very diffuse at the large surface electrode, destroys the tissue around the cerebral electrode tip by the combination of heat and the transference of metallic ions to the tissue. The latter process is called electrolysis, and hence lesions produced in this way are called electrolytic lesions. A more recently developed procedure involves passing a current, alternating at radio frequencies (RF), through the tissue. This destroys the tissue through the generation of large amounts of heat. In a recent systematic comparison made of the tissue-destroying properties of DC and RF currents, DiCara, Weaver, and Wolf (1974) conclude that the former is preferred in situations

---

[1] *Ablation* implies the complete removal of some part of the brain, whereas a *lesion* implies some damage to a part of the brain. The former term is usually used to refer to cortical damage involving the removal of some region of the cortex; the latter term is usually used to refer to subcortical damage. The two terms are, however, often used quite interchangeably, especially in general or theoretical discussions.

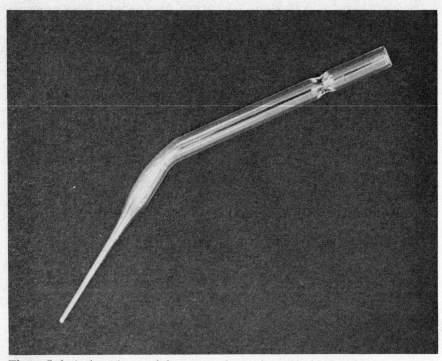

Figure 5–2. A glass pipette of the type used to make cortical lesions by aspiration. This will be used in Laboratory Exercise IV, and instructions for making one are included in Appendix B.

requiring the destruction of nuclear groups while the latter is preferred in situations requiring the destruction of white matter.

Both these contemporary ablation or lesion techniques, aspiration and electrolysis, produce permanent brain damage, but there are techniques that allow for making apparently temporary lesions. The great advantage of such temporary functional blockades (as they are aptly called) is that the behavior of an animal with some part of its nervous system nonfunctional can be subsequently compared with itself with that part of the nervous system again functional.

One of the better known and widely used of these involves the application of potassium chloride (KCl) to the surface of the dura. This induces a wave of functional depression that slowly spreads across the cortex. The phenomenon was first observed by Dusser de Barenne and McCullock (1941), who found that strong repetitive electrical stimulation applied directly to the cortex often resulted in the cortical surface becoming electrically depressed at the site of stimulation. This depression then slowly moved across the surface of the cortex, leaving the cortex in a temporarily nonfunctional state. Leaõ

(1944, 1947) studied the phenomenon and found that it could be initiated in several ways, such as electrical stimulation, the application of various chemicals (especially KCl), mechanical deformation of the cortex, and even partial drying of the cortical surface. The phenomenon is characterized by a negative wave of electrical activity that moves slowly across the cortex at a rate of 2 to 3 mm per minute (Bures, Petran, and Jachar, 1967), followed by a longer lasting but smaller amplitude positive wave; then slowly, over a period of an hour or more, the cortex returns to normal. During this time, the normal electrical activity of cortical neurons is disrupted.

Spreading depression initiated in one hemisphere has the interesting and useful property of being restricted to that hemisphere; it does not cross the corpus callosum to the opposite hemisphere. Consequently, it can be used to create a temporary hemidecorticate preparation that has proved useful in research problems concerned with interhemispheric relations. Unfortunately, however, its use is restricted to smooth brained, or lissencephalic, animals, since the passage of spreading depression through the depths of the sulci of convoluted brains is rather unpredictable and erratic.

The mechanism of spreading depression is obscure, but one generally accepted hypothesis is that of Grafstein (1956), which suggests that its initiation and propagation depend on the liberation of potassium ions from the neurons. This depolarizes the adjoining neurons, liberating more potassium, and hence there is a slow movement or chain reaction across the cortex. In Laboratory Exercise IX, an attempt will be made to record the EEG changes associated with the induction of spreading depression.

Figure 5–3 shows, in a diagrammatic form, one method used to initiate spreading depression. With the rat under anesthesia, a trephine hole is made in the parietal bone of each hemisphere and a small cup is cemented to the skull over each trephine hole. After the animal has recovered fully from the anes-

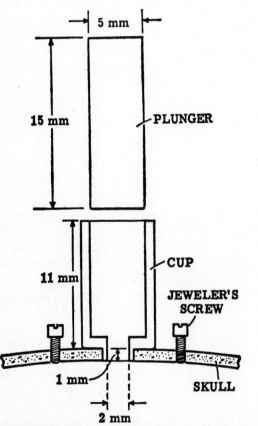

Figure 5–3. Diagram of one assembly used for inducing cortical spreading depression in a chronic preparation. Dental cement is built up around the sides of the cup and is held firmly to the cranium with the jeweler's screws, which act as anchors. The plunger is left in the cup to keep out dirt. (From I. S. Russell and S. Ochs, Localization of a memory trace in one cortical hemisphere and transfer to the other hemisphere. *Brain,* 1963, **86,** 37–54, Figure 1.)

thesia, KCl can be applied to the surface of the dura at will by the experimenter. Russell (1971) and Dimond (1972) have recently reviewed some of the applications of spreading depression in physiological psychology; suffice it to say here that the focus of attention has been principally on questions of the learning and memory capabilities of one hemisphere functioning in the temporary absence of the other, and secondarily on questions concerned with the integration of function of the two hemispheres.

A second method of making a reversible functional blockade exploits the fact that when tissue is cooled, its metabolic rate drops drastically and, in the case of nervous tissue, the cells no longer support the transmission of axon potentials. The principles involved in using subcortical cryogenic blockade devices are analogous to making electrolytic lesions in that a probe, thermally insulated except at the tip, is inserted into the brain tissue with the aid of stereotaxic procedures, and a coolant is passed through this which puts the brain tissue at the tip in a reversibly nonfunctional state. As might be suggested by a close examination of the cryoprobe in Figure 5–4 which can be permanently implanted in the brain, the actual procedures are technically much more complicated than those involved in making electrolytic lesions. The coolant must flow constantly through the probe to maintain cooling, and the rate of flow must be adjusted on the basis of the temperature of the tip, which must be constantly monitored. The thermal insulation along the length of the probe is provided by heating a coil; to avoid permanent tissue damage due to excess heat or a temporary functional blockade due to too little heat, the temperature along the length of the probe must also be monitored and the heat adjusted. However, with the temperature feedback system described by Skinner and Lindsley (1968), it is possible to have well-controlled tissue cooling in the awake animal.

THE ANALYSIS OF BEHAVIORAL CHANGE

It was not until the beginning of this century that the effects on behavior of neurological manipulation began to be assessed by objective and quantifiable measures. Because the shift in orientation that occurred was away from sensory-motor concerns toward concerns of intelligence, problem solving, learning, and memory, the objective measures were largely derived from animal learning techniques, which had just begun to be developed and studied by psychologists. It is far beyond the scope and intent of this

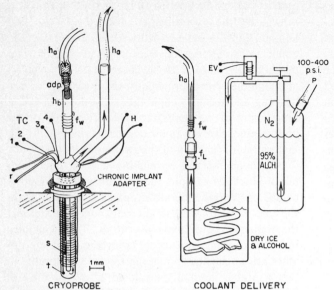

Figure 5–4. Part of a cryogenic system. The cryoprobe is inserted in the brain and is cemented to the cranium. The coolant is circulated through h_a, the temperature is monitored with thermocouples s and t, and temperature information is sent to a feedback control system (not shown here) by the thermocouple leads, TC. (From J. E. Skinner and D. B. Lindsley, Reversible cryogenic blockade of neural function in the brain of unrestrained animals. *Science,* 1968, **161,** 595–597, Figures 1(c), 1(d). Copyright © 1968 by the American Association for the Advancement of Science.)

chapter to explore the methods that have developed for the study of behavioral change, for these are the methods of experimental psychology. For purposes of later discussion and for purposes of commenting on certain logical problems, however, it is instructive to consider briefly one or two classes of testing situations commonly used in contemporary physiological psychology. One class is discrimination learning situations, usually involving approach learning, in which the animal is required to make differential responses to two or more stimuli, that is, to respond one way to one stimulus and another way to another. Figures 5–5 and 5–6 show two types of discrimination learning apparatuses that can be used to illustrate certain features common to virtually all discrimination learning situations. Figure 5–5 shows a Lashley jumping stand, designed for use with laboratory rats, consisting basically of a small jump stand and two doors on which are mounted stimulus panels. The animal must jump from the stand to one of the two doors, and if it jumps to the door containing the stimulus panel that the experimenter has designated as correct

(S^+), the door opens and the rat receives a piece of food from behind it. If it jumps to the incorrect stimulus panel (S^-), the door is locked and there is no food reward. Some versions of this apparatus incorporate punishment for incorrect responses; there is no ledge to jump to and an incorrect response leads to the animal falling into a net located below the apparatus. The Wisconsin General Test Apparatus (WGTA), shown in Figure 5–6, is used for larger animals like monkeys and cats, and the animal must again respond in a differential manner to the two stimuli. If it responds correctly to S^+, it receives a piece of food from the well located beneath the displaced object; if it responds incorrectly to S^-, there is no food reward.

Two features are common to most such discrete trial discrimination learning situations. First, all cues apart from the differential cues in which the experimenter is interested are either equalized or balanced across trials. The most obvious such cue is position, and so the positions of S^+ and S^- are varied according to a specified sequence of right and left which is

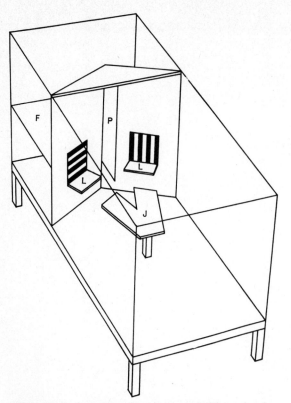

Figure 5–5. A Lashley jumping stand. The animal must jump from one of the arms of the platform, J, to one of the two ledges in front of the doors. If the animal is correct, it gets access to the food located through the door. The partition between the two ledges prevents the animal from correcting errors. (From N. S. Sutherland, The learning of discrimination by animals. *Endeavour,* 1964, **23,** 148–152, Figure 1.)

irregular and balanced but not random (Gellerman, 1933; Fellows, 1967).[2] Such sequences will be used in Laboratory Exercise IV. The second feature is that training proceeds until the animal reaches some learning criterion, some level of performance deemed by the experimenter to constitute evidence sufficient to claim that the animal has "learned" the problem. Such criteria as 10 consecutive correct responses,

11 out of 12 correct responses, 90 percent correct responding on 3 consecutive test sessions, and so on are quite commonly encountered, and the dependent variable is either trials or errors to the criterion (sometimes including the criterion trials, sometimes not). In normal animals and in most learning situations, these criteria produce similar results in terms of trials and errors to criterion, and trials and errors to criterion are themselves highly correlated.

It is, however, not difficult to imagine treatments whose effects would be enhanced or diminished depending on the choice of criterion and dependent variable. Consider a treatment that, in fact, makes the animal more distractible. This might not even be detected if a criterion of 18 out of 20 correct responses were used, for the animal could have a few brief lapses in attention but still reach criterion. Furthermore, if errors to criterion rather than trials to criterion were the dependent variable, the few extra blocks of 20 trials it might take the treated animals to reach criterion would not appreciably alter the total errors, since there would be but a few errors being made. On the other hand, if the criterion were 10 consecutive correct responses, and if trials to criterion was the dependent variable, the treated group might be very different from normals, since their occasional lapses of attention would prevent them from achieving 10 *consecutive* correct responses. Although they might be making only a very small proportion of errors, their total trials would quickly accumulate. The exercise simply illustrates that certain treatments may have differential effects on various performance criteria and may disrupt the normally good correlation between trials and errors to criterion. This makes the choice of a criterion a most important consideration is designing research as well as in evaluating behavioral deficits.

Certainly as common as discrimination learning situations are avoidance learning situations, some of which do involve discrimination. We can distinguish between two general categories of avoidance learning, one being active avoidance, in which the animal is required to perform some response in order to avoid an aversive event, the other being passive avoidance, in which the animal is required to withhold a response to avoid punishment. An example of the latter will be used in Laboratory Exercise V in conjunction with evaluating the effects of amygdaloid lesions in rats. In addition to discrete trial situations such as these in which individual trials are run and each trial is scored for correctness and/or response time, operant learning situations are finding increasing use in physiological psychology. These situations

[2] In any random bivalent sequence, there will quite frequently occur runs of surprisingly long length of one value or the other. To follow such a sequence might then require positioning the stimuli in the same position for six or eight or even more consecutive trials, which is certainly not conducive to extinguishing positional response habits and facilitating attending and responding to visual cues. A balanced irregular sequence is designed so that there will be no more than three consecutive trials with the stimuli in the same position.

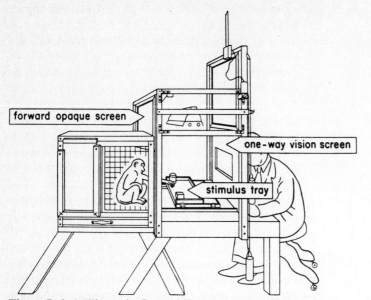

Figure 5–6. A Wisconsin General Test Apparatus. This can be used with large laboratory animals such as cats or monkeys. Between trials, the stimuli are baited while the forward opaque screen is closed; during trials, the one-way vision screen is closed. (From H. F. Harlow, The formation of learning sets. *Psychological Review,* 1949, **56,** 51–56, Figure 1. Copyright 1949 by the American Psychological Association. Reprinted by permission.)

involve the animal performing some response, such as bar pressing, in order to receive food pellets, and it is the rate of response that serves as the dependent measure. Treatment effects are then assessed in terms of change in response rate from some baseline.

There can be no dispute that the shift from an essentially neurological examination of animals to the use of objective measures of behavior to assess treatment effects represented a major advance in the experimental study of brain-behavior relations. But in many respects this advance was more technical than conceptual, for an objective and quantifiable measure of behavioral change is no better than a subjective description of a change, if it is lacking validity. What is of interest to the psychologist is the meaning or interpretation of a behavioral change rather than the change per se, and consequently any behavioral measure must have validity in the sense that it must indeed be a measure of some process. Most important, changes in the behavioral measure must indeed reflect change in the process. This problem of task validity is no trivial matter and is fundamental to physiological psychology, yet for some peculiar reason it has been benignly ignored.

In the context of discrimination learning, the problem of task validity can be exemplified with two illustrations. The first is derived from the experimenter who assumes that his method of classifying stimuli is the same as that used by his experimental subject, that is, the experimenter who assumes that he and his animals see their worlds in the same way. Consider the experimenter who is studying spatial perception using a discrimination learning paradigm and assumes two problems to be spatial problems because they involve differences in stimulus orientation, an apparent dimension of spatial perception. These might be the problems shown for purposes of illustration in Figure 5–7, which are taken from Webster (1972). To assume that the animal is discriminating between these pairs of stimuli on the basis of their differential orientation requires, *as a minimum,* that the animal is attending to the entire stimulus configuration. Animals, however, are notorious for attending only to where they respond and for ignoring those aspects of the stimulus display that are not in the immediate proximity of the locus of the response (Cowey, 1968; Meyer, Treichler, and Meyer, 1965). Consequently, a cat being trained in a WGTA on the problems in Figure 5–7 will likely respond to the base of the stimuli and hence will

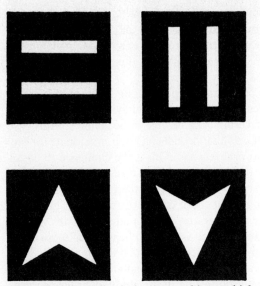

Figure 5–7. Two discrimination problems which, under certain conditions, could be, but under other conditions might not be, considered valid tests of spatial perception.

probably treat the arrowhead problem as a V-shape (the bottom of the downward-pointing arrowhead) versus a somewhat flat edge (the bottom of the upward-pointing arrowhead) and treat the horizontal-vertical problem as the presence of a brightness change (the vertical lines) versus the absence of any brightness change (the horizontal lines). How the animal in fact views his world can be determined only by rather extensive equivalence and transfer testing (see Butter, 1968, for an example of the use of such testing). Without such testing, there is simply no justification for the psychologist to consider discrimination test performance in terms of human perceptual categories. Without such testing, the use of problems in Figure 5–7 as tests of spatial perception would be an example of a probably invalid behavioral test, for despite objectivity, quantifiability, and reliability, there is no assurance that the tests measure what they are supposed to.

A second and more general problem bearing on test validity is derived from the multideterminacy of task performance: Performance on a task has many nonindependent determinants and a change in performance may be due to change in any one or more of these determinants. This makes the interpretation of a behavioral change a most complicated enterprise. One need only consider the years of research and debate since Jacobson (1936) observed delayed response decrements in monkeys with frontal lobe

ablations and since Kluver and Bucy (1939) observed changes in visual behavior in monkeys with temporal lobe ablations to appreciate the subtleties and complexities there can be in attempting to sort out, first, which variables influence task performance under various conditions, and second, which of the task determinants have been altered in some way by the treatment.

Even performance on a "simple" two-choice visual discrimination task is multidetermined; changes in performance cannot be unambiguously attributed to any one particular variable although the basic problem may seem quite obvious. A striking example of this is provided by Schneider (1967). Hamsters with bilateral lesions of the superior colliculus or with bilateral lesions of the visual cortex or with control sham operations were required to discriminate a horizontal grating from a vertical grating in a two-choice discrimination box that required the animal to leave the start box, enter one or the other response compartment, and press on a stimulus panel at the end of the compartment. If the animal correctly pressed S⁺, it was rewarded with access to water, but if it incorrectly pressed S⁻, it was simply returned to the start box for a new trial. As in most such discrimination situations, the positions of S⁺ and S⁻ were varied according to a Gellerman sequence. As might be expected, animals with visual cortex lesions were grossly impaired and never performed above chance. But of more immediate interest was the very poor (chance) performance of the animals with bilateral superior colliculus lesions. The "obvious" interpretation is that both treatments impair pattern perception.

Schneider, however, went on to demonstrate very elegantly that while this may have been so for the animals with cortical lesions, the deficits of the animals with superior colliculus lesions were due to problems in spatial orientation and in moving through space from the start box to the correct goal box. In other words, these animals could perceive the patterns and discriminate between them quite normally, but could not locomote themselves through space from the start box to the response panel to make the correct response. Consequently, when the apparatus was arranged as shown in the lower part of Figure 5–8 and a response was defined as entering one or the other response compartment (demarcated by the barrier between the response panels), the animals performed at no better than chance; their mode of responding (edging along one wall until they eventually reached a panel with S⁺) of course would lead them to the correct response compartment on only 50 percent of the trials. When the apparatus

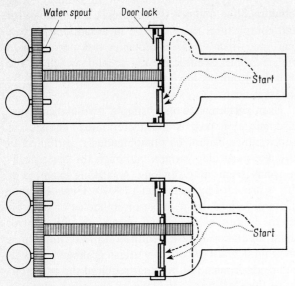

Figure 5–8. Two views of the two-choice discrimination apparatus used by Schneider. The dashed line shows the path usually followed by a hamster with bilateral lesions of the superior colliculus (SC) and the dotted line that followed by a normal subject. In the initial experiment, when the barrier between response compartments was in place and a response was defined as entering one response compartment or the other, SC animals showed only a 50% correct response rate. When the barrier was removed (upper diagram) or when the definition of a response was changed to be the pressing against one door or the other (lower diagram), then the choice behavior of the SC animals was similar to that of the normals. (From G. E. Schneider, Contrasting visuomotor functions of tectum and cortex in the golden hamster. *Psychologische Forschung,* 1967, **31**, 52–62, Figure 5.)

was modified so that the barrier was removed (upper diagram of Figure 5–8) and/or the response definition was changed to pressing against one panel or the other, the choice behavior of the animals was almost perfect.

One of several important points that this study illustrates is that just as a behavior is controlled by multiple variables, a change in behavior (in this case visual discrimination deficits) can take place for any one of several reasons. This is the challenge to physiological psychologists. Much of the rest of this book is concerned with the techniques of physiological psychology, but these can be learned in a matter of hours by a moderately bright undergraduate. What is of real importance is the application of these techniques to the problems of behavioral analysis.

The validity of the use of ablation and postoperative behavioral testing in the study of brain-behavior relations assumes the validity of the behavioral testing, and this is why it is of such critical importance for the physiological psychologist to be a psychologist, to be concerned about the validity of behavioral tasks as indicators of psychological processes, about the validity of changes in task performance as indicators of change in psychological processes, and hence to be concerned with the study of variables that influence behavior and with how variables interact in task influence. Only by studying behavior can we begin to understand the multideterminants of behavior and be in a position to begin to study and to understand the effects of treatments on behavior. The physiological psychologist must not only be working in and thinking about what is traditionally included in physiological psychology, but also be enthusiastically involved in comparative and experimental psychology.

6 LABORATORY EXERCISE III

BASICS OF SMALL ANIMAL SURGERY

This is one of the more important laboratory exercises because it forms the procedural foundation for most of those that follow; you should pay careful attention to all details.

Figure 2–1 showed most of the surgical instruments you will be using in this and subsequent labs. Use it to help identify your instruments and consult the equipment list below. Be sure that everything you will need from beginning to end of the surgery is available, clean, in good operating condition, and laid out in an orderly fashion. The key to working quickly but effectively is organization and forethought. Once surgery begins, you should work quickly so that the animal will not begin to recover from the anesthetic before you are finished. Supplementary anesthetic doses can be given should your animal begin to wake up before you are finished, but should be avoided when possible.

Equipment and supplies for each group

Rat headholder on base
High-intensity lamp (if necessary)

Surgical instruments
#3 scalpel handle
#10 blade
2 mosquito forceps
Rat-tooth forceps
Thumb forceps
Needleholder
Large scissors
Size 16 suture needle
18 in. size 00 silk thread
Instrument sterilizer tray and Zephiran chloride solution
6-in. ruler
Saline bowl with saline
10 2"×2" gauze sponges
2 1-cc syringes with 26G needles
Dishpan with detergent
2 towels
Lab coats

Equipment and supplies to be shared by groups

Animal balance
Nembutal anesthetic, 60 mg/cc
Atropine sulfate, 0.4 mg/cc
70% alcohol and sponges
Animal clippers
Respirator
Heating pad
Heavy gloves

Pour Zephiran, which is an antiseptic, into the instrument tray and place the instruments and thread in it. In the case of a cat or monkey, one would want to follow sterile procedures completely to minimize the chance of infection, but rats are a sufficiently hardy species that only minimal precautions are necessary.

Handling and anesthetizing the rat

Each group will be assigned a rat for use in this lab (and to be used again in Laboratory Exercise VI). A few minutes should be spent handling and getting to know it to both calm the animal's fear of humans and the human's fear of the rat. Remember that these laboratory rats are only distant relatives of wild rats and much of the aggressiveness so characteristic of the wild rat has been bred out of these strains. They also should have been handled previously and so should not be wild or vicious. Those who are hesitant, however, might want to use a glove when handling their rat for the first time or two.

Never pick up the rat by the tail; instead, reach confidently into the cage, slip your fingers under the animal's chest, and grip it firmly with your thumb across the back. Be careful not to lift it from the cage too quickly, since it may be holding onto the grid floor with its toes. Breaking its nails will result in profuse bleeding. When the rat has been lifted from the cage, transfer it to the arm of your laboratory coat as shown in Figure 6–1 and rub the fur on the head and neck for a short time. Practice picking up the animal and handling it for short periods of time with your bare hands; when you feel confident, proceed to anesthetize it.

Your animal will have been deprived of food for 24 hours, which should facilitate anesthetization. Place the animal in the scale and weigh it to the nearest five grams. The animal will be anesthetized with sodium pentobarbital (Nembutal) using an anesthetic dosage of 60 milligrams of anesthetic per 1000 grams of body weight, conventionally expressed as 60 mg/kg. The anesthetic is dissolved in solution for easy administration, and this solution has a concentration of 60 mg of anesthetic per cubic centimeter of solution (60 mg/cc). To calculate the required dosage for your animal, (1) determine the quantity of anesthetic required—for example, 268 g × 60 mg/1000 g = 16.8 mg; (2) determine the volume of anesthetic required—for example, 16.8 mg × 1 cc/60 mg = 0.268 cc. Calculate the dosage for your animal. Double-check your calculations and make sure that units cancel properly. Be sure you understand the basic logic behind calculating dosages. (Note that because of the particular concentration (60 mg/cc) and dosage (60 mg/kg) used, if an animal weighs 0.*xxx* kg, it will require 0.*xxx* cc.)

Using a piece of gauze sponge soaked in 70% alcohol, wipe the rubber

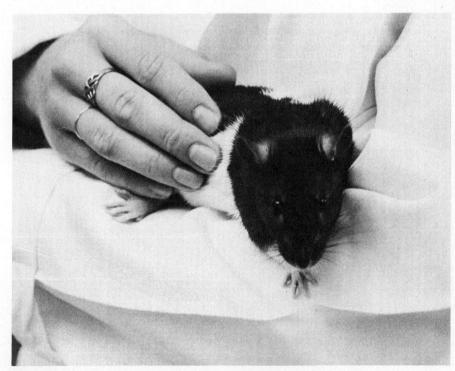

Figure 6–1. A laboratory hooded rat being handled and tamed on the arm. The albino rat, which is white with pink eyes, is another strain often used in physiological psychology.

diaphragm top of the anesthetic vial. If disposable syringes and needles are used, remove them from their packages by peeling apart the wrappers. Hold the needle by the clear plastic casing and firmly press the needle onto the syringe, twisting slightly. Note that the syringe may have two sets of calibrations; you will be using the cc calibrations. Pull off the clear plastic cap, fill the syringe with about as much air as anesthetic you will remove, turn the vial upside down, push the needle through the rubber stopper, inject the air (this prevents a vacuum from forming in the vial), and withdraw slightly more anesthetic than you require. Remove the needle and syringe, pull back on the plunger, lightly tap the side of the syringe with your fingernail to get rid of any air bubbles, and then push the plunger up until there is no longer any air in the syringe. Now squirt into the air any excess anesthetic.

Figure 6–2 demonstrates how the animal should be held for an intraperitoneal injection. The animal is held in the left hand; by squeezing the elbows together with the thumb and middle finger, the forepaws are crossed under the chin, which prevents the animal from biting. The lower legs are pressed against a table top or other firm surface, which stretches the abdominal muscles and allows for the easy penetration by a needle. For the first one or two injections, it is strongly suggested that the animal be held with a glove so that attention can be paid more to the mechanics of injecting the animal than to the details of restraining it.

(a)

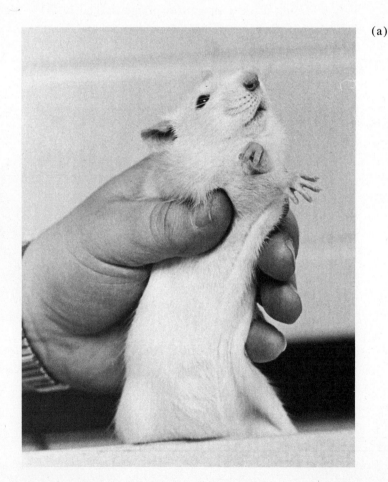

(b)

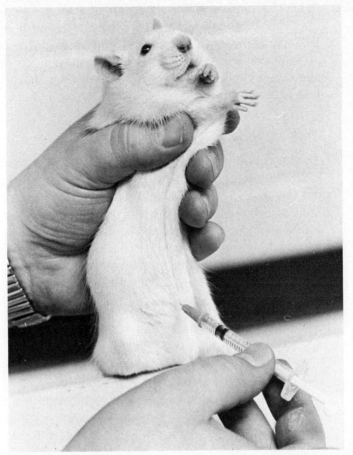

Figure 6–2. Holding the rat for an IP injection. Note that the forelimbs have been crossed by pressing together the elbows. It is most important that during the injection the abdominal muscles be tightly stretched and the needle be inserted perpendicular to the abdominal wall.

Now, orienting the needle perpendicular to the abdominal wall, jab the needle sharply (do not push) just lateral to the midline in the lower left quadrant of the abdomen, inject the anesthetic by pushing in the syringe plunger, and withdraw the needle. Good practice dictates that before the anesthetic is actually injected, the plunger should be withdrawn slightly (aspirated). If the needle tip is in the peritoneal cavity, there will be a slight vacuum. Blood in the syringe barrel indicates that the needle has penetrated an organ and that the tip is not in the peritoneal cavity; if this occurs, remove the needle and start again with a fresh needle, syringe, and anesthetic dose.

The importance of stretching the abdominal muscles and having the angle of the needle perpendicular to the abdominal wall cannot be overemphasized. One of the most common reasons for anesthetic failure is that the needle does not penetrate the abdominal muscles and the anesthetic is just injected subcutaneously. With some experience, this can be detected by rubbing the site of injection with the thumb; a subcutaneous injection will leave a bubble, whereas a successful IP injection will not.

Return the animal to its cage. Within 5 to 10 minutes the anesthetic should have taken effect. Once the animal is at least partially unconscious, the depth of anesthesia can be determined readily by pinching the tail with the thumbnail. Movements of the hind limbs indicate that the necessary depth of anesthesia has not been reached. If movements still occur after 15 to 20 minutes, inject a supplementary dose of anesthetic (15 to 20 percent of the original dose).

Clipping fur

The fur from the head can be clipped before the animal is fully anesthetized. Hold the electric clippers in your right hand and, keeping the animal's ears out of the way with the thumb and middle finger of your left hand, shave the head as closely as possible. If fur gets into the eyes, be sure to remove it later with a sponge or cotton swab dampened with saline. Clipping the fur facilitates making the incision and reduces the possibility of pieces of fur getting into the incision and causing infection later.

Mounting the animal in headholder

After the animal is clipped but before mounting it in the headholder, inject intraperitoneally about 0.1 cc of atropine (0.4 mg/cc). For reasons discussed in Chapter 16, this will prevent the development of respiratory problems that sometimes occur with barbiturate anesthetics.

A stereotaxic instrument similar to one shown at the end of this chapter is usually used to hold the animal during surgery, but in these labs a headholder will be used instead. Figure 6–3 demonstrates the steps involved in mounting

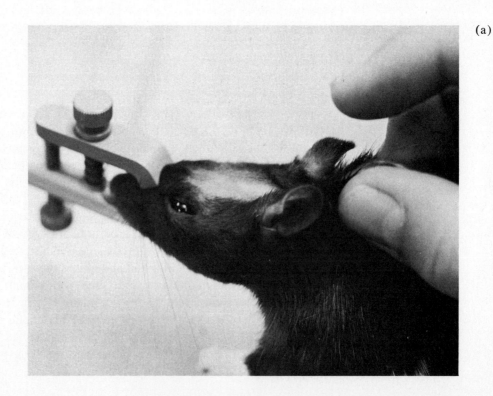

(a)

(b)

(c)

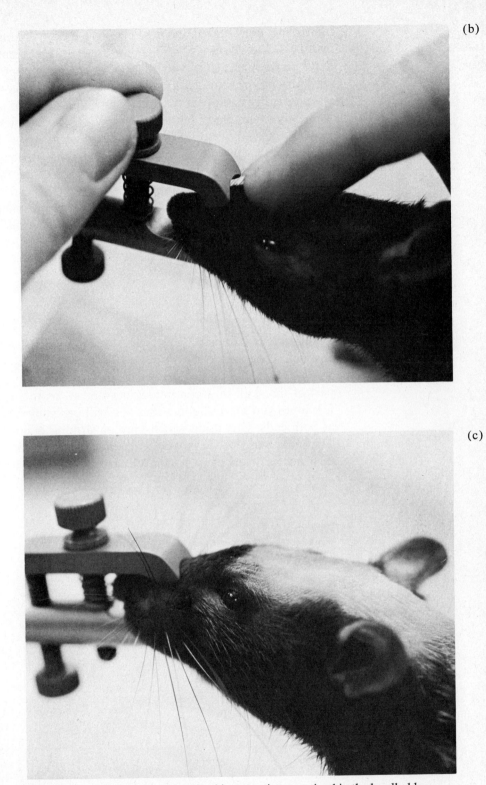

Figure 6–3. The three stages involved in mounting an animal in the headholder.
(a) The rat is held by the scruff of the neck by the thumb and middle finger of
the right hand, and the upper incisor teeth are slipped into the slot in the
support bar. (b) The snout is held down with the index finger of the right hand while
the left hand tightens the nose clamp. (c) The angle of the headholder is
adjusted so that the head is almost horizontal.

the animal in it. Loosen the nose clamp so that the animal's upper incisor teeth can be slipped through the opening on the support bar. To do this you may have to open the jaws with the blunt end of your probe. Be careful not to inadvertently occlude the trachea with your finger. As in Figure 6–3(a), with your right hand, support the animal by holding the fur on the back of the neck with your thumb and middle finger; then, as in Figure 6–3(b), push the snout against the support bar with your right index finger and tighten the noseholder on the animal's snout. First thumb-tighten the upper screw until the noseholder is level with the support bar and then thumb-tighten the lower screw. If the screws are tightened too much, especially the lower one, you could crush the snout, so be careful to tighten just enough to ensure that the animal's head is firmly held. The head must not be able to be moved laterally. Adjust the universal clamp so that the head is flat and level as shown in Figure 6–3(c).

Incision

Make the incision as illustrated in Figure 6–4. Using the thumb and middle finger of your left hand, stretch the skin laterally, as shown in Figure 6–4(a), and with the round edge of the #10 blade (not the point), apply *firm pressure* against the skull and move the scalpel from the anterior to the posterior part of the skull in a continuous movement, as in Figure 6–4(b). The first few times you make the incision, you will probably have to expand it slightly at both ends. One thing which may be striking is how little bleeding occurs. There are very few large vessels running through the scalp (this is not true of primates), and most of the bleeding after your incision is made will be

(a)

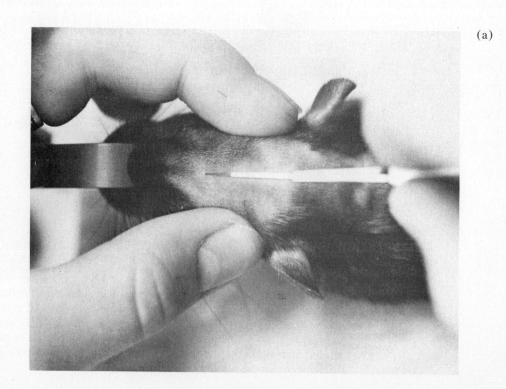

(b)

(c)

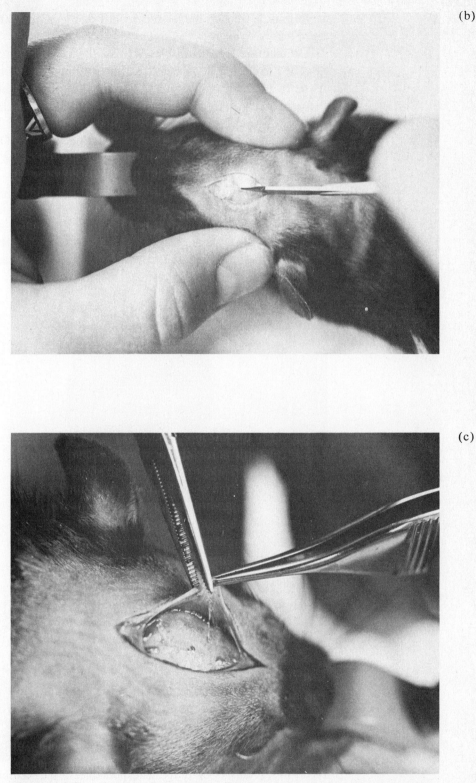

Figure 6–4. Steps involved in making the initial exposure. (a) The skin is stretched laterally with the thumb and index finger of the left hand and (b) the scalpel is pressed firmly against the skull and drawn posteriorly in a continuous movement. (c) After the periosteum has been scraped from the cranium, it is caught with the thumb forceps while mosquito forceps are attached.

from muscle fiber in the posterior part of the head that has been inadvertently cut.

Immediately beneath the skin is the periosteum, a thin layer of tissue attached to the skull, especially at the midline. Use your scalpel to loosen this tissue from the bone by *firmly* scraping from the midline to both sides. Catch the periosteum with your thumb forceps and attach a mosquito forcep to it on each side about two-thirds of the way posterior, as in Figure 6–4(c). Do not attach the forceps to the skin, just to the periosteum. Orient the forceps so the handles point away from the animal's head to keep the skin retracted from the working area, as shown in Figure 6–5.

Mapping cortical areas

After the skull dries slightly, it will become clear that the skull consists of a number of bones. The points at which these join are called sutures. Locate the

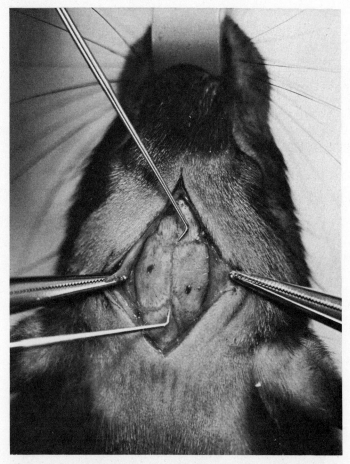

Figure 6–5. A dorsal view of the final appearance of the exposure. Note the position and the angle of the mosquito forceps. The upper probe is pointing to bregma and the lower probe to lambda. These reference points are where the anterior and posterior bone sutures, respectively, intersect the midline suture. (The dark spots on the bone are from bone bleeding. This oozing usually stops soon after the incision is made.)

midline suture. The junction of the midline suture with that between the frontal and parietal bones is called bregma, and the junction of the midline suture with that between the parietal and occipital bones is called lambda. The location of these is shown in Figure 6–5.

There is quite good consistency from one laboratory rat to the next as to the location of bregma and its relationship to underlying brain structure. The student should be aware, however, that one does occasionally encounter an animal with an anomalous suture pattern, such as the midline suture being off the midline or the frontoparietal suture having a marked posteriorly oriented "dip" so that it intersects the midline too posteriorly. The first condition can be coped with easily because the sagittal sinus, located in the midline between the two hemispheres, can be seen through the cranium (the cranium must be moist) as a bluish band. The middle of this can be taken as the midline. The second condition is the more difficult, and the appropriate anterior-posterior reference point must be guessed by ignoring the dip and estimating on the basis of the entire frontoparietal suture just where the suture should have intersected the midline.

Figure 6–6 shows three views of the rat brain surface, a lateral view, a

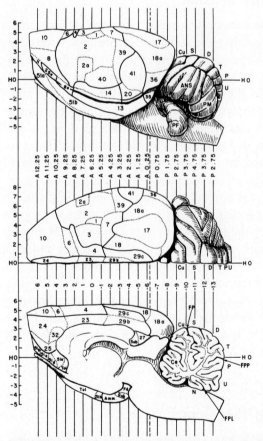

Figure 6–6. Three views of the rat brain showing Brodmann cortical areas. Calibrations are stereotaxic and expressed in millimeters. The anterior-posterior calibrations with an A or P prefix are millimeters anterior or posterior to earbar zero; those without a prefix are millimeters from bregma. (From J. E. Skinner, *Neuroscience: A laboratory manual*, Philadelphia: Saunders, 1971, Figure 6–1.)

dorsal view (of one hemisphere), and a medial view, all with stereotaxic calibrations indicated. For the lateral and medial views, the left calibration markings indicate millimeters of depth above and below an imaginary horizontal line through the brain, as discussed in Chapter 3. For the dorsal view, the left calibration markings refer to millimeters from the midline. The calibration markings for the anterior-posterior plane are given in two forms. Those prefixed with A and P indicate millimeters anterior and posterior, respectively, from where the ear bars would be if the animal were held in a stereotaxic instrument. Those without the prefix are millimeters anterior and posterior from the bregma reference point. It is this latter set of calibrations that we will use extensively in this and subsequent labs.

Using the dorsal view, locate that area of the bone that overlies area 17, the visual cortex of the rat, and the area of bone that overlies areas 3 and 4, the motor cortex. Use your ruler to measure from bregma and from the midline the anterior, posterior, lateral, and medial extent of these areas on both hemispheres. In Laboratory Exercise IV, the bone overlying one of these areas of one hemisphere will be removed and a cortical lesion will be made.

Closing the incision

Remove the mosquito forceps from the periosteum, and with the thumb forceps pull together the skin. Cut a piece of suture thread about 8 inches long with your *large* scissors, thread it through the needle eye an inch or two, and hold the needle in your needleholder. Use the thumb forceps to hold first the right side of the incision and then the left side and pass the needle through the skin, as shown in Figure 6–7(a). Catch the needle with the forceps or with your fingers and pull the suture thread through until there is only about 1 inch left, as in Figure 6–7(b). Make an overhand loop with the long portion of the thread around the needleholder jaws, as in Figure 6–7(c), catch the short portion of the thread in the needleholder jaws, and then pull the short portion of the thread through the loop. Tighten the knot until firm. Now repeat the process, making a second overhand loop, but make it in the reverse direction of the first loop (otherwise you will end up with a slip knot rather than a square knot). Again, catch the short end of the thread in the needleholder jaws, as in Figure 6–7(d), pull it through the loop, and tighten it. Using the large scissors, snip the suture thread quite close to the knot. Repeat the entire process, making four or five knots about ⅜ in. apart, as in Figure 6–7(e). It should be noted that the knots could be tied by hand without the needleholder, but the needleholder does make it easier to work in small spaces. (See pages 78–79.)

Removing the animal

Remove the animal from the headholder by loosening the screws and removing the incisor teeth from the support bar. Normally after surgery involving lesions, it is a good idea to leave the animal in the headholder for a few minutes to allow any blood clots to become very firm before the animal is moved. But since there will have been no bleeding from your animal today, it can be removed from the headholder immediately. One of the effects of pentobarbital anesthesia is that body temperature control is lost, so the animal should be placed on a heating pad or under a heat lamp after marking its tail in some distinctive manner (for example, a particular number of stripes).

When the animal begins to show signs of moving, place it back in its cage, indicate the surgical treatment on the cage label, put the cage back in the rack, and replace the water bottle.

Cleaning up

In this and all labs, the equipment you use is to be cleaned carefully and left in an orderly fashion.

>   Remove the scalpel blade from the handle and discard. Remove the needle from the syringe; if they are disposable, discard them in the box provided.
>   Wash in detergent and warm water and rinse all instruments, glassware, and the headholder. Dry everything well with the cloth towels.
>   Return the instruments, equipment, and any unused supplies to the supply room as instructed.
>   Sponge off your work area and leave it clean.

Headholders and stereotaxic instruments

Figures 6–8 through 6–10 (pages 80–81) demonstrate several headholders and stereotaxic instruments designed for work with rats, cats, monkeys, and other species. The stereotaxic instruments have in common the feature discussed in Chapter 3; the animal is held with ear bars inserted into the external auditory meatus.

(a)

(b)

(c)

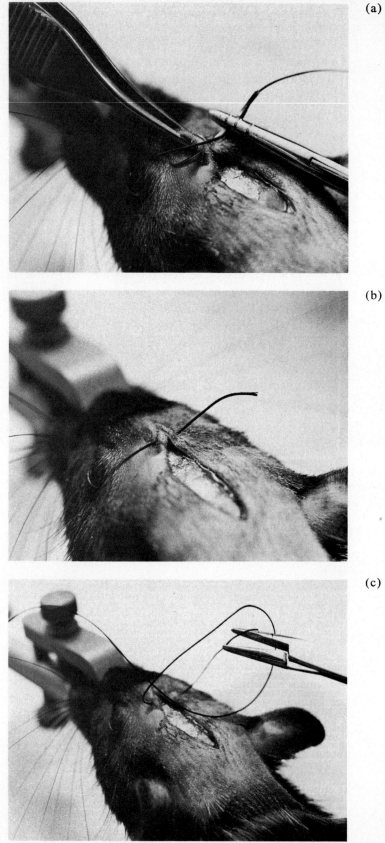

(d)

(e)

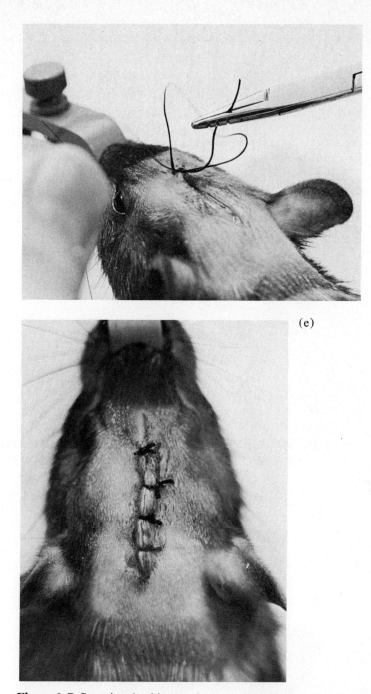

Figure 6–7. Steps involved in suturing. (a) The skin is caught and lifted with the thumb forceps, and the threaded needle, held in the needleholder, is pushed through both sides of the incision. (b) The suture thread is pulled through until about 1 to 2 inches remain. (c) The long piece of thread is looped around the opened jaws of the needleholder, and the short end is then caught in the jaws. When the short end is held firmly in the jaws, it is pulled through the loop, the knot is pulled firmly, and then the short end of the thread is released from the needleholder jaws. (d) A second loop is then made around the open needleholder jaws, but in a direction opposite to the first. Again, the short end of the thread is caught in the jaws and pulled through the loop. This second loop is pulled firmly and the two pieces of thread are cut with large scissors quite close to the knot. (e) Knots should be placed about ⅜ to ½ inch apart.

Figure 6–8. A stereotaxic instrument for use with cat or monkey. Note that it has four independent and removable electrode holders. (Courtesy David Kopf Instruments.)

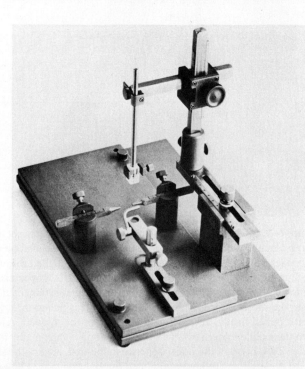

Figure 6–9. A stereotaxic instrument designed for laboratory rats. It has just one electrode holder. (Courtesy David Kopf Instruments.)

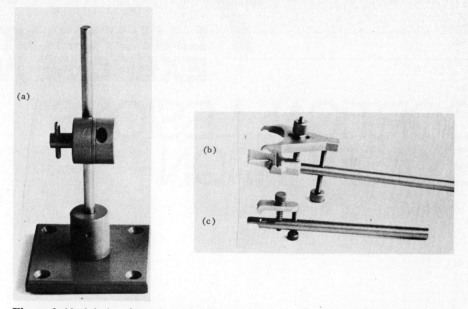

Figure 6–10. (a) A universal stand, which is used in conjunction with either the headholder for (b) the cat or (c) the rat. Note that the cat is held by the inferior orbit of the eye and the rat by the snout. (Courtesy David Kopf Instruments.)

7 LABORATORY EXERCISE IV

CORTICAL LESIONS BY ASPIRATION

It is now well established that man is not the only species to manifest lateral preferences. Members of many nonhuman species have rather distinct paw preferences in that individual animals tend to use one paw more than the other when put into situations involving unimanual responding, situations such as reaching for food from a narrow trough or other small enclosure (Warren, Abplanalp, and Warren, 1967). In laboratory rats and cats, these preferences are reversed if lesions are made in the sensory-motor cortex of the hemisphere contralateral (that is, opposite) to the preferred paw (Forward, Warren, and Hara, 1962; Peterson and Fracarol, 1938; Warren, Cornwell, Webster, and Pubols, 1972). So, if in reaching for food pellets an animal has a preference for using its right paw, relatively small cortical lesions in the anterior part of the cortex of the contralateral hemisphere (in this case the left hemisphere) will lead to the animal shifting its preference when tested postoperatively.

In this laboratory exercise, cortical lesions will be made by the aspiration technique to demonstrate that a unilateral anterior cortical lesion in the hemisphere contralateral to the preferred paw reverses paw preference, while a comparable lesion of the posterior cortex does not. Such a demonstration requires as a minimum, of course, that some laboratory groups make an *anterior* lesion in the hemisphere opposite the preferred paw and other groups make a *posterior* lesion, also in the hemisphere opposite the preferred paw. However, to make the argument of locus specificity of effects (and, implicitly, the argument of localization of function), it is really necessary to include a task that is impaired by the posterior unilateral lesion but not by the anterior one. This is the double-dissociation paradigm briefly discussed in the introduction to the Brush, Mishkin, and Rosvold reading in Chapter 9. Unfortunately, there are few, if any, tasks that can be conveniently used to demonstrate visual field losses (or other losses) in the rat which follow unilateral posterior damage (bilateral damage is, of course, a different story). It would also be desirable to include animals that receive anterior or posterior cortical lesions, but in the hemisphere ipsilateral (that is, on the same side) to the preferred paw. This would allow one to argue firmly that the effects are indeed restricted to damage to the hemisphere contralateral to the preferred paw and that shifts in paw preference will not follow *any* anterior cortical damage, regardless of hemisphere. Given, however, the crossed neuroanatomical organization of the motor system and the fact that there is no reason whatsoever for thinking such damage should produce changes in preference, these groups can be omitted for the sake of convenience.

Consequently, following preoperative assessment of paw preference, each animal will be classified as having either a right paw preference or a left paw preference, and all will receive a cortical lesion in the hemisphere opposite the preferred paw. At least half the laboratory groups will be asked to attempt to make the lesion in their animal in the anterior cortex (in the so-called motor cortex), and the remainder will be asked to attempt their lesion in the posterior cortex (in the so-called visual cortex, or area 17). A week after recovery from surgery, all animals will be retested for paw preference, following which the extent of damage will be verified histologically.

A. PREOPERATIVE PAW PREFERENCE ASSESSMENT

Equipment and supplies

Handedness testing box (see Figure 7–1 and Appendix B–2)
45 mg Noyes pellets
Thumb forceps for handling pellets
Data sheets (Tables 7–1 and 7–2)

Procedures

In order to assess paw preferences by having the animal reach for food pellets, it is necessary to ensure that the animal is somewhat hungry. Three or four days prior to when testing begins, the animal should be placed on a food deprivation schedule so that it receives only a limited amount of food at the time of the day immediately following when it will be tested. Three or four Purina Lab Chow pellets is usually sufficient, but because the ration is partly dependent on factors such as the strain of laboratory rat being used, its size, age, and sex, you will be instructed as to the appropriate amount for your

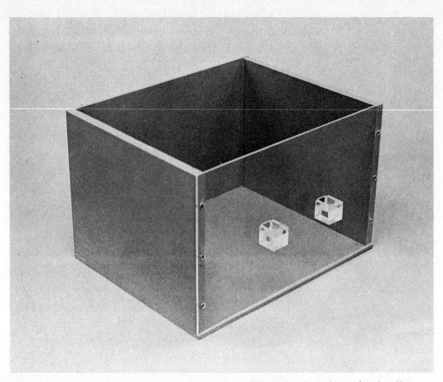

Figure 7–1. A paw preference assessment box. The animal retrieves food pellets placed in the food wells and the paw used on each trial is recorded.

animals. All animals on food deprivation must be weighed every other day to ensure normal weight maintenance.

Prior to attempting to assess paw preference, the animal should be allowed to explore the handedness box briefly. Then place food pellets on the floor of the box itself, being sure that the pellets are near the front of the box. Once the rat will eat these from the floor, place pellets in front of the food wells. Let the animal retrieve the pellet with its snout and tongue the first few times, but then put the pellets farther and farther back, and if necessary hold them with the forceps so that it has to use its paw. During this adaptation, it will probably be necessary to tap the food well with the forceps to attract the animal's attention, and it may be necessary to help the animal somewhat by pushing the pellet with your forceps while the rat is trying to retrieve it with its paw. Throughout, use a series of successive approximations, rewarding the animal whenever it attempts a response closer to the desired end. At first, reward the animal for just putting the paw anywhere near the food well, but then slowly make the criterion for reward increasingly stringent. There is considerable variability in how long it will take to complete this adaptation. Some animals will be fully adapted in a very few minutes while others may require two or three sessions. Once the animal will readily reach for pellets, the actual paw preference assessment trials can begin.

The data sheet in Table 7–1 contains 100 trials of a balanced irregular sequence of left and right as devised by Gellerman (1933) and discussed in Chapter 5. Each trial consists of placing a food pellet into the food well

Table 7–1
Paw Preference Data Sheet

Subject_____   Date_____
                                    Group_____

TRIAL	POSITION	RESPONSE	TRIAL	POSITION	RESPONSE	TRIAL	POSITION	RESPONSE	TRIAL	POSITION	RESPONSE
1	R		26	R		51	L		76	L	
2	L		27	L		52	R		77	R	
3	R		28	R		53	L		78	L	
4	L		29	L		54	R		79	R	
5	L		30	L		55	R		80	R	
6	R		31	L		56	L		81	R	
7	R		32	R		57	L		82	L	
8	R		33	R		58	L		83	L	
9	L		34	L		59	R		84	R	
10	L		35	L		60	R		85	R	
11	L		36	R		61	R		86	L	
12	R		37	R		62	L		87	L	
13	R		38	L		63	L		88	R	
14	L		39	L		64	R		89	R	
15	R		40	R		65	L		90	L	
16	L		41	R		66	R		91	L	
17	L		42	R		67	R		92	L	
18	L		43	L		68	R		93	R	
19	R		44	L		69	L		94	R	
20	R		45	R		70	L		95	L	
21	R		46	R		71	L		96	L	
22	L		47	L		72	R		97	R	
23	L		48	L		73	R		98	R	
24	R		49	R		74	L		99	L	
25	R		50	L		75	L		100	R	

In terms of S's right and left:
$\Sigma R =$ _____ $\Sigma R/L =$ _____
$\Sigma L =$ _____ $\Sigma L/R =$ _____

specified on the data sheet and recording the paw or paw sequence (L, R, L/R, R/L, R/L/R, etc.) used by the subject to retrieve the pellet. The Ls and Rs on the data sheet indicate the food-well position as seen by the experimenter, and the paw used by the animal should be recorded in terms of the experimenter's left and right.

Administer 50 trials of testing on the first day following adaptation and then return the animal to its home cage and give it the food ration. On the following day administer a second 50 trials. Tally up the number of left and right paw responses (this time in terms of the subject's right and left). The unilateral lesion will be made in the hemisphere contralateral to the animal's preferred paw. Whether the lesion should be made in the anterior cortex or posterior cortex will be worked out with the instructor.

Be sure to return the animal to *ad libitum* feeding from the day testing ends until the day before surgery.

B. CORTICAL LESIONS BY ASPIRATION

Your animal should be completely deprived of food and water for 24 hours prior to the laboratory period.

The initial and terminal procedures to be followed are similar to those used in Laboratory Exercise III, but the cerebral cortex contralateral to each animal's preferred paw will be exposed by removing the cranium and dura overlying it.

Figure 6–6 of Laboratory Exercise III showed the cerebral cortex of the rat from a lateral, a dorsal, and a medial view. Those who have been assigned to make posterior lesions should attempt to remove all of area 17, and those who have been assigned to make anterior lesions should attempt to remove all of areas 3 and 4. Before coming to the lab, be sure to identify (using Figure 6–6 of Laboratory Exercise III) the coordinates, with respect to bregma, of the lesion you will be attempting.

Equipment and supplies for each group

Rat headholder
Osteological drill
High-intensity lamp (if necessary)
Magnifier
Surgical instruments
    #3 scalpel handle
    #10, #11 blades
    2 mosquito forceps
    Rat-tooth forceps
    Thumb forceps
    Lempert rongeurs
    Large scissors
    Fine-tipped scissors
    Dental probe
    Drill bit (#8)
Instrument sterilizer and Zephiran chloride solution
6-in. ruler
Beaker with saline
Saline dish—fill two-thirds with saline
Glass pipette (see Figure 5–2 and Appendix B–1)
Distillation flask and rubber stopper
Surgical tubing and Hoffman clamp (clamp optional)

Diaper towels
2"×2" gauze sponges
Small cotton pledgets
2   1-cc syringes with 26G needles
Lab coats
Towels

Equipment to be shared by groups

Nembutal anesthetic, 60 mg/cc
Atropine sulfate, 0.4 mg/cc
Gelfoam sponge
Animal clippers
Animal balance
Wound clip applicator and clips
Suction pump (see Appendix B–3)
Tubing and connectors
Heating pad
Respirator
Heavy gloves

Connecting to the vacuum pump

You will share access to the vacuum pump with the other groups. Connect the distillation flask and rubber stopper to your outlet as shown in Figure 7–2.

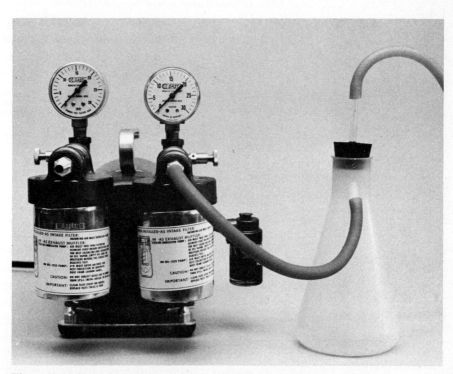

Figure 7–2. Connections between the vacuum pump and flask and between the flask and pipette.

Either there will be one collection flask to which all groups are connected through tubing and three-way connectors, or each group will have its own collection flask connected to a common vacuum source. Whichever the setup, double-check that your connections are basically as indicated in Figure 7–2; if they are not correct, fluid may get into the pump and damage it. Connect your pipette immediately. If during the lab you need to change pipettes, be sure to close off the tubing with a Hoffman clamp or by bending it so that other groups will not lose their vacuum pressure while you are doing so.

Initial stages

Follow the instructions from last week's lab. Then

1. Check the instruments and supplies and place all instruments in Zephiran.
2. Obtain and weigh your animal.
3. Calculate the dosage of anesthetic required on the basis of a dosage level of 60 mg/kg and a concentration of Nembutal of 60 mg/cc. Double-check calculation.
4. Fill your syringe with the required amount of anesthetic, following the aseptic procedures outlined last week.
5. Inject the animal intraperitoneally (IP), using the procedures outlined in the last lab. 15 to 20 minutes after the animal is fully anesthetized, inject IP 0.1 cc of atropine.
6. Clip the hair from the animal's head, removing about the same amount as in the last lab.
7. Mount the animal in the headholder.
8. Make the initial incision using your #10 blade, scrape the periosteum to either side of the midline, and retract it with the mosquito forceps. With a gauze sponge, wipe the cranium clean of excess blood or moisture.
9. Identify bregma and lambda. Visualize the area of the skull overlying the cortex that will be exposed based on calculations made before the lab.

Drilling the cranium

In order to expose the cortex, it is necessary to remove the bone overlying that area as well as some of the adjacent bone. An easy way to do this is to use the drill like a sanding device. Insert the drill bur tightly. With the drill operating at a moderate speed, and with the bur oriented at about 45° to the skull, as shown in Figure 7–3, apply only a slight amount of pressure and evenly move the drill bur back and forth across the area of bone you want to remove. *Do not drill a hole.* Instead, sand down the cranium until it is paper thin and has a spongy texture. Take care not to inhale bone dust. If you find the bur gets clogged with pieces of bone, wipe it with a moist gauze sponge and if necessary pick it clean using the used #10 blade (not the unused #11 blade).

Thin an area several millimeters in diameter and centered roughly over the area of cortex you will expose. Stop drilling periodically and use the

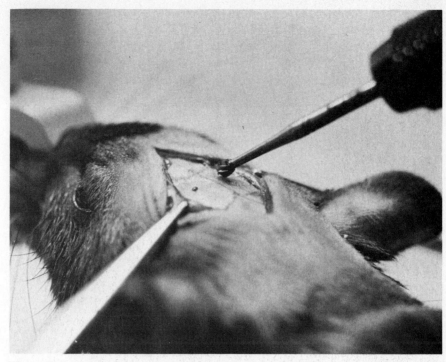

Figure 7–3. The exposure just prior to drilling. Note the angle of the drill bur that will produce an efficient "sanding" action.

pipette to vacuum away the pieces of bone chips and dust from the entire exposure. If there is any dust left after the incision is closed, it may become a source of infection while the animal is recovering.

There are two ways to tell when you are almost through the cranium. First, if you touch the area of the bone being drilled with a blunt instrument, it will be spongy or soft to the touch. Second, if you use a gauze sponge to apply a little saline to the area being drilled, the bone will become translucent and you may be able to see blood vessels through it.

When you can see you are just about through the bone, use the sharp dental probe to hook the bone and break through by pulling *up*. This pick is very sharp and can easily puncture the bone, dura, and cortex if pushed against the drilled area with any pressure. Simply try to catch the bone with the pick and lift, making a small hole. This can then be expanded by using the pick and thumb forceps to peel back some of the remaining thined bone.

Now, keeping the Lempert rongeurs moist with saline, expand the exposure. Angling the rongeurs at about 45°, as shown in Figure 7–4, carefully slip the tips under the edge of the bone (this will necessarily involve depressing the cortex slightly) and snip a small piece of bone. The rongeurs should be used to produce a nibbling action, not a twisting, bending, or breaking action. Nibble away at the bone in all directions but be careful about going near the midline. You need the midline as a reference point to determine exactly where the cortical area you will remove is located (remember there are no surface features on the cortex of the rat to indicate this). Also, there is a large venous sinus, the sagittal sinus, which runs between the

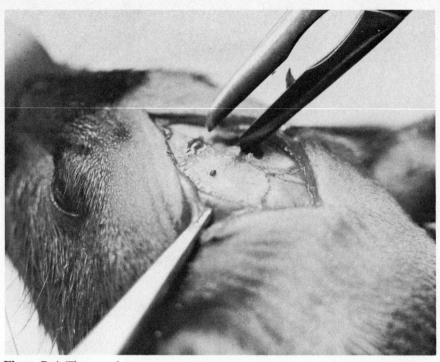

Figure 7–4. The use of rongeurs to "nibble" bone in order to enlarge the exposure.

hemispheres and drains the blood from the cortex. If your rongeurs get too close to the midline, you will likely break into the sinus, which could prove fatal for the animal.

Remove an area of bone about twice as large as the cortex you will remove so that you get a good exposure of the cortical surface. Just be sure that all of areas 3 and 4 or area 17 is exposed.

Cutting the dura mater

The entire brain is surrounded by the dura mater, which must be cut before the cortex is actually exposed. *Visualizing it through the magnifier,* carefully nick the dura with the point of the #11 scalpel blade with the sharp edge of the blade pointed up. You can usually tell when the dura has been nicked because there will be a flow of clear cerebrospinal fluid. Continuing to use the scalpel with the sharp edge pointed up, and not applying any downward pressure, make a small slit in the dura that would correspond to slit A in Figure 7–5. It is of critical importance not to cut any of the vessels below the dura in the pia mater. Then, using the fine-tipped scissors, catch the edge of the slit and cut the dura anteriorly (slit B). Make the two other slits (C and D) to form an I-shaped cut in the dura. Finally, expand the cut posteriorly by making slit E with the fine-tipped scissors. Use the thumb forceps to retract the edges of the dura.

If there is any bleeding at this time, simply place a cotton ball soaked in saline on the exposure for a short time. Any excess blood can be removed by applying suction through the cotton ball. *Do not touch the cortical surface*

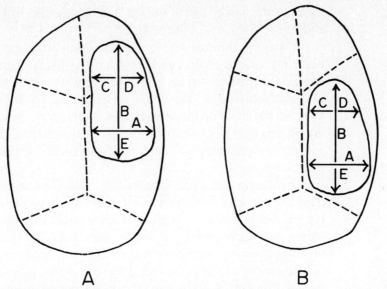

Figure 7–5. Diagrams of anterior and posterior exposures, showing the pattern of cuts that should be made in the dura.

with your pipette tip or you will make a lesion. From this point on, the cortical surface must be kept moist with frequent applications of saline.

The lesion

Double-check the extent of the cortical area you are going to remove and try to imagine it in relation to landmarks in your exposure. Now, touch the surface of the cortex with the pipette. It should readily penetrate the pia mater, and some tissue will be drawn into the pipette (this is cortex). What you want to do is to suck all the cortical tissue making up either areas 3 and 4 or area 17. To do this, move your pipette under the pia mater almost parallel to the cortex, as diagramed in Figure 7–6. Remember that the cortex is only

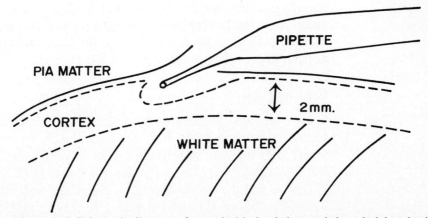

Figure 7–6. Schematic diagram of a cortical lesion being made by subpial aspiration.

about 2 mm thick, and if you go below this you will cut the fibers going to and from other parts of the brain.

It may be difficult to see the transition from gray (really yellowish) to white matter, the main cue being that the tissue begins to reflect more light and glistens because of the fatty myelin sheaths. You may also detect a change in tissue consistency, the white matter being considerably tougher than the gray. If the flaps of dura mater get in the way, hold them back with your thumb forceps. Note the consistency of the cortical tissue and compare this with the consistency of the preserved tissue worked with in Laboratory Exercises I and II.

Constantly check the dimensions of the lesion you are making with the objective of striving to make a complete lesion of the area but (1) not invading the white matter beneath (which would "disconnect" other parts of the cortex to which and from which the fibers are projecting) and (2) not invading the surrounding cortical areas.

Be careful of the veins that drain the cortex into the sagittal sinus and try to avoid nicking a large one. If you encounter a vein where you are trying to make the lesion, try to orient the pipette underneath it. If a vein is punctured, bleeding can be quickly and easily controlled by applying a cotton ball soaked in cold saline and waiting a few minutes.

Closing the exposure

Do not begin to close the exposure until all signs of bleeding have ceased.

When the bleeding has ceased, check that all cotton balls have been removed from the exposure. Using the *large* scissors, cut a piece of Gelfoam (made of gelatin and which will be absorbed in the body) slightly larger than the size of the bone opening. Soak this in saline, squeeze out the excess moisture, and gently lay it over the exposure with your thumb forceps. The scar tissue will form around this. The incision is now ready to be closed.

In the last lab we closed the animal using silk sutures. In this lab we will close the incision using a different means, wound clips. This is a much easier and faster means of closing a wound and involves simply clamping the two sides of the incision with the clip while holding the tissue up in the thumb forceps. Your animal will require two or three clamps (Figure 7–7). After the wound clipping is complete, let the animal stay in the headholder for a few minutes before removing it, unless it is clear it is on the verge of walking away. As in the last lab, place it on the heating pad after marking its tail and indicate on a cage label your names, the date, the type of surgery, and the tail marking you have used.

Cleaning up

Follow the same procedures as outlined in the last lab to clean your instruments and work area. As there will undoubtedly be more blood on the instruments after this lab, rinse them briefly in cold water before washing in hot water and detergent. This will keep the blood from setting. Be sure to wash glassware and the headholder. Dry everything well with a cloth towel. Cold water must be run through the tubing to remove all blood; the instructor will set up facilities for this.

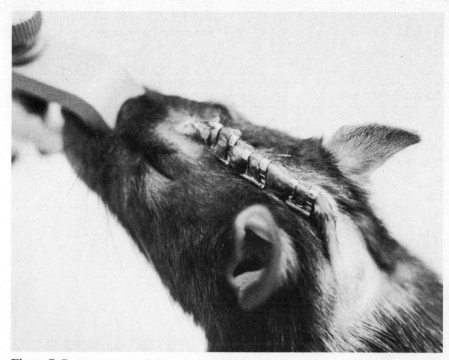

Figure 7–7. Appearance of the animal in the headholder after wound clips have been applied.

A reminder that all unused supplies should be returned to the supply room, along with the instruments, headholder, drill (be sure you washed the bur and removed any particles of bone from the sharp edges), lamp, and magnifier.

C. POSTOPERATIVE PAW PREFERENCE ASSESSMENT

One week after the animal has recovered from surgery, place it on a 23-hour food deprivation schedule and several days later begin postoperative handedness assessment. Again administer 50 trials of testing per day for two days, using the data sheet in Table 7–2. Following completion of testing, the preoperative and postoperative data from all groups will be pooled, and your instructor may request a laboratory report.

D. RECONSTRUCTION OF THE LESION

In making your cortical lesion, it probably became evident that considerable skill and experience are necessary to make well-defined lesions in which one can be confident of surface extent and depth. As there are few situations in neuropsychology when it is not desirable to have at least some indication of the extent of damage, verification of the intended lesion is usually imperative.

After the postoperative testing, your laboratory instructor will perfuse your animal and extract its brain from the cranium. Perfusion is done in the

Table 7–2

Paw Preference Data Sheet

Subject_____   Date_____
                                     Group_____

TRIAL	POSITION	RESPONSE	TRIAL	POSITION	RESPONSE	TRIAL	POSITION	RESPONSE	TRIAL	POSITION	RESPONSE
1	R		26	R		51	L		76	L	
2	L		27	L		52	R		77	R	
3	R		28	R		53	L		78	L	
4	L		29	L		54	R		79	R	
5	L		30	L		55	R		80	R	
6	R		31	L		56	L		81	R	
7	R		32	R		57	L		82	L	
8	R		33	R		58	L		83	L	
9	L		34	L		59	R		84	R	
10	L		35	L		60	R		85	R	
11	L		36	R		61	R		86	L	
12	R		37	R		62	L		87	L	
13	R		38	L		63	L		88	R	
14	L		39	L		64	R		89	R	
15	R		40	R		65	L		90	L	
16	L		41	R		66	R		91	L	
17	L		42	R		67	R		92	L	
18	L		43	L		68	R		93	R	
19	R		44	L		69	L		94	R	
20	R		45	R		70	L		95	L	
21	R		46	R		71	L		96	L	
22	L		47	L		72	R		97	R	
23	L		48	L		73	R		98	R	
24	R		49	R		74	L		99	L	
25	R		50	L		75	L		100	R	

In terms of S's right and left:
$\Sigma R =$_____ $\Sigma R/L =$_____
$\Sigma L =$_____ $\Sigma L/R =$_____

following manner: The animal is deeply anesthetized and its thoracic cavity is opened (this will be done at the end of Laboratory Exercise VI), exposing the beating heart. The heart is held with forceps, a blunt 20-gauge hypodermic needle is inserted through the left ventricle into the aorta, and a small hole is snipped in the right ventricle. The needle is connected to a 20-cc syringe filled with physiological saline (an NaCl solution having the same concentration [0.9%] as the body fluids), and this is injected. Because of the anatomy of the circulatory system, the saline will replace the blood that drains from the system through the hole in the right ventricle. A 50-cc syringe, filled with a 10% Formalin solution (a solution of NaCl and the preservative formaldehyde) is then connected to the perfusion needle and Formalin is quickly injected, replacing the saline. The animal's head is then removed and left for 24 hours in a Formalin solution, which allows the tissue to harden well before being removed. Your instructor will also extract the brain from the cranium, which will allow you to examine the surface extent of the tissue damage.

Use Figure 6–6 of Laboratory Exercise III to trace a lateral, a dorsal, and a medial view of the hemisphere in which the lesion was made. Do not indicate Brodmann areas. You should now attempt to sketch a diagram of the surface extent of the ablation on these. In the case of small lesions, a dorsal view is quite sufficient, but with larger lesions, it is necessary to sketch the extent of the damage on all three views of the cortex.

The problem of estimating the depth of the lesion to ascertain whether all cortical tissue was in fact removed from the area of damage and whether there was an invasion into the underlying white matter, the corpus callosum, the hippocampus, the caudate nucleus, and so on, requires that the brain tissue be sliced and stained as described in Chapter 3. After you have sketched the surface extent of the ablation, return the brain in a clearly identified bottle to the instructor, who will slice the brain on a microtome and stain the sections through the region of the damage. In order to facilitate the identification of brain structures, he will attempt to slice it in the same plane as that used in preparing the stereotaxic atlas you are using. This requires "blocking" the brain, a procedure to be discussed in some detail in connection with the verification and reconstruction of subcortical lesions.

Figure 7–8 is a photomicrograph of a stained section through a cortical

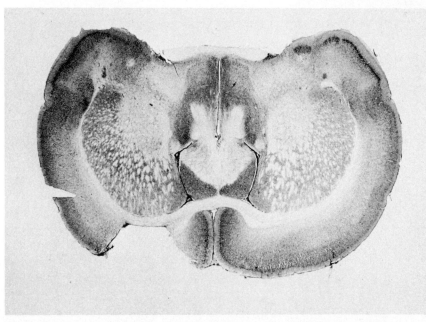

Figure 7–8. Photomicrograph of a Nissl stained section showing an anterior cortical lesion. Note the undercutting into the white matter.

lesion and illustrates two things you should look for in the microslides of your rat brain. First, it illustrates how an invasion of the white matter appears. Second, it illustrates that around the limits of the cortical damage there is a proliferation of glial cells. These stain with a Nissl stain and can be seen as a dark edge around the lesion. This phenomenon of gliosis greatly facilitates distinguishing between damage associated with an ablation and damage associated with a sloppy removal of the brain.

In Chapter 3, the use of patterns of thalamic retrograde degeneration as a means of describing or characterizing cortical lesions when thalamocortical projections are well known was also discussed. Certainly in the case of a lissencephalic brain like that of a rat, on which there are no landmarks, the argument that all of a particular cortical area was removed would have to be based on an analysis of thalamic retrograde degeneration. This type of histological analysis is beyond the scope of this laboratory exercise, but the student should be aware that it is often necessary for such an analysis to be done in order to completely characterize the extent of cortical damage.

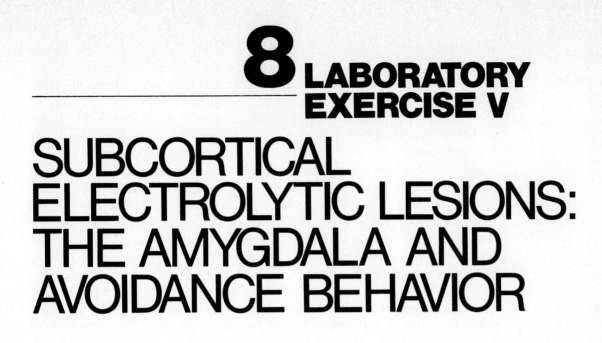

8 LABORATORY EXERCISE V

SUBCORTICAL ELECTROLYTIC LESIONS: THE AMYGDALA AND AVOIDANCE BEHAVIOR

The basic principles associated with making subcortical electrolytic lesions using stereotaxic procedures were discussed in Chapters 3 and 5. Basically, these principles involve localizing a neuroanatomical structure of interest in terms of three right-angled coordinates having as their reference the bone sutures of the skull or, in the case of using a stereotaxic instrument, the center of the ear bars. A piece of wire, electrically insulated except at the tip, is inserted into the brain so that its tip is in the area of interest, and the lesion is made by passing a DC current (anodal) between the electrode tip and a large-area electrode inserted into the rectum or attached to a large muscle.

In this laboratory exercise, these principles will be used in attempting to make bilateral lesions of the amygdala. The effects of the lesions on passive avoidance behavior will be assessed, and the brains will be examined for verification of the lesion site.

A. STEREOTAXIC LESIONS

Each laboratory group will be assigned two rats which have been randomly selected from the colony. One will have been designated at random as being the experimental subject and the other as the control subject. Bilateral lesions of the amygdala will be made in the experimental subjects; the control subjects will serve as "operated controls" in the sense that they will undergo the same surgical operation as the experimental animals (including the insertion of the electrode), but no current will be passed through the electrode. The order in which the experimental and control subjects are operated on should be counterbalanced across groups—that is, some groups should operate on their experimental animal first and on the control animal second while other groups should do the opposite (this may be omitted because of possible time limitations in surgery). It is suggested that the experimental animal be operated on first by all groups; after this is done, the same procedures should be repeated with the second animal except that no current is passed through the electrode. There may be insufficient time to complete the sham operation, but do as much of it as possible.

The laboratory instructions have been written for use with a headholder and micromanipulator, but in actual research the lesions would be made using a stereotaxic instrument, the advantages of which will become evident as the lab progresses. If stereotaxic instruments are available, your instructor may suggest you use one and will show you how to mount your animals in it, but it is to be emphasized that a headholder and micromanipulator are quite sufficient for demonstrating the principles of stereotaxic surgery.

As in all labs, be sure all your equipment and supplies are present and laid out in an orderly fashion before anesthetizing your subject.

Equipment and supplies for each group

Rat headholder
Osteological drill
Stereotaxic atlas of the rat brain [1]
High-intensity lamp (if necessary)
Micromanipulator with single electrode holder (see Appendix B–14)
Lesioning electrode, insulated except at the tip (see Appendix B–5)
Cathode electrode (see Appendix B–5)
Surgical instruments
    #3 scalpel handle
    2 #10 blades
    1 #11 blade
    2 mosquito forceps
    Thumb forceps
    Rat-tooth forceps
    Large scissors
    Dental probe
    Medium cutting bur (#8)
    6-in. ruler
Instrument container and Zephiran antiseptic

---

[1] Recommended atlases include de Groot (1959), Pelligrino and Cushman (1967), and Skinner (1971), all of which were constructed with the stereotaxic incisor bar positioned 5 mm above the stereotaxic ear bars.

6-in. length of copper wire

2   12-in. leads, one red, one black, each with alligator clip on one end and
        banana plug on other end

Saline bowl with saline

$2'' \times 2''$ gauze sponges

Cotton pledgets

2   1-cc syringes with 26G needles

Lab coats

Dishpan with detergent

Towels

Equipment and supplies to be shared by groups

Animal balance

Animal clippers

Nembutal anesthetic, 60 mg/cc

Atropine sulfate, 0.4 mg/cc

Gelfoam sponge, 3 or 7 mm

Electrode testing circuit (see Appendix B–6)

Gloves

Lesion maker with leads (see Appendix B–4)

Wound clip applicators and clips

Heating pad

Place surgical instruments in the Zephiran antiseptic solution.

Operation of lesion maker

A lesion maker is simply an electronic device that provides a regulated and constant amount of DC current. Some of these are available commercially, but quite satisfactory lesion makers can be made for a lot less cost. Appendix B shows a diagram of one such circuit.

If you are using a commercial lesion maker like that shown in Figure 8–1, turn on the power when you arrive at the lab so that the tubes will warm up before you use it. Note on the upper right of the panel [2] the needle dial that indicates the output current in milliamperes. With the RANGE switch set to 10 ma (do not flip the switch to this position without first turning the ADJUST CURRENT knob fully anticlockwise), the lesion maker has a range of currents from 0 to 10.0 milliamperes (ma); we will be using a current of 2.0 ma. The amount of current that will be passed can be determined by placing the switch, which is immediately to the left of the dial, into the SET position; the amount of current can be adjusted using the ADJUST CURRENT knob located just to the left of the switch. When you are ready to make the lesion, the switch is depressed to the FIRE position and the output current is what was, and is, indicated on the current dial. If you are using some other type of lesion maker, the instructor will give you instructions on its use.

---

[2] The description of the controls is for a Lehigh Valley lesion maker, but other commercial lesion makers have similar controls which can be easily identified.

Figure 8–1. A Lehigh-Valley electrolytic lesion maker. The current flow, in milliamperes, can be adjusted by the RANGE switch and the ADJUST CURRENT knob and monitored with the needle dial.

Testing the electrode

Instructions for making an electrode are contained in Appendix B, but basically an electrode is a stainless steel needle or insect pin of ½ mm diameter that has been electrically insulated with epoxylite. The tip of the needle is then scraped with an old scalpel blade. To ensure that the insulation on the electrode is not chipped or cracked (which would allow for a flow of current from the shaft of the electrode), the electrode should be tested with a small beaker of saline and batteries. Simply connect the electrode and the saline to the battery as shown in Figure 8–2 and watch for bubbles at the tip of the electrode. If the insulation has chipped or cracked, you will also see bubbles at those sites along the electrode shaft; discard the electrode.

Micromanipulator

A micromanipulator is a precision instrument that holds the electrode in a fixed position and allows it to be moved in precisely calibrated amounts in the three right-angled planes. The particular micromanipulator shown in Figure 8–3 has two controls for vertical movements, the large black knob on the side for gross movements and the small silvered knob for very fine movements. Movement in the other two planes is controlled by the knobs facing away from the electrode holder. Note that the entire micromanipulator can be raised on the base by releasing the clamp lever located on the side of it just above and behind the silvered vertical control knob. It may be necessary to use this when inserting the electrode into the brain.

All three axes have vernier calibrations, which allow for movements of the electrode holder to be accurate to a tenth of a millimeter. Figure 8–4

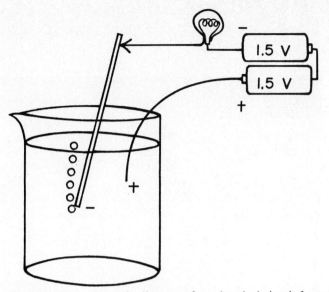

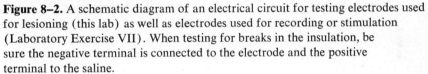

Figure 8–2. A schematic diagram of an electrical circuit for testing electrodes used for lesioning (this lab) as well as electrodes used for recording or stimulation (Laboratory Exercise VII). When testing for breaks in the insulation, be sure the negative terminal is connected to the electrode and the positive terminal to the saline.

Figure 8–3. A micromanipulator that allows for the movement of the electrode holder in the three right-angled planes.

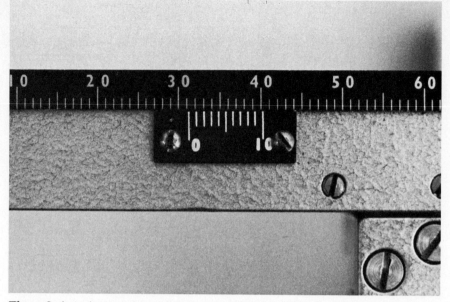

Figure 8–4. A closeup of one of the vernier scales on the micromanipulator. The setting is 31.2 mm.

demonstrates the use of a vernier scale. On the larger scale, the numbers and calibration markings are in millimeters; the millimeter decimal is indicated by determining which of the ten calibration markings on the smaller scale is aligned with a marking on the larger scale. For example, if as in Figure 8–4 the second marking on the smaller scale is aligned with a marking on the larger scale, then the decimal is 2 (so the setting in Figure 8–4 is 31.2 mm). Practice moving the scales until you can quickly and accurately set any particular reading and can move the electrode holder any specified amount in any direction. Note that the micromanipulator on a stereotaxic instrument works in precisely the same way, each axis having a venier calibration scale.

Determination of electrode coordinates

Before coming to the lab, use a rat stereotaxic atlas to determine the coordinates of the center of the amygdaloid complex with reference to bregma. To do this, find the atlas plate that appears to be best in terms of anterior-posterior position, determine how far lateral the amygdala is from the midline, and determine how far you would have to lower the electrode from the dura mater so that the tip will be located in the center of the amygdala. In certain atlases, the anterior-posterior coordinates are given using only the ear-bar reference system, but since bregma is located 6.25 mm anterior to ear bar 0, the conversion to the bregma reference system can be made easily. It should be evident that for the coordinates to have meaning, the head of your animal will have to be positioned in the headholder in the same orientation as that used to construct the atlas. If you are using an atlas constructed for use with the orientation of the head such that the incisor tooth bar is 5 mm above the interaural line, the head of the animal will have to be level in its lateral orientation and, as shown in Figure 8–5, positioned so that lambda is located

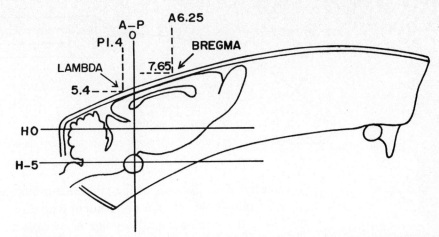

Figure 8–5. Diagram of the appropriate head orientation showing the horizontal and vertical stereotaxic planes, and showing the relation of bregma and lambda to those planes in reference to ear-bar zero. (Adapted from J. E. Skinner, *Neuroscience: A laboratory manual*. Philadelphia: Saunders, 1971, Figure 6–2.)

2.25 mm ventral to bregma (7.65 mm — 5.40 mm). One of the real advantages of using a stereotaxic instrument is that if the animal is properly positioned in the instrument (a skill that requires considerable practice), the head is automatically oriented correctly.

Preparation of the subject

Follow the same basic procedures outlined in Laboratory Exercises III and IV.

1. Obtain and weigh your experimental subject.
2. Calculate the amount of Nembutal anesthetic required on the basis of a dosage of 60 mg/kg and an anesthetic concentration of 60 mg/cc and inject the animal IP. Be sure to stretch the abdominal muscles well and insert the needle perpendicular to the wall.
3. Clip the hair from the top of the head, and inject 0.1 cc of atropine.
4. Mount the animal firmly in the headholder. It is important that the head be held firmly without moving from this point on. Make the initial incision as in past labs using one of the #10 blades in the #3 handle. Scrape the periosteum from the midline to either side and retract it with the mosquito forceps. With a gauze sponge, wipe the cranium clean and identify bregma and lambda.
5. At this point it will be necessary to adjust the animal's head so it conforms to the orientation illustrated in Figure 8–5. Set up your micromanipulator with the copper wire (*not* the insulated electrode) held in the electrode holder, as illustrated in Figure 8–6. The difference in vertical height of lambda and bregma can now be measured by first positioning the wire so it touches bregma and reading the vertical scale, and then positioning the wire so it touches lambda and reading the scale. Adjust the animal's head so that it is level, so that the midline is parallel with the side of the headholder box and parallel to the

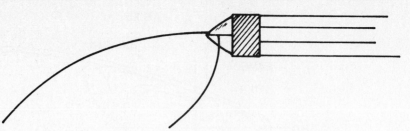

Figure 8–6. Diagram showing copper wire held in electrode holder.

anterior-posterior axis of the micromanipulator, and so that bregma is 2.25 mm above lambda (be content with an error of ±0.05 mm).

6. Using the micromanipulator again as a measuring device, determine the anterior-posterior and lateral position (both right and left) of the amygdala nuclei in reference to bregma and mark these two points on the skull with the point of the dental probe. Do not mark these with a pencil, as the lead may become a source of infection.

7. Drill a trephine hole in the skull at each of the points you have marked. Use a fairly high speed and light pressure and try not to pierce the dura.

8. Use the point of the #11 blade to pierce the dura at each site if it was not cut by the drill. This will allow an easier penetration of the brain by the electrode.

The lesion

Insert the rectal electrode into the rectum of the animal and connect it to one lead with the alligator clip. Be sure that this lead goes to the black negative or cathode terminal of the lesion maker. Insert the lesion electrode into the micromanipulator electrode holder as shown in Figure 8–7 and make it as vertical as possible. This can be done using a ruler as a set square against which the electrode orientation can be compared. Now, attach the other lead to an uninsulated portion of the electrode and connect this to the red positive or anode terminal. Position the electrode tip at bregma and then using your coordinates, move the electrode posterior and lateral to the first trephine hole; if your original measurements and your drilling were good, the electrode should be positioned immediately above the hole. Lower the electrode until the tip touches the cortex. Note the vertical reading on the micromanipulator and be sure that the micromanipulator can be lowered sufficiently to put the electrode tip into the amygdala. Slowly lower the electrode the correct distance into the brain. *Double-check.* The lesion will be made by passing a 2.0 ma current for 10 seconds.[3] Press and hold the ON switch (in the FIRE position in the case of the Lehigh Valley lesion maker) for 10 seconds. As soon as the current is turned on, the animal will probably show a flinching response and

---

[3] The size of the lesion will depend on the parameters of current strength, time of current flow, and the size of the uninsulated electrode tip. One way to determine the approximate size of a lesion for a given set of parameters is to make a "lesion" in a small beaker of egg white. On the basis of such a test using your particular electrode dimensions, you may be instructed to use lesion parameters different from those included in these instructions.

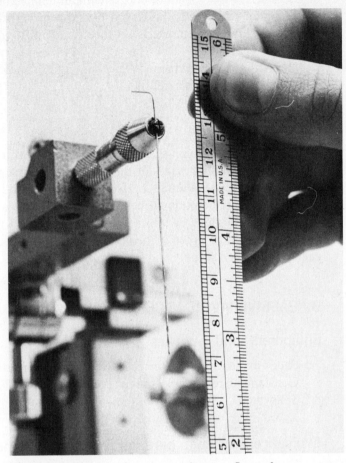

Figure 8–7. The use of a ruler, resting on a flat surface, as a set square to align the lesion electrode vertically.

perhaps whisker twitching. This is a good sign; if you do not see it there may be something wrong with the electrical connections and a current may not be passing through the electrode tip. The only way to determine this, however, is when histology is done. Raise the electrode from the brain slowly, carefully wipe the tip clean with a damp gauze sponge, and repeat exactly the same procedures for lesioning the other side.

Now place a small piece of Gelfoam soaked in saline into each of the trephine holes, remove the mosquito forceps, and close the incision with wound clips. Leave the animal in the headholder for a few minutes and then transfer it to the heating pad. At this time place an identification mark on the animal's tail and indicate on the label of the animal's cage what this identification marking is, what treatment it was that the animal received, (in this case, bilateral amygdala lesions), and what your names are.

Control subject

Before obtaining and weighing your control subject, place all your surgical instruments into the Zephiran solution, and replace the #10 blade. Repeat all the preceding steps but of course without connecting the animal electrically to the lesion maker and passing a current through the electrode. After the sham operation is completed, be sure to identify your animal as described above.

Wash all your instruments, glassware, and the headholder in hot water and detergent and dry them carefully.

Postoperative care

It is not at all uncommon that after bilateral lesions of the amygdala the feeding and grooming behaviors of the animals are disrupted. It is suggested that during this time the animals be fed a wet mash food rather than the regular dry pellets. As the emotional behavior of the animals may also be upset, it is suggested that a glove be worn when handling them until it is clear that they will not show rage types of behavior. All animals should be handled briefly each day between surgery and testing.

B. PASSIVE AVOIDANCE BEHAVIOR

Equipment and supplies

Shock avoidance box (see Figure 8–8 and Appendix B–8)
Constant current shock source (see Appendix B–7)
Stopwatch

Avoidance learning: paradigms and problems

It was pointed out in Chapter 5 that two general classes of avoidance learning paradigms can be distinguished on the basis of what the subject must do in order to avoid some aversive event such as an electric shock. In active avoidance paradigms, the animal must actively do something, such as run from one compartment to another or press a bar, in order to avoid shock. In passive avoidance paradigms the animal is required to remain still or to refrain from making some response that would "normally" occur in order to avoid punishment. Because many passive avoidance responses are learned by normal animals in a single trial, they have been used quite extensively in the study of treatment effects on memory. Since the "learning" demands of these tasks are minimal, retention deficits following some treatments have been attributed to the effect of the treatment administered following acquisition on the storage or consolidation of the learning. However, as Weiskrantz (1968a) has pointed out, it is impossible to determine whether a retention deficit indicates that the treatment interfered with the storage of information or that the treatment somehow interfered with the retrieval of the information. However, performance deficits might best be understood or interpreted in terms quite different from storage and retrieval, such as motivation, and the student should consider other reasonable interpretations or inferences by considering those variables that influence passive avoidance performance.

The passive avoidance apparatus used in the present exercise is illustrated in Figure 8–8. It consists of a large box with a grid floor, inside which is a start box with a guillotine-type door. The grid is wired to a shock source in

Figure 8–8. A passive avoidance apparatus. Note that resting on the grid is a lighted start box with guillotine door.

such a way that when the animal steps on adjacent bars it receives a mild but aversive electric shock.

A normal animal, placed into the start box, will readily leave it and explore the large box, especially if the start box is made somewhat aversive by suspending a bright light over it. If the animal is shocked as soon as it steps onto the grid, then when it is subsequently returned to the start box some hours or days later, it will not leave the box, or if it does it is only with a latency considerably longer than originally. The purpose of this laboratory is to compare the performance of the animals having sustained amygdala lesions with that of the control animals for retention of a passive avoidance response. The dependent variables are the time it takes the subjects to leave the start box on both the acquisition trial and the retention trial and, not independent of this, the proportion of animals in each group showing successful avoidance on the retention trial.

The flow of current through an electrical circuit is directly proportional to the voltage and inversely proportional to the resistance of the circuit.[4] An animal receiving an electric shock can be conceptualized as being part of an electric circuit (Figure 8–9). One fundamental problem with shock circuits is that the resistance of that part of the circuit made up by the animal changes while the animal is being shocked. This is due both to changes in the skin resistance of the animal and to changes in the distribution of skin contact with the bars. As it is usually considered desirable to shock the animal with a constant current, a high-voltage transformer (about 1000 volts) is connected to the grid with a large resistor in series that limits the current flow. Since the

[4] Principles of electricity are discussed in more detail in Chapter 15.

resistance of the animal makes up but a small proportion of the total resistance of the circuit, changes in the resistance of the animal produce only negligible changes in current flow (Figure 8–9).

In certain situations like the present one it is sufficient to connect the terminals of the shock source directly to alternate bars of the grid so that the animal is shocked if it is in contact with at least one even-numbered and one odd-numbered bar. But it should be evident that if the animal were placed in the situation for several trials, it would happen occasionally that it would be standing only on even-numbered or on odd-numbered bars and hence there would be no current flow and no shock. Animals learn very readily that shock can be avoided by simply stepping on alternate bars. Hence, in those situations involving multiple trials or extended durations of shock exposure, it is necessary to "scramble" the shock, that is, to make the distribution of shock to the grid bars unpredictable and random so that it is impossible for the animal to avoid shock by standing on any particular pair or combination of bars.

In this lab the shock source is operated manually and time is measured simply with a stopwatch. In most research settings, it would be desirable to use a clock that can be started and stopped electronically and to use a timer to control the duration of shock. If these are wired together with relays and microswitches, it is easy to achieve good control over the measurement of latency, over the relationship between stepping from the start box and the

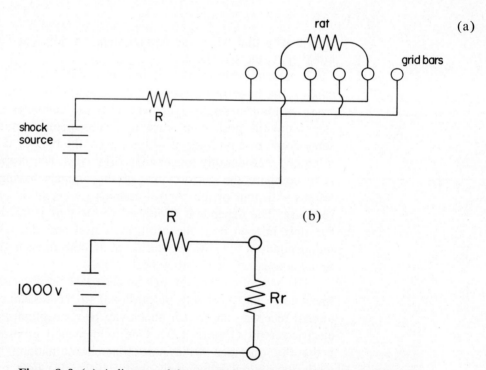

Figure 8–9. (a) A diagram of the completion of the electrical circuit when the rat steps on the grid bars. Note that the animal will not get a shock if it steps only on every other bar, as the circuit will not be completed. (b) An approximation to a constant current shock source. Note that with a high-voltage source and a large-value current-limiting resistor (R), the resistance of the animal R_r accounts for but a small proportion of the total resistance of the circuit. Hence, changes in the resistance of the animal during testing will result in only small changes in the current flow. See Appendix Figure B–3 for an operational circuit diagram.

onset of shock, and over the duration of shock itself. Students interested in pursuing how this can be done semiautomatically are referred to Cornsweet (1963) for a very understandable discussion.

Passive avoidance acquisition

Each group will test its own experimental and control subjects; the order in which the animals should be tested will be specified by the instructor. Care must be taken to treat the two animals in as similar a manner as possible.

1. Turn out the room lights and turn on the apparatus light.
2. Wearing a glove, transfer the animal from its cage to the start box with the start box door closed.
3. Lower the apparatus light over the start box.
4. As soon as the animal is facing the door, open the door and turn on the stopwatch. The stopwatch stays on until the animal has left the start box. The operational definition of "leaving the start box" is that all four feet are on the grid. The time from when the door opens to when the watch is stopped is the response latency.
5. Contiguous with turning off the stopwatch, close the start box door to prevent the animal from returning, switch on the shock source, and leave it on for 4 to 5 seconds. This time can be estimated by counting "1 steamboat, 2 steamboats," etc.
6. Turn off the shock and, *wearing a glove,* remove the animal from the apparatus and return it to its cage.
7. Record the response latency and set the watch back to zero.
8. Repeat the same procedure for the second animal.

Retention testing

The same procedures used for acquisition should be used for retention testing except that no shock is administered at all. The retention testing can be carried out on the same day after all animals have received the acquisition trial. The order in which the subjects receive retention testing should be the same as that used for acquisition in order to keep the intertrial interval as constant as possible.

1. Place the subject in the start box with the door closed (it is strongly suggested that a glove be used).
2. Lower the apparatus light above the start box.
3. As soon as the subject faces the start box door, open the door and start the watch. Stop the watch when the animal leaves the start box (4 feet outside the box on the grid) and then return the animal to its cage. Record the response latency. If the animal does not leave the box within 180 seconds (3 minutes), remove the animal from the start box and return it to its cage; this is a successful avoidance response.

Data analysis

The data from all subjects of all groups should be pooled. The instructor will discuss various ways to approach the examination and analysis of data, but a complete analysis will have to await lesion verification.

C. VERIFICATION OF LESIONS

In the case of cortical ablations, considerable information on lesion size and locus could be derived from an examination of the external features of the brain, but of course with subcortical lesions this is not the case. Nevertheless, the brain is still worth examining to ensure that there is not severe infection around the electrode tracts.

Again the instructor will perfuse your experimental and control subjects and remove the brains from the crania. So the brain can be sliced in an orientation corresponding to the plane of the stereotaxic atlas you used, it must be "blocked." This is often done by putting the animal's head into a stereotaxic instrument after perfusion and after the brain is partially exposed. With a blade held in the electrode carrier, a vertical slice is made through the brain 2 to 3 mm anterior to the electrode tract and another vertical slice is made 2 to 3 mm posterior to the electrode tract. This block of tissue then contains the lesion. If it is mounted on a microtome pedestal (see Figure 3–1) with a cut edge parallel to the knife blade, the brain will be cut so that the sections correspond to the stereotaxic atlas plates. Although it is less precise, blocking can be done by hand. Consideration of Figure 8–5 should indicate that if the brain is placed upside down so that the cerebellum and cerebrum rest on a flat surface, cuts made through the brain on an angle of about 20 to 25° posterior to the vertical should be in the same plane as the atlas. This is illustrated in Figure 8–10. Accuracy can be improved somewhat by constructing a box similar to a miter box with slits cut at the correct angle to guide a razor blade.

The importance of tissue blocking and slicing in the stereotaxic plane is illustrated in Figures 8–11 and 8–12. They show rat brain sections sliced in the stereotaxic plane, and sections sliced at 22° and 45° off the stereotaxic

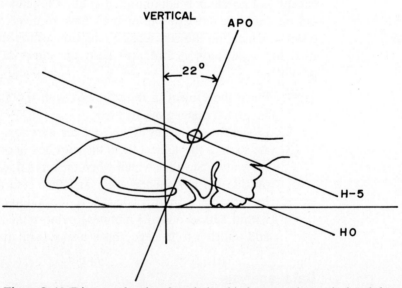

Figure 8–10. Diagram showing the relationship between the vertical and the stereotaxic plane for a rat brain oriented so that the cerebrum and cerebellum rest on a flat surface. Compare this diagram with Figure 8–5.

(a)

(b)

(c)

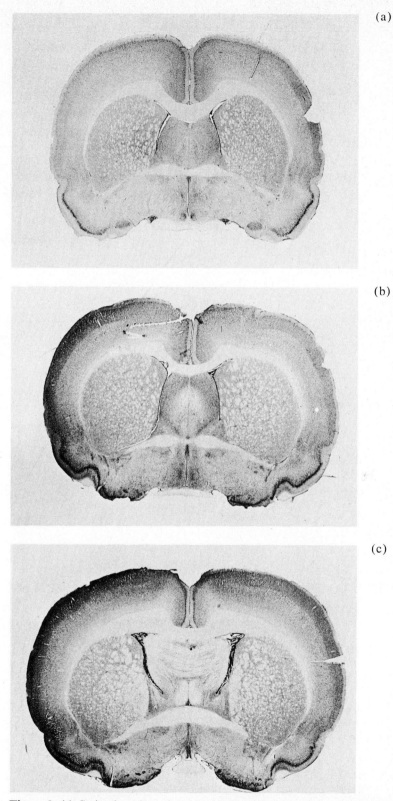

Figure 8–11. Stained sections through the anterior commissure of a normal rat brain, having been blocked and cut (a) in the stereotaxic plane, (b) in the vertical plane 22° from the stereotaxic plane (as shown in Figure 8–10), and (c) in a plane 22° from the vertical plane and 44° from the stereotaxic plane.

(a)

(b)

(c)

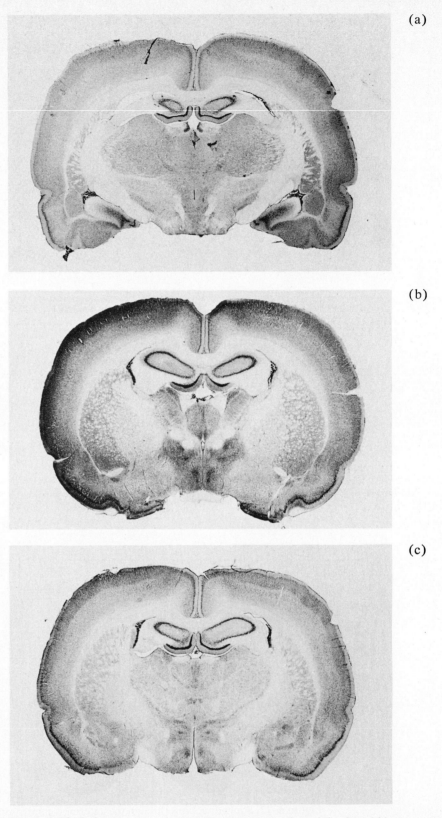

Figure 8–12. Stained sections through the anterior portion of the dorsal hippocampus of normal rat brains, having been blocked and cut in the same three planes described in Figure 8–11.

plane (that is, sections approximately 22° posterior to the vertical, sections on the vertical, and sections approximately 22° anterior to the vertical plane of Figure 8–10). The latter sections are clearly quite different in appearance from the stereotaxic plates.

If the brain is sliced into sections of 25μ thickness, a 5-mm block of tissue will of course yield some 200 sections. Mounting on slides and staining every section would represent considerable waste, and although all sections may be saved and stored for possible future use, only every fifth or tenth section is actually mounted on slides and stained. This is usually quite sufficient to allow one to determine the limits of the lesion. In working with the rat brain, it is almost imperative to use a microprojector (like that used in Laboratory Exercise II to examine stained slides). Each slide can be projetced onto a piece of paper and the lesion and the principal structures can be drawn for later comparison with an atlas. It is not difficult to make quantitative statements about the actual size of a lesion or the proportion of a structure damaged. The reader is referred to Wolf (1971) for a discussion of some of the methods involved.

Compare your brain sections and drawings with the brain atlas and try to specify the extent of the lesion in terms of (1) the approximate proportion of the amygdala left intact and (2) any invasion of surrounding tissue. Be sure also to study carefully the electrode tract. If there was any leak in the electrical insulation, there will probably be some damage along the tract. Be sure to examine any damage associated with the sham operation. Ideally, the experimental and control animals should be identical except for damage to the amygdala.

9

SELECTED READINGS FOR PART TWO

K.S. Lashley
IN SEARCH OF THE ENGRAM

In this paper Lashley reviews some thirty years of
work that represented an attempt both to identify the
nature of the engram (or the memory trace or that
change which must occur somewhere in the nervous
system during learning) and to localize it in the brain.
To understand his work, it is important to note that
the model of nervous system organization implicit at
the time of his early work was derived from the
sensory-motor physiology and psychology of the late
nineteenth century and from the conditioned reflex
psychology of Pavlov. The part of the nervous system
seen as being involved in learning and memory was
the cerebral cortex. Its organization was conceptualized

as consisting of sensory areas, which functioned to
receive the conditioned stimulus (CS) in a learning
situation, the motor area which mediated the conditioned responses (CRs), and the association areas,
intercalated between the various sensory areas and
the motor area. The association areas were viewed as
being where learning took place, as being where the
Pavlovian reflex arcs between CSs and CRs were
formed, as being where associations between stimuli
and responses were established, and as being the
actual storehouses of memory traces and engrams.

The first part of Lashley's paper examines the proposition that the motor cortex plays a major role in the
formation and storage of memory traces and the proposition that well-defined pathways (Pavlovian reflex
arcs) linking sensory and motor areas are formed
across the cortex during learning. The absence of major
retention disturbances following motor cortex ablations
and following the interruption of presumed cortical

From *Symposia of the Society for Experimental Biology. IV:
Physiological mechanisms in animal behaviour*. Cambridge,
Eng.: The University Press, 1950, pp. 454–482. Reprinted
by permission of the Society for Experimental Biology
Symposia.

pathways formed the basis of his rejection of both propositions. The lack of retention deficits following association cortex lesions similarly led him to reject the proposition that the association areas of the cortex are "associational" in function. Instead Lashley found evidence that they modulate or control behavioral strategy. The only areas of the cerebral cortex for which he found evidence of memory trace storage were the cortical sensory projection areas, and he identified two properties of these areas that are really characterizations of the behavioral effects of lesions on learning and retention. The first is equipotentiality, which refers to his observations that small portions of sensory cortex left intact seem to be sufficient for discrimination retention and performance. The second is mass action, which refers to his observations that regardless of locus, the larger the amount of tissue damage, the greater the retention deficit in the case of difficult mazes, suggesting a general facilitative function for the cortex.

The last part of the paper, an attempt to specify what the memory trace must be like, is a clear statement as to what may go on in an animal discrimination learning situation. As a convenient shorthand the psychologist may characterize discrimination learning in terms of CSs and CRs, but Lashley's discussion should make it very clear that the processes involved in learning and memory are much more complex than often assumed. It is not without reason that Lashley concludes, "I sometimes feel, in reviewing the evidence on localization of the memory trace, that the necessary conclusion is that learning just is not possible."

Finally, in reading this paper, the student should keep clearly in mind the uses to which Lashley put the techniques of lesions and ablations and the types of inferences he made from studying their effects on behavior.

I. INTRODUCTION

'When the mind wills to recall something, this volition causes the little [pineal] gland, by inclining successively to different sides, to impel the animal spirits toward different parts of the brain, until they come upon that part where the traces are left of the thing which it wishes to remember; for these traces are nothing else than the circumstance that the pores of the brain through which the spirits have already taken their course on presentation of the object, have thereby acquired a greater facility than the rest to be opened again the same way by the spirits which come to them; so that these spirits coming upon the pores enter therein more readily than into the others.'

So wrote Descartes just three hundred years ago in perhaps the earliest attempt to explain memory in terms of the action of the brain. In the intervening centuries much has been learned concerning the nature of the impulses transmitted by nerves. Innumerable studies have defined conditions under which learning is facilitated or retarded, but, in spite of such progress, we seem little nearer to an understanding of the nature of the memory trace than was Descartes. His theory has in fact a remarkably modern sound. Substitute nerve impulse for animal spirits, synapse for pore and the result is the doctrine of learning as change in resistance of synapses. There is even a theory of scanning which is at least more definite as to the scanning agent and the source of the scanning beam than is its modern counterpart.

As interest developed in the functions of the brain, the doctrine of the separate localization of mental functions gradually took form, even while the ventricles of the brain were still regarded as the active part. From Prochaska and Gall through the nineteenth century, students of clinical neurology sought the localization of specific memories. Flechsig defined the association areas as distinct from the sensory and motor. Aphasia, agnosia and apraxia were interpreted as the result of the loss of memory images, either of objects or of kinaesthetic sensations of movements to be made. The theory that memory traces are stored in association areas adjacent to the corresponding primary sensory areas seemed reasonable and was supported by some clinical evidence. The extreme position was that of Henschen, who speculated concerning the location of single ideas or memories in single cells. In spite of the fact that more critical analytic studies of clinical symptoms, such as those of Henry Head and of Kurt Goldstein, have shown that aphasia and agnosia are primarily defects in the organization of ideas rather than the result of amnesia, the conception of the localized storing of memories is still widely prevalent (Nielsen, 1936).

While clinical students were developing theories of localization, physiologists were analysing the reflex arc and extending the concept of the reflex to include all activity. Bechterew, Pavlov and the behaviourist school in America attempted to reduce all psychological activity to simple associations or chains of conditioned reflexes. The path of these conditioned reflex circuits was described as from sense organ to cerebral sensory area, thence through associative areas to the motor cortex and by way of the pyramidal paths to the final motor cells of the medulla and cord. The discussions of this path were entirely theoretical, and no evidence on the actual course of the conditioned reflex arc was presented.

In experiments extending over the past 30 years I have been trying to trace conditioned reflex paths through the brain or to find the locus of specific memory traces. The results for different types of learning have been inconsistent and often mutually contradictory, in spite of confirmation by repeated tests. I shall summarize to-day a number of experimental findings. Perhaps they obscure rather than illuminate the nature of the engram, but they may serve at least to illustrate the complexity of the problem and to reveal the superficial nature of many of the physiological theories of memory that have been proposed.

I shall have occasion to refer to training of animals in a variety of tasks, so shall give a very brief description of the methods used. The animals studied have been rats and monkeys with, recently, a few chimpanzees. Two lines of approach to the problem have been followed. One is purely behavioural and consists in the analysis of the sensory excitations which are actually associated with reactions in learning and which are effective in eliciting the learned reactions. The associated reactions are similarly analysed. These studies define the patterns of nervous activity at receptor and effector levels and specify certain characteristics which the memory trace must have. The second approach is by surgical destruction of parts of the brain. Animals are trained in various tasks ranging from direct sensori-motor associations

to the solution of difficult problems. Before or after training, associative tracts are cut or portions of the brain removed and effects of these operations on initial learning or postoperative retention are measured. At the termination of the experiments the brains are sectioned and the extent of damage reconstructed from serial sections. The brains are also analysed for secondary degeneration, so far as available histological methods permit.

II. ELIMINATION OF THE MOTOR CORTEX

I first became sceptical of the supposed path of the conditioned reflex when I found that rats, trained in a differential reaction to light, showed no reduction in accuracy of performance when almost the entire motor cortex, along with the frontal poles of the brain, was removed. This observation led to a series of experiments designed to test the part played by the motor cortex or Betz cell area in the retention of various habits. The matter can be tested either by removing the motor cortex or by severing its connexions with the sensory areas of the brain. Both methods have been used with the rat and the monkey.

The sensory and motor areas of the brains of these animals have been mapped by anatomic methods and by electric stimulation. Figure 1 shows the principal areas of the rat's brain, the separate auditory and visual areas and the overlapping sensory and motor areas. Figure 2 is a composite from sev-

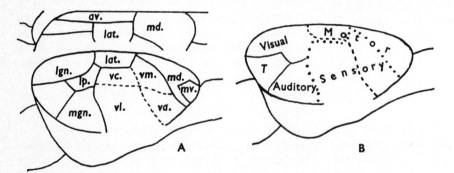

Figure 1. Functional divisions of the rat's brain. A. The projection fields of the principal thalamic nuclei. *av.* anteroventral; *lat.* lateral; *lgn.* lateral geniculate; *lp.* lateral, pars posterior; *med.* median dorsal; *mgn.* median geniculate; *mv.* median ventral; *v.* the various divisions of the ventral nucleus. The projection fields of the median nuclei (*md., mv.*) correspond to the prefrontal areas of primates. B. Location of visual, auditory, and overlapping sensorimotor areas (after Lashley, 1944). The region marked T is probably homologous with the temporal association area of primates.

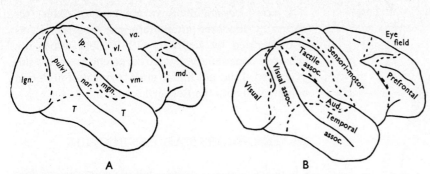

Figure 2. Functional divisions of the monkey's brain. A. The projection of the principal thalamic nuclei. Abbreviations as in Figure 1. The homologies between the divisions of the ventral and lateral nuclei are uncertain. B. Location of functional areas.

eral sources of the chief sensory and motor areas of the brain of the macaque monkey.

Incisions were made through the cortex and underlying fibres of the rat's brain such as to sever the visual areas more or less completely from the motor regions of the brain. The rats were then trained in what I have called the conditional reaction. They are taught to jump to a white triangle and to avoid a white × when both figures are on a black background, but to choose the × and avoid the triangle, if the background is striped; the direction of choice is conditional upon the character of the background. This is the most difficult visual generalization that we have been able to teach the rat. Animals with incisions like those shown in Figure 3, which practically separate the motor regions from the visual, were able to learn this reaction as quickly as did normal controls (Lashley, 1942b).

Monkeys were trained to open various latch-boxes. The motor areas were then removed, as shown in Figure 4. Note that these lesions involved both the

Betz cell area and the premotor area, including parts of the eye fields around the arcuate sulcus. This operation produces a temporary paralysis, but after 8–12 weeks this paralysis recovers to such an extent that the animals are capable of the movements required to open the boxes. During this recovery period they did not have access to the training boxes. When sufficiently recovered, they were tested and opened the boxes promptly without random exploratory movements. The tasks require both a visual recognition of the latches and semi-skilled movements, such as turning a crank. Removal of the motor areas did not produce a loss of memory for the movements (Lashley, 1924). Jacobsen has since confirmed these observations with a chimpanzee from which the motor cortex was removed (Jacobsen, 1932).

These experiments seem to rule out the motor cortex or Betz cell area as containing any part of the conditioned reflex arc. The traditional view of the function of this area regards it as the region of final integration of skilled voluntary movements. My own

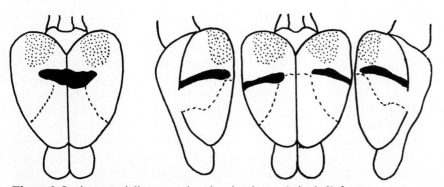

Figure 3. Lesions partially separating the visual area (stippled) from the motor areas (outlined by dashes) of the rat's brain without disturbing visual learning.

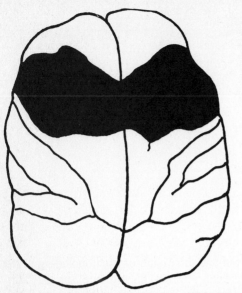

Figure 4. Extent of cortical lesion which did not abolish latch-box habits. The lesion is bounded caudally by the central fissure and extends forward to include the arcuate sulcus.

interpretation, to which few neurologists would subscribe, is that it has no direct concern with voluntary movement, but is a part of the vast reflex postural system which includes the basal nuclei, cerebellar and vestibular systems. Certainly there is no evidence that it forms a part of the conditioned reflex circuit.

For the rat the experiments rule out the whole frontal region of the brain from participation in visual habits. In the monkey there remains another possibility. The so-called visual associative area (area 18) has direct connexion with the cortex of the arcuate sulcus (area 8), and this in turn with the premotor cortex (area 6). This last area is also motor and perhaps equivalent in function with the Betz cell area (Bucy, 1934). The cortex of the arcuate sulcus and of a considerable surrounding area was removed from five monkeys that had been trained in a variety of visual discriminative reactions. After the operations they showed perfect retention of all their visual habits (Lashley, 1948). Jacobsen (1932) has reported loss of certain latch-box habits in monkeys after removal of area 6, but there are indications that this may be a kinaesthetic-sensory area (Walker, 1938; Gay & Gelhorn, 1948), and the loss cannot be ascribed to disturbance of its function as a final common motor path. I have removed it in combination with area 4 without disrupting motor habits (Lashley, 1924).

I have occasionally seen the type of defect reported by Jacobsen after prefrontal lobe lesions, as also reported by Kennard (1939), but it has not occurred consistently and its occurrence remains unexplained. I did not find it after removal of area 6 in conjunction with the Betz cell area.

III. TRANSCORTICAL CONDUCTION

There is evidence, not only that the motor cortex does not participate in the transmission of the conditioned reflex pattern, but also that the transmission of impulses over well-defined, isolated paths from one part of the cortex to another is inessential for performance of complicated habits. The maze habit of the rat almost certainly involves the utilization of several sensory modalities, visual, tactile and kinaesthetic. In a rather complicated set of experiments I attempted to test the importance of connexions across the cortex for maze performance. Rats were trained on the maze, then knife cuts were made through the cortex and underlying fibres, separating different functional areas or cutting through functional areas. The incisions were long, averaging half of the entire length of the cerebral hemispheres. After recovery the animals were tested in retention of the maze habit. In other experiments the incisions were made before training and their effect upon the rate of initial learning was tested. In neither initial learning nor in retention could any certain effect of separating the various parts of the cortex be demonstrated. If the incisions interrupted sensory tracts to the cortex, there was loss of the habit, but uncomplicated separation of cortical areas produced no effect on performance. Figure 5 gives composite diagrams of incisions which were without effect on maze performance (Lashley, 1944).

Both the anatomic evidence of Le Gros Clark (1941) and the physiological evidence from strychninization of the cortex (Bonin, Garol & McCulloch, 1942) shows that the primary visual area has direct axon connexions only with the immediately adjacent cortex. In experiments which I shall report in more detail in considering the function of associative areas, I removed the greater part of this band of cortex surrounding the visual areas from five monkeys that had been trained in a variety of visual habits (Figure 6). This operation almost certainly destroyed all the relay connexions across the cortex from the macular fields. It produced no loss of visual habits based on discrimination of the colour, brightness, or form of objects (Lashley, 1948).

Miss Wade trained monkeys in habits which are

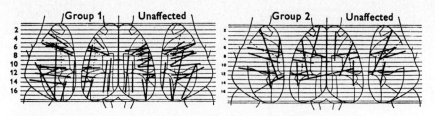

Figure 5. Composite of incisions through the cortex of the rat which
did not disturb maze learning (Group 1) or retention (Group 2). One pair of
lines, roughly symmetrical in the two hemispheres, represents the lesion in
each animal studied (after Lashley, 1944).

abolished by destruction of the frontal lobes and which require visual, tactile and kinaesthetic adjustments. I cut the transcortical fibres of the frontal lobes in these animals, leaving only the projection fibres for the area. There was no disturbance of performance after the operations (unpublished experiments).

Such results are certainly puzzling. They leave us with almost no understanding of the function of the associative fibres which extend across from one part of the cortex to another. The results are difficult to accept, yet they are supported by various other lines of evidence. Smith (1947) and Akelaitis (1944) have reported careful studies of human patients in whom the corpus callosum (the great commissure of fibres connecting the two hemispheres) had been severed in an effort to stop the spread of Jacksonian epilepsy. These investigators were not able to demonstrate any effects of the operation except a slight slowing of reaction time, which was equally great, whether the reaction was on the same or opposite side of the body to that stimulated. Sperry (1947) has divided the arm motor and sensory areas of the mon-

key's brain into a number of small square divisions (Figure 7) by careful subpial section. Although the operations were intended to sever only the intrinsic fibres of the cortex, they actually destroyed most of the longer loop fibres as well. Such animals do not show any postoperative inco-ordination of the movements of the different segments of the arm and use the arm efficiently in the performance of habitual movements.

It is difficult to interpret such findings, but I think that they point to the conclusion that the associative connexions or memory traces of the conditioned reflex do not extend across the cortex as well-defined arcs or paths. Such arcs are either diffused through all parts of the cortex, pass by relay through lower centres, or do not exist.

There is the possibility that the chief associative connexions between functional areas of the cortex are by connexions through the thalamus. I doubt this for two reasons. The techniques that have been used to demonstrate cortical efferents to the thalamus, the Marchi stain and strychninization of the cortex, are unreliable indices of the direction of fibres. The sup-

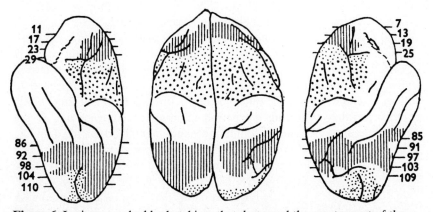

Figure 6. Lesions, marked by hatching, that destroyed the greater part of the
so-called visual associative areas in a monkey without affecting visual functions.

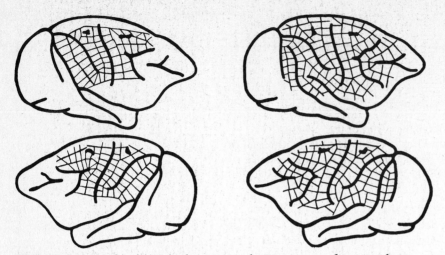

Figure 7. Pattern of incisions in the motor and sensory areas of two monkeys which did not produce incoordination of movements (after Sperry, 1947).

posed cortico-thalamic fibres follow the paths of the afferent fibres and may not be efferent. Secondly, in the rat at least there is little evidence of an elaborate system of intrathalamic association fibres. After a cortical injury thalamic nuclei degenerate completely without leaving a residue of internuncial cells. The question of the importance of intrathalamic association is not settled, and none of the available anatomic or physiological techniques is capable of giving conclusive evidence.

A few experiments by Ingebritsen (1933) on the spinal cord suggest that the essential pattern of a learned reaction can be transmitted by a diffuse nervous network. Ingebritsen made double hemisections of the spinal cord of rats, severing one-half at the second, the other at the fifth cervical level. These lesions cut all long fibres connecting the brain with the spinal motor centres of the limbs. Nevertheless, such rats retained maze-habits and were able to learn to operate latch-boxes requiring that they rise on the hindfeet and depress a lever with the forepaws. There are no long fibres, either sensory or motor, crossing over between the two levels of these sections. Habit patterns cannot be acquired by the isolated spinal cord (Kellogg, Deese, Pronko & Feinberg, 1947). Somehow, the control of the motor pattern essential for the performance of the complex acts traverses the network of short internuncial cells of the spinal cord.

IV. THE PROBLEM OF THE 'ASSOCIATION AREAS'

In anatomic theories of the memory trace the association areas of the cortex have played a major part. Frontal, parietal, occipital and temporal associative areas have been distinguished as regions of the cortex, relatively lacking in massive connexions with the lower centres of the brain. On the basis of some clinical evidence, but chiefly because of their anatomic relations, these areas have been considered as associative and as the storehouses of memory images of sensations derived from the adjacent sensory areas. Thus areas 18 and 19 of Brodmann's questionable divisions have been called the visual associative areas, areas 5 and 7 tactile associative, and areas 20, 21 and 22 of the temporal lobe the auditory association areas. The prefrontal area was considered by Hitzig to be a higher integrative region because he believed that it showed the greatest evolutionary growth in the primate brain. Special memory functions were also ascribed to it, however.

S. I. Franz reported that the removal of the frontal association areas of cats destroyed recently formed habits but left old, well-established habits unaffected (Franz, 1907). The actual observation was that the cats lost their habits of opening latch-boxes but would still come when called. His operations destroyed much of the motor areas as well as the prefrontal cortex. I later trained monkeys on latch-boxes and removed the prefrontal cortex, in an experiment designed to test the influence of the operation on learning ability. During the period allowed for recovery one of the animals found the experimental boxes piled in the corner of the room and promptly opened them. Tests of the other animals showed perfect retention of the manipulative habits. There was no indication that the recently acquired habits had been lost. Jacobsen took up the problem at this point and carried it further. He found that visual discriminative habits and simple habits of latch-box manipulation are unaffected by loss of the prefrontal association areas. Habits requiring a series of acts, such as opening a box with several independent latches, may be lost. This is not, however, a simple removal of memory traces. The animals are incapable of relearning the functions which they have lost. They fail because of a difficulty in going on from one task to the next, not from loss of memory of the individual items of the task (Jacobsen, 1936).

Loss of the delayed reaction after removal of the prefrontal lobes of the monkey has been interpreted as a loss of immediate memory. However, this task and others, which are affected by prefrontal injury, all involve a series of conflicting actions. Difficulty in maintaining a constant set or attitude is the real basis of the loss. Such an interpretation fits better with clinical findings than does the hypothesis of memory defect.

We have recently been testing the relation of other associative areas to memory functions in the monkey. Five spider monkeys were trained on a variety of visual tasks. A band of cortex surrounding the primary visual areas and including the visual associative areas of Campbell and Brodmann was then removed (Figure 7), and the animals were tested for retention of habits based on discrimination of colours, of geometric forms, and of a number of familiar objects, such as visual recognition of their home cages, of the caretaker, and the like. No loss of any visual memories could be demonstrated (Lashley, 1948).

Similar experiments with habits of tactile discrimination are now being completed. The monkeys are required to reach through a hole in a partition and to distinguish variously shaped covers of food dishes by touch alone. They learn readily such tasks as to choose a cylinder and reject a prism, if both are smooth, but to choose the prism, if both are coated with sandpaper. When they had reached a standard criterion of accuracy, the parietal associative areas (Brodmann's areas 5 and 7) were removed. No animal has shown significant loss of the habits based on tactile discrimination after removal of these areas alone (Dr Josephine Blum).

Removal of the lateral surfaces of the temporal lobes alone has also not affected visual or tactile habits.

A number of experiments with the rat have shown that habits of visual discrimination survive the destruction of any part of the cerebral cortex except the primary visual projection area. Similarly for auditory habits and the auditory cortex. There is no indication of specialized memory areas outside the primary sensory fields. Although there are not clearly distinguished associative areas in the rat's cortex, I have become somewhat sceptical of the existence of any great difference in the extent of associative areas, as between the rat and monkey. The best anatomic index that we have of the functional differentiation of a cortical area is its connexions with the thalamus. The prefrontal cortex of man is the projection field of the dorsomedial and ventromedial nuclei. The corresponding nuclei in the rat's thalamus project to a large frontal region, perhaps proportionately as large as the prefrontal lobes of man (Lashley, 1941). This region also includes the electrically excitable points for the head and part of that for the forelegs. It has therefore been classed as motor, but it is equally justifiable to class it as corresponding to the human prefrontal cortex.

It has been claimed that the differentiation of a number of cerebral areas contributes to man's superior intelligence by avoiding confusion of functions, but, if the anatomic relations in man and the rat were reversed, it would be concluded with equal assurance that, because intellectual activity requires close integration of different functions, the advantage lies with the brain in which functional areas are not sharply set off. Such *post hoc* arguments based on anatomic grounds alone have little value for functional interpretations. Many current conceptions of cerebral physiology are based upon just such dubious inferences from anatomic data.

The outcome of the experiments involving removal of the associative areas of the monkey was unexpected, in spite of the fact that it confirms the earlier results with the rat. The conclusion, which seems to be forced by the accumulated data, runs counter to the accepted tradition concerning the organization of the cerebral cortex. Memory traces, at least of simple sensori-motor associations, are not laid down and stored within the associative areas; at least not within the restricted associative area supposedly concerned with each sense modality. Memory disturbances of simple sensory habits follow only upon very extensive experimental destruction, including almost the entire associative cortex. Even combined destructions of the prefrontal, parietal, occipital and temporal areas, exclusive of the primary sensory cortex, does not prevent the animal from forming such habits, although pre-existing habits are lost and their reformation is greatly retarded.

These results, showing that the so-called associative areas are not essential to preservation of memory traces, have been obtained with rats and monkeys. Is there a greater cortical differentiation in anthropoid apes and man? We have experimental data only on the prefrontal associative cortex of the chimpanzee and of man. Bilateral removal of the entire prefrontal granular cortex in five chimpanzees in our laboratory has not resulted in any memory defect. One two-year-old animal, lacking prefrontal and parietal areas, removed in early infancy, falls well within the normal range in all aspects of development. Adult chimpanzees, trained in such complicated habits as choosing an object, like a model shown, retain the habits after removal of the entire prefrontal cortex. We have not been able to demonstrate loss of any memory or, in fact, of any function after such operations.

Clinical data, with amnesias following apparently small lesions, seem to contradict such experimental findings. However, lesions in the human brain are mostly the result either of tumor growth or of severe traumatism, both of which probably produce widespread changes in addition to the local injury. The surgical removal of parts of the frontal lobes in the recent topectomy studies has not produced such severe defects as usually result from traumatic destruction of the lobes (Mettler, 1949).

V. THE ROLE OF SUBCORTICAL STRUCTURES

Perhaps we have been looking in the wrong place for the conditioned reflex arcs or memory traces. Are they formed somewhere else than in the cortex? Experiments on the thalamus and other subcortical structures are technically difficult, and there is little direct evidence on this question. Since the classical experiments of Goltz a number of investigators have studied the capacity of the totally decorticate animal to learn. The outcome of these experiments is that such animals can form simple sensori-motor associations, although with extreme slowness in comparison with the rate of the normal animal (Polterew & Zeliony, 1930; Girden, Mettler, Finch & Culler, 1936). We must ask, however, whether such learning occurs when the cortex is intact.

When the sensory or associative areas of the cerebral cortex are destroyed, the corresponding nuclei of the neo-thalamus degenerate, so this portion of the subcortex is eliminated from consideration by the same experiments which rule out the cortical association areas. The only experiments bearing upon the participation of other subcortical centres suggest that subcortical learning does not occur when the cortex is functioning.

Fischel (1948) has maintained, solely from comparative psychological studies, that the basal ganglia are the seat of the space-co-ordinate elements of mo-

tor habits. I have destroyed the greater part of these structures in rats, trained in the discrimination box, without producing loss of orientation. The animals may perform forced circus movements but, in spite of this, they maintain their orientation in the problem box (Lashley, 1921b). The basal ganglia in man are subject to various degenerative diseases. The symptoms of such diseases are, in general, tremors and other disturbances of co-ordination at a primitive level, but without evidence of apraxia or other disorder of the learned patterns of motor co-ordination. The evidence seems conclusive that in mammals the basal nuclei are not an essential link in the patterning of learned activities.

It has been widely held that although memory traces are at first formed in the cerebral cortex, they are finally reduced or transferred by long practice to subcortical levels. The evidence for this has been the apparently greater fragility of recently formed habits than of old habits; the supposedly greater resistance of the latter to brain injuries. The amnesias following electroshock therapy indicate that it is the age of the trace and not the amount of practice that has built it up which determines its survival, and a difference of a few minutes in the age of memories may suffice to determine their loss or survival. This is scarcely evidence for reduction to lower levels of the nervous system. The chief argument for the dropping out of memory traces from the cortex has seemingly run somewhat as follows: Consciousness is a function of the cerebral cortex; long-practised habits become automatic and are performed without conscious control; therefore they are no longer mediated by the cerebral cortex. Both premises of this syllogism are probably false, and the conclusion would not follow if they were true.

When rats are trained in a habit based upon the discrimination of intensities of light, to choose a brightly lighted alley and avoid a dimly lighted one, the removal of the striate cortex completely abolishes the habit. The animals are able to relearn the reaction and require as much practice as they did for initial learning. One group of animals was trained in this habit and given 1200 trials of overtraining, daily practice for a period of 3 months. Their behaviour strongly suggested automatization of the habit. The striate areas were then removed. The habit was lost, just as in the case of animals which are operated as soon as they give evidence of the presence of the habit. The long overtraining did not eliminate the participation of the cortex (Lashley, 1921a).

This visual habit can be formed in the absence of the visual cortex, and the rates of learning with and without the visual area are exactly the same. The average for 100 normal animals is 125 trials; for nearly 100 without the visual areas it is 123 trials. After such animals, lacking the visual cortex, have learned the brightness reaction, any other part of the cerebral cortex may be destroyed without disturbing the habit. Apparently no other part of the cortex takes over the learning function (Lashley, 1922). If, in addition to removal of the striate areas, the pretectile region of the thalamus and the optic tectum are destroyed, the animals cannot learn the discrimination reaction (Lashley, 1935b). These facts indicate that, in the absence of the visual cortex, the learning of the brightness reaction is carried out by the optic tectum. However, so long as the visual cortex is intact, removal of the tectum has no effect whatever upon the performance of visual habits. The tectum apparently does not participate in visual learning so long as the cortex is intact (Lashley, 1935b).

Dunlap (1927) has advanced the hypothesis that complex serial habits such as that of maze-running, playing a musical passage, or speaking a sentence, are at first chains of sensori-motor reactions in which excitations from muscular contractions in one movement of the series serve as stimuli to elicit the next. He holds that, with continued practice, there is a short-circuiting of these conditioned reflex pathways through the cerebellum and that the peripheral elements drop out. McCarthy and I (1926) attempted to test this hypothesis by training rats in the maze, removing the cerebellum, and testing for retention. The operations greatly disturbed the motor coordination of these animals. Some of them practically rolled through the maze, but they rolled without entering the blind alleys. There was no loss of memory of the sequence of turns in the maze.

These few experiments are, of course, by no means conclusive. They constitute, however, the only direct evidence available, and they definitely point to the conclusion that, if the cerebral cortex is intact, the associative connexions of simple conditioned reflexes are not formed in the subcortical structures of the brain.

The studies which I have reported thus far point to the conclusion that habits based upon visual discrimination are mediated by the striate areas, by the primary visual cortex, and do not involve the activity of any other part of the cerebral cortex. The conduction of impulses is from the retina to the lateral geniculate nuclei, thence to the striate areas, and from them down to some subcortical nervous mechanism. The path beyond the striate cortex is unknown. It may be direct to the spinal cord. There is some evidence that the pyramidal paths contain many fibres from all parts of the cerebral cortex, not from the Betz cell area only.

It seems probable that the same restriction of simple discriminative habits to the primary sensory areas holds also for other sensory modalities. The evidence is less complete, but what there is is consistent with the data on the visual system.

The evidence thus indicates that in sensori-motor habits of the conditioned reflex type no part of the cerebral cortex is essential except the primary sensory area. There is no transcortical conduction from the sensory areas to the motor cortex, and the major subcortical nuclear masses, thalamus, striatum, colliculi and cerebellum do not play a part in the recognition of sensory stimuli or in the habit patterning of motor reactions.

VI. THE ENGRAM WITHIN SENSORY AREAS (EQUIPOTENTIAL REGIONS)

The experiments reported indicate that performance of habits of the conditioned reflex type is dependent upon the sensory areas and upon no other part of the cerebral cortex. What of localization within the sensory areas? Direct data upon this question are limited, but point to the conclusion that so long as some part of the sensory field remains intact and there is not a total loss of primary sensitivity, the habit mechanism can still function. Thus, in a series of experiments attempting to locate accurately the visual cortex of the rat, parts of the occipital lobes were destroyed in a variety of combinations. In these experiments it appeared that, so long as some part of the anterolateral surface of the striate cortex (the projection field of the temporal retina corresponding to the macula of primates) remained intact, there was no loss of habit. Any small part of the region was capable of maintaining the habits based on discrimination of intensities of light (Lashley, 1935b).

In a later experiment an attempt was made to determine the smallest amount of visual cortex which is capable of mediating habits based upon detail vision. The extent of visual cortex remaining after operation was determined by counting undegenerated cells in the lateral geniculate nucleus. Discrimination of visual figures could be learned when only one-sixtieth of the visual cortex remained (Lashley, 1939). No comparable data are available on postoperative retention, but from incidental observations in other experiments I am confident that retention would be possible with the same amount of tissue.

In an early study by Franz (1911) the lateral surfaces of the occipital lobes of the monkey were destroyed after the animals had been trained in pattern and colour discrimination. These operations involved the greater part of what is now known to be the projection field of the macula. There was no loss of the habits. I have destroyed the cortex of the retrocalcarine fissure (the perimacular field) without destroying visual memories. The results with monkeys thus support the more ample data for the rat; the visual memory traces survive any cortical lesion, provided some portion of the field of acute vision remains intact.

This lack of definite habit localization might really have been predicted from psychological data alone. Analysis of the effective stimuli in discriminative learning reveals that the association is independent of particular sensory nerve fibres. It is a response to a pattern of excitation which may vary widely in position on the sensory surface and consequently in cortical projection. The reactions involved in motor habits show the same sort of functional equivalence; a motor habit is not a predetermined set of muscular contractions but is a series of movements in relation to bodily posture and to the complex pattern of the environment. The writing of one's name, for example, is not a stereotyped series of contractions of particular muscles but is a series of movements in relation to the body planes which can be performed with any motor organ and with any degree of amplitude.

I have not time here to report in detail the experiments which justify the conclusion that neither the afferent path nor the efferent is fixed by habit. The mass of evidence accumulated by gestalt psychologists shows conclusively that it is the pattern and not the localization of energy on the sense organ that determines its functional effect. Similar motor equivalence is demonstrated by a variety of less systematic evidence. The psychological studies, like the more limited direct experiments on the brain, point to the conclusion that the memory trace is located in all parts of the functional area; that various parts are equipotential for its maintenance and activation.

VII. FACILITATIVE FUNCTIONS IN LEARNING AND RETENTION (MASS ACTION)

The experiments thus far reported have been concerned almost entirely with discriminative habits requiring only an association between a single sensory stimulus and a motor response. A very different picture develops in experiments with other types of learning. If rats are trained in the maze and then have portions of the cortex removed, they show more or less loss of the habit. If a small amount of cortex is destroyed, 5–10%, the loss may be scarcely detectable. If large amounts, say 50% or more, are destroyed, the habit is completely lost, and relearning may require many times as much practice as did initial learning. The amount of loss, measured in terms of the practice required for relearning, is, on the average, closely proportional to the amount of cortex destroyed. Figure 8 shows the relation for one group of rats on a relatively difficult maze with eight *culs de sac*. There is some evidence that the more difficult the task, the greater the relative effect of the larger lesions (Lashley, 1929; Lashley & Wiley, 1933). Similar results have been obtained with latch-box learning and retention (Lashley, 1935a). So far as it is possible to analyse the data from more than 200 diverse operations, the amount of loss from a given extent of cortical destruction is about the same,

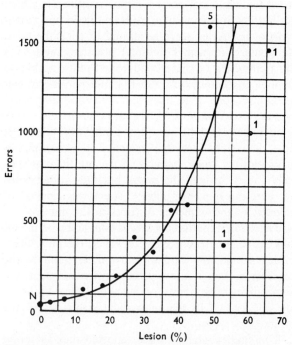

Figure 8. The relation of errors in maze learning to extent of cerebral damage in the rat. The extent of brain injury is expressed as the percentage of the surface area of the isocortex destroyed. Data from 60 normal and 127 brain-operated animals are averaged by class intervals of 5 percent destruction. The curve is the best fitting one of logarithmic form. For lesions above 45 percent the number of cases (indicated by numerals on the graph) is too small for reliability (After Lashley & Wiley, 1933).

no matter what part of the cerebral hemispheres is destroyed, provided that the destruction is roughly similar in both hemispheres.

The explanation of this quantitative relationship is difficult. In learning the maze the rat certainly employs a variety of sensory cues, visual, tactile, kinaesthetic, olfactory, possibly auditory. Brain injuries destroy various sensory fields and the larger the lesion the greater the reduction in available sense data. The production of different amounts of sensory deficit would thus appear to be the most reasonable explanation of the quantitative relation between habit loss and extent of lesion (Hunter, 1930; Finley, 1941). Sensory deficit certainly plays a role in it. In the experiment on effects of incisions through the cortex, which was described earlier, the severity of loss of the maze habit correlated highly with the interruption of sensory pathways, as determined from degeneration of the thalamus.

However, sensory loss will not account for all of the habit deterioration. There is evidence which shows that another more mysterious effect is involved. In the first place, destruction of a single sensory area of the cortex produces a far greater deficit in maze or latch-box performance than does loss of the corresponding sense modality. A comparison was made of the effects on retention of the latch-box habits of combined loss of vision, vibrissae touch, and the anaesthesia to touch and movement produced by sectioning the dorsal half of the spinal cord at the third cervical level. This latter operation severs the columns of Gall and Burdoch, which convey tactile and kinaesthetic impulses, and also severs the pyramidal tracts which have a dorsal position in the rat. The combined peripheral sense privation and section of the pyramids produced less loss of the latch-box habits than did destruction of a single sensory area of the cortex (Lashley, 1935a). Secondly, when blind animals are trained in the maze, the removal

of the primary visual cortex produces a severe loss of the habit with serious difficulty in relearning, although the animals could have used no visual cues during the initial learning (Lashley, 1943).

A possible explanation of this curious effect was that the rat forms concepts of spatial relations in visual terms, as man seems to do, and that the space concepts are integrated in the visual cortex. The visual cortex might then function in the formation of spatial habits, even when the animal loses its sight. To test this Tsang (1934) reared rats blind from birth, trained them as adults in the maze, then destroyed the visual cortex. The resultant loss of the maze habit by these animals was as severe as in animals which had been reared with vision. The hypothesis concerning the formation of visual space concepts was not confirmed.

Our recent studies of the associative areas of the monkey are giving similar results to those gained with rats. Visual and tactile habits are not disturbed by the destruction singly, either of the occipital, parietal, or lateral temporal regions, so long as the primary sensory fields remain. However, combined destruction of these regions, as shown in Figure 9, does produce a loss of the habits with retarded relearning. Higher level functions, such as the conditional reaction, delayed reaction, or solution of the multiple stick problem, show deterioration after extensive damage in any part of the cortex. The capacity for delayed reaction in monkeys, for example (to remember in which of two boxes food was placed), may be seriously reduced or abolished by removal either of the prefrontal lobes or of the occipital associative cortex or of the temporal lobes. That is, small lesions, embracing no more than a single associative area, do not produce loss of any habit; large lesions produce a deterioration which affects a variety of habits, irrespective of the sensori-motor elements involved.

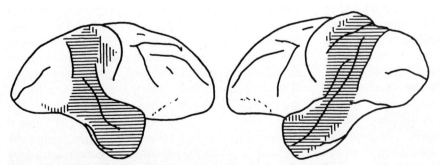

Figure 9. Minimal lesion which produces disturbances in tactile or visual memory in the monkey.

Results such as these have led me to formulate a theory of mass action or mass facilitation. It is, essentially, that performance of any function depends upon two variables in nervous activity. The reaction mechanism, whether of instinctive or of learned activity, is a definite pattern of integrated neurons with a variable threshold of excitability. The availability of such patterns, the ease with which they can be activated, is dependent upon less specific facilitative effects. This facilitation can come from a variety of sources. Some instinctive behaviour seems to require hormonal activation, probably a direct chemical effect upon specific nervous elements. Emotional facilitation may produce a temporary activation. Continued activity of related mechanisms may facilitate the whole group of associated reactions; a sort of warming-up effect.

There are indications (Krechevsky, 1936), although little systematic evidence, that the severity of postoperative amnesia varies with the intensity of motivation. Rats trained in a discrimination without punishment with electric shock for errors may show loss of the habit after lesions which do not produce loss in animals which were trained with punishment. The greater effects of cortical lesions in monkeys than in rats may be in part a result of the greater difficulty in getting consistent motivation in the higher animals. In man an amnesia often seems to be a difficulty rather than impossibility of recall; recall may be possible but only with extreme effort and fatigue. I believe that the evidence strongly favours the view that amnesia from brain injury rarely, if ever, is due to the destruction of specific memory traces. Rather, the amnesias represent a lowered level of vigilance, a greater difficulty in activating the organized patterns of traces, or a disturbance of some broader system of organized functions.

In interpreting apparent loss of memory after cerebral damage, extreme caution is necessary. The poor performance in tasks may be due to the destruction of specific associative connexions, but is instead generally, I believe always, the result rather of interference with a higher level functional patterning. Some experiments of Dr Klüver's (personal communication) illustrate this point. Monkeys were trained in a variety of discriminative reactions calling for use of different sense modalities by a method that required them to pull in the stimulus objects by attached strings. Extensive lesions in different cortical areas all caused loss of these habits. The monkeys simply pulled the strings at random. They were retrained in the discrimination of weights. When this was learned, the habits based on other sense modali-

ties (reactions to intensities of light, for example) returned spontaneously. What had been disturbed by all the operations was the set or attitude to compare stimuli, not the specific memory of which one was correct.

This example perhaps illustrates at a primitive level the characteristic of amnesias as seen clinically. Apparent loss of memory is secondary to a disorder in the structuring of concepts. Some physiological mode of organizing or integrating activity is affected rather than specific associative bonds.

VII. THE COMPLEXITY OF THE MEMORY TRACE

The experiments that I have reviewed deal with only a small part of the whole problem of the memory trace; with those aspects which can most readily be studied in experiments with animals. Immediate memory presents a different type of problem. It is highly probable that immediate memory is maintained by some sort of after-discharge of the originally excited neurons. Such persistent activity can scarcely be the basis of more permanent memory, although Ebbecke (1919) and Edgell (1924) have formulated theories of memory in terms of persistent states of excitation. It is by no means certain that all memory is mediated by a single type of mechanism; that motor skills and eidetic images, for example, have any physiological properties in common. The attempt to account for all memory by any single theory involves assumptions which are not supported by any evidence now available.

Much of learning theory has been based upon supposedly isolated and simple instances of association, on the assumption that these represent a primitive prototype of all memory. However, an analysis of even the conditioned reflex indicates that it is not the simple, direct association of stimulus and response that it has been thought to be. I served as experimenter and subject for several years in experiments employing both the salivary method of Pavlov and the motor reactions of Bechterev. The experience convinced me that, far from being a simple sensorimotor reaction, the conditioned reflex is very complicated (Lashley, 1916). The S-R diagram is misleadingly schematic. The effective stimulus is not only the object which the experimenter designates as S, but a whole background of other objects constituting the situation in which the experiment is conducted. Every stimulus has a space setting. When, for example, the rat is trained to react to a triangle, he fails to respond, if the figure is rotated through more than 10–15° (Fields, 1932). This means that the memory trace of the figure is tied in with the space co-ordinates of the animal's postural system. This system of space co-ordinates is a part of the postural reflex system which pervades every aspect of behaviour. There is scarcely a memory which does not have spatial orientation, either with reference to the planes of the body or to external space in addition.

Most skilled acts, from running a maze to playing a musical phrase or speaking a sentence, involve a timed series of actions which cannot be accounted for as a single chain of conditioned reflexes (Lashley, 1949). The serial timing of actions is among the most important and least studied of behavioural problems. Almost all memories except those of automatized motor habits are dated, as Bergson (1896) has emphasized; that is, they have a temporal position in the series of memories which constitutes the individual's past. The memory trace is associated with this series as well as with the particular objects which make up its central core.

The conditioned reflex also includes an element of affective reinforcement. Corresponding to the nature of the conditioning stimulus, there is fear of electric shock, objectively demonstrable by cardiac and respiratory changes, anticipation of acid in the mouth with slight nausea, or expectation of food(Lashley, 1916). Unless this affective element is aroused, the conditioned reflex does not occur. So-called extinction of the conditioned reflex is not a weakening of the specific association, but a waning of this affective reinforcement. Other types of association also have dynamic aspects. The amnesic aphasias seem to be due less to a weakening of specific associations than to a reduction in some general form of facilitation. Henry Head has expressed this as a reduction of 'vigilance,' without attempting to define further the nature of the function which is disturbed.

A variety of evidence (McGeoch, 1942) shows that, in a memorized series of nonsense syllables, associations are formed, not only between adjacent words but also between words remote from each other in the series. This, I believe, is an illustration at a primitive level of the fact that every memory becomes part of a more or less extensive organization. When I read a scientific paper, the new facts presented become associated with the field of knowledge of which it is a part. Later availability of the specific items of the paper depends upon a partial activation of the whole body of associations. If one has not thought of a topic for some time, it is difficult to recall details. With review or discussion of the subject, however, names, dates, references which seemed to be forgotten, rapidly become available to memory. Head (1926) has given instances of such recall by multiple reinforcement in his studies of aphasia. Although there are no systematic experiments upon this 'warming-up' effect, it is a matter of common experience and is evidence, I believe, that recall involves the subthreshold activation of a whole system of associations which exert some sort of mutual facilitation.

All this is by way of indicating the probable complexity of the memory trace of even the simplest associations. The engram of a new association, far from consisting of a single bond or neuron connexion, is probably a reorganization of a vast system of associations involving the interrelations of hundreds of thousands or millions of neurons.

IX. SOME QUANTITATIVE CONSIDERATIONS

It has been customary to assume that, since the nervous system contains so many millions of neurons, there must be a large reservoir of cells or of synaptic connexions which can be modified and reserved for specific memory functions. Dunlap (1930) has expressed the view that every individual has far more brain cells than he is ever called upon to use, and has urged this as an argument against any congenital restriction of ability. A similar view has been implied in the identification of intelligence as the individual's number of unpreempted and available memory bonds. However, only the vaguest sort of anatomic data have been available to support such theories. Analysis of actual cell numbers involved in a reaction system gives little indication of a reserve of unused connexions and raises a very difficult question as to the way in which the same system can mediate different functions.

I have counted or estimated the number of cells at different levels in the visual system of the rat. The numbers, which I believe are correct within approximately 10%, are given in Table 1. You will note that there is a marked concentration of paths from the retinal myoids to the lateral geniculate nucleus, such that an average of nearly 300 myoids feed into each thalamo-cortical path. At the cortical level there is some dispersion, but it is not great. In the receptive layer (lamina iv) there are fewer than four neurons for each afferent fibre, and in the whole visual cortex there are only nineteen neurons for each afferent fibre.

The rat's maximal visual acuity is about 30 min.

Table 1 The number of neurons at each level in the visual system of the rat (unilateral)

LEVEL	TOTAL NO. OF NEURONS	RATIO TO FIBRES IN RADIATION
Retinal cells		
Rods	9,180,000 ⎱	273.0
Cones	120,000 ⎰	
Bipolar	3,530,000	104.0
Ganglion	260,000	13.1
Lateral geniculate	34,000	1.0
Cortical cells		
Lamina vii	68,800	2.0
Lamina vi	135,400	4.0
Lamina v	147,700	4.3
Lamina iv (granular)	127,000	3.7
Laminae ii–iii	176,000	5.2
Total cortical	654,900	19.2

of arc, as determined by behavioural tests and from the resolving power of the lens system. Because of the extreme curvature of the cornea and lens the visual field of one eye subtends about 210°. If acuity were uniform throughout the retina, it would require more than 80,000 fibres to represent each acuity unit of the retina by one central fibre. The concentration of ganglion cells falls off from 130 per hundredth square millimetre at the fixation point to 65 at the ora serrata (Lashley, 1932). Assuming that acuity decreases proportionately, some 40,000 separate paths are required to represent each acuity unit at the cortex by a single afferent fibre. This corresponds fairly well to the 34,000 geniculo-striate paths actually counted. Since acute vision is continuous under light stimulation, it follows that all of the geniculo-striate cells must be firing constantly when the eye is stimulated by the usual lighted environment. Further, since there are not more than nineteen neurons in the visual area for each afferent fibre, it is almost certain that every cell in the striate cortex is firing during light stimulation. Certainly there is no large reserve of cells which can be set aside for excitation only in specific habits.

Corresponding counts of cells in the visual system of the monkey have recently been made by Chow & Blum (personal communication). The number of neurons in the lateral geniculate nucleus and visual cortex is enormously greater than in the rat, about 1 and 140 millions respectively, but the ratio of cortical cells to central pathways is only 140 to 1, so again there is no great reserve of cells for mnemonic purposes.

The rat is capable of retaining scores, probably hundreds, of visual habits involving discrimination of complex figures (Lashley, 1938), and retention may sometimes be demonstrated a year after training. As I reported earlier, there is good evidence that visual habits are dependent upon the striate cortex and upon no other part of the cerebral cortex. The efferent path from the striate cortex is not known. It is not via cortico-tectile fibres. If by cortico-thalamic fibres, there are far fewer neurons within the thalamic nuclei than in the corresponding cortical areas, and there is certainly no reserve of cells there for the storing of memories. There seems to be no justification for assuming that the specific shunting of nervous impulses constituting various memories occurs at some level beyond the visual cortex or that memory traces are stored elsewhere than in the cortex.

If the data on the restriction of visual memory to the striate cortex are correct, and they are supported by a variety of experiments, the conclusion seems inevitable that the same cells which bear the memory traces are also excited and play a part in every other visual reaction of the animal. In all probability, the same sort of quantitative relations holds for the other sense modalities.

Even if the associative areas are functional in memory, they do not provide the supposed excess of cells. The visual cortex is directly connected only to a band of cortex directly adjacent, the visuo-psychic area of Campbell. The boundaries of this are indeterminate, but it certainly contains no more cells than does the striate area, probably fewer. There is no geometrical multiplication of cells and pathways. Many millions of cells of the striate cortex must be firing constantly into the adjacent area, so that its cells also must be constantly bombarded with nervous impulses and constantly firing. The conclusion is justified, I believe, by such considerations and is supported by electrical studies, that all of the cells of the brain are constantly active and are participating, by a sort of algebraic summation, in every activity. There are no special cells reserved for special memories.

Lorente (1934) has shown that each neuron may bear a hundred or more end-feet or separate synapses. However, considering the enormous complexity of the nervous activity involved in performance of even the simplest habit, it is doubtful that even the multiplication of cell number by a hundredfold will provide separate connexions that function only for single specific memories.

The alternative to the theory of preservation of memories by some local synaptic change is the postulate that the neurons are somehow sensitized to react to patterns or combinations of excitation. It is only by such permutations that the limited number of neurons can produce the variety of functions that they carry out. Local changes in the cell membrane, such that combined excitation by several synapses excites the cell, would provide a possible mechanism for such response to patterns, but speculation about this mechanism without direct evidence is likely to be as futile as speculation concerning changes in resistance in the synapse has been.

X. SUMMARY

This series of experiments has yielded a good bit of information about what and where the memory trace is not. It has discovered nothing directly of the real nature of the engram. I sometimes feel, in reviewing the evidence on the localization of the memory trace, that the necessary conclusion is that learning just is not possible. It is difficult to conceive of a mechanism which can satisfy the conditions set for it. Nevertheless, in spite of such evidence against it, learning does sometimes occur. Although the negative data do not provide a clear picture of the nature of the engram, they do establish limits within which concepts of its nature must be confined, and thus indirectly define somewhat more clearly the nature of the nervous mechanisms which must be responsible for learning and retention. Some general conclusions are, I believe, justified by the evidence.

(1) It seems certain that the theory of well-defined conditioned reflex paths from sense organ via association areas to the motor cortex is false. The motor areas are not necessary for the retention of sensori-motor habits or even of skilled manipulative patterns.

(2) It is not possible to demonstrate the isolated localization of a memory trace anywhere within the nervous system. Limited regions may be essential for learning or retention of a particular activity, but within such regions the parts are functionally equivalent. The engram is represented throughout the region.

(3) The so-called associative areas are not storehouses for specific memories. They seem to be concerned with modes of organization and with general facilitation or maintenance of the level of vigilance. The defects which occur after their destruction are not amnesias but difficulties in the performance of tasks which involve abstraction and generalization, or conflict of purposes. It is not possible as yet to describe these defects in the present psychological terminology. Goldstein (1940) has expressed them in

part as a shift from the abstract to the concrete attitude, but this characterization is too vague and general to give a picture of the functional disturbance. For our present purpose the important point is that the defects are not fundamentally those of memory.

(4) The trace of any activity is not an isolated connexion between sensory and motor elements. It is tied in with the whole complex of spatial and temporal axes of nervous activity which forms a constant substratum of behaviour. Each association is oriented with respect to space and time. Only by long practice under varying conditions does it become generalized or dissociated from these specific co-ordinates. The space and time co-ordinates in orientation can, I believe, only be maintained by some sort of polarization of activity and by rhythmic discharges which pervade the entire brain, influencing the organization of activity everywhere. The position and direction of motion in the visual field, for example, continuously modifies the spinal postural adjustments, but, a fact which is more frequently overlooked, the postural adjustments also determine the orientation of the visual field, so that upright objects continue to appear upright, in spite of changes in the inclination of the head. This substratum of postural and tonic activity is constantly present and is integrated with the memory trace (Lashley, 1949).

I have mentioned briefly evidence that new associations are tied in spontaneously with a great mass of related associations. This conception is fundamental to the problems of attention and interest. There are no neurological data bearing directly upon these problems, but a good guess is that the phenomena which we designate as attention and interest are the result of partial, subthreshold activation of systems of related associations which have a mutual facilitative action. It seems impossible to account for many of the characters of organic amnesias except in such general terms as reduced vigilance or reduced facilitation.

(5) The equivalence of different regions of the cortex for retention of memories points to multiple representation. Somehow, equivalent traces are established throughout the functional area. Analysis of the sensory and motor aspects of habits shows that they are reducible only to relations among components which have no constant position with respect to structural elements. This means, I believe, that within a functional area the cells throughout the area acquire the capacity to react in certain definite patterns, which may have any distribution within the area. I have elsewhere proposed a possible mechanism to account for this multiple representation. Briefly, the

characteristics of the nervous network are such that, when it is subject to any pattern of excitation, it may develop a pattern of activity, reduplicated throughout an entire functional area by spread of excitations, much as the surface of a liquid develops an interference pattern of spreading waves when it is disturbed at several points (Lashley, 1942a). This means that, within a functional area, the neurons must be sensitized to react in certain combinations, perhaps in complex patterns of reverberatory circuits, reduplicated throughout the area.

(6) Consideration of the numerical relations of sensory and other cells in the brain makes it certain, I believe, that all of the cells of the brain must be in almost constant activity, either firing or actively inhibited. There is no great excess of cells which can be reserved as the seat of special memories. The complexity of the functions involved in reproductive memory implies that every instance of recall requires the activity of literally millions of neurons. The same neurons which retain the memory traces of one experience must also participate in countless other activities.

Recall involves the synergic action or some sort of resonance among a very large number of neurons. The learning process must consist of the attunement of the elements of a complex system in such a way that a particular combination or pattern of cells responds more readily than before the experience. The particular mechanism by which this is brought about remains unknown. From the numerical relations involved, I believe that even the reservation of individual synapses for special associative reactions is impossible. The alternative is, perhaps, that the dendrites and cell body may be locally modified in such a manner that the cell responds differentially, at least in the timing of its firing, according to the pattern of combination of axon feet through which excitation is received.

References

Akelaitis, A. J. (1944). A study of gnosis, praxis and language following section of the corpus callosum and anterior commissure. *J. Neurosurgery,* **1,** 94–102.

Bailey, P., Bonin, G. v., Davis, F. W., Garol, H. W. & McCulloch, W. S. (1944). *J. Neuropath. Exp. Neurol.* **3,** 413–15.

Bergson, H. (1896). *Matière et mémoire.* Paris.

Bonin, G. von, Garol, H. W. & McCulloch, W. S. (1942). The functional organization of the occipital lobe. *Biol. Symp.* **7,** 165–92.

Bucy, P. C. (1934). The relation of the premotor cortex to motor activity. *J. Nerv. Ment. Dis.* **79,** 621–30.

Bucy, P. C. & Fulton, T. F. (1933). Ipsilateral representation in the motor and premotor cortex of monkeys. *Brain,* **56,** 318–42.

Clark, W. E. L. (1941). Observations on the associative fibre system of the visual cortex and the central representation of the retina. *J. Anat., Lond.,* **75,** 225–36.

Dunlap, K. (1927). The short-circuiting of conscious responses. *J. Phil. Psychol. Sci. Meth.* **24,** 263–7.

Dunlap, K. (1930). Psychological hypotheses concerning the functions of the brain. *Sci. Mon., N.Y.,* **31,** 97–112.

Ebbecke, U. (1919). *Die kortikalen psychophysischen Erregungen.* Pp. x+306. Leipzig: Barth.

Edgell, B. (1924). *Theories of Memory.* Pp. 1–174. Oxford: Clarendon Press.

Fields, P. E. (1932). Studies in concept formation. I. The development of the concept of triangularity by the white rat. *Comp. Psychol. Monogr.* **9,** no. 2, pp. 1–70.

Finley, C. B. (1941). Equivalent losses in accuracy of response after central and after peripheral sense deprivation. *J. Comp. Neurol.* **74,** 203–37.

Fischel, W. (1948). *Die höheren Leistungen der Wirbeltiergehirne.* Pp. iv+96. Leipzig: Barth.

Franz, S. I. (1907). On the functions of the cerebrum: The frontal lobes. *Arch. Psychol.* no. 2, pp. 1–64.

Franz, S. I. (1911). On the functions of the cerebrum: The occipital lobes. *Psychol. Monogr.* **13,** no. 4, pp. 1–118.

Gay, J. R. & Gelhorn, E. (1948). Cortical projection of proprioception. *Amer. J. Physiol.* **155,** 437.

Girden, E., Mettler, F. A., Finch, G. & Culler, E. (1936). Conditioned responses in a decorticate dog to acoustic, thermal, and tactile stimulation. *J. Comp. Psychol.* **21,** 367–85.

Goldstein, K. (1940). *Human Nature in the Light of Psychopathology.* Pp. x+258. Cambridge: Harvard University Press.

Head, H. (1926). *Aphasia and Kindred Disorders of Speech.* Vol. 2, pp. xxxiii+430. New York: Macmillan.

Herrick, C. J. (1926). *Brains of Rats and Men.* Chicago: University Press.

Hunter, W. S. (1930). A consideration of Lashley's theory of the equipotentiality of cerebral action. *J. Gen. Psychol.* **3,** 455–68.

Ingebritsen, O. C. (1933). Coordinating mechanisms of the spinal cord. *Genet. Psychol. Monogr.* **13,** no. 6, pp. 485–553.

Jacobsen, C. F. (1932). Influence of motor and premotor area lesions upon the retention of skilled movements in monkeys and chimpanzees. *Proc. Ass. Res. Nerv. Ment. Dis.* **13,** 225–47.

Jacobsen, C. F. (1936). Studies of cerebral function in primates. *Comp. Psychol. Monogr.* **13,** no. 3, pp. 1–68.

Kellogg, W. N., Deese, James, Pronko, N. H. & Feinberg, M. (1947). An attempt to condition the *chronic* spinal dog. *J. Exp. Psychol.* **37**, 99–117.

Kennard, M. A. (1939). Alterations in response to visual stimuli following lesions of frontal lobe in monkeys. *Arch. Neurol. Psychiat.* **41**, 1153–65.

Krechevsky, I. (1936). Brain mechanisms and brightness discrimination. *J. Comp. Psychol.* **21**, 405–45.

Lashley, K. S. (1916). The human salivary reflex and its use in psychology. *Psychol. Rev.* **23**, 446–64.

Lashley, K. S. (1921a). Studies of cerebral function in learning. II. The effects of long continued practice upon cerebral localization. *J. Comp. Psychol.* **1**, 453–68.

Lashley, K. S. (1921b). Studies of cerebral function in learning. III. The motor areas. *Brain,* **44**, 256–86.

Lashley, K. S. (1922). Studies of cerebral function in learning. IV. Vicarious function after destruction of the visual areas. *Amer. J. Physiol.* **59**, 44–71.

Lashley, K. S. (1924). Studies of cerebral function in learning. V. The retention of motor habits after destruction of the so-called motor areas in primates. *Arch. Neurol. Psychiat.* **12**, 249–76.

Lashley, K. S. (1929). *Brain Mechanisms and Intelligence.* Pp. xiv+186. Chicago: University Press.

Lashley, K. S. (1932). The mechanism of vision. V. The structure and image-forming power of the rat's eye. *J. Comp. Psychol.* **13**, 173–200.

Lashley, K. S. (1935a). Studies of cerebral function in learning. XI. The behavior of the rat in latch-box situations. *Comp. Psychol. Monogr.* **11**, 1–42.

Lashley, K. S. (1935b). The mechanism of vision. XII. Nervous structures concerned in the acquisition and retention of habits based on reactions to light. *Comp. Psychol. Monogr.* **11**, 43–79.

Lashley, K. S. (1938). The mechanism of vision. XV. Preliminary studies of the rat's capacity for detail vision. *J. Genet. Psychol.* **18**, 123–93.

Lashley, K. S. (1939). The mechanism of vision. XVI. The functioning of small remnants of the visual cortex. *J. Comp. Neurol.* **70**, 45–67.

Lashley, K. S. (1941). Thalamo-cortical connections of the rat's brain. *J. Comp. Neurol.* **75**, 67–121.

Lashley, K. S. (1942a). The problem of cerebral organization in vision. *Biol. Symp.* **7**, 301–22.

Lashley, K. S. (1942b). The mechanism of vision. XVII. Autonomy of the visual cortex. *J. Genet. Psychol.* **60**, 197–221.

Lashley, K. S. (1943). Studies of cerebral function in learning. XII. Loss of the maze habit after occipital lesions in blind rats. *J. Comp. Neurol.* **79**, 431–62.

Lashley, K. S. (1944). Studies of cerebral function in learning. XIII. Apparent absence of transcortical association in maze learning. *J. Comp. Neurol.* **80**, 257–81.

Lashley, K. S. (1948). The mechanism of vision. XVIII. Effects of destroying the visual 'associative areas' of the monkey. *Genet. Psychol. Monogr.* **37**, 107–66.

Lashley, K. S. (1949). The problem of serial order in behavior. *Hixon Symposium on Cerebral Mechanisms in Behavior.*

Lashley, K. S. & McCarthy, D. A. (1926). The survival of the maze habit after cerebellar injuries. *J. Comp. Psychol.* **6**, 423–33.

Lashley, K. S. & Wiley, L. E. (1933). Studies of cerebral function in learning. IX. Mass action in relation to the number of elements in the problem to be learned. *J. Comp. Neurol.* **57**, 3–55.

Lorente de Nó, R. (1934). Studies on the structure of the cerebral cortex. II. Continuation of the study of the Ammonic system. *J. Psychol. Neurol.* **46**, 113–77.

McGeoch, J. A. (1942). *The Psychology of Human Learning.* Pp. xviii+633. New York: Longmans, Green.

Mettler, F. A. (1949). Physiologic effects of bilateral simultaneous removal of Brodmann's cytoarchitectural areas in the human. *Fed. Proc.* **8**, 109.

Nielsen, J. M. (1936). *Agnosia, Apraxia, Aphasia, their Value in Cerebral Localization.* Pp. vii+210. Los Angeles: Waverly Press.

Polterew, S. S. & Zeliony, G. P. (1930). Grosshirnrinde und Assoziationsfunction. *Z. Biol.* **90**, 157–60.

Smith, K. U. (1947). Bilateral integrative action of the cerebral cortex in man in verbal association and sensori-motor coordination. *J. Exp. Psychol.* **37**, 367–76.

Sperry, R. W. (1947). Cerebral regulation of motor coordination in monkeys following multiple transection of sensorimotor cortex. *J. Neurophysiol.* **10**, 275–94.

Tsang, Yu-Chuan (1934). The function of the visual areas of the cortex of the rat in the learning and retention of the maze. *Comp. Psychol. Monogr.* **10**, 1–56.

Walker, A. E. (1938). *The Primate Thalamus.* Pp. xxiv+321. Chicago: University Press.

Ward, A. A. Jr., Peden, J. K. & Sugar, O. (1946). Cortico-cortical connections in the monkey with special reference to Area 6. *J. Neurophysiol.* **9**, 453–61.

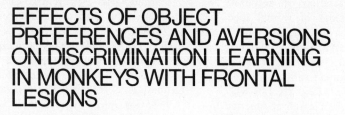

E. S. Brush, M. Mishkin,
and H. E. Rosvold

EFFECTS OF OBJECT PREFERENCES AND AVERSIONS ON DISCRIMINATION LEARNING IN MONKEYS WITH FRONTAL LESIONS

In the previous paper, Lashley reported finding no retention loss with lesions of the "association cortex." In this paper, which is a contemporary example of ablation methodology in physiological psychology, Brush, Mishkin, and Rosvold discuss some of the impairments that do result from frontal and from temporal lobe ablations. These are clearly not "memory" deficits, at least in the usual sense of the word. The method section of the paper is quite clear in describing the details of the procedures actually used in the behavioral testing of the animals and should complement the discussion of testing methods in Chapter 5. A few comments about the problems are necessary. First, it should be noted that there are really only three problems of importance: the learning set problem, the pattern discrimination problem, and the delayed alternation problem. The first part of the procedure section, including the acquisition of three object discrimination problems,[1] is a discussion of how the animals were adapted to or familiarized with the apparatus and the general "rules" of the situation. Animals do not just start to perform what an experimenter wants them to do; they must be shaped and trained to do so.

Note that the animals were trained to a performance criterion in both the pattern discrimination problem and in the delayed alternation problem. In the former problem, each subject had to learn to respond consistently to the + sign, while in the latter it had to learn to alternate its responses from the left plaque to the right plaque across trials separated by 5-second intervals. The learning set problem was different in that it did not involve a criterion. Instead, pairs of objects were presented for a fixed number of trials (one preference trial

and 10 discrimination trials), and performance on the discrimination trials was recorded. Training ended after the animals had been exposed to a total of 200 such problems. Note that the "preference trial" is really an information trial informing the animal of the reinforcement contingencies for the 10 discrimination trials. For those problems in which both stimulus objects were baited, the one chosen by the animal was designated as S+ and the animal had to continue to respond to it during the discrimination trials. For those problems in which neither stimulus object was baited, the one chosen by the animal was designated as S− and the animal had to shift its response and respond to the other stimulus during the discrimination trials.

The results of the experiment illustrate two important concepts. First, they illustrate double dissociation, a procedure or set of results which, in its ideal form, allows one to argue for localization of function and qualitative differences between the effects of different brain lesions or treatments. The animals with frontal lobe damage showed deficits in delayed alternation performance but not in pattern discrimination performance, while the animals with temporal lobe damage showed exactly the opposite pattern of deficits. This is quite strong evidence that these two parts of the brain function in quite different ways in the mediation of these two tasks. However, it is necessary to assume linear treatment effects, for as Weiskrantz (1968c) has shown with a very elegant hypothetical example, two treatments with quantitatively rather than qualitatively different effects can give rise to a double dissociation outcome if the treatment effects on some process are curvilinear. Note also that while double dissociation allows one to argue for localization of brain function, it tells very little about the nature of brain function.

Second, the paper provides a clear example of how two different treatments can have the same behavioral effects for quite different reasons. Attention is drawn to Table 1, which indicates that both the animals with frontal lobe lesions and those with temporal lobe lesions were impaired on object quality learning set, yet Figure 1 and Experiment 2 make it very clear that the

From *Journal of Comparative and Physiological Psychology*, 1961, **54**, 319–325. Copyright © 1961 by The American Psychological Association. Reprinted by permission.

[1] The essential difference between an "object" discrimination and a "pattern discrimination" is that the former involves three-dimensional forms or objects while the latter involves two-dimensional patterns mounted on plaques or projected on screens, which themselves provide no differential cues.

reason for the impairment is quite different for the two groups. As discussed in Chapter 5, great care must be exercised not to assume that because two treatments result in the same behavioral deficit, the reason for the deficits is the same in both cases.

Lesions of anterior and posterior "association cortex" in monkeys produce clearly dissociable deficits in behavior. Thus, Harlow (1952) and Pribram (1954), each summarizing the results of an independent and extensive series of experiments in which the effects of the two types of damage were directly compared, conclude that bilateral posterior damage produces severe impairment in visual discrimination but little or none in delayed response, while bilateral frontal damage produces severe impairment in delayed response but little or none in visual discrimination.

This conclusion is, however, subject to one very important qualification. In both series of studies cited the differential effects of the two lesions with respect to visual discrimination are clearest when animals are trained to a criterion in a simple choice reaction between two stimuli that are difficult to discriminate, such as a pair of painted patterns. But as the testing procedure is made more complex, even though the difficulty of the discrimination itself is reduced, then not only are animals with posterior lesions impaired, but animals with frontal lesions also begin to show considerable impairment. This result has been obtained in object-quality learning set, a task in which numerous pairs of easily discriminable objects are presented for only a few trials each, and even more strikingly in oddity learning, where three such objects are presented simultaneously (two of which are identical) with the animal's task being always to choose the odd object (Harlow, 1952). In referring to the results on oddity learning, where the impairment of the frontal group was found to be just as severe as that of the posterior group, Harlow (1952, p. 250) states: "Observational data suggest, however, that the kinds of errors made by the two groups may differ."

The proposal that the deficit of frontal animals on visual discrimination tasks, when it appears at all, is qualitatively different from that of animals with posterior lesions is supported by the results of the present experiments on multiple object-discrimination learning. The first experiment to be reported suggests that while animals with posterior (inferotemporal) lesions are impaired in forming learning sets largely because of difficulty with the visual-discrimination requirements of the test, the deficit of frontal animals stems primarily from their difficulty in overcoming spontaneous object preferences and aversions. The second experiment supports this interpretation by demonstrating that if the approach or avoidance tendencies toward specific objects are established experimentally, significant impairment in discrimination learning is found only in the frontal group and only when they are required to suppress the experimentally induced tendencies.

METHOD

Subjects

The *S*s were 12 experimentally naive, immature rhesus monkeys (*Macaca mulatta*), ranging in weight from 3 to 5 kg. Four of the animals (F1 to F4) received anterior frontal lesions, 4 (T1 to T4) received lesions of inferotemporal cortex, and 4 (N1 to N4) remained as unoperated controls.

Operations

Animals were anesthetized with Nembutal (40 mg/kg body weight), and surgery was carried out under aseptic conditions. All lesions were one-stage bilateral cortical resections. In the case of the frontal lesions the attempt was to ablate the entire dorsolateral convexity, including the banks and depths of the *sulcus principalis*, from the frontal pole to the arcuate sulcus including its anterior bank. In the case of the temporal lesions, the aim was, starting with the inferior bank of the superior temporal sulcus, to remove the middle, inferior, and fusiform temporal gyri, sparing the temporal pole; the posterior boundary was a line approximately 0.5 cm. anterior and parallel to the inferior occipital sulcus. Reconstructions of the lesions will be presented in a later report.

EXPERIMENT 1

Method

Apparatus. Animals were trained in a modification of the Wisconsin General Test Apparatus which was located in a sound-proofed, darkened room. The stimuli used for the learning-set series were 200 small objects of the sort obtainable at a dime store. The objects were paired randomly for 100 problems and then re-paired at random to provide 100 additional problems. Six other objects were used for preliminary training.

In addition to the multiple object-discrimination problems, animals were trained on single alternation and on a visual pattern discrimination. The plaques for the single-alternation task were identical 3-in. squares of steel-gray mat board; for the pattern-discrimination task, similar gray plaques had white paper patterns pasted on them—one a plus sign, the other an outline square. The two patterns contained approximately equal amounts of white.

Procedure. Training was begun ten days after operation, at which time the animals were taught to obtain blanched peanut-halves by pushing aside white matboard plaques which covered two food wells spaced 14 in. apart. Three preliminary problems were then presented in order to familiarize the *S* with the object-discrimination procedures. On the first trial of the first problem a peanut-half was placed in each well and each well was covered with an object; whichever object the *S* chose became the positive stimulus for this discrimination. The position of the positive stimulus over the left and right food wells was varied according to a pre-determined balanced sequence, and the animal was not permitted to correct an error. Training was continued at the rate of 30 trials a day until the animal achieved 27 correct responses in one day's session. For the second problem, neither food well was baited on the first, or "preference," trial; whichever object the animal selected was designated as incorrect, and discrimination training proceeded as before with the other object being rewarded. For the third problem, the preference trial was again run with both objects baited, and the stimulus chosen by the animal was designated as correct.

After completing the three preliminary discriminations, the learning-set series proper was begun. The series consisted of 200 problems, each involving a new pair of objects. Each pair was presented for ten discrimination trials preceded by a preference trial. On half the problems, predetermined by a balanced sequence, both objects were baited on the preference trial and the object chosen was designated as correct; on the other half, neither object was baited on the preference trial and the object chosen was designated as incorrect. Three problems were presented daily until a total of 100 "baited" and 100 "unbaited" problems had been completed.

Following the learning-set series all animals were trained on the visual pattern discrimination, with the plus sign as the positive stimulus. This task was run for 30 trials a day to a criterion of 90 correct responses in 100 trials. As with learning set, a noncorrection technique was used and the position of the positive stimulus was varied in a balanced sequence.

After reaching criterion on pattern discrimination, or after a maximum of 1,000 trials, the animals were trained on single alternation for 30 trials a day. A day's session on this test began with a free trial in which both plaques were baited; thereafter, the left and right plaques were baited alternately unless the animal made an error, in which case the bait was left in place on succeeding trials until the *S* responded correctly. The delay interval between trials, during which the opaque screen was lowered, was 5 sec. As with pattern discrimination, the animals were trained to the criterion of 90 correct responses in 100 trials, or for a maximum of 1,000 trials.

Results

The group means for trials and errors preceding criterion on the preliminary object discriminations, the pattern discrimination, and delayed alternation are presented in Table 1. On the preliminary discriminations (the scores for which are summed over the three problems), the animals with temporal lesions exhibited impairment; there was no overlap between their scores and those of the animals in the other two groups. On the pattern discrimination, the temporal group was again significantly inferior to each of the other two groups (the differences for trials and errors, tested by Dunnett's [1955] *t* test, are all significant beyond the .05 level). It should be noted that in neither type of visual discrimination did the frontal animals differ from the controls. On the alternation problem, however, the results for the operated groups are reversed; the temporal animals learned as quickly as the controls, while the frontal animals failed to achieve the criterion.

The group means for total errors in the 2,000 trials of the learning-set series are given in the final column of Table 1. In contrast with the results on the other tests, here *both* operated groups exhibited impairment. There was no overlap between the normal animals' scores and those of the operated ani-

Table 1 Performance on the four tasks in Experiment 1

GROUP	PRELIMINARY OBJECT DISCRIMINATIONS		PATTERN DISCRIMINATION		DELAYED ALTERNATION		OBJECT-QUALITY LEARNING SET
Normal	50	(19)	142	(49)	515	(144)	(148)
Frontal	55	(25)	122	(50)	1000	(526)*	(416)*
Temporal	268	(107)*	565	(219)*	490	(133)	(354)*

Note. Scores are mean no. of trials (and errors). An asterisk denotes impairment.

mals, but among the two groups of operated animals total error scores overlapped extensively.

While from these results it would appear that the frontal and temporal groups were about equally impaired, a different picture of their impairment emerges when error scores are analyzed separately for the two baiting conditions. In Figure 1, the data for the 100 "baited" and the 100 "unbaited" problems are graphed separately, with the error scores on each type of problem plotted as five successive blocks of 20 problems each. An analysis of variance revealed that all groups made more errors on "unbaited" than on "baited" problems ($p > .001$). It may be seen, however, that the difference between errors on the two types of problems is much larger for the frontal group than it is for either of the other two groups. This was reflected as a significant interaction ($p < .05$) between groups and type of problem in the analysis of variance. Using Dunnett's (1955) t test it was found that the frontal group differed significantly from both the temporal group ($p < .05$) and the normal controls ($p < .01$). The difference between the temporal and control groups, on the other hand, was not significant.

An additional point to be noted in Figure 1 is that the differences among the groups relative to the "baited-unbaited" dichotomy varied with the length of training. This was indicated by a significant second-order interaction ($p < .05$) between groups, type of problem, and blocks. In the first block of problems, the difference between errors on "baited"

and "unbaited" problems was the same for the normal and temporal groups, but more than twice as large as this in the frontal group. Thereafter, the difference between errors on the two types of problems disappeared quickly in the normal group, disappeared by the end of training in the temporal group, but remained large throughout training in the frontal group.

The severe impairment of the frontal animals on "unbaited" problems was reflected in their high frequency of both initial and perseverative errors. An analysis of first-trial errors yielded performance curves similar in pattern to, though less stable than, those for all ten trials shown in Figure 1, indicating that the frontal group committed more errors than the other groups even on the initial trials of "unbaited" problems. As for perseverative errors, defined here as a score of either nine or ten errors out of the ten trials on a given problem, there were only 4 such instances in the normal group, 7 in the temporal group, but 31 in the frontal group, all on "unbaited" problems. There was no overlap between the frontal group and the others in the number of times individual animals made perseverative errors.

EXPERIMENT 2

The procedure used in the "unbaited" problems of Experiment 1 was such that if an object was "preferred," it automatically became the negative stimu-

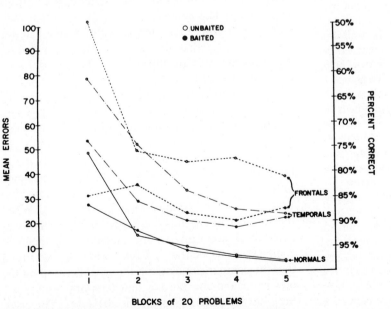

Figure 1. Object-discrimination learning, Experiment 1.

lus for that discrimination; or, conversely, if an object was "aversive," it became the positive stimulus. One possible interpretation of the frontal animals' impairment is that they had abnormal difficulty in overcoming these specific object preferences and aversions. In the second experiment an attempt was made to test this hypothesis directly, by first bringing object preferences and aversions under experimental control, viz., building them in by presenting single stimuli either with or without reward, and then pairing such stimuli with other, indifferent stimuli in simultaneous discrimination tests. If the proposed interpretation of the frontal animals' impairment is correct, they should have greater difficulty than their controls only on those tests in which they are required to suppress the experimentally induced preferences and aversions.

Method

Apparatus. From among the 200 stimulus objects used in the first experiment 80 "indifferent" objects were selected. (An "indifferent" object was defined as one that was chosen by no fewer than 5 but no more than 7 of the 12 monkeys on each of the two preference trials in which that object had appeared.) This procedure was adopted in order to eliminate at least those objects which were most consistently selected or rejected spontaneously in the first experiment.

Procedure. The 80 objects were paired at random, with the restriction that no pairing used in Experiment 1 was repeated. One member of each of the 40 pairs was designated as the "training" stimulus for that problem. At the beginning of each problem the training stimulus was presented alone for five trials, with its position over the left or right food well predetermined according to a balanced sequence. On half the problems the well covered by the training stimulus was baited; on the other half the well remained empty, the S in this case being forced to make five successive unrewarded responses to a negative training stimulus. Immediately following the five training trials, ten test trials were run in which the training stimulus was presented with the other member of its pair in a simultaneous discrimination. On half the problems, cross-cutting the training procedure, the training object was the positive stimulus for the discrimination; for the other half it was the negative stimulus.

The combination of two training and two testing procedures yielded the four types of problems: $++$, $+-$, $--$, and $-+$, where the signs refer to whether or not the training stimulus was baited when it was presented alone (that first sign in each pair) and when it was presented in the discrimination test (the second sign). The prediction was that the frontal animals would have greater difficulty than their controls in overcoming a preference $(+-)$, an aversion $(-+)$, or both, but not

in persisting in a preference $(++)$ or an aversion $(--)$.

Four problems, one of each type, were presented each day for ten days. The order in which the four problems appeared within a day's session was varied in a balanced sequence.

Results

The response to the training stimulus on the first trial of the discrimination provides one measure of the effectiveness of the training procedures in producing the desired object preferences and aversions. The analysis of first-trial performance revealed that animals avoided a negative training object in favor of a new indifferent object 95% of the time, whereas they chose a positive training object in preference to a new indifferent object only 55% of the time. These percentage levels, which were approximately the same for all three groups, would appear to indicate that negative training was far more effective in producing an aversion than was positive training in producing a preference.

In examining the influence of the training procedures on discrimination learning, however, it was found that positive and negative training were more nearly equivalent in their effects. Figure 2 shows, for each group, the mean number of errors on Trials 2 to 10 for each of the four types of problems. (Here performance on Trial 1 is excluded, since this trial, and not the training trials preceding it, indicated for the first time which object would be the positive stimulus for the discrimination.) That both positive and negative training did produce the desired effects (i.e., preferences and aversions, respectively) is indicated by the fact that irrespective of which training procedure preceded the discrimination, all groups made more errors on the reversal than on the nonreversal problems ($p < .001$).

It may also be seen in Figure 2, however, that the difference between errors in the reversal and nonreversal conditions is not the same for the three groups. The difference is small *and equal* for the normal and temporal groups but is nearly twice as large as this in the frontal group. This was reflected in the analysis of variance as a significant interaction ($p < .05$) among groups, training, and testing. When the variance due to this second-order interaction was partitioned according to the method of orthogonal comparisons (Cochran & Cox, 1950), it was found that the comparison between the frontal group on the one hand and the normal and temporal groups on the other was significant at the .01 level. The comparison between the normal and temporal groups, on

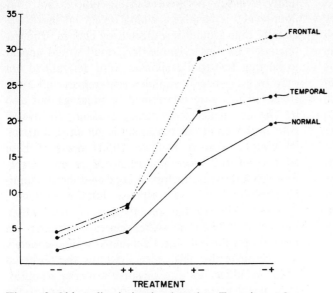

Figure 2. Object-discrimination learning, Experiment 2.

the other hand, was not significant. The results demonstrate that whereas the temporal group was inferior to the normal controls equally (though not significantly) on all types of problems, the frontal group was significantly inferior to both, but on the reversal problems only.

DISCUSSION

The results of the first experiment duplicate in several important respects the results of the series of experiments summarized by Harlow (1952). Thus, only the frontal lesion produced impairment on a delayed-response type of test, only the posterior lesion produced impairment on single visual discriminations, while both lesions produced impairment in the formation of an object-quality learning set.

The consistency of the results both within and between operated groups on delayed alternation and on the single visual discriminations provides evidence, independently of anatomical reconstructions, that the lesions were appropriately placed. The result on the learning-set task, which showed the over-all deficits of the frontal and posterior groups to be approximately the same, differs somewhat from the result reported by Harlow in that the posterior lesions studied in the Wisconsin experiments produced an over-all learning-set deficit which was both more severe and more lasting than that following frontal lesions. This difference in the two sets of results is

probably attributable to the fact that in the Wisconsin studies the posterior lesions were far more extensive than in the present study, where they were limited to the inferotemporal area.

For the present analysis, however, a more important difference was the use in Experiment 1 of baited and unbaited preference trials (cf. Riopelle, Francisco, & Ades, 1954), a procedure which revealed a *qualitative* difference in the deficits of the two operated groups. Thus, whereas throughout the learning-set series the temporal group exhibited impairment under both conditions of baiting, the impairment of the frontal group, at least at the beginning of training, was confined to "unbaited" problems (see Figure 1). Initially, the frontal animals' performance on "baited" problems, as with their performance on the three object discriminations which preceded the learning-set task and on the pattern discrimination which followed it, was equal to that of the normals. It seems reasonable to conclude from this that the frontal group's atypical increase in errors from the first to the second block of "baited" problems, as well as their failure to show ultimate improvement on these problems, was a secondary impairment caused by interference from the "unbaited" condition.

There are a number of plausible explanations for the frontal animals' primary impairment, which may be viewed as a difficulty in reversing their initial choices on the unbaited preference trials. One possibility is that initial choices were in fact determined not by preferences (or aversions) but by chance, with the frontal group displaying abnormal difficulty in learning to inhibit unrewarded responses to stimuli which, on first exposure, were "indifferent." Such an interpretation seems unlikely, however, in view of the frontal group's high frequency not only of initial but also of perservative errors, a phenomenon which strongly suggests that the frontal animals often did prefer one object to the other and in many of the "unbaited" problems persisted in this tendency for as many as ten more unrewarded trials. This finding, in turn, might be interpreted as indicating that the frontal animals had abnormally strong, frequent, or persistent preferences and aversions. But the difficulty for this interpretation is that the frontal animals were not superior to the normal controls on "baited" problems, where persisting in strong preferences and aversions should have facilitated performance.

An explanation which does seem to be consistent with these data, and the one that was tested in Experiment 2, is that the initial choices of all animals were frequently guided by the specific object preferences and aversions (accounting for the somewhat poorer performance of all groups on "unbaited" as compared with "baited" problems), the frontal group differing from the others only in that they had relatively greater difficulty in learning to suppress these normal tendencies. The origins of these tendencies in Experiment 1 were probably numerous. Thus, it was frequently observed that animals approached warily, if at all, objects that were tall and unstable, or others that were fuzzy; on the other hand, there were many brightly colored plastic objects, for example, which they not only chose quickly but attempted to manipulate, inspect, and sometimes even taste. In addition to these spontaneous fears and attractions there were undoubtedly many other instances in which the approach to or avoidance of particular objects was due to generalization from other similar objects that had been positive or negative earlier in the series. Whatever their origin, however, the evidence suggests not that these tendencies were initially more prevalent among frontal animals, but rather that for the frontal animals such tendencies were more difficult to suppress.

In Experiment 2 an attempt was made to induce "preferences" and "aversions" experimentally, by presenting single stimuli either with or without reward. Before commenting on the major findings of this experiment it is pertinent to consider the incidental finding that the initial effects of positive and negative training were grossly unequal: On the first trial of each discrimination, the animals did consistently avoid a negative training object, but they approached a positive training object no more frequently than would be expected by chance. The explanation for this asymmetrical result would appear to be that first-trial responses were determined not only by (a) specific stimulus preferences and aversions (in this case established in training) but also by (b) an unexpectedly strong tendency to investigate new stimuli. In his analysis of discrimination learning in monkeys, Harlow (1950) identified these as two of the more important of several error-producing response factors, and labeled them "stimulus perseveration" and "response shift," respectively. It is likely that in the present study the two factors interacted as follows: After negative training, an aversion for the old object combined with a tendency to investigate the new object, yielding the observed 95% avoidance of the negative training stimulus; after positive training, a specific preference for the old object came in conflict with the tendency to investigate the new object, resulting in only a 55%, or chance, selection of the positive training stimulus.

Presumably, the influence of "response shift" was quickly dissipated after negative training, since under this condition nearly all animals did in fact select the new object on the very first discrimination trial. After positive training, however, with about half the animals refraining from selecting the new object on the first trial, "response shift" would be expected to exert some influence beyond Trial 1. The effect of this residual tendency to approach the new object on Trials 2 to 10 following positive training only, would be to interfere slightly with the maintenance of a preference $(++)$ as compared with the maintenance of an aversion $(--)$, and to facilitate slightly the reversal of a preference $(+-)$ as compared with the reversal of an aversion $(-+)$. It may be seen in Figure 2 that such a result was in fact obtained, and it was reflected in the analysis of variance as a significant effect of testing procedures $(p < .05)$. It is important to note, however, that there were no differences in the effect of this variable among the groups.

According to the preceding analyses, differences between the effects of the positive and negative training procedures can be traced to their interaction with the animal's tendency to approach new stimuli. With these differences accounted for, the remaining results of the second experiment confirm in detail the predictions derived from Experiment 1. First, the frontal animals had no difficulty in learning to inhibit unrewarded responses to "indifferent" stimuli. This is shown by the fact that on nonreversal problems the frontal animals benefited as much as the controls not only from positive but also from negative training with single "indifferent" objects. Secondly, neither the approach nor avoidance responses established in training were abnormally strong in the frontal animals. This is suggested by the finding that frontal animals were not superior to normals on nonreversal problems, where abnormally strong initial response tendencies should have facilitated performance. Finally, the frontal animals were severely impaired on reversal problems, confirming the prediction that they would have difficulty overcoming the previously established approach or avoidance response to a particular stimulus.

That animals with frontal lesions are impaired on visual-discrimination reversals was first demonstrated by Harlow and Dagnon in 1942. What has been demonstrated by the present experiment, using a modified reversal procedure, is that the same result is obtained when either an approach or an avoidance response, trained to only one of the discriminanda, must be reversed only half the time. The situation is clearly analogous to that in learning-set experiments, with the exception that in learning set whatever response must be reversed is elicited by one of the discriminanda on its initial presentation. It is important to emphasize that an abnormal difficulty in suppressing either trained or spontaneous stimulus preferences or aversions would appear to be specific to frontal animals, since under all these conditions, though all involve visual discrimination, the impairment of frontal animals exceeds even that of animals with inferotemporal lesions.

It may be concluded from this analysis that two quite different factors are responsible for the deficits of frontal and temporal animals on visual learning tasks. At one extreme are those tasks in which only discrimination learning is involved and on which only the temporal animals are impaired. Difficult painted-pattern discriminations clearly belong to this category. In many other tasks, however, discrimination learning is complicated by error-producing preferences and aversions. Included in this category are object-quality learning set, ordinary discrimination reversal, and probably oddity learning as well. Such tasks reveal impairment in both operated groups, though whether or not both groups will be impaired to the same extent will depend, in each instance, on the difficulty of the discrimination and the strength of the error-producing tendencies. If discrimination difficulty is reduced to a minimum and the difficulty of suppressing preferences and aversions is increased, a third category of tests is obtained on which only

frontal animals show significant impairment. Such a result was obtained with the modified reversal procedure that was employed in the present study.

SUMMARY

In the first experiment, four monkeys with anterior frontal lesions, four with inferotemporal lesions, and four unoperated controls received 200 ten-trial object discriminations, each preceded by a preference trial. On half the preference trials both objects were baited, and the one selected became the positive stimulus; on the other half, neither object was baited, and the one selected became the negative stimulus. The over-all learning-set deficits of the two operated groups were approximately the same, but their deficits relative to the two baiting procedures differed from each other. Compared with the controls, the temporal group was affected about equally in both conditions, from which it was concluded that their impairment in forming a learning set was closely related to the discrimination aspects of the test. The frontal group, in contrast, was much more markedly affected in the unbaited than in the baited condition, an analysis of their errors suggesting that they had abnormal difficulty in overcoming spontaneous object preferences and aversions.

This hypothesis was investigated in a second experiment, in which the tendency to approach or avoid specific objects was brought under experimental control by presenting single objects either with or without reward before pairing these with other indifferent objects in simultaneous discrimination tests. Under these conditions significant impairment in discrimination learning was found only in the frontal group, and only when they were required to suppress the experimentally induced object preferences and aversions. This finding, with a modified discrimination-reversal test, was the opposite of that obtained with standard visual discrimination tests, each presented to a criterion, on which only the temporal group was impaired.

The results demonstrate a dissociation of deficits within the category of visual discrimination learning following frontal and temporal lesions.

References

Cochran, W. G., & Cox, G. M. *Experimental designs.* New York: Wiley, 1950.

Dunnett, C. W. A multiple comparison procedure for comparing several treatments with a control. *J. Amer. Statist. Ass.,* 1955, **50,** 1096–1121.

Harlow, H. F. Analysis of discrimination learning by monkeys. *J. exp. Psychol.,* 1950, **40,** 26–39.

Harlow, H. F. Functional organization of the brain in relation to mentation and behavior. In, *The biology of mental health and disease.* New York: Hoeber, 1952. Pp. 244–264.

Harlow, H. F., & Dagnon, J. Problem solution by monkeys following bilateral removal of the prefrontal areas: I. The discrimination and discrimination-reversal problems. *J. exp. Psychol.,* 1942, **32,** 351–356.

Pribram, K. H. Toward a science of neuropsychology. In, *Psychology and the behavioral sciences.* Pittsburgh: Univer. Pittsburgh Press, 1954. Pp. 115–142.

Riopelle, A. J., Francisco, E. W., & Ades, H. W. Differential first-trial procedures and discrimination learning performance. *J. comp. physiol. Psychol.,* 1954, **47,** 293–297.

part three

STIMULATION OF THE BRAIN IN PHYSIOLOGICAL PSYCHOLOGY

10

ELECTRICAL STIMULATION OF THE BRAIN

ORIGIN OF BRAIN STIMULATION PARADIGMS

One of the truly classical studies in physiological psychology is that of G. Fritsch and E. Hitzig (1870), an edited translation of which is reprinted in Chapter 14 at the end of Part Three. They reported that in partially anesthetized dogs, electrical stimulation of specific points in the anterior region of the cerebral cortex produced discrete muscle movements in the neck, face, and contralateral limbs, and they argued that this could not be accounted for in terms of the spread of current to peripheral nerves, in terms of the spread of current to subcortical areas, or in terms of the evocation of withdrawal reflexes.

[1] The reader is referred to Valenstein (1973) for a most readable and stimulating discussion of the history of the experimental study of the brain using electrical stimulation and of the clinical and social applications of brain stimulation, specifically psychosurgery.

In retrospect, their basic observations seem quite straightforward and perhaps mundane, but the consequences of the study were profound. First, the study provided evidence that, like the rest of the nervous system, the cerebral cortex is electrically excitable. This allowed for the eventual extension of Mueller's law of specific nerve qualities from the peripheral nerves to the highest levels of the brain itself and provided the foundation for sensory-motor conceptions of nervous system organization and the impetus for the subsequent study of the sensory cortical regions. Second, the findings were regarded as critical evidence against Flourens' arguments concerning the cerebral hemispheres having a unitary functional nature, for here indeed was evidence of localization of function. Not only did stimulation of the anterior cortex produce motor movements whereas stimulation of the posterior cortex did not, but there was apparent localization of function with respect to the specific movements that could be elicited at each anterior stimulation site. The third, and perhaps the most important reason for regarding this as a classic study, is that it provided an entirely new paradigm for brain research during the subsequent years of the nineteenth century. Literally hundreds of studies were reported that made direct reference to Fritsch and Hitzig and that employed essentially the same method.

It is interesting to note that despite the profound consequences of the study, the results are a good example of serendipity. Fritsch and Hitzig point out that what motivated their investigation was the observation of Hitzig that, in humans, eye movements could be produced by passing a current through the posterior part of the head. Although it is now known that this was due to stimulation of the labyrinth, Fritsch and Hitzig interpreted these eye movements in terms of a cerebral motor movement center. Their study was an attempt to identify the locus of that presumed center.

In the thirty years following their report, there were numerous attempts to localize other cortical centers. One name that stands out in this regard is that of David Ferrier, who successfully replicated and extended the findings of Fritsch and Hitzig in other species. Furthermore, he combined the older technique of ablation with that of stimulation to identify what became known as the sensory areas of the cortex, which received input from the receptor surface and which, if ablated, led to sensory loss. These sensory-motor developments in physiology combined with the flourishing associationist psychology formed the foundation of sensory-motor psychology, the idea that the functions of the brain or the faculties of the mind can be understood and conceptualized in sensory and motor terms. As pointed out in Chapter 1, this is a conception of the nervous system still very much with us today.

RESEARCH TRADITIONS INVOLVING BRAIN STIMULATION

The general approach of Fritsch and Hitzig of observing the effects of electrical stimulation of the exposed cortex on some response has continued to the present and is seen most dramatically in the work of Penfield, who has stimulated the cerebral cortex of humans in the course of clinical neurosurgery. In this work, the cortical exposure is typically made while the patient is under anesthetic, but when the cortical tissue is stimulated, the patient is awake, is able to communicate with the surgeon, and can verbally report what is experienced during stimulation. Although the dura mater is exquisitely sensitive (something to be noted when reading the Fritsch and Hitzig paper and in evaluating some of their arguments), there are in the brain itself no receptors that respond to touch or pressure; the patient does not feel anything, nor is there any experience of pain.

Stimulation of the sensory and motor cortex produces the general types of response that might be expected from Ferrier's work: Stimulation of the motor cortex, that tissue lying just anterior to the central sulcus, produces reflexive types of motor responses over which the patient reports little or no control; stimulation of the occipital cortex gives rise to reports of seeing lights, shadows, and colors, often moving; stimulation of Heschl's gyrus, located in the depths of the superior temporal gyrus, produces sensations of humming, buzzing, and ringing sounds; and stimulation of the postcentral gyrus produces sensations of tingling, numbness, and the sense of limb movement. However, stimulation of other regions of the cortex outside the classical sensory or motor areas also produces certain experiences. Right temporal lobe stimulation evokes what Penfield has called "psychic responses" of two general types. First are "experiential flashbacks." During stimulation, the patient has a vivid and clear image of selected past experiences that retain their correct temporal order. It is not a complete reliving of the experiences, though, as the patient is fully aware of the hallucinatory nature of the images and is able to talk to the surgeon about them. The second type of psychic response described by Penfield is "interpretative response." During stimulation the patient reports having a *déjà vu* experience, the false sense that he has been in the situation before and having the false impression of knowing what will happen.

Responses produced by stimulation of the left temporal cortex are related to speech and language functions and are always negative in the sense that stimulation produces an arrest reaction and interference with speech production.

A second general line of research paradigmatically similar to that of Penfield and of Fritsch and Hitzig was initiated by W. R. Hess in Zurich in the late 1920s. Hess combined stereotaxic procedures developed by Horseley and Clark (1908), which have been discussed in Chapters 3, 5, and 8, with techniques for permanently implanting electrodes in the brains of animals. This allowed the examination of the effects of electrical stimulation of cortical and subcortical areas of the brain in unrestrained and unanesthetized animals. His usual procedures involved inserting three pairs of electrodes (¼ mm diameter wires, insulated except for about 1 mm at the tips) into the region of the hypothalamus of the cat while the animal was anesthetized. The electrodes were held in a ceramic holder which in turn was screwed to the cranium of the animal. Soon after the anesthetic wore off, electrical pulses (typically from ¼ to 4 volts and having a frequency of 8 pulses per second) were passed between the tips of the electrode pairs for a duration of anywhere from 1 to 60 seconds. The dependent variables were observed changes in the "spontaneous" and "directed" behavior of the animal.

The types of behaviors Hess observed were generally affective defensive reactions that included such somatic responses as growling, spitting, retraction of the ears, crouching and arching of the back, and such autonomic responses as piloerection, urination, dilation of the pupils, and salivation. There were also changes in water and food intake, in sleep, in responses to temperature, and in general sympathetic arousal. These behavioral observations were combined with the histological determination of electrode placements to produce what were called electrical maps of the diencephalon indicating the loci from which particular behaviors could be elicited with particular parameters of stimulation.

This approach has recently become more technically sophisticated with the development of telemetry devices that obviate the necessity for wires and that allow for a greater degree of freedom of movement of the animals. The animal is equipped with a small battery-powered stimulation circuit that can be activated by a radio receiver responding to the transmission of radio signals. An equally common application of telemetry is in transmitting physiological signals such as heart rate, temperature, or brain potentials from the animal to the experimenter. Again, the need for wires is obviated by having the recording electrodes connected to a small amplifier and transmitter, allowing for the transduced signals to be transmitted from the subject to the receiving, amplifying, and recording equipment.

A rather different dimension of brain stimulation was added to the study of brain function by the observations of J. Olds and P. Milner (1954) that electrical stimulation of certain subcortical regions, through electrode implants similar to those used by Hess, did not evoke particular responses but had what seemed to be a rewarding effect on the animal. The animals were willing to work for stimulation in much the same way as a hungry animal in willing to work for food reward. Instead of behavior being evoked by stimulation, stimulation could be made contingent upon the animal performing some response. Other sites were found to have an opposite—that is, a punishing—effect. Most stimulation sites, however, seem to have rather ambiguous effects in that the animal will press a bar for stimulation while simultaneously showing behavioral signs of great fear, and even minor changes in the stimulation parameters will result in complete termination of responding. A massive body of literature has been generated around such issues as critical loci of stimulation, the similarity of electrical stimulation to conventional reward, and how to best conceptualize the effects of such stimulation.

THE PROBLEM OF LOCALIZATION OF FUNCTION

Underlying most of the studies done involving electrical stimulation of the brain is the issue of localization of brain function. The conclusions of such studies are often expressed in terms of the region of the brain stimulated being in some sense responsible for, or controlling, or causing the behavior observed to accompany the stimulation. Implicit in such conclusions is the basic assumption that stimulation in some way mimics normal brain activation. Several issues bear on this assumption. First, if electrical stimulation of some discrete area of the brain produces a complex response that can be conceptualized only in terms of being the product of complex spatial and temporal patterning of excitatory and inhibitory influences, then in no way can the locus of stimulation be considered a "center" for that complex response. Electrical stimulation is physiologically meaningless, and for it to produce complex, meaningful, and integrated responses the nervous system must first transform the stimulation into a pattern of neural activation that is physiologically meaningful. It would not seem unreasonable to assume that such a transformation must involve several synaptic links, and if the behavior is in any way caused by the stimulation, it must be conceptualized as being caused not by the activation of the stimulated region, but by activation by the transformed pattern of impulses in some other relatively remote area. A second issue bears on the assumption that electrical stimulation of the brain has an activating or excitatory effect on the neural tissue in close proximity to the electrode. It is not difficult to imagine that at least some behavioral effects of electrical stimulation are due to the blocking of ongoing activity in the area being stimulated, for the currents and voltages usually involved are physiologically massive and must interfere with and block the normal spatial and temporal patterning or sequencing of activity.

Apart from such issues as these concerned with the effects of electron flow on ionic flow of neurons, there is the problem in attempting to infer brain function from stimulation that the effects of electrical stimulation are only to a limited degree a function of stimulation parameters (such as current and electrode locus) and are largely a function of organismic and environmental variables. The effects of stimulation on behavior are clearly influenced by such fundamental variables as environmental setting (for example, attack responses may be manifest only if there is an object to attack in the environment), by hormonal level (for example, the rewarding effect of stimulation of the posterior hypothalamus is contingent upon the level of androgen hormone), or by even satiety level (for example, the rewarding effects of lateral hypothalamic stimulation and the elicitation of stimulation-bound feeding behavior depends on the amount of food deprivation). In Chapter 13 there will be a consideration of possible implications of such interactions for the use of stimulation or lesions in the study of brain function. Finally, although stimulation of many regions of the brain (for example, sensorimotor cortex) does produce highly reliable and consistent results, the effects of stimulation in other regions are highly transient.

An argument has been made that some of these problems can be circumvented with the use of chemical stimulation of the brain. The assumption is that when presumed neural transmitter substances like acetylcholine, serotonin, and norepinephrine are injected into neural tissue or into the ventricles, the resulting activation more closely approximates normal activation than it does in the case of electrical stimulation. Certainly one of the most compelling arguments validating chemical stimulation is that there are at least certain sites from which different physiological and behavioral responses can be obtained with the microinjection of different substances, whereas electrical stimulation of these same sites produces only one response. Presumably overlapping neural systems selectively activated with the different substances would all be activated (or blocked) with electrical stimulation. In this way, chemical stimulation of the brain may indeed be, as Myers (1972) claims, a refinement or extension of the method of electrical stimulation. But there is still a loss of temporal organization with chemical stimulation, and it is still a moot point whether the presumed difference between electron activation and ionic activation of the neurons is of any significance.

These are issues of concern only when electrical stimulation of the brain is used in an attempt to determine the functions of the brain and localization of function, and certainly not all research using electrical stimulation of the brain is oriented toward these questions. An example of a different orientation involves the use of electrical stimulation of the brain as an unconditioned stimulus (UCS) that produces an unconditioned response (UCR), such as a limb flexion, in the absence of motivation. One of the central problems in learning theory has been whether motivation is a necessary condition for learning to occur or whether simple spatial and temporal contiguity of stimulus and response is sufficient. In a normal Pavlovian conditioning paradigm, the UCS, food, produces the UCR, salivation, provided the animal is hungry. If some neutral stimulus precedes the presentation of the UCS, and if a reward follows the evocation of the UCR, then that neutral stimulus becomes a conditioned stimulus (CS) capable of eliciting a conditioned response (CR) similar to the UCR. With electrical stimulation of the motor cortex, the UCR can be produced in the absence of a motivational state in the organism. In an early study Loucks (1935) attempted to determine whether a neutral stimulus could in fact come to elicit the UCR when that was produced by electrical stimulation of the brain. Although Loucks was unsuccessful, more recent studies such as that by Doty and Giurgea (1961) have indicated that such learning proceeds rapidly and efficiently provided a sufficiently long intertrial interval has been used. If either the presentation of an external stimulus or electrical stimulation of some region of the brain not producing a motor response precedes electrical stimulation of the motor cortex (UCS), that CS can come to elicit the UCR.

This phenomenon of learning in the absence of motivation has been exploited by Doty and his colleagues in the study of the neural substrates of learning, discrimination, generalization, and related phenomena, and some of this work has recently been discussed and summarized in a thoughtful review by Doty (1969).

11 LABORATORY EXERCISE VI

ELECTRICAL STIMULATION OF THE CEREBRAL CORTEX OF THE ANESTHETIZED RAT

This laboratory exercise represents an attempt to replicate the observations of Fritsch and Hitzig discussed in the previous chapter. Their classic paper, published in 1870, is reprinted in Chapter 14. It is important to read it carefully before coming to the lab so you can relate it to what you are doing.

As in all labs, be sure your equipment is all there and in good operating condition, properly adjusted, and laid out in an orderly fashion before anesthetizing the subject.

Equipment and supplies for each group

Rat headholder
Osteological drill
High-intensity lamp (if necessary)
Magnifier on base
Micromanipulator with single electrode holder (see Appendix B–14)
Stimulator (instructions below)
2 wires, each with banana plug on one end and alligator clip on the other
end

4-in. length of uninsulated 28-gauge copper wire (to serve as stimulating electrode)

Surgical instruments

    #3 scalpel handle

    #10 and #11 blade

    2 mosquito forceps

    Thumb forceps

    Rat-tooth forceps

    Lempert rongeurs

    Large scissors

    Fine-tipped scissors

    Dental probe

    Medium cutting bur (#8)

    Fine cutting bur (#½) for bonescrew

    6-in. ruler

Jeweler's screw

Saline dish with saline

Eyedropper for mineral oil

10   2″×2″ gauze sponges

2   1-cc syringes with 26G needles

Dishpan with detergent

Towels

Lab coats

Equipment and supplies to be shared by all groups

Nembutal anesthetic, 60 mg/cc

Atropine sulfate, 0.4 mg/cc

70% alcohol, sponges

Animal clippers

Gloves

Mineral oil

Heater

Thermometer

Bonescrew-driver (see Appendix B–10)

Stimulator

The circuit diagram for the stimulator shown in Figure 11–1 is included in Appendix B. If the stimulator you are using was built with a Plexiglas bottom, you can see that it consists principally of either a small step-down transformer, which reduces the voltage of the power lines from 120 volts to smaller voltages, or an isolation transformer. The output voltage depends on the positioning of a variable resistor connected to the black rotating knob on top. When this knob is turned fully toward zero, there is no voltage output; when it is turned fully the opposite way, the voltage between the two output terminals on the top of the stimulator is at maximum. The frequency of the output is the same as the line frequency, that is, 60 cycles. An ON-OFF switch on the top of the stimulator should be turned to the ON position when you are ready

Figure 11–1. External view of a simple AC brain stimulator with variable voltage. The circuit diagram is included in Appendix B–9.

to stimulate. The momentary switch on the side allows you to control when the stimulus will actually be delivered. It should be noted that this circuit is electrically isolated from the power mains; this means that you do not have to worry about being electrocuted should you touch certain parts of the stimulator and electrical ground at the same time (which could happen if the circuit were not electrically isolated).

It is to be emphasized that most stimulators used in biological research are considerably more sophisticated than the one used in this lab, which has only an AC output of variable intensity. There is usually the facility for applying DC voltage, either positive or negative, and the stimulating voltage can be pulsed in either a sine-wave or a square-wave form at various frequencies. It is usually possible also to vary the duration that the voltage is applied during each cycle so that the brain can be stimulated, for example, at a frequency of 5 times per second, and during those stimulations the voltage is applied for only a small fraction of 0.2 seconds. Finally, research stimulators can usually be triggered electronically from some source other than the experimenter. Of great importance for work involving simultaneous stimulating and recording from the central nervous system, the output of the stimulator can be used to trigger the movement of the beam of an oscilloscope. It is to be emphasized, however, that despite the technical sophistication often associated with brain stimulation research, all that is really needed to observe interesting and theoretically important effects of brain stimulation is simply a battery or doorbell transformer and a piece of wire.

Initial stages

Follow the same operating procedures outlined in previous labs to expose the cerebral cortex.

1. You will use the same subject used in Laboratory Exercise III in which you made the initial incision and then sutured the animal. Obtain and reweigh the subject.
2. Calculate the dosage of anesthetic required on the basis of a dosage level of 60 mg/kg and a concentration of Nembutal of 60 mg/cc. Inject the animal IP, ensuring that the abdominal wall is well stretched and the needle penetration perpendicular to the abdomen.
3. After your animal is anesthetized, use the large scissors and forceps to remove any sutures remaining in the skin from Laboratory Exercise III. Then clip the fur from the animal's head, shaving anterior to the eyes.
4. Inject about 0.1 cc of atropine IP.
5. Mount the animal firmly in the headholder and position the head as in Laboratory Exercises III and IV.
6. Starting far anteriorly, make the initial incision using the #10 blade in the #3 handle. Remove the periosteum by scraping it from the midline to either side and retract it with the mosquito forceps. With a gauze sponge, wipe the cranium clean and identify bregma, the approximate position at which the mosquito forceps should be attached. Be sure to note the extent to which the tissue has healed since Laboratory Exercise III.
7. Using the medium cutting bur, thin the cranium of one hemisphere and very carefully break through the bone with the dental pick. Be sure not to puncture the dura and cortex. With the rongeurs, expand the exposure posteriorly to almost the lambdoidal suture and a few millimeters anterior to bregma. Try to get quite close to the midline but be careful of the sagittal sinus running down the midline. Try also to get a good lateral exposure.

Applying bonescrew

Before cutting the dura, drill a hole through the cranium of the hemisphere opposite to that exposed at a position quite far anterior (about 4 or 5 mm anterior to bregma) and just slightly off the midline. Use the small bur (it may be necessary to change the drill collet to hold it), hold the drill in a vertical orientation as if you were a human drill-press (Figure 11–2), and drill only until you go through the bone into the frontal sinus. Then, apply the bonescrew with the bonescrew-driver as shown in Figure 11–3. Leave

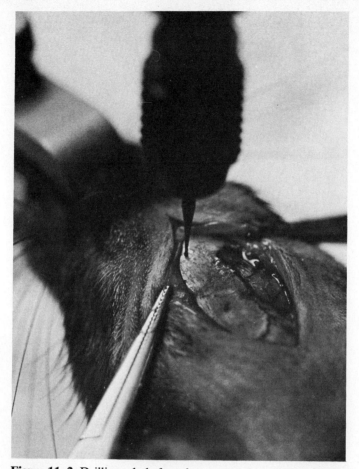

Figure 11–2. Drilling a hole for a bonescrew. Locate bregma and lambda, note the position of the mosquito forceps, and note the size of the exposure.

about one-fourth of the shank above the bone; this will be used to attach one electrode during stimulation.

Completing the exposure

Cut the dura in the pattern described in Laboratory Exercise IV, exposing as much of the cortex as possible. It is important that a clean cut be made through the dura and that the flaps be retracted to either side of the exposure as far as possible.

From this point it is important to keep the cortex moist, as any drying may lead to the induction of cortical spreading depression (discussed in Chapter 5) and the cortex will simply stop functioning. So, until you are ready to stimulate, keep the cortex covered with a cotton pellet moistened with saline. Once you start to stimulate, the cortex should be kept moist with a small amount of warm heavy mineral oil. Besides keeping the cortex moist, it acts as an electrical insulator (this is, of course, opposite to saline) and will restrict the stimulation to that part of the cortex immediately below the electrode. Furthermore, being warm, the oil will help keep the cortex at

(a)

(b)

(d)

(c)

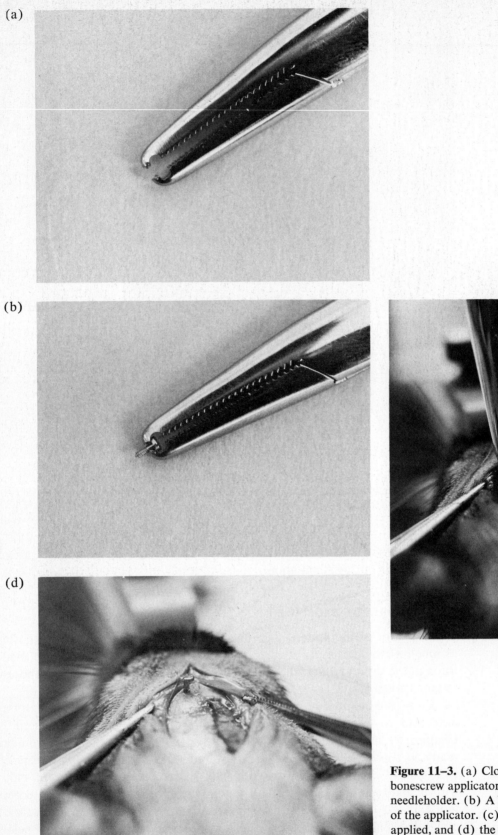

Figure 11–3. (a) Close-up of the jaws of a bonescrew applicator constructed from a needleholder. (b) A bonescrew held in the jaws of the applicator. (c) The bonescrew being applied, and (d) the final appearance of the exposure with the bonescrew in place.

approximately body temperature, which is important for the maintenance of normal electrophysiological properties.

Preparation for stimulation

The electrode is simply a piece of copper wire that should be placed into the electrode holder as shown in Figure 11–4 in the same way as was the copper measuring wire used in Laboratory Exercise V. The longer piece of wire will serve as the electrode proper and will rest on the cortex; the shorter piece is where the stimulator will be attached to the electrode. Lower and adjust the headholder so the animal's head is level with the rest of the body. This will enable you to spread the forelimbs laterally, making any evoked movements of the forelimbs quite evident. Position the calibration on all three scales of the micromanipulator in such a way that the electrode tip can be moved to any part of the cortex. It may be necessary to actually raise the manipulator from its base (by releasing the clamp on the side of the micromanipulator), although it is probably easier to simply bend the electrode so it is the appropriate height. Try to orient the manipulator so its planes are as parallel as possible to the principal planes of the rat's head.

Turn the stimulator on and attach the leads to the terminals. No current will pass between these unless the momentary switch is depressed. Attach the alligator clip of one lead to the bonescrew and that of the other lead to the short end of the electrode wire. Turn the variable resistor about one quarter of a turn from the zero voltage point.

Position the electrode so it is on about a 45° angle, as shown in Figure 11–5. Such an angle will prevent the electrode from piercing the cortex. Now lower it so the tip just touches bregma. Note the anterior-posterior (A-P) reading and the lateral reading on the micromanipulator. All future readings will be made in reference to bregma, so care must be taken not to alter the orientation of the electrode with respect to the manipulator nor the orientation of the manipulator with respect to the animal. If you do alter it, you will have to recalibrate.

Position the electrode about 1 to 2 mm lateral to the midline at the A-P level of bregma. (Note: 1 to 2 mm lateral to midline is not the same as 1 to 2 mm lateral to the edge of your exposure.) Lower the electrode so it just *touches* the surface of the pia. Do not treat the cortex as a pincushion, for after several such penetrations, the cortex could become nonfunctional due to the induction of spreading depression. Be sure the cortex is moist with

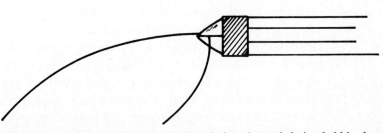

Figure 11–4. Diagram showing the stimulating electrode being held in the electrode holder and the angle at which the wire should be bent.

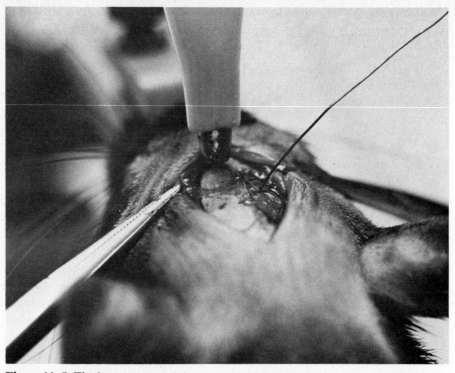

Figure 11–5. Final appearance of the exposure with the alligator clip attached to the bonescrew and the electrode resting on the cortical surface. Note the angle of the electrode with respect to the cortical surface. Before stimulating, ensure that the alligator clip is not touching the skin or periosteum.

mineral oil. Press the momentary switch for approximately a half-second, watching the body of the rat, especially the limbs, for any signs of movement. (Do not stimulate more than once every 5 seconds.) Spreading the limbs as much as possible from the sides of the body will help you to detect muscle contraction. Make a note of any movements you observe on either side of the body. Now decrease the voltage slightly and repeat the procedures until there are no longer any detectable movements. The voltage just higher than this will be referred to as the threshold voltage.

If there was no movement from the original stimulation, increase the intensity until one is elicited or until the intensity is half maximum. You must work with threshold voltages because when you stimulate you are passing a current between your electrode tip and the bonescrew, and any neurons lying between these points will tend to be activated. At high voltages, there will be a great spread of current and large parts of the brain will be stimulated. As the voltage is decreased, you will reach the activation threshold of only those cells immediately below the electrode tip. In many respects, it is easier to work with a bipolar electrode in which the electrode tips are in close proximity so all that is stimulated, regardless of voltage, is the small amount of tissue lying between and around the electrode tips.

Remember that you are using a 60 cps alternating current. This means that 60 times per second the tissue will alternate between a state of depolarization (during the negative phase of each cycle) and hyperpolarization (during the positive phase).

It is important to note that each stimulation should be of no more than 1-second duration and that you should not stimulate more than once every 4 or 5 seconds. More frequent stimulation may trigger off a wave of spreading depression.

Mapping the cortex

Once you have observed some movements, you should attempt to map the cortex for electrically excitable points. Imagine a grid with 1-mm squares applied to the surface of the cortex.[1] Using the micromanipulator, move the electrode in 1-mm steps and record any movements evoked by stimulation of each square in the imaginary grid. For each point, carefully lower the electrode so it just touches the pia mater, record the relationship of the point to bregma (expressed as x mm anterior or posterior to bregma and y mm lateral to the midline), and record any movements and their latency observed on either side of the body with suprathreshold and threshold stimulus intensities. Make a note of any apparent changes in the intensity or speed of movements evoked at increasingly high stimulus intensities.

Concentrate your attention on the more anterior portions of the cortex, those areas that correspond to areas 3, 4, and 6 as diagramed in Figure 6–6 of Laboratory Exercise III. These are areas from which you should be able to evoke some movements at least some of the time. But do stimulate some sites posterior to this (for example, area 17) and some sites anterior (for example, area 10). Figure 11–6 is an illustration of a somatic sensory and motor "homunculus" of the rat taken from Woolsey (1958). This may prove useful to you in placing your electrode. In your lab report, you should discuss the degree of correspondence you observe between this illustration and the motor homunculus of your rat. Some groups will find excellent correspondence, others may find very little.

Stimulate the dura and the temporal muscles using the same stimulation procedures. Compare the types and intensities of responses with those observed following stimulation of the motor cortex and note especially differences in threshold. Recall the use to which similar observations were put by Fritsch and Hitzig.

Sacrificing and disposing of the subject

At the end of the exercise, your subject should be sacrificed. If we were interested in saving the brain to determine where, for example, we had made a lesion or, in the case of subcortical stimulating electrodes, where we stimulated, we would want to follow the procedures discussed in Chapter 3 and in Laboratory Exercises IV and V for perfusing the animal and removing its brain.

---

[1] An *actual* grid can be made on the surface of the cortex using black India ink and a fine piece of wire. An array of small black dots, spaced one millimeter apart, obviates the necessity for continual reference to bregma and the midline, and facilitates replication of stimulation effects.

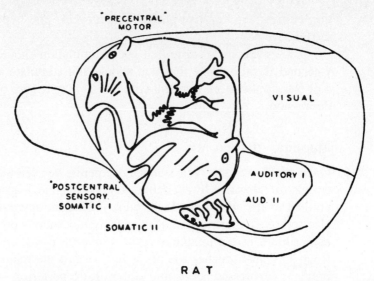

Figure 11–6. Diagram of the somatic sensory and motor "homuculi" of the rat cortex. (From C. N. Woolsey, Organization of somatic sensory and motor areas of the cerebral cortex. In H. F. Harlow and C. N. Woolsey (Eds.), *Biological and biochemical bases of behavior.* Madison: University of Wisconsin Press, 1958, Figure 19.)

Inject the subject IP with about 1 cc of Nembutal, which is a lethal overdose. The heart will probably stop beating within 5 to 10 minutes. To confirm that it has, and to ensure that death would follow even if it had not, the thoracic cavity should be exposed. After the animal is deeply anesthetized, use your #10 scalpel blade to make a midline incision through the skin overlying the rib cage, which can be easily felt. Then push the pointed blade of the *heavy* scissors underneath the lower boundary of the rib cage, which can also be easily felt. The ribs and muscles of the rat are very soft and can be cut with the large scissors (Figure 11–7). You should now be able to see the heart. The pinkish tissue located to the sides and slightly behind the heart is the lungs (note that the rat was not a smoker, for they would be black if it were). Note that separating the thoracic and peritoneal cavities is the diaphragm, a structure important in the control of the expansion of the lungs. Immediately below this you may be able to see the dark red liver tissue.

Identify the right and left ventricles of the heart. If the animal were to be perfused, a blunt hypodermic needle connected to a syringe of saline and then one of Formalin would be inserted through the left ventricle into the aorta and the right ventricle would be cut. Students wishing to attempt a perfusion should consult with their instructor.

Discard the subject into the bag provided and carefully clean all the instruments and your work area as described in previous labs.

(a)

(b)

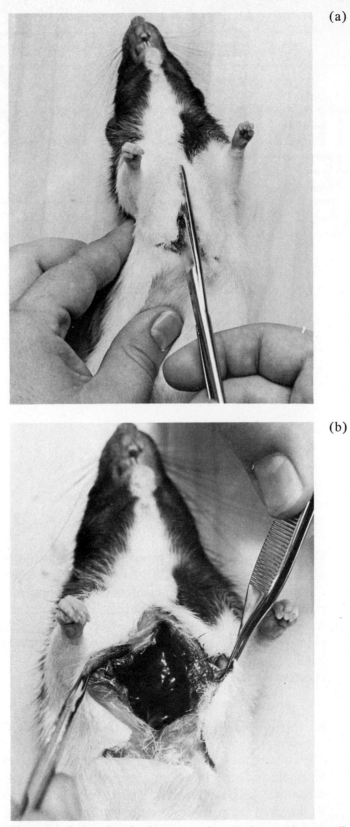

Figure 11–7. Opening the thoracic cavity. (a) Large scissors easily cut through the soft ribs revealing (b) the heart and lungs in the thoracic cavity.

12 LABORATORY EXERCISE VII

ELECTRICAL STIMULATION OF THE BRAIN: REWARDING EFFECTS

Certainly as dramatic, and probably as theoretically important as the findings of Fritsch and Hitzig (1870), were the observations of Olds and Milner (1954) that electrical stimulation of the septal area of the rat brain had positive reinforcing effects on behavior in that the animal would work for stimulation. In this laboratory exercise, a stimulating electrode will be permanently implanted into the lateral hypothalamus or medial forebrain bundle, and following recovery from surgery, the potentially reinforcing effects of stimulation will be assessed.

A. IMPLANTING A STIMULATION ELECTRODE

The procedures described for implanting chronic stimulating electrodes are the same as those that would be used to implant electrodes for recording subcortical EEGs (Chapter 17). As was the case with Laboratory Exercise V, however, the procedures described involving the use of a headholder and micromanipulator are not those that would be used in actual research. Instead, a stereotaxic instrument, having the virtues of convenience and accuracy, would normally be used. If a stereotaxic instrument is available, your instructor may encourage you to use it and will demonstrate how to mount the animal in it. In that case, it will be unnecessary to use a micromanipulator or to follow the procedures for adjusting the head orientation using the difference in the vertical heights of bregma and lambda.

Equipment and supplies for each group

Stereotaxic atlas of the rat brain (see Laboratory Exercise V)
Rat headholder
Osteological drill
High-intensity lamp (if necessary)
Micromanipulator with single electrode holder (see Appendix B–14)
4-in. length of wire for measuring head orientation
Bipolar stimulation electrode (see Figure 12–1 and Appendix B–11)
Headplug with ring screw (see Figure 12–2 and Appendix B–12)
Surgical instruments
    #3 scalpel handle with #10 and #11 blade
    2 mosquito forceps
    Thumb forceps
    Rat-tooth forceps
    Large scissors
    Dental explorer
    Medium (#8) cutting bur
    Fine (#½) bur for bonescrews
    Cement spatula for spreading dental cement and applying bone wax
    6-in. ruler
Instrument container and Zephiran chloride solution
Bone wax
Watch glass
Dental cement and solvent
4 jeweler's screws
Petri dish with Zephiran for sterilizing electrode and bonescrews
2"×2" gauze sponges
Cotton pledgets
2   1-cc syringes with 26G needles
Dishpan with detergent
Towels
Lab coats

Equipment and supplies to be shared by groups

Animal balance
Animal clippers
Nembutal anesthetic, 60 mg/cc
Atropine sulfate, 0.4 mg/cc

Electrode testing circuit (see Laboratory Exercise V and Appendix B–6)
Bonescrew-driver
Glove
Wire cutters or specially designated scissors to trim electrodes

Electrode construction and testing

The electrode to be implanted into the brain is simply a piece of insulated wire twisted on itself and cut at the looped end to make two separate wires. On the end of each wire has been soldered a Relia-Tac male contact pin (Amphenol No. 220–PO2). Detailed instructions for making these electrodes are included in Appendix B–11, and Figure 12–1 shows an electrode before and after trimming. The electrodes must be prepared well ahead of time, but they can be trimmed to the proper length at the time of the lab.

Figure 12–2 is a photograph of the three component parts of the head-plug assembly recommended for use in this lab and in certain of the independent projects described in Part Five. Designed by Molino and McIntyre (1972), the assembly provides excellent electrical contact and obviates the problem of plugs becoming disconnected during testing. The only disadvantage at this time is that the plugs are not yet available commercially and

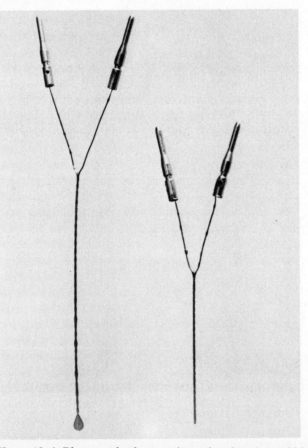

Figure 12–1. Photograph of an untrimmed and a trimmed bipolar electrode similar to that which may be used in this laboratory exercise.

Figure 12–2. Photograph of the headplug, ring screw, and connecting plug described in this laboratory exercise and in Appendix B.

must be made to order.[1] Some of the technical details are provided in Appendix B. The component with the threaded portion is the actual headplug to be cemented to the skull after the pins from the implanted electrode have been inserted into the appropriate holes. The mating component, which is connected by wire to the stimulator, fits the headplug and is held firmly to it by the ring screw. It is very important to note into which holes the female pins have been placed, since the electrode pins must be inserted into the appropriate corresponding holes in the headplug. It is also important to note that when cementing the headplug to the skull, dental cement must not get into the threaded portion. Accordingly, the spare ring screw with which you have been provided should be threaded on the headplug during surgery.

Before beginning surgery, the electrode shaft must be trimmed to the proper length, but to do this it is necessary to know where the electrode tip will be positioned. Consult a stereotaxic atlas and determine the coordinates for the middle of the lateral hypothalamus and medial forebrain bundle, which extend through several atlas plates. Determine the A-P coordinates with respect to bregma, the lateral coordinate with respect to the midline, and the depth of the site with respect to the cortical surface. It does not matter into which hemisphere the electrode is implanted. (If your atlas is calibrated with respect to stereotaxic ear bars, recall that bregma is 6.25 mm anterior to the ear bar 0).

---

[1] If facilities are not readily available, headplugs, connector plugs, and brass ring screws can be obtained, at cost, through the author, at least until the time the assembly is available commercially. As described in Appendix B–12, similar connectors are available commercially from the Plastic Products Company. Another alternative, which is probably the least expensive and certainly as satisfactory for much brain stimulation work (but not for recording because of "noise" problems) involves the use of Amphenol 221 series strip connectors, which are meant for use with the Amphenol Relia-Tac contact pins described in this exercise and in Appendix B–12. The narrower connector strip (Amphenol No. 221–2253) can be cut to a length having the right number of holes (in the case of this lab, two holes) and after the electrode pins (Amphenol No. 220–P02) have been inserted into the holes, cemented to the skull in exactly the way described for the Molino-McIntyre assembly. The connecting plug is made in a similar way with the corresponding wider connector strip (Amphenol No. 221–2153) fitted with female Relia-Tac pins (Amphenol 220–S02) to which lead wires have been soldered.

With wire cutters or with specially designated scissors, trim the electrode so that the length of the twisted shaft is about 4 to 5 mm longer than the depth of the intended site from the cortical surface. The electrode should now be tested using the battery circuit described in Laboratory Exercise V. First test that there are no short circuits in the electrode wires by connecting one battery lead to each of the pins. If the bulb lights up, indicating a flow of current through the circuit, it means that somewhere there is an electrical contact between the wires and the electrode should be discarded. If there is no short circuit, proceed to check that there are no breaks in the insulation by placing the electrode into a beaker of saline with the negative battery terminal attached to both electrode pins and the positive terminal in contact with the saline. As in Laboratory Exercise V, bubbles should appear only at the electrode tips and not along the shaft.

Place the electrode in a dish of Zephiran so that it will become reasonably sterile, and from this point on handle it by the pins and avoid letting anything touch the shaft. Since the electrode will be left in the animal's brain for a reasonably long period of time, bacteria on the shaft can cause infection. The bonescrews, which will be placed in the skull as anchor points, and the tips of the bonescrew-driver should also be placed in the Zephiran.

Procedures

Up to the point of lowering the electrode into the brain, connecting the pins to the headplug, and cementing the headplug to the skull, the procedures to be followed are identical with those used in Laboratory Exercise V for making subcortical lesions.

1. Obtain and weigh your subject and anesthetize it with Nembutal anesthetic (60 mg/kg). When injecting the animal, be sure to stretch the abdominal muscles well and insert the needle perpendicular to the abdominal wall. After the animal is completely anesthetized, inject it with 0.1 cc of atropine.

2. Clip the fur from the animal's head.

3. Mount the animal firmly in the headholder and, using the #10 blade in the #3 handle, make the initial incision. Try to make this incision a little shorter than those made in previous labs. Scrape the periosteum from the cranium and retract it with the mosquito forceps.

4. Use the micromanipulator and wire to measure the difference in the vertical height of bregma and lambda and adjust the head so that its orientation corresponds to that illustrated in Figure 8–5 of Laboratory Exercise V. It should be level; the midline suture should be parallel to the side of the headholder box and parallel to the anterior-posterior axis of the micromanipulator; and bregma should be 2.25 mm above lambda. As in Laboratory Exercise V, be content with an error of ±0.05 mm.

5. Using the coordinates previously determined, find exactly where on the skull you should drill to implant the electrode. Mark this with the point of the dental explorer (not a pencil), but do not drill at this time.

6. To keep the headplug firmly fastened to the skull, it is necessary to put several bonescrews into the skull to serve as anchors. Four screws should be placed around the site of the intended electrode trephine hole and located so that two are anterior and two posterior to the intended hole and so that two are in the cranium overlying each hemisphere. Use the #½ bur to drill the four holes just through the skull and apply each bonescrew with the bonescrew-driver as described in Laboratory Exercise VI, so that about one-third or one-half of it remains above the surface of the skull. If the hole is too large, be sure to drill a new one, as it is most important that the bonescrew be firmly in the skull. Now use the #½ bur to roughen the surface of the cranium, a procedure that will increase the bond between the dental cement and cranium. Be sure to remove all bone dust with a moist cotton pledget before continuing.

7. Double-check the coordinates of the electrode and then use the medium bur (#8) to drill a hole through the cranium for the electrode. Then carefully nick the dura with the tip of the #11 blade.

8. Use cotton pledgets to dry the cranium as thoroughly as possible, for dental cement will not form a good bond unless the cranium is completely free of moisture.

9. Clamp the electrode into the electrode holder of the micromanipulator. *Do not clamp it by the shaft,* as this may break the insulation; instead, clamp it between the twisted shaft and pins with one or both wires. Orient the electrode vertically, using the ruler as a set square. Line up the micromanipulator, locate bregma with the electrode tip, and move the electrode the appropriate distance posterior and lateral from bregma. It should be positioned immediately over the hole previously drilled. (If it is not, check the atlas to determine where the electrode tip would end up if it were implanted into the hole as drilled. As the lateral hypothalamus–medial forebrain bundle is a large area, especially in the anterior-posterior plane, a small deviation may not be serious. If the deviation is large, however, you might want to drill a new hole, either in the same or the contralateral hemisphere.) Lower the electrode tip so it just touches the cortex, note the vertical scale reading, check the vertical scale of the micromanipulator to ensure that the electrode can in fact be lowered the required distance, and then proceed to lower it into the brain.

10. If excess moisture appears on the cranium, remove it with small cotton pledgets. Use your dental probe and spatula to carefully pack a little bone wax in the hole around the electrode. This will prevent the dental cement from running down the hole and coming into contact with the cortex.

11. Sprinkle a small amount of dental cement powder into the watch glass, add some solvent, and mix. You will have to determine the proper proportions by trial and error, but you should strive for a smooth and somewhat liquid consistency. The mixture hardens rapidly, so as soon as it is properly mixed, apply it with the spatula. First apply a thin layer of cement around the electrode shaft itself

and let this dry well (about 5 to 10 minutes).[2] Then the electrode can be released from the electrode holder and the micromanipulator put aside.

12. The part of the twisted electrode shaft that remains above the layer of cement should now be bent flat against the cranium and a small amount of cement applied to hold it. This layer of cement can then be extended around the bonescrews. At this point, the periosteum can be released from the mosquito forceps to become adhered to the cement.

13. Insert the electrode pins into the appropriate headplug holes and snap each into place using mosquito forceps. Position the plug upright, roughly in the middle of the head, and align the electrode wires so they do not touch one another. (Note that the insulation may have cracked on one or both of these when they were held in the electrode holder, but the cement will insulate them again.) Mix still more cement and slowly build a mound that encases the wires and the base of the headplug and that runs up the sides of the headplug almost to the threads. Make the mound as smooth as possible, using your finger if necessary. Figure 12–3 shows the final appearance of the animal with a headplug in place. Note that there is no need to suture or use would clips to close the incision, as the tissue has become firmly attached to the cement. Just be sure that the cement is in contact with the tissue all around the incision and that there are no pockets in which infection can develop.

14. Remove the animal from the headholder and let it recover. Be sure to remove the ring screw from the headplug before the animal awakens. The animal should be allowed several days for recovery before any attempt is made to connect the stimulator plug to the headplug. Check the animal each day. If there is any sign of infection around the incision, be sure to tell the instructor, who may administer antibiotics.

B. ASSESSMENT OF REWARDING EFFECTS OF BRAIN STIMULATION

The essential criterion as to whether some event is rewarding or positively reinforcing is whether the occurrence of that event increases the probability or the liklihood of occurrence of behavior that precedes it and upon which the event is made contingent. One simple way to assess whether electrical stimulation of the brain is rewarding, punishing, or neutral for the animal would be to place it in an open-field situation, such as that shown in Figure 12–4, and stimulate it when it is in certain parts of the box but not when it is in other parts. The floor of the box can be divided into quarters and one quarter can be defined as a stimulation area, that is, an area which when

---

[2] Do not let excess dental cement harden completely in the watch glass, for it becomes extremely difficult to remove. While the leftover cement is still somewhat soft, scrape the glass clean so it is ready for mixing additional cement.

(a)

(b)

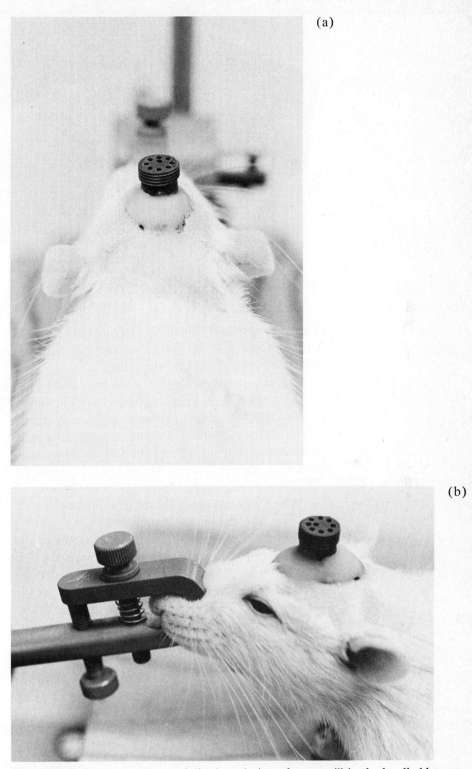

Figure 12–3. (a) A posterior and (b) lateral view of a rat, still in the headholder, with headplug cemented to the skull.

Figure 12–4. An open-field maze.

entered or remained in will be accompanied by brain stimulation. An opera‹ tional definition of the animal entering or leaving an area might be that its front feet have crossed over some line.

The stimulator can be the same one used in Laboratory VI, but it should be equipped with a thumb-operated switch that will allow manual administration of brief pulses of stimulation. A very lightweight and flexible connection between the stimulator and the animal can be made by using phono-pickup wire suspended from the ceiling with long, large rubber bands. This allows the animal to move about freely without the wires dragging behind it or pulling excessively at the skull.

When you are ready to test the animal, insert the mating plug into the headplug and fasten the ring screw. Now place the animal in the middle of the open-field maze and turn the voltage of the stimulator to just above the zero point. Whenever the animal enters the area you have defined as the stimulation area, deliver a very short stimulating pulse once every 2 or 3 seconds. If the animal leaves the stimulation area, cease stimulation. One lab partner should administer stimulation and the other should record the amount of time spent in the stimulation and in the nonstimulation areas of the box. If the stimulation is neither rewarding nor punishing, the animal should spend approximately one-quarter of the time in the stimulation area. Spending significantly more or less time in that area can be taken as evidence of a rewarding or a punishing effect, respectively.

Continue the procedure for a 5- or 10-minute period and then return the animal to its home cage. Analyze the data and determine the proportion of time spent in the two areas of the box. The following day repeat the observations but increase the voltage [3] slightly if the stimulation seemed to

[3] What is of importance is the current flow, which is a direct function of the voltage and an inverse function of the resistance through the electrodes and animal. In principle,

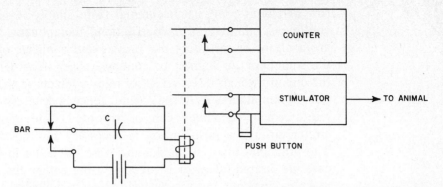

Figure 12–5. A schematic diagram of a circuit that will deliver a brief pulse of stimulation whenever the bar is depressed or continuous stimulation for as long as the push button is pressed and that will count the frequency of bar presses. The relay must be DC and needs to be double-pole, double-throw. The actual value for the capacitor (C) would depend on the characteristics of the relay and the desired duration of the stimulation pulse.

have little or no effect the previous day. The observations should be repeated for a number of days with appropriate changes in the stimulation voltage.

Much more information of a parametric nature can be derived from the use of operant conditioning techniques which, in fact, constitute the most commonly used approach to the assessment of the reinforcing effects of brain stimulation. If Skinner boxes are available, the instructor may wire them up to demonstrate the use of these techniques.[4] Each box must be wired so that whenever the bar is depressed, the stimulator turns on briefly. The electrical circuit involved is, in principle, very straightforward and is sketched in Figure 12–5. The bar in the box is connected physically to a microswitch and when depressed allows current to flow from the battery through the coil of a relay; this closes the relay contacts and the stimulator is then on. However, the current flows through the coil only until the capacitor in the circuit becomes charged; at that time, the relay contacts open and the stimulator is then off. For the stimulator to be turned on again, the capacitor must first discharge, which occurs when the bar is released. When the bar is again depressed, the stimulator turns on. This

---

this can be measured by placing a resistor of known value between the stimulator and the animal, measuring the voltage drop across the resistor using an oscilloscope (Chapter 15), and then calculating the current flow through the circuit using Ohm's law. However, it is strongly recommended that this *not* be done in these labs without at least the advice of an electrical engineer. By itself, the stimulator described in Chapter 11 does not pose a serious shock hazard because it is electrically isolated from ground through a transformer. But if an oscilloscope, which is connected to ground, is placed between the stimulator and the subject, there is a serious shock hazard unless special precautions are taken. Consequently, for this lab, which is designed simply to demonstrate principles of research methodology, it is suggested that whatever quantification is done be in terms of voltage rather than current although the instructor will discuss, and perhaps demonstrate, what these voltages mean in terms of current flow.

[4] An excellent half-hour film that demonstrates the use of lever pressing in the assessment of reinforcing effects of brain stimulation is *Hypothalamic reward in feeding, running, and mating behavior,* by B. G. Hoebel (Psychological Cinema Register, film number 2182K).

sort of circuit prevents the animal from simply leaning on the bar to get continuous stimulation. Two additional components needed in this circuit are a means of recording bar presses and a means of manually controlling the stimulator. A counter or cumulative pen recorder can be connected to the circuit through a second set of relay contacts so that the frequency or the rate of stimulation over time (and hence, bar pressing on this continuous reinforcement schedule) can be recorded. The manual operation of the circuit through a push button is necessary for the shaping of the animal. The principles involved in shaping were discussed in Chapter 7, but in this case the desired behavior is pressing a bar rather than making a unimanual reaching response and the reward, which is delivered by the experimenter as successive approximations to the desired response are made by the animal, is a brief pulse of brain stimulation rather than a food pellet.

After the animal has been shaped, record the bar pressing rates over a period of days. Depending upon available equipment and facilities, your instructor may suggest other manipulations to attempt.

C. VERIFICATION OF ELECTRODE PLACEMENT

Principles of verification of subcortical lesions were discussed in Laboratory Exercise V. The verification of a subcortical electrode site often involves very similar principles as it is, in fact, the identification of an electrolytic lesion.

After the animal is deeply anesthetized, but before it is perfused, the stimulating electrodes are used to make a small lesion in the brain. A connecting plug that can be attached to the lesion maker must be prepared and is wired in such a way that both electrode pins are connected to the anode of the lesion maker. The cathode is connected to a rectal electrode as discussed in Laboratory Exercise V. A 2 ma current passed through the electrode for about 5 seconds produces a small lesion around the electrode tip that can be subsequently identified histologically.

Two things should be noted about the procedure. First, removing the brain from the cranium can be a little tricky; the electrode, connected to the headplug which is in turn still cemented to the cranium, must be removed without damaging the tissue. This can be done using rongeurs to cut the bone all around the headplug. Second, after a chronic stimulation or recording electrode has been in the brain for a long period of time, and especially if it is in the brain during perfusion, the electrode tract is very clear and distinct. Slicing the brain slightly off the stereotaxic plane will allow one to see the beginning of the electrode tract several slices prior to the appearance of those sections that contain the lesion, and this prevents the possibility of carelessly slicing through and discarding those sections of critical interest.

ABLATION, STIMULATION, AND THE SEARCH FOR THE FUNCTIONS OF THE BRAIN

Much of the history and contemporary concern of physiological psychology centers upon the related issues of the identification of the functions of the brain and cerebral localization of those functions. The reason for this is as obvious (at least superficially) now as it was to Gall in the late eighteenth and early nineteenth century: If behavior and other processes of psychological interest have their origin in the activity of the brain, if one understands the functions of the brain one should understand the organization of behavior and the nature of these other processes.

These issues of brain-behavior relations are often identified with cortical functioning, perhaps in part because of the controversy that surrounded Lashley's concepts of equipotentiality and mass action (discussed in his paper in Chapter 9), concepts derived from research concerned with cortical function. The

attempt to identify and to localize function in subcortical neuroanatomical structures is certainly as real. It is reflected, for instance, in discussions of speech and sleep centers, of homeostatic feeding and satiety centers, of centers for the regulation of water balance and body temperature, of neural substrates of maternal, sexual, and aggressive behaviors, of approach and avoidance responding, of response inhibition and facilitation, and so on. It is reflected in such titles in the contemporary literature as "Functions of the amygdala" (Goddard, 1964), "Hippocampus internal inhibition" (Kimble, 1968), "Septum and behavior: A review" (Fried, 1972), "Functional dissociation within the hippocampus" (Grant and Jarrard, 1968), "The lateral hypothalamic syndrome" (Teitelbaum and Epstein, 1962), "Pleasure centers of the brain" (Olds, 1956), and "Approach-avoidance dissociation in rat brain" (Olds, 1960), to name but a few, as well as in the chapter and section headings of most contemporary textbooks of physiological psychology.

One of several reasons to study the history of a discipline is to gain insight into the current condition of that discipline, and indeed the reason for examining in Chapters 5 and 10 some of the modern history of localization of function is that certain issues associated with this problem come into sharp focus when viewed with such perspective. In those chapters it was pointed out that two of the principal methods used in the empirical study of brain-behavior relations have been ablation (usually presumed to abolish the functioning of a neural area) and electrical or chemical stimulation (usually presumed to activate it). It was also pointed out that the logical foundation underlying the use of these methods is that formulated in the nineteenth century by Pierre Flourens: Remove (or stimulate) a part of the brain, observe what the organism ceases to do (or begins to do), and infer what that part of the brain normally does.

This same logic permeates much research and thought in contemporary physiological psychology, and the purpose of this chapter is to examine certain issues of a conceptual nature that are implicit in its application. Two partially interdependent facets of the formulation will be of particular concern. The first supposes that the functions of the brain can be determined by observing what behavioral alterations occur following ablation or stimulation. The second supposes that function can be localized in at least the sense of that part of the brain manipulated being a component of a larger system mediating a function underlying the behavioral alteration.

OBSERVATION OF BEHAVIORAL CHANGE

A major problem in relation to the first facet is derived from the fact that it is impossible to objectively and impartially observe all behaviors of an organism under all conditions. If we plan to observe what an organism ceases to do or begins to do after some manipulation, we must decide at some point just what it is we are going to observe and how we are going to observe it. To do this, we must decide which categories of behavior, or which categories of experience—or, to put it in more classical terms—which faculties of the mind we should use in characterizing alterations in behavior. If the decision is based upon the categories of the medieval philosophers, categories such as memory, judgment, percep-

tion, volition, and so forth, having their origin in common language and experience, we would look at behavior we might guess reflects these presumed functions and would characterize behavioral change in these terms. If instead we use the sensory-motor categories of the late nineteenth century, we would classify behavioral change in terms of alterations in underlying sensory and motor processes. Or if we use categories that have in some sense biological significance for the organism, we would look for changes perhaps in feeding or sexual behavior or in patterns of social interaction, but not in behaviors reflecting memory processes or volition. Implicit in the classic formulation of Flourens and encountered occasionally in contemporary thought is the notion that this need not be of concern, for the functions of the brain should and will become evident, even obvious, in the nature of the alterations which follow brain lesions or which accompany electrical stimulation. There are, however, several grounds for questioning such a supposition.

First, as Teuber (1959) has emphasized in reference to the study of the psychological effects of penetrating brain wounds in humans, changes in behavior are "often subtle, elusive, require very special tasks for their discovery, and even then might go undiscovered" (Teuber, 1959, p. 158). A striking example of the subtle nature of behavioral alteration that can follow *major* neurological insult is the notable absence of effects that follows sectioning of the corpus callosum, that massive bundle of fibers interconnecting the two cerebral hemispheres. Indeed, there is such an absence of observable effects following commissurotomy that it was suggested half seriously in the 1940s that the function of the corpus callosum must be to physically hold the cerebral hemispheres together. The development and utilization of special testing procedures, however (Gazzaniga, Bogen, and Sperry, 1962, 1963, 1965), clearly indicated the major role played by the corpus callosum in interhemispheric integration.

If special tests are required to detect behavioral change, the importance of recognizing assumptions regarding functional categories and implicit conceptualizations concerning the organization of the nervous system should be very evident. Whether an organism is tested following some treatment for changes in sensory thresholds, or on a perceptual task, or in a situation involving social interaction, or in one involving the assessment of a motivational state, and considerations such as the type of environment in which the organism is tested, the internal state of the organism at the time of testing, or the specific tasks employed to detect and measure behavioral change (and hence the manifestation of behavioral change), all depend upon the assumptions and conceptualizations of the experimenter. For example, if the organization and the functions of the hypothalamus are viewed in terms of homeostatic regulatory mechanisms, the effects of manipulation of hypothalamic functioning will tend to be assessed in those terms and not in terms of changes in, for instance, memory or sensory-perceptual processes (see Marshall, Turner, and Teitlebaum, 1971).

The research reviewed by Hoebel (1969) and discussed in the introduction to the study by Valenstein et al. (1968) reprinted in Chapter 14, and the Valenstein study itself, illustrate that the observed effects of electrical stimulation of the hypothalamus are as much a function of the method of assessing the effects as of the stimulation parameters. Similarly, the reinforcing effects of electrical stimulation of the hypothalamus interacts with the internal state of the organism; for example, Hoebel and Teitlebaum (1962) have shown that if the animal is tested after being force-fed, rates of bar pressing for lateral hypothalamic stimulation are substantially lower than when the animal is tested hungry. These types of interactions are not evident in the behavior of an animal standing in the middle of an isolated chamber and would seldom be detected unless looked for, yet they are of critical importance for the interpretation to be given to a treatment effect.

The student should also seriously consider the possibility that "objective" observations are neither totally objective nor impartial and are not representations of reality, but interpretations of reality based on the assumptions and the conceptualizations of the observer. As Brush (1974) has pointed out, recognition of this often comes as a great, disillusioning shock to students, for acceptance of this notion is inconsistent with their view of science and scientists, a view often based on the "professional ideal and public image of scientists as rational, open-minded investigators, proceeding methodically, grounded incontrovertibly in the outcome of controlled experiments, and searching objectively for truth, let the chips fall where they may" (Brush, 1974, p. 1164). This is not to imply that scientists do not try to work objectively or rationally, for without doubt most do. It is to simply suggest that contrary to what is required by the formulation of Flourens, observations are not free from theory and are not made in a theoretical vacuum. What the experimenter looks

for and how he looks for it are determined by his theory, or his assumptions, or his conceptualizations, whether or not he is able to articulate them. Accordingly, inferences about brain function based on alterations in behavior will tend to be in terms of the original (explicit or, more usually, implicit) conceptualizations.

A second reason for questioning the supposition that the functions of different parts of the brain are clearly evident in observations of behavioral change which accompany manipulation of them is based on the fact that behavior and the brain are described functionally in quite different terms. As Oatley points out, the problem arises

. . . from supposing that if the brain is the organ that generates behaviour, then if we can separate behaviour into discrete categories, the brain too must be divisible into parts each separately responsible for one category of behaviour. We can easily see that this is a mistake by thinking about any moderately complicated mechanism with which we are familiar, for instance a motor car. Its behaviour can easily be categorized in various ways, e.g. speediness, hillclimbing ability, noisiness and so forth, or if one prefers less phrenological categories: going forward, going backwards, back-firing, etc. However, none of the functional components of the car is alone responsible for any of the whole car's behavioural attributes. This does not mean that parts of the car have functions which are unconnected with its behaviour. It is simply that the functions of the parts are described in quite different terms, and at what may conveniently be called a lower level. For instance, the distributor applies a voltage to the spark plug of each cylinder in turn so that the mixture of fuel and air is ignited at the correct point in each piston stroke. It is the combined operation of such lower-level functions that makes the whole engine work. We understand the car in terms of how electrical and mechanical components with defined properties interact to produce in various circumstances the whole gamut of motor vehicular behaviour. (Oatley, 1972, pp. 54–55. Reprinted by permission of the publishers, Thames and Hudson of London, England, and E. P. Dutton & Co., Inc. of New York, U.S.A.)

To manipulate the brain and to expect the behavioral changes to indicate the function of the brain requires essentially an assumption of there being a one-to-one correspondence between one's conception of just what the "parts" of the brain are (usually assumed to be the neuroanatomically distinct nuclei and fiber tracts, but recall what Flourens conceived them to be and the implications this had for his technique of ablation) and what categories of behavior or experience are used. This, as will be recalled from Chapter 5, was the basic assumption made by Gall, and it is also the implicit assumption of some contemporary physiologists, clinical neurologists, and physiological psychologists who attempt to assign various psychological or behavioral functions to the brain.

METHODOLOGICAL IMPLICATIONS OF SERIAL AND PARALLEL PROCESSING MODELS OF BRAIN ORGANIZATION

Arising from a consideration of mechanical and/or electronic analogs of brain function, such as that described by Oatley, is a serious criticism of the use of any form of direct neurological manipulation for the study of brain-behavior relations. It is a criticism that warrants careful consideration, first because it suggests that there may be serious limitations to the use of ablation, stimulation, and so on for the study of brain-behavior relations; second, because it leads to a suggestion as to conditions under which it might be possible to in some sense localize function in specific brain structures; and third, because it again points to how conceptualizations dictate methodology.

The criticism can be exemplified with the argument of Gregory (1961) that there would be serious difficulty in attempting to deduce the functioning of an electronic circuit, such as a computer or television, by observing the effects on the circuit output of either "ablating" or removing component parts, or "stimulating" the parts of the circuit with high-voltage probes. If a tube or a resistor is removed from a radio circuit and it is found that the radio begins to howl, it is unlikely that the function of the tube or resistor would be considered in terms of howling. That is, it is unlikely that it would be inferred that the normal function of the tube or resistor is to suppress or inhibit howling. Yet as Gregory points out, this type of inference of some system having the function of inhibiting some other system or behavior is very often encountered in physiological psychology, for example in hypotheses about the inhibitory functions of the hippocampus or the excitatory functions of nuclei in the reticular formation.

The basic reason for the difficulty is that suggested earlier: In any complex serial processing circuit, such as a radio or a television or Oatley's automobile, the output is very dissimilar to the functioning of any of the component parts. It is described in terms different from those likely to be used to describe the function

of the parts, and consequently it is unlikely that removing a part will indicate what the normal functioning of the part really is. (Those who have paid for a television repairman need no reminding of the converse that even when the circuit diagram is known and the principles of operation of each part are understood, it can be very difficult to trace a malfunction given some abnormal output.) Part of this problem is that of distinguishing primary from secondary effects. In a complex circuit, the removal of a particular part does not produce an effect only because the part is absent, but because removal of the part disrupts the normal functioning of other components with which it interacts, and this induced malfunctioning also produces alterations in the output. Consequently, the output alteration of such a system might be due to the primary effects of the treatment and/or to secondary effects due to the alteration of the normal functioning of other parts of the system.

The problem is especially complicated in the case of analyzing behavioral change in biological organisms, for unlike most electronic circuits, they are adaptable and respond to changes in their behavior with other changes in their behavior. Within any syndrome produced, for instance, by a brain ablation, certain changes may be *primary* and independent of others while other changes are *secondary* and are produced by or in response to the primary changes. The relationship between any two behavioral alterations can be conceptualized as being either independent or hierarchical. If they are related in a hierarchical manner, the organism shows a behavioral alteration A because of behavioral alteration B, a direct consequence of the treatment; or conversely, it shows B because of A. (One could also imagine a double hierarchy of mutually reinforcing alterations.) If the alterations are independent, they can be independent in one of at least two ways. Either the lesion or stimulation or other treatment produces the two alterations in behavior quite independently (as might be the case if there were a high degree of localization of function and the lesion invaded two different areas of the brain), or the two behavioral alterations are independent but are both secondary effects due to the treatment producing some underlying primary effect that causes both. For example, if following some treatment an organism shows increased food consumption and increased drinking, the two effects could be produced quite independently by the treatment, or one of the effects, such as increased drinking, might be due to the treatment having the primary effect of increasing food consumption. These various relationships can be diagramed as follows:

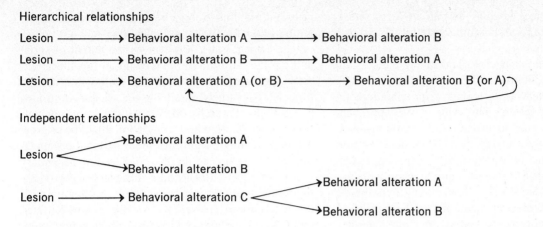

Weiskrantz (1968c) has argued that it is possible, at least theoretically, to establish that behavioral alterations are independent within certain limits. He proposes that this can be done by producing behavioral alteration A by some means other than the original treatment showing that behavioral alteration B does not occur, and conversely showing that the induction of B by some means other than the original treatment does not produce behavioral alteration A. (It is of some interest that this is conceptually similar to the procedures suggested by Gall to demonstrate that two talents or propensities or other striking behaviors were independent and not different manifestations of some faculty; instead of experimentally manipulating one or the other, however, he suggested looking for persons displaying one but not the other attribute or talent.) But Weiskrantz argues that it is logically impossible to establish the existence of a hierarchical relationship, that is, to distinguish between primary and secondary effects.

It should be noted that this problem is simply a special case of the more general problem of inferring causality as raised by the English philosopher David Hume (1711–1776). It was the position of Hume that although two events can be shown to be not causally related, events cannot be shown to be causally related. All that can be shown, according to the argument, is that two events occur in close spatial and/or temporal conjunction, but it cannot be deduced whether this conjunction is derived from one event causing the other (a hierarchical relationship in the previous discussion) or whether the two events are themselves independent but are both caused by some unknown third event (an independent relationship).

These problems, among others, obviously raise serious questions about the utility of any form of direct neurological manipulation in the study of brain-behavior relations. Gregory since has in fact suggested that "to deduce the functioning of a part from

the effect upon the output of removing or stimulating this part we must know at least in general terms how the machine works" (Gregory, 1961, p. 322). Returning to the analogy of the television set, he suggests that to interpret the effects of removing a part, it is necessary first to know the circuit diagram and second to understand the principles of operation of the circuit. Even as forceful an advocate of the use of direct manipulation of the brain in studying brain function as Weiskrantz concedes that "we can make judgments about how some treatments affect the inner workings of the organism only if we already know something about the way they work already" (Weiskrantz, 1968b, p. 401). This is not an assessment that should lead to optimism, but it does point to the necessity of thinking about brain function in terms of what Hebb (1955, 1958) has called a "conceptual nervous system."

A conceptual nervous system, as opposed to the central nervous system, is one that is inferred principally from behavior and that is a specification of how the nervous system might be organized in order to give rise to behavior having certain properties and bearing a certain relationship to other behaviors and to the environment. It is most important to note that a conceptual nervous system is a specification only of how the nervous system *might,* as opposed to must, be organized. This is so, of course, because it is a specification derived from the output of the system, and any given function or output could logically be mediated by any one of a number of different structural configurations. In Chapter 5 it was argued that the physiological psychologist must be a psychologist and must be well versed in the principles of behavior and highly cognizant of problems of diverse areas of psychology. Indeed, this is a prerequisite for the formulation of a conceptual nervous system. The physiological psychologist, however, must also be sophisticated in neurophysiology, neuroanatomy, and the other neurosciences so that he can at least reject alternative conceptual nervous systems which are clearly untenable.

Methods of direct neurological manipulation can perhaps be of utility in testing the adequacy of various conceptual nervous systems as approximations to the real nervous system. The value of this approach is that it forces one to articulate assumptions and allows one easily to modify them if the data are not consistent. It must be emphasized that this approach involves not logical deduction, but working with intuitive hunches and guesses, formulating hypotheses and models of brain organization based on psychological considerations, and testing their implications. Weiskrantz (1968b) maintains that neuroscientists in fact work in this way and has argued that as a consequence, Gregory's (1961) indictment of ablation and stimulation is not as serious as it would be if neuroscientists did attempt to work within a strictly logical framework.

Perhaps more important for the present consideration of the argument against the use of direct neurological manipulation is Weiskrantz's (1968b) argument that the analogy between the brain and a television set or other electronic circuitry is misleading and invalid. First, the basic units of the nervous system, the neurons, are unlike electronic components in that they are digital and either fire or do not fire, and information presumably is encoded and processed partly in terms of frequency and patterning of firing. But since the processes that determine the digital output are the analog processes of excitation and inhibition, Weiskrantz (1968b) is much less skeptical of inferences about excitatory and inhibitory functioning based on dysfunction caused by ablation and stimulation than is Gregory (1961). Indeed, he argues that this type of hypothesis has in fact been most fruitful in the past in generating research.

A second reason for rejecting the electronic circuit analogy is that the mammalian nervous system is the product of multiple stages of evolution, with new sets of components and functional principles being superimposed upon previous sets and thus maintaining the evolutionary history of the nervous system very much intact. In contrast, newer models of electronic devices are not the product of new components being added to old but often consist of entirely new types of integrated designs. In essence, then, Weiskrantz argues that because of its evolutionary development, the brain is not a serial information processor like many electronic circuits, but is organized in a hierarchical manner, allowing for methods of neu-

rological manipulation to be of use in suggesting the nature of the functional organization.

The critical issue, however, is the extent of serial and parallel information processing in this hierarchically organized nervous system. If the information processing is largely parallel in the sense that various levels of the hierarchy operate with relative independence, then ablation and stimulation might be of great use in providing insight into the functional organization of the brain, as there would be few secondary treatment effects. But if there is much serial processing and if the interactions between and among various levels are extensive, then for the reasons outlined by Gregory, methods of direct neurological manipulation may indeed be of questionable value.

How the organization of the nervous system is conceptualized, then, has enormous implications for methodology. If the analogy of the brain and electronic circuits is valid, that is, if the brain acts largely as a serial information processor, even if organized hierarchically, so that information is taken in bit by bit and processed bit by bit by the operation of the entire circuit, Gregory's analysis of the utility of methods of direct neurological manipulation for the study of brain function would seem valid and well founded. Given a conceptualization of the brain that emphasizes the parallel processing aspects of nervous system organization, a conceptualization that treats the brain as being comprised of a number of relatively independent processing units, then even Gregory would probably concede the utility of methods like ablation and stimulation for the study of the nature of these independent units. It is no coincidence that those parts of the nervous system which, through the use of such methods as ablation and stimulation are *apparently* best understood in functional terms at present, are those that seem to act as parallel information processors—the sensory, motor, and certain homeostatic regulatory systems. The problem is that while ablation and stimulation are appropriate for the analysis and dissociation of parallel processing systems, they are simply not tuned for the detection and study of the serial processing aspects of the nervous system, if there are such aspects.

It was previously emphasized that the types of behavioral change looked for after neurological manipulation (as well as the methods of neurological manipulation themselves, as Webster [1973] has pointed out), are greatly influenced by how the functions of the brain and the structure of the brain are conceptualized. A comparison of the position represented by Gregory (1961) with that represented by Weiskrantz (1968b) further suggests that if the organization of the brain with respect to the processing of information relevant to some behavior is serial in nature, such methods as ablation and stimulation are unlikely to be of utility in unraveling questions of brain-behavior relations and functional localization; if it is parallel in nature, however, they may be. One of the important consequences of conceptualizing the nervous system as being a parallel information processing system and then proceeding to study it with methods like ablation and stimulation is that the results of such study will tend to support the validity of the conceptualization and will tend not to provide evidence against it. This is precisely the problem pointed out in Chapter 5 in reference to the methodology of Flourens.

Flourens himself said, "Everything in experimental research depends upon the method, for it is the method which gives the results" (1842, p. 502). An attempt has, however, been made to demonstrate that method is very much influenced by the assumptions and conceptualizations of the experimenter. It is these that determine the conditions under which the dependent variables are assessed and indeed the choice of the dependent variables themselves, and it is these that determine the choice of the independent variables. To the extent that method is dictated by assumptions and conceptualizations, then (to overstate it somewhat) everything in experimental research depends upon assumptions and conceptualizations. It must be emphasized, though, that it is impossible to work without some set of assumptions. This chapter has been an attempt to make evident the importance of explicitly recognizing them and of recognizing the implications for methodology and data interpretation of working within one conceptual framework or another.

14

SELECTED READINGS FOR PART THREE

G. Fritsch and E. Hitzig

ON THE ELECTRICAL EXCITABILITY OF THE CEREBRUM

This is a difficult reading for many students because it was published more than a century ago when equipment, methods, and general philosophical orientation were very different. Perhaps identifying the three quite distinct sections of which it is composed will be of help. The first section outlines the basic procedures that were used to expose the cortex and to apply the electrical stimulation. The second part outlines the major findings of the study, and the types of motor movements observed with variations in stimulation parameters are carefully described. The final part of the paper consists of arguments that the results obtained were due to excitation of the cerebral cortex itself and not to the spread of current to subcortical areas (known

Archiv. f. Wissenschaftliche Medizin, 1870, pp. 300–332. From an edited translation by D. Harris in K. H. Pribram (Ed.), *Brain and Behaviour 2.* London: Penguin Books Ltd., 1969, pp. 353–364. © K. H. Pribram, 1969.

and accepted at the time to be electrically excitable) or to reflex movements.

Although it is a difficult paper, for reasons discussed in Chapter 10 it is worthy of careful consideration as a classic paper in physiological psychology. Editor's footnotes have been added to help clarify various passages; these are indicated by arabic numerals to distinguish them from the original Fritsch and Hitzig footnotes, for which lower case italic letters are used.

[. . .] The starting point of the present investigations were observations one of us had the opportunity to make on human subjects (1), which concerned the first movements of voluntary muscles produced and observed after direct stimulation of the central organs. It was found quite easy to obtain eye movements by leading constant galvanic currents through the posterior part of the head, movements which in their very nature could only have been provoked by direct stimulation of cerebral centres. Inasmuch as these movements occurred only after galvanization of a certain area of the head, as mentioned above, numerous factors suggested that they were caused by stimulation of the corpora quadrigemina or adjacent parts. However, since similar eye movements occurred after galvanization of the temporal region, after application of certain techniques capable of increasing the excitability, the question arose whether in the latter case loops of current penetrating down to the base caused the eye movements or whether the cerebrum possessed after all—contrary to the generally accepted views—a certain electrical excitability.[1]

After preliminary experiments carried out by one of us on rabbits produced a generally positive result, we chose the following method to settle this point:

In the first experiments the animals (dogs) were not narcotized, but later the skull was trephined [2] under narcosis, on an as far as possible plane area. The whole half of the calvaria, or only the part of it covering the anterior lobe of the brain, was then removed by means of cutting bone with forceps with rounded tips.[3] In most cases the procedure was repeated exactly with the other half of the calvaria after one of the hemispheres had been used up. After we had lost a dog by exsanguination due to a slight injury of the longitudinal sinus we left in all cases a median bony bridge intact, which protected the above vessel. Now a slight incision was made in the hitherto untouched dura mater, and the latter was grasped with forceps and removed up to the edges of the bone. During this procedure the dogs showed signs of great pain by cries and characteristic reflex movements. Later, however, after exposure for some time to the stimulating effect of the open air, the dura mater becomes much more sensitive, a fact that must be taken into account in the arrangement of experiments involving stimulation. On the other hand, injury of the pia mater by mechanical and/or other stimuli, evoked no signs of pain.

The electrical apparatus used for stimulation was arranged as follows: [4] The poles of a battery of ten

Daniell cells were led via a commutator to the terminals of a Pohl turnover switch from which the cross had been removed. Wires leading the current of a secondary induction coil ended in the two opposite terminals. Two wires led from the middle pair of terminals to a rheostat included as a shunt, with a resistance of 0–2,100 S.U. The main circuit continued via a du Bois key to two small isolated cylindrical terminals carrying the electrodes in the form of very thin platinum wires ending in small knobs. These platinum wires run through two pieces of cork, the forward of the two pieces being bored so as to obtain two slightly non-parallel channels, as a result of which the distance between the knobs could be easily altered by a small movement of the cork. As a rule, this distance measured 2–3 mm. It was necessary to ensure that the platinum wires moved with only slight mechanical resistance and to provide them with the knobs mentioned above, as otherwise any trembling of the hand or even the respiratory movements of the brain itself could have led to injuries of the soft mass of the central organ.

The battery used by us consisted of tar-paper cells produced by Siemens and Halske, which had—as shown by earlier investigation—less than the full e.m.f. of a Daniell cell and a resistance of 5 S.U. The resistance of the shunt circuit was generally rather low, measuring between 30 and 40 S.U. The current was so weak that touching the tongue with an electrode produced only a slight sensation.[5] Much higher currents and exclusion of the shunt circuit were used only in control experiments. In the much smaller number of experiments in which we used induction currents, the resistance of the shunt circuit naturally depended on the given position of the induction coils. Here too we used for most of the experiments just currents of sufficient strength to cause a slight sensation on the tongue.

Using this method we obtained the following results, presented here as the outcome of a very high number of experiments on the brain of dogs, consistent down to the smallest detail without going into detailed description of each separate experiment. In view of the exact description of the method, and taking into account some factors to be mentioned below, it is in any case so easy to reproduce our experiments that we shall not have to wait very long for their confirmation.

Part of the convexity of the cerebrum in the dog is of motor character (this expression is used in Schiff's sense) and another part of non-motor character.

---

[1] Note the serendipitous origins of this study. It is now known that the eye movements evoked by stimulation across the temporal region were due to activation of the labyrinth, or inner ear, and were not due to activation of more central regions of the brain.

[2] Meaning, a hole was made in the skull.

[3] Similar to the rongeurs used in the laboratory exercises.

[4] Students should not be too concerned with the details of the apparatus since the items discussed are of course not used today. Basically, however, it consisted of a battery that provided DC stimulation through two platinum electrodes (bipolar electrode configuration) which rested on the cortex. Note that in Laboratory Exercise VI, the stimulator is AC and a monopolar electrode configuration is used.

[5] Note that as little as a century ago, galvanometers were not routinely used for calibration purposes.

Generally speaking, the motor part is situated more in the anterior and the non-motor part more in the posterior regions. Electrical stimulation of the motor part can produce combined muscle contractions in the contralateral half of the body.

If very weak currents are used, these muscular contractions can be localized to certain narrowly defined groups of muscles. With stronger currents, stimulation of the same or closely adjacent spots immediately leads to the participation of other muscles, including those of the corresponding half of the body. Using very weak currents, however, the possibility of exciting a well-defined group of muscles is limited to very small spots which may be called centres for the sake of brevity. A very slight shift in the position of the electrode still causes movement in the same extremity, but if initially the stimulus caused extension, for example now, after the change of position flexure or rotation would be evoked. The parts of the cerebral surface lying between the centres were found to produce no response to the method of stimulation used by us if only currents of minimum strength were used. If we increased the distance between the electrodes, however, or if we increased the strength of the applied current, contractions were obtained, but these extended over the whole body in such a manner that it could not be decided even whether they were unilateral or bilateral.

The localization of the centres, discussed in greater detail below, is fairly constant in the dog. Precise establishment of this fact initially caused some difficulties, which could be overcome by first trying to find the spot producing with the smallest effective strength of the current the most marked contraction of the muscle group in question. A pin was then placed in the brain of the still living animal between the two electrodes, and after removal of the brain the various points marked in this manner were compared with the alcohol-fixed preparations from earlier experiments.[6] The high degree of constancy in the position of identical centres appears best of all from the fact that we repeatedly succeeded in finding the desired site in the centre of a single trepanation hole without having to open the skull anywhere else.

After resection of the dura mater the corresponding muscles contracted with the same degree of certainty as if we had uncovered the whole hemisphere. Initially, we encountered somewhat greater difficulties, even when the whole field of operation was uncovered. Although the gyri of the brain are fairly

constant, as is well known, their individual development and their relative position still vary appreciably from case to case. It is almost a rule rather than an exception that even the corresponding gyri of the two hemispheres in one and the same animal are different with regard to various parts. Moreover, in some cases the central part of the convexity is better developed, and in other cases this applies more to the anterior or the posterior parts (2). If one adds the necessity to spare to a considerable extent the brain membranes and the blurring of the picture by the continuously varying structure of the blood vessels which cover the gyri, it is hardly surprising that initially we encountered certain difficulties.

To facilitate even more reproduction of our experiments, we now present exact data concerning the localization of individual motor centres, following the nomenclature recommended by Owen (3).

The centre for the neck muscles (O in Figure 1) is situated in the middle of the prefrontal gyrus where the surface of this gyrus begins to fall steeply downwards. The extreme end of the postfrontal gyrus lies near the end of the frontal fissure (● in Figure 1) the centre for the extensor and adductor muscles of the anterior extremity. A little farther back, nearer the coronal fissure (● in Figure 1), lie the centres governing the flexure and rotation of the limb. The centre for the posterior extremity (△ in Figure 1) is also situated in the postfrontal gyrus, but more in the median direction from the centre, and somewhat more dorsally, for the anterior extremity. The facial part ++ in Figure 1) is innervated from the middle part of the suprasylvian gyrus. The site in question frequently extends over more than 0.5 cm. and extends from the main bend above the sylvian fissure forward and downward.

To this we have to add that we did not always succeed in moving the nuchal muscles from the first of the centres mentioned above. Although we frequently succeeded in causing movements in the back, tail, and abdominal muscles from parts situated between the points enumerated above, we were unable to pinpoint a circumscribed spot from which isolated stimulation of these muscles could be reliably achieved. We found the whole part of the convexity [a] situated behind the facialis centre to be completely refractory, even to currents of disproportionate

---

[6] Note this relatively early use of histological verification of electrode placement.

[a] We deliberately avoid the term lobe, as there are no clear-cut lobes in the dog nor do the formations that might be regarded as lobes fully correspond in their position to human brain lobes; finally, we do not know at all as yet which parts of the canine brain correspond to certain parts of the human brain.

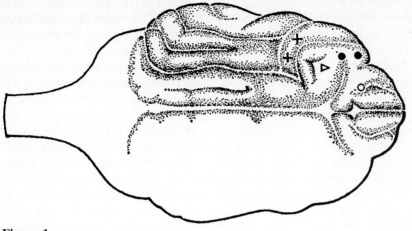

Figure 1.

strength. No muscular contraction could be achieved even if the shunt circuit was excluded, i.e. a current of ten Daniell cells was used.

The character of the contractions produced by stimulation of the motor centres varies depending on the nature of the stimulus. Stimulation by a single metallic closure of the circuit produces only a single quickly transient contraction. If the circuit is not closed in its metallic part but by putting on the electrodes, greater strength of current is required to achieve the same effect. In other words, here too the du Bois Reymond law is valid. All other things being equal, the metallic switch always has a more marked stimulating effect than mere closure of the circuit, but two contractions (the second being for the opening of the circuit) do not arise. Not infrequently, however, the same type of stimulation produced tetanus in the muscle group in question, particularly in the case of the flexor muscles of the toes, although no further stimulation had been applied. If one electrode had exerted its effect, even for a short period, the other electrode would produce a greater effect at the same spot than it would have had before or shortly after.

Although the described facts are fully consistent with our knowledge regarding the properties of the peripheral nerves, we feel obliged, for a reason that will be mentioned below, to call attention to a stimulating factor which does not fit in and which seems highly interesting from the physiological point of view. This factor is the constant predominance of the anode. It even seems that with the minimum strength of current only the anode is capable of evoking contractions.[7] To ascertain this point—primarily because

knowledge of the fact would greatly facilitate the investigation—we carried out and frequently repeated the following experiments:

1. Keeping the two electrodes at the usual distance from each other, we tried to find the spot from which the minimum current evoked contractions, and to be absolutely certain we closed the circuit several times by means of the metallic switch. We then kept the circuit open and reversed the direction of the current, keeping the electrodes in their place, and closed the circuit again. Now no contraction occurred. If we opened the circuit once more, reversed it, and closed it, the stimulating effect was somewhat more marked than on the first occasions. This procedure could be repeated any number of times. If we now moved away one or the other electrode from its site while the circuit was repeatedly closed, the effect of the stimulation remained the same if it was the cathode that had been removed. The anode, however, could not be moved away any distance from the point of stimulation without producing contractions, or else it produced contractions in a different group of muscles.

2. The anode was placed onto the centre for the extensor muscles and the cathode onto the centre of the flexor muscles for the anterior extremity. Closing of the circuit evoked extension, reversion of polarity (with the circuit still closed) produced flexure, and so on. In other words, it was always the centre corresponding to the anode that proved to be stimulated.

In view of recent physiological investigations it

---

[7] Recall that the processes of neuronal depolarization and hyperpolarization were not known at the time and conse-

quently this observation would be very interesting and peculiar. In Laboratory Exercise VI, it was not possible to observe the same thing as an AC stimulator was used and so the electrode alternated 60 times per second between being an anode and being a cathode.

seems rather tempting to relate the above facts to considerations concerning chemical processes participating in the nervous function. However, for the moment we prefer to refrain from doing so. The new facts uncovered in the present investigation are so varied, and their consequences extend in so many directions, that it would be hardly in the interest of the cause to try to follow all the paths requiring thorough further investigation.

To this we have to add that with a slightly prolonged closure of the circuit the greater stimulating effect of reversal of the electrodes also became manifest in the following manner. If we had produced a contraction by putting the anode on a centre and the cathode on a spot known to be indifferent for the current used, and if we continued closure of the circuit for a time, then sometimes opening and subsequent closure of the reversed circuit produced a single contraction: in very rare cases we produced a series of contractions. In other words, after a prolonged action of the anode the substance of the central nervous system reacted for a short time even with a very small current to the cathode as well. This experiment succeeds only if very weak currents are used, particularly because stronger currents immediately destroy the substance by electrolysis.

If tetanizing induction currents are used for the stimulation, the effects achieved are not so constant in their character. Frequently tonic contractions of the muscle groups in question will occur, the intensity of which subsides only after a considerable time. An initial contraction maximum can often be observed, followed by such considerable relaxation—even if the action of the current lasted only for a second—that one could consider the contraction to be completely gone were it not for a slight movement in the direction of the subsiding contraction occurring at the moment the circuit is opened. The individual features of the experimental animal—its greater or lesser excitability—seem to be in a causal relation to these differences, as well as to some other phenomena that will be mentioned below.

Thus, continuous use of stronger currents causes symptoms of exhaustion: such as the need for stronger currents to achieve the same effects, as well as complete absence of contractions. In these cases sanguineous suffusion of the cortical substance can frequently be observed. In other cases, however, particularly after application of weak currents, a number of phenomena can be observed which must be interpreted in the opposite sense.

It has been reported (4) that opening of a circuit tetanizing the spinal cord of frogs caused subsequent movements in all muscles of the body. This fact seems to have been forgotten, as otherwise the defenders of the view that the spinal cord possessed excitability could have used it as an argument.

Similar facts can be observed after tetanization of the brain substance. Even a stimulation of only a few seconds' duration is followed by after-movements in the dependent musculature. These movements are clearly of tremor character in the facialis region. In the extremities the picture rather resembles clonic convulsions. The above differences depend apparently on the different types of muscle insertions. These local fits of convulsions may reoccur even if the brain is not stimulated any more. In some cases fits of convulsions also occurred after maltreatment of the brain substance by closing of the circuit, but as a rule such fits were not observed after stimulation with these currents. In two of our experimental animals these after-movements developed into well-defined epileptic fits. The fits began in one half of the body, with contractions in the previously stimulated musculature, but later spread to all muscles of the body leading to a complete extensor tetanus. During the fit the pupils were maximally dilated. One of these animals had two and the other three fits. It could be argued that the dogs may have been epileptic before the experiment, but one of them had been with one and the same mistress for six years without ever having suffered from convulsions. The antecedents of the second dog remained unknown.

We shall now try to counter the arguments which could be raised against our experiments.

The first argument, always raised by experts [b] and by the not so expert in relation to experiments with electrical stimulation is based on the assumption that the current may reach more distant parts of the brain.[8] Disregarding the question whether the cortical or the medullar substance of the cerebrum is excitable, this argument is easier to answer than any other. The currents used by us in the experiments in question were very weak, the brain substance has a very high electric resistance, there are no other conducting parts in the vicinity, and finally, the distance between

[b] It may be of interest that the great number of doctors to whom our experiments were demonstrated included several specialists highly competent in the field, such as Prof. Nasse (Marburg) and Munk (Berlin).

[8] Recall that it was not accepted that the cerebral cortex was electrically excitable and consequently the onus was on Fritsch and Hitzig to demonstrate that the effects they observed were due to cortical excitation and not to a spread of current to regions of the nervous system which were accepted as being excitable—specifically, the peripheral nerves and subcortical areas of the brain.

the electrodes was small, so that according to the laws of distribution of currents in nonprismatic conductors the current density could only be minimal even at a very small distance from the point of entry. This alone would be sufficient to counter *a priori* the argument in question. We have, moreover, a whole series of direct further proofs in our favour. If one assumed that the current first of all reached the peripheral nerves, the nerves on the same half of the body would always have been nearer, there would be no reason for the currents to reach exclusively the nerves of the contralateral half of the body. Furthermore, the oculomotor nerves of the same side were much nearer to the source of current than any other nerve in question. The bulbus formation, always balanced in a state of labile equilibrium, would constitute an excellent physiological rheoscope without any preliminary preparation, and would be much more likely to move when touched, even by a very small current, than an anterior extremity let alone a posterior extremity. The whole convexity, however, as far as it can be uncovered, does not contain a single point from which movement of the bulbus can be evoked, even with currents stronger than those usually employed by us. This argument would settle part of the question which induced one of us to take up the present investigation. Finally, we quote one more fact of considerable physiological and pathological interest. The excitability of the brain decreases rapidly when the animal is bled and is extinguished almost completely prior to the animal's death. Immediately after death the excitability is completely lost, even against the strongest currents, whereas the muscles and nerves still react perfectly. This fact apparently makes it necessary to carry out experiments regarding the excitability of the central nervous system with unimpaired circulation.

The second argument is that even if the current failed to reach the peripheral nerves or the spinal cord to which latter the same counter arguments would apply as to the former, it might reach regions of the brain other than the cerebral hemispheres. If this was the case, demonstration of electrical excitability in other parts of the brain would still represent an important discovery. Even experts in the field still maintain in general that not all parts of the brain are susceptible to direct stimulation. This, however, is not the case, as can be shown with regard to electrical stimulation. The parts which have been at all accepted as being excitable, though only by a few authors, are the posterior part (cauda) of the corpus striatum, the thalamus opticus, the crus cerebri, the corpora quadrigemina, and the pons. Disregarding for

the moment the corpus striatum, all other morphologic parts of the brain quoted above are situated so far backward that they are only intersected by frontal sections through the more posterior parts of the brain, which do not react. The only exception is the corpus striatum although the cauda of this formation is also situated in the non-excitable zone.[c] It would therefore be possible that it was just the anterior or middle part of this ganglion—allegedly a non-excitable part— which proved excitable and was the source of our stimulation effects. This latter view seems *a priori* improbable, as despite the unchanged strength of the current the contractions ceased as soon as the electrodes were shifted by a few millimetres. If we were to draw straight lines through the two assumed points of entry and also through a third point situated in the corpus striatum vertically under the line connecting the two points, we would obtain an equilateral triangle the equal sides of which would represent pathways offering the smallest resistance to the current. As the resistance would be necessarily identical in both pathways, all other things being equal, the stimulating effect should be the same, but this was not the case.

Not content with these *a priori* proofs, however convincing these might be, we also made attempts to provide direct evidence. To this purpose we provided Carlsbad-type insect pins with a dense insulating cover by dipping them repeatedly into a solution of guttapercha in chloroform.[9] Only the tip and the head of the pin retained their conducting properties. No trace of contractions was obtained when these pins were stuck into the posterior part of the cerebrum even if the currents used were very much stronger, until the rheophores had penetrated to a depth of several centimetres and touched the crura cerebri. At that moment the animal jumped violently and displayed general muscular convulsions. The results were quite different if the anterior part of the cerebrum was stimulated in the same manner. If we were to assume that current reaching the corpus striatum had provoked the observed contractions after superficial stimulation, one would simply expect intensification of the contractions in step with the penetration of the electrodes. But this was not the case; instead, the convulsions extended to quite different groups of muscles and generally behaved in a different manner, which we are not going to discuss in greater detail at this point. It follows with great certainty that

[c] We call 'non-excitable'—without prejudice—all those areas from which we were unable to elicit contractions.

[9] Note this early use of an insulated electrode (made from an insect pin) for subcortical stimulation.

neither the above-mentioned ganglion nor the formations constituting the brain stem took part in the contractions evoked from the convexity.

Another counter-argument that could be raised (as had been the case in all previous successful experiments concerning stimulation of the central nervous system—spinal cord, brain stem) is that the contractions came about on a reflex basis. This argument, too, can be answered by the following convincing proof:

Reflexes could have been elicited via the nerves in the dura mater and the pia mater, as we were protected against stimulation of adjacent nerves in the calvaria by wide uncovering of the brain surface. Besides, the partly freed bulk of the temporal muscles was lying at one edge of the wound. These structures, which presumably retained their excitability, would have immediately indicated even weak current. So far, however, nobody has demonstrated or even assumed the presence of sensory fibres in the cerebrum itself. Moreover, the complete insensitivity of the latter substance does not give the slightest indication of this kind.

As far as the dura mater is concerned, we have said above that it has a certain sensitivity even under physiological conditions, a sensitivity which increases rapidly after opening of the skull. For this reason it is advisable to operate very quickly as otherwise the experimental animal, however tightly it may be strapped in, performs violent jumps and makes it very difficult to preserve the brain substance during removal of the dura membrane. Once the dura has been removed up to the edges of the bones, however, one is sufficiently protected against reflexes from the dura nerves. We made sure of this fact in a variety of ways. First of all our stimulation experiments elicited crossed contractions, whereas reflexes always appear on the same side (Pflueger). Secondly, the reflexes ceased after a slight shift in the position of the electrodes, although the distance from the remaining parts of the dura had not been altered. Thirdly, the reflexes ceased even when the electrodes were applied nearer to the dura, provided we did not hit upon motor centres. If the latter condition was observed we did not even obtain contractions when the electrodes were applied very close to the dura but still on the brain substance. If we touched the dura itself, frequently even in the absence of electrical current and always with electrical stimulation, extremely violent and highly characteristic reflex movements could be observed. However, these were completely different from our usual stimulation effects. First of all, these movements always appeared to be purpose-ful. The head was thrown back, the back muscles contracted, and the animal cried and whimpered, even when narcotized with morphine; the extremities moved only rarely. Quite a different picture was obtained in our stimulation experiments. Here frequently even non-narcotized animals were lying still, indifferently, while we caused movements in an anterior or in a posterior extremity by applying electrical stimuli.[10]

The pia mater cannot be removed in a similar manner by preparation; on the contrary, it has to be dealt with as carefully as possible. Injury to any one of its innumerable abundantly filled blood vessels can cover the whole field of operation with blood, and can cause failure of the whole experiment, when the animal has been sacrificed in vain. This, however, does not invalidate our evidence showing that the pia does not take part in the provocation of our stimulatory effects. In addition to all the arguments already enumerated during the discussion of the dura mater, the following evidence will be more than sufficient. Similarly to Longet et al. (5), we found that the pia mater was insensitive. We excised the pia over a motor centre, sparing the large vessels, without any change in the effect of stimulation. Even if the pia was removed from such a site, the contractions never failed to appear. If we stabbed the brain substance with needles the muscles would still contract if this had been done within a motor area, but under all these conditions no contraction would occur if we went beyond the posterior border of the motor sphere in question. It might be of interest to add that neither morphine nor ether narcosis had any appreciable effect on the success of the experiments.

Finally, the question will arise why so many earlier authors, including some of the most illustrious ones, had come to the opposite conclusion. To this we have only one answer: 'It is the method that brings the results.'[11] Our predecessors could not have uncovered the whole convexity, as otherwise they would have been bound to obtain contractions. The posterior lateral wall of the skullcap in dogs, under which there are no motor parts, is highly suitable because of its formation for the application of the first trepanation hole. The earlier authors presumably started the operation at that spot and failed to proceed further, breaking away more anterior parts of the skullcap, erroneously assuming that the various areas of

---

[10] The difference in effect between stimulation of the dura mater and stimulation of the cortex will be especially apparent in Laboratory Exercise VI in terms of both the laterality and the intensity of movements.

[11] Note this allusion to Flourens.

the brain surface were equivalent. This belief was based on the assumption, discussed in the initial part of this paper [not included in this excerpt] and still generally held, according to which all parts of the cerebral cortex took part in all psychic functions.[12] If the idea of a possible localized character of the psychic functions had arisen at all, the apparent failure of certain parts of the substrate to react to stimulation would have been regarded as an obvious fact, only to be expected, and the authors concerned would not have failed to investigate all parts of that substrate. After all, it can be safely stated that none of the earlier workers assumed that the stimuli used by us were capable of producing psychic conceptions or

[12] This assumption had, of course, its origin with Flourens, whose influence was still strongly felt at the time.

of bringing about the manifestation of already evoked conceptions in the animal under vivisection. [. . .]

References

1. Hitzig, 'On the galvanic vertigo and a new method of galvanic excitation of the eye muscles', *Berl. Klin. Wochenschrift*, vol. 11 (1870).
2. Reichert, *Der Bau des Menschl. Gehirns* (The structure of the human brain), Leipzig, 1861, p. 77.
3. Owen, *On the Anatomy of Vertebrates,* London, 1868, vol. 3, p. 118.
4. R. Wagner, *Handworterb. d. Physiol.,* vol. 3, p. 15 [Date not known but probably *c.* 1860.]
5. Longet *et al., Anatomie et Physiologie du Systéme Nerveux de l'Homme et des Animaux Vertébrés* (Anatomy and physiology of the nervous system in man and other vertebrates); Paris 1842, vol. 1.

E. S. Valenstein, V. C. Cox, and J. W. Kakolewski

MODIFICATION OF MOTIVATED BEHAVIOR ELICITED BY ELECTRICAL STIMULATION OF THE HYPOTHALAMUS

Electrical stimulation of various regions of the brain, including the lateral nucleus of the hypothalamus, has a rewarding or reinforcing effect in that an animal will work to receive stimulation. Continuous stimulation also elicits behavioral activities such as feeding or drinking or gnawing. These are referred to as stimulus-bound behaviors because they can be elicited even when the animal is fully satiated. Until quite recently, it was believed that the behavior elicited by stimulation was almost exclusively a function of the stimulation parameters, and the interpretation of this was that the stimulation somehow aroused a natural drive state in the organism. This paper, however, casts serious doubt on that interpretation and on the model of neural centers mediating drive states that is implicit in it. It demonstrates that there is a considerable degree of plasticity in that the elicited stimulus-bound behavior is not just a function of stimulation parameters. This finding is very similar to those reviewed by Hoebel (1969) showing that different behaviors can be elicited with constant stimulation parameters as a function of there

From *Science,* 1968, **159**, 1119–1121. Reprinted with permission of E. S. Valenstein and the American Association for the Advancement of Science. Copyright © 1968 by the American Association for the Advancement of Science.

being the opportunity for the animal to perform them. Stimulation of the lateral hypothalamus elicits not only the behaviors described in this paper, but running behavior if a running wheel is provided (Rosenquist and Hoebel, 1968). It is findings like these that make the interpretation of brain stimulation effects most ambiguous.

ABSTRACT: *Previous reports demonstrated that hypothalamic stimulation may elicit either eating, drinking, or gnawing and emphasized both the specificity of the neural circuits mediating these behaviors and the similarity to behavior during natural-drive states such as hunger and thirst. We find that, after a period of very consistent elicitation of one of these behaviors, the animal may exhibit an equally consistent alternate behavior. A learning component is implicated in the association of hypothalamic stimulation with a particular behavior pattern.*

Hypothalamic stimulation in the rat may elicit behaviors such as eating, drinking, and gnawing (*1, 2*); previous reports have emphasized both specificity of the neural structures activated and similarity of the behavior to that occurring during natural-drive states. As satiated animals exhibit the behavior only during the period of stimulation, the term "stimulus-bound" behavior has been applied. From the fact that animals that exhibit such behavior will perform some learned task (instrumental behavior) to obtain a relevant goal, it has been concluded that the stimulation does not trigger a stereotyped motor act, but activates a motivational state such as hunger or thirst.

We studied the development of "stimulus-bound" behavior and the possibility of modifying the elicited behavior in the absence of any change in stimulation site or stimulation parameters. Our results indicate that there is a learning component involved in the association of hypothalamic stimulation with such behavior as eating, drinking, or gnawing. Hence, we question those theoretical positions based on the conclusion that electrical (and perhaps chemical) stimulation activates fixed neural circuits mediating natural-drive states.

Bipolar electrodes (3) were implanted in the lateral hypothalamus of mature Holtzman albino rats of both sexes. With the dorsal surface of the skull level between bregma and lambda, the electrodes were positioned 2.50 to 3.50 mm posterior to bregma, 1.25 to 1.50 mm lateral, and 8.25 to 8.50 mm below the top of the skull (4). Animals were stimulated with either 30-second trains of 60-cycle sine waves or biphasic rectangular pulses (frequency, 100 pulses per second; pulse duration, 0.2 msec). The stimulus parameters used with each animal are provided in Table 1. All stimulation was programmed by automatic equipment and was not delivered under the experimenter's control.

After surgery but before any stimulation, the animals were placed individually in Plexiglas cages which served as living quarters and testing chambers. Light in the room was on from 7:00 a.m. to 7:00 p.m. each day. The cages contained three goal objects: pellets (Purina Lab Chow), a water bottle with a metal drinking tube, and a pine wedge mounted either on the wire-mesh floor or one of the walls. During preliminary screening to determine an appropriate stimulus intensity, animals were stimulated for a 30-second period followed by a 60-second interstimulus interval. The intensity was adjusted until the stimulus elicited a forward-moving "searching" behavior. If, after a period of time, the animal did not exhibit either eating, drinking, or gnawing in response to stimulation, the intensity was raised or lowered to what appeared to be a more promising level. If no specific behavior pattern emerged, the animal was stimulated throughout the night for 30 seconds every 5 minutes (night schedule). If no "stimulus-bound" behavior was evident, the sequence was repeated dur-

ing at least one additional night before the animal was rejected. With this procedure, approximately 25 percent of the animals exhibited "stimulus-bound" eating, drinking, or gnawing on the pine wedges.

The animals that exhibited "stimulus-bound" behavior were then given a series of three standard tests (30 minutes in duration, with twenty 30-second stimulation periods, each separated by a 60-second interstimulus period). There was a minimum of 30 minutes between each test. During these tests, the three goal objects were present. After this first series of tests, the goal object to which the rat oriented was removed, and the animal was left overnight with the other two goal objects and stimulated on the night schedule. If, for example, the rat exhibited "stimulus-bound" drinking during the first series of tests, the water bottle was removed during the night, and only the wood and food pellets were left in the cage. *The stimulus parameters remained unchanged.* If the animal did not exhibit a new "stimulus-bound" behavior, it was stimulated additionally on consecutive nights. In most cases, however, one night was sufficient time for a new behavior to emerge, although for animals 60S and 89S several nights were necessary. In general, the earlier the onset of the first behavior during the preliminary stimulation sessions and the more consistently this behavior was displayed, the sooner the animal switched to a second behavior pattern when the first goal object was removed. Animals were then given two additional standard tests with the initial goal object still absent. Finally, the animals were given a competition test with all three goal objects present. Prior to all tests, animals were provided with an opportunity to satiate themselves on food and water.

Eating and drinking were scored only when there was clear evidence of consuming the food or water (Table 1). The food pellets were held with the front paws, and pieces were bitten off; the drinking tube was lapped, and the animal could be observed ingesting the water. Gnawing consisted of biting off pieces of wood from the wedge. In most cases, the animal began the "stimulus-bound" behavior within 1 to 2 seconds after the onset of the stimulus and stopped abruptly after its termination. The duration of the "stimulus-bound" behavior was variable. In a number of instances, the animal ate, drank, or gnawed for the entire 30-second stimulation period, and in a few cases the behavior was observed for only a 5-second period. Only in rare instances was any scoreable behavior observed during the interstimulus period. Table 1 illustrates that the "stimulus-bound" behavior

Table 1 Eating (E), drinking (D), and gnawing (G) behavior elicited during hypothalamic stimulation. Each test had 20 stimulation periods. Maximum score for any one behavior is 20, but the animal could exhibit different behaviors during each period. The dash (—) in the second series of tests indicates which goal object had been removed. RP, rectangular pulses; SW, sine wave. All animals except 80S were males.

ANIMAL	BEHAVIOR	TEST SERIES					COMPE-TITION	STIMULUS PARAME-TERS (μA)
		FIRST SERIES			SECOND SERIES			
		1	2	3	1	2		
	E	0	0	0	15	17	11	RP, 80
60S	D	20	20	20	—	—	14	RP, 80
	G	0	0	0	0	0	0	RP, 80
	E	0	0	0	20	20	15	RP, 120
61S	D	20	20	20	—	—	12	RP, 120
	G	0	0	0	0	0	0	RP, 120
	E	0	0	0	0	0	0	RP, 500
63S	D	0	0	0	20	20	12	RP, 500
	G	20	20	20	—	—	8	RP, 500
	E	0	0	0	20	20	12	SW, 20
74S	D	20	20	20	—	—	13	SW, 20
	G	0	0	0	0	0	0	SW, 20
	E	19	16	12	—	—	10	RP, 120
80S	D	1	5	8	19	16	10	RP, 120
	G	0	0	0	2	2	6	RP, 120
	E	0	0	0	18	20	16	SW, 24
89S	D	19	19	20	—	—	4	SW, 24
	G	0	0	0	0	0	0	SW, 24

during the first series of tests was exhibited consistently with almost every stimulus presentation. The second series was administered after the animal spent a variable amount of time receiving stimulation without the first goal object present. In most cases the second "stimulus-bound" behavior was exhibited as consistently as the first behavior (Table 1). During the competition test, when all three goal objects were present, approximately equal amounts of the two "stimulus-bound" behavior patterns were displayed in most instances, although the second behavior—eating—dominated the behavior of 89S during the competition test. In the case of 80S (an animal that exhibited two behaviors initially), a third behavior pattern—gnawing—was observed during the second series of tests and the competition test. This animal had been placed on the night schedule for two consecutive nights with only wood and water present. In addition to eating, drinking, and gnawing, other behavior was observed to be elicited by the stimulation in some animals; for example, 80S frequently positioned itself in one part of the cage, and with the onset of stimulation a specific path was traversed on the way to the drinking bottle.

There were no cases of "stimulus-bound" behavior which could not be switched to another behavior with the stimulus parameters held constant. We cannot be certain that such a case might not exist, but, in addition to the data in Table 1, there were a number of instances in which there were "spontaneous" switches from one "stimulus-bound" behavior to another. For example, an animal that might exhibit "stimulus-bound" gnawing approximately 50 percent of the time might switch to drinking with approximately the same consistency. We regard these cases of "spontaneous" switching as additional evidence of the lack of specificity of the behavior evoked by electrical stimulation. This conclusion is also supported by animal 80S, as well as others that did not complete the test series, which exhibited more than one behavior from the beginning of stimulation.

In stressing the lack of specificity between a given behavior pattern and lateral hypothalamic stimulation, we are not advancing a position of neural equipotentiality. We were not able to evoke either eating, drinking, or gnawing from a number of lateral hypothalamic sites. Furthermore, in several animals in which electrodes were placed in somewhat different lateral hypothalamic sites on the left and right side, the animal exhibited "stimulus-bound" behavior only when stimulated on one of the sides.

It might be argued that all the animals used in our experiment were special cases in which stimulation activated simultaneously the neural circuits mediating two motivational systems. We disagree for several reasons. We did not select the animals, and we studied all that exhibited any "stimulus-bound" behavior. Only one of the animals exhibited more than one behavior pattern before our effort to modify their responses. Of the animals exhibiting only one behavior initially, those that displayed the most vigorous pattern (judged by the brief latency, long duration during stimulation, and great consistency) required the least amount of training for a second pattern to emerge.

As far as we could determine, most investigators of "stimulus-bound" behavior focused on a specific behavior. As a result, the animals received either or both special training or limited opportunity to display different patterns. Those few instances in which an animal was given a brief "competitive" test with another goal object present usually followed an extensive amount of opportunity to display the initial behavior pattern. We found that the more opportunity an animal has to exhibit a specific "stimulus-bound" behavior, the longer it may take for a new pattern to emerge.

A number of experiments demonstrated that animals exhibiting "stimulus-bound" eating, drinking, or gnawing have much in common with animals under the influence of natural drives such as those induced by deprivation. Animals will work to obtain appropriate goal objects and appear willing to tolerate aversive stimulation, such as shock or quinine additives, in order to obtain the desired objects (2). However, the fact that in our experiment animals that were "stimulus-bound" drinkers appear just as motivated to obtain food, for example, raises the question of whether thirst and hunger motives are involved at all (5). Apparently, there is considerably more plas-

ticity in establishing connections between hypothalamic circuits and motivated behavior than commonly advanced interpretations of "stimulus-bound" behavior suggest.

References and notes

1. E. E. Coons, thesis, Yale University (1964), (microfilm obtainable from University Microfilms, Inc., Ann Arbor, Mich., order 64–13, 166); ———, M. Levak, N. E. Miller, *Science* **150,** 1320 (1965); L. Fantl and H. Schuckman, *Physiol. Behav.* **2,** 355 (1967); M. A. Greer, *Proc. Soc. Exp. Biol. Med.* **89,** 59 (1955); J. Mendelson, *Science* **157,** 1077 (1967); ——— and S. L. Chorover, *ibid.* **149,** 559 (1965); N. E. Miller, *Fed. Proc.* **19,** 846 (1960); P. J. Morgane, *Nature* **191,** 672 (1961); G. J. Mogenson and J. A. F. Stevenson, *Physiol. Behav.* **1,** 251 (1966); ———, *Exp. Neurol.* **17,** 119 (1967); W. W. Roberts and R. J. Carey, *J. Comp. Physiol. Psychol.* **59,** 317 (1965); E. A. Steinbaum and N. E. Miller, *Amer. J. Physiol.* **208,** 1 (1965).
2. P. J. Morgane, *Science* **133,** 887 (1961); *Amer. J. Physiol.* **201,** 838 (1961); S. S. Tenen and N. E. Miller, *J. Comp. Physiol. Psychol.* **58,** 55 (1964).
3. E. S. Valenstein, W. Hodos, L. Stein, *Amer. J. Psychol.* **74,** 125 (1961).
4. The electrode tips were located in neural sites previously reported to yield "stimulus-bound" behavior. The electrode tips of animals 60S and 61S were located in the zona incerta dorsal to the fornix, and the electrode tips of animals 74S, 80S, and 89S were located in the dorsal part of the lateral hypothalamus. No histology is available for 63S due to dislodgement of its electrode pedestal.
5. Animals that were switched from "stimulus-bound" drinkers to "stimulus-bound" eaters have been observed to eat the dry pellets in the absence of water almost to the point where they appeared to be choking.
6. Supported by NIH grants M–4529, career scientist award MH–4947, and research grant NsG–437 from NASA. We thank Laura Lande and Debra Singer for assistance.

part four

ELECTRO-PHYSIOLOGICAL RECORDING

15

BASICS OF BIOELECTRICAL AMPLIFICATION AND RECORDING

A familiarity with basic principles of electricity and electronics has become imperative for the contemporary student of physiological psychology. Most physiological measures are electrical in nature, reflecting the fact that most physiological processes are accompanied by electrical changes. Even those measures that are not necessarily electrical (such as certain measures of blood flow or blood pressure) usually involve electronic equipment in their measurement. Furthermore, most behavioral testing situations can be made more efficient or more reliable through the use of simple electronic circuits involving timers, switches, and relays. Some knowledge of the elements of electricity is necessary for understanding this important aspect of psychotechnology.

Although this chapter lays the theoretical groundwork for Laboratory Exercise VIII (Chapter 16) involving the operation of the oscilloscope, the student should note that that laboratory exercise can be done quite successfully without a thorough understanding of principles of electronic amplification or recording. In fact, all that is necessary is that the student know that an oscilloscope is a device that allows one to draw a graph of voltage with respect to time. Instead of the drawing being on paper, it is on a tube (similar to a television screen); since the drawing "pen" is free of inertia, it can accurately record very rapid fluctuations in voltage.

BASIC CONCEPTS OF ELECTRICITY

There are four concepts basic to an understanding of electricity and electrical forces. First is the concept of an electric charge, which is a fundamental property of electrons. The student is referred to any introductory chemistry or physics textbook for a detailed discussion of atomic structure, but suffice it to say here that according to the Bohr model of the atom, a positively charged nucleus consisting of protons and neutrons is conceptualized as being surrounded by negatively charged electrons. These charges have an electrical field associated with them through which the charges interact with and influence each other. Like charges repel one another and unlike charges attract one another. In an electrical circuit such as that diagramed in Figure 15–1, the force exerted between charges and the tendency for electrons to move through the circuit is referred to as the potential difference or voltage. It is to be emphasized that voltage refers to a difference between two points, and it is not meaningful to talk about the voltage at a single point unless there is some implied referent.

When electrons move in response to the electric field forces, we refer to this movement per unit time as current, the usual unit of measure of which is the ampere, or amp. Finally, resistance (or its reciprocal, conductance) refers to the ease with which the charges can move or the ease with which the current can flow, and is measured in terms of ohms. The three concepts of potential difference, current, and resistance are interrelated through Ohm's law, which states that in a closed electrical circuit, such as that in Figure 15–1, the flow of current through the circuit (measured in amperes) is directly proportional to the voltage (in volts) and inversely proportional to the resistance (in ohms), or $I = E/R$. The greater the voltage (E), the greater the current flow (I); the greater the resistance (R), the less the current flow. If any two of these variables are known, the third can be easily determined.

It is sometimes useful to conceptualize the relationships among voltage, current, and resistance in terms of a hydraulic model, as illustrated in Figure 15–2. The water pressure at any point is a function of the height of the water above that point, and this would be analogous to the voltage or potential difference of an electrical circuit. Note that the water pressure, like voltage, is a difference between two points. The flow of water per unit time through the faucets is analogous to the flow of current, and the resistance of the system resulting from such physical constraints as the diameter of the pipes and the viscosity of the fluid is analogous to electrical resistance. Within this model then, given a constant pressure P, the water flowing from each faucet depends on the resistance of each faucet; given a constant resistance, the flow of water per unit time depends on the pressure.

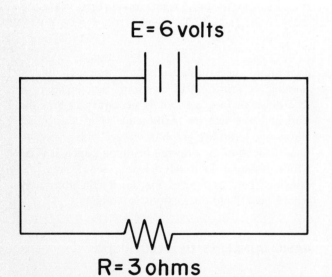

Figure 15–1. A simple electrical circuit consisting of a power source E (in this case a 6-volt battery) and some source of resistance, R (such as a light bulb). The current flow, I, through such a circuit is directly proportional to the voltage and inversely proportional to the resistance (i.e., $I = E/R$).

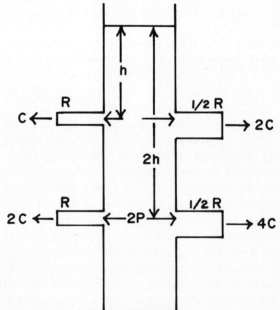

Figure 15–2. A hydraulic model of electrical circuits. P: Pressure (analogous to voltage), a function of the height of the water, h. R: Resistance to water flow (analogous to electrical resistance). C: Quantity of water per unit time (analogous to current). (Adapted from J. E. Skinner, *Neuroscience: A laboratory manual.* Philadelphia: Saunders, 1971, Figure 4–1.)

PRINCIPLES OF ELECTRONIC AMPLIFICATION

In the study of biological systems we are often interested in the variations in electrical activity that accompany certain physiological processes and events. For example, accompanying the beating of the heart are electrical changes associated with cardiac muscle contractions. These are of sufficient magnitude to be detectable through electrodes placed on either side of the body across the heart. Usually it is fluctuations in voltage that are measured rather than fluctuations in current or resistance, in part because voltage is relatively easy to measure and in part because changes in voltage seem meaningfully to reflect physiological changes. In contrast to the voltages of common batteries and electrical power lines, however, the magnitude of the voltage fluctuations in physiological preparations is typically very small, in the order of microvolts or millivolts; in order to detect, record, and measure them, it is necessary first to amplify them.

An amplifier is an electronic device, the heart of which is a vacuum tube or transistor, and the output of which is a magnified version of the input. The ideal amplifier produces no distortion, so that the output is identical with the input, but greater. Although vacuum tubes are seldom used in contemporary amplifiers, the basic principles of electronic amplification can be easily understood by considering their construction and operation. Figure 15–3 illustrates a typical triode vacuum tube. It consists

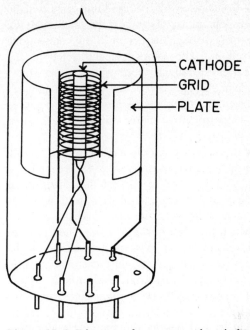

Figure 15–3. Diagram of a vacuum tube triode. The flow of electrons from the cathode to the plate is modulated by the charge applied to the grid.

of three parts (hence the name, *tri*ode): cathode, plate, and grid. When heated, the cathode emits negatively charged electrons. If the cathode is connected to the negative terminal of a battery and the plate is connected to the positive terminal of the battery as shown in Figure 15–4, there will be an

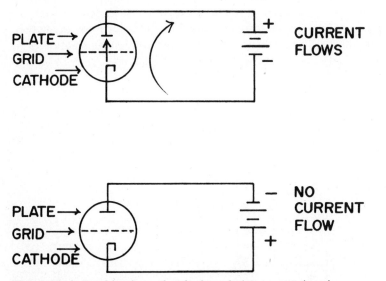

Figure 15–4. Combinations of cathode and plate connections in an electrical circuit. When the grid is not connected, the triode acts as a diode limiting current flow to one direction.

excess of electrons at the cathode and they will be attracted to the plate. Consequently, there will be current flowing through the circuit. If the connections are reversed and the cathode is connected to the positive battery terminal, there will be few excess electrons available and those that are available will not be attracted to the plate (as it now has a negative charge). Consequently, there will be no flow of current.

A tube that consists of only a cathode and a plate (which is all we have considered so far) is called a diode and can be used to control the direction of flow of current. A triode includes the grid, which is a screen located between the plate and the cathode through which the electrons must pass. The extent to which the electrons can pass is a function of the charge applied to the grid. When there is no charge, electrons can pass freely from the cathode to the plate, but as the grid becomes increasingly negative the flow of electrons is reduced because the electrons are repelled by it. Consider the simple amplification circuit illustrated in Figure 15–5. Normally the power supply on the input side of the amplifier biases the grid negatively so that electrons are repelled from it; hence there is little flow of electrons from the cathode through the grid to the plate and minimal current flow through the output side of the circuit. If a negative voltage is applied to the lead connected to the grid, the grid biasing will become more negative and there will be even less current than before flowing through the cathode-plate circuit; if a positive voltage is applied to the input lead, there will be a decrease in the negative biasing and more current will flow through the cathode-plate circuit. Since the grid is close to the cathode, very small changes in the input voltage can produce large changes in the flow of current through the cathode-plate circuit. In an ideal amplifier, changes in the flow of current through the output circuit are linearly related to changes in the degree of biasing and so the output is the same as the input in all respects except, of course, amplitude.

Most amplifiers now use transistors rather than tubes. They have advantages of cost, size, durability, and life span. Their use also obviates the necessity for the high-voltage power supplies necessary to heat the tube cathode. A transistor consists of three pieces of semiconductor material sandwiched together (Figure 15–6). A voltage applied to the center piece, the base, controls or modulates the flow of current through the base between the outer two pieces, the emitter and the collector. As with the tube, a small voltage applied to the base controls the flow of a much larger current in the emitter-collector circuit and so again there is amplification. The analogy between the transistor and the triode can be seen clearly in a comparison of Figure 15–5 with Figure 15–7. In the case of the triode, the flow of current in the cathode-plate circuit is governed by the charge applied to the grid; in the transistor, the flow of current in the emitter-collector circuit is governed by the charge applied to the base. But note there is only an analogy: the principles of operation of the two types of amplification devices are totally different.

There are severe limitations on the extent to which signals can be amplified in any simple amplification circuit like those illustrated in Figures 15–5 and 15–7, because the linear relationship between the output of an amplifier and its input extends over only a restricted range of input and output values. Consequently, amplifiers are often cascaded so that the output from one amplifier forms the input to another. This allows for very large amplification ratios to be achieved without a loss in linearity.

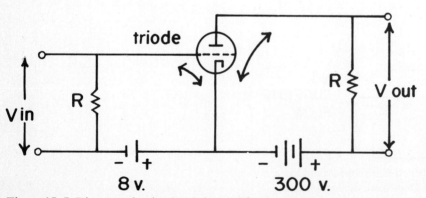

Figure 15–5. Diagram of a simple triode amplification circuit.

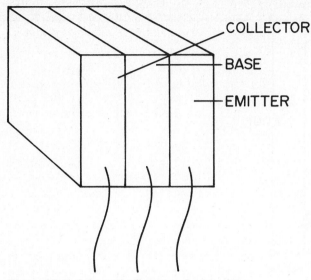

Figure 15–6. Schematic diagram of a transistor.

DIFFERENTIAL AMPLIFICATION AND FILTERING

A special type of amplifier commonly encountered in physiological psychology is the differential or push-pull amplifier, so called because it amplifies the difference between two signals. Basically it consists of two matched amplification circuits, as illustrated in Figure 15–8. The input in one lead with respect to ground is amplified in one circuit and the input in the other lead with respect to ground is amplified in a matched circuit. The outputs then converge. When the amplified signals in the two circuits are the same, they cancel out. The final output is only the *difference* between the two amplified signals. The adequacy of this type of amplification system clearly depends upon there being a perfect match between the two halves of the system. This type of amplifier is commonly used because one of its features allows the blocking of unwanted signals. When measuring low-level signals, the two leads will sometimes pick up much stronger biological signals, such as those from the heart. If the signals are amplified with a differential amplifier the extraneous signals picked up by the two leads are blocked or canceled out, leaving only the signal of interest. Similarly, extraneous nonbiological electrical interference can be reduced. The environment is saturated with electrical interference coming from power wires, generators, elevator motors, and so on, and when recording low-level biological signals involving high-gain amplification, the input leads often act as antennae picking up this electrical noise. By using a differential amplifier, the noise can be reduced because the interference will be picked up equally on both leads and canceled out. This subtraction process is illustrated in Figure 15–9. The degree to which unwanted signals are rejected or

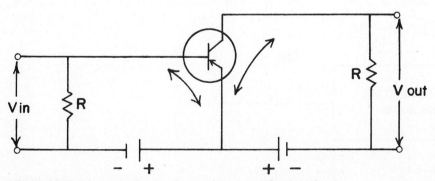

Figure 15–7. Diagram of a simple transistor amplification circuit.

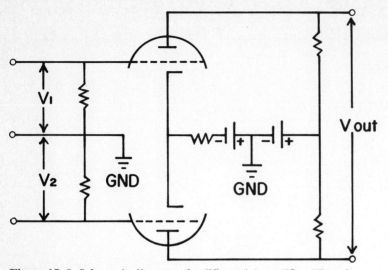

Figure 15–8. Schematic diagram of a differential amplifier. The tube that is half open indicates a dual triode, that is, a triode tube with matched cathodes, grids, and plates.

canceled is referred to as the common mode rejection ratio.

Two other common methods of reducing electrical interference should be noted. The first involves the use of an electronic filter, which is a circuit comprised of a capacitor and a resistor connected in a particular way and placed between the input leads and the first amplification stage. The particular values of the capacitor and the resistor determine the upper or lower signal frequency that can pass unattenuated into the amplifier circuit. Figure 15–10(a) is a circuit diagram of a low-pass filter, one that allows signals of low frequency to pass through but that blocks or filters high-frequency signals. Figure 15–10(b) is a circuit diagram of the converse, a high-pass filter that allows high-frequency signals to pass but blocks or filters low-frequency signals. The reason for this differential filtering effect is beyond the scope of this discussion, but its importance should be evident. For instance, if recording an electro-encephalogram (Chapters 17 and 18) having signals of interest in the frequency range of from 2 to 30 Hz (that is, signals recurring at a frequency of from 2 to 30 times per second), it is possible to select values of R and C for a low-pass filter so that signals with a frequency of greater than 30 Hz will be filtered or blocked, hence reducing the amount of 60 Hz interference. Note that filters are not absolute; they do not eliminate all signals above or below a frequency but simply *attenuate* signals above or below it. Consequently, the ratio of the amplitude of the signals of interest to the amplitude of the background or irrelevant noise is increased.

A second method of reducing irrelevant signals is through the use of a Faraday cage. If the preparation is completely enclosed in a wire-mesh cage connected to a ground, electrical interference impinging upon the cage will follow the path of least resistance and be conducted to ground rather than passing through the cage to be picked up by the recording electrodes.

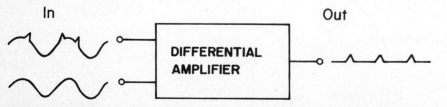

Figure 15–9. Diagram illustrating the effect of the operation of a differential amplifier. The noise common to both input leads is blocked, leaving only the signal. Input and output signals are with respect to ground (not shown).

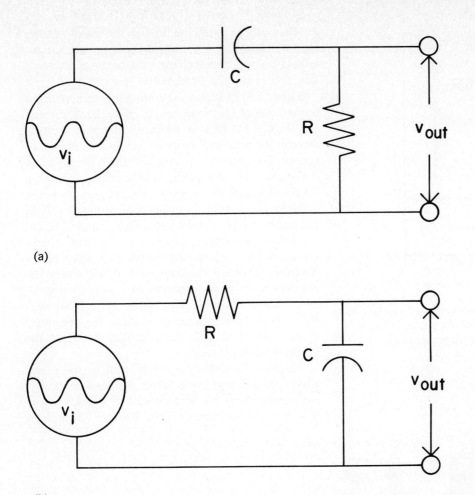

(a)

(b)

Figure 15–10. Schematic diagrams of (a) a high-pass filter and (b) a low-pass filter.

RECORDING AMPLIFIED SIGNALS

Electrical shielding is still commonly used in conjunction with filters and/or differential amplifiers to attenuate unwanted noise and will be used in the laboratory exercises.

The final stage of the amplification process involves increasing the power of the signals so they can drive or activate recording and measurement devices. One type of recording system makes use of a galvanometer or pen-writing device. The output from the signal amplifier is fed into a "power amplifier," the output of which has sufficient power to drive a rotating coil on which a pen is mounted (Figure 15–11). The extent to which the coil turns and consequently moves the pen back and forth is a function of the amplitude of the amplified signal and hence reflects the characteristics of the input signal. Knowing the "gain" or the amount of amplification of the system, the size of the input signal can be easily determined given any particular amount of pen deflection. As the pen moves back and forth, a continuous sheet of paper moves beneath it at a constant speed, leaving a permanent record of voltage changes with respect to time. Most pen-writing systems are polygraphs with multiple amplification channels and associated output recording pens that allow for a comparison to be made of several simultaneously occurring signals. This is one of the great strengths of this type of system. One of the major problems, however, is that of frequency response, since the pens, having a finite mass, have inertia and cannot move or respond fast enough to keep up with the high-frequency components of certain biological signals. This particular

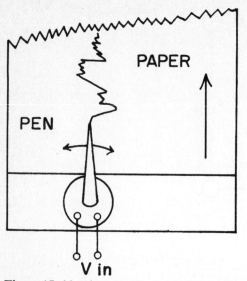

Figure 15–11. Diagram of a pen-writing coil and moving paper. The extent to which the pen is deflected is a function of the input voltage. Paper speed can be varied.

problem can be overcome through the use of another type of recording and measurement device, the oscilloscope, which makes use of a beam of electrons that acts essentially as an inertia-free pen.

Figure 15–12 shows the front panel of an oscilloscope commonly encountered in research laboratories and Figure 15–13 is a schematic diagram showing some of the principal components found in all oscilloscopes. The cathode ray tube, of which the screen is the visible part, has at the rear a cathode that is a source of negatively charged electrons (similar to the cathode of a triode previously described). These electrons can be accelerated, aimed, and shot toward the front screen, which is coated with a substance that will cause phosphorescence when hit by electrons. Between the cathode and the screen the electron beam passes between two pairs of electromagnetically charged plates. When there is an electromagnetic field between two plates, the negatively charged beam of electrons is deflected toward the positively charged plate.

The vertical deflection plates, that is, the plates which when charged will deflect the beam vertically, are connected to the signal amplifier in such a way that the electromagnetic field between them is a

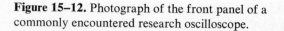

Figure 15–12. Photograph of the front panel of a commonly encountered research oscilloscope.

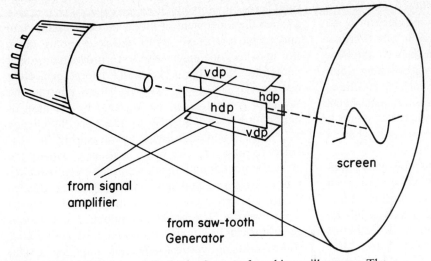

Figure 15–13. Diagram of the basic elements found in oscilloscopes. The electron beam from the cathode is deflected by the horizontal deflection plates (hdp) and the vertical deflection plates (vdp).

function of the amplifier output. Hence, the extent to which the electron beam is deflected vertically as it passes between these plates is directly proportional to the input signal (assuming good linear amplification). Consequently, the vertical deflection of the spot of light on the screen is proportional to the input voltage, and again, knowing the gain of the signal amplifier, the size of the input signal can be determined given some vertical deflection.

The horizontal deflection plates allow for changes in the input voltage to be related to time. These plates are connected to an electronic circuit called a *sawtooth generator,* the output from which is diagramed in Figure 15–14. This output is connected to the horizontal deflection plates so that the electromagnetic field between them changes continuously a constant amount with respect to time. This in turn causes the beam of light to move horizontally from left to right across the screen with respect to time. When the beam has reached the far right side of the screen, a "blanking" circuit is activated that turns off the electron beam while the sawtooth generator returns to its initial voltage, and then the entire process repeats itself. The beam of light is therefore seen to move only one way across the screen.

All oscilloscopes have controls for the brightness and the focusing of the electron beam on the screen and most have a means of controlling the illumination of the ruled calibration markings on the screen. There is usually also a device that generates electronic pulses of some known amplitude which can be fed into the oscilloscope amplifiers for calibration purposes.

Many oscilloscopes, like that shown in Figure 15–12, have two completely separate amplifiers so that two signals can be recorded simultaneously. In *dual-beam* oscilloscopes, there are also two completely separate sources of electrons, two completely separate sets of vertical deflection plates and hence two completely separate beams. Usually, however, there is a common set of horizontal deflection plates,

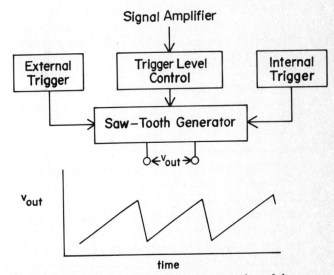

Figure 15–14. Modes of triggering the operation of the sawtooth generator and a schematic representation of the output of the generator with respect to time.

which means that the two beams are related with respect to time. In *dual-trace* oscilloscopes, the two separate amplifiers share access to the electron beam according to a time-sharing principle; the vertical deflection plates alternate between the two amplifier channels at a very high frequency (switching times in the order of nanoseconds are usual), and so there appear to be two separate beams. A dual-beam oscilloscope will have two separate sets of controls for beam intensity, focus, and astigmatism, whereas a dual-trace oscilloscope has only one set.

Regardless of the type of oscilloscope, each channel has a completely separate amplifier. For each channel there is a control for specifying the "gain" of the amplifier or the magnitude of voltage in the input signal that will produce a vertical deflection of the electron beam of 1 division on the screen. For example, if the amplifier is set at 0.5 volts per division, there will be a deflection in the beam of one screen division for each half-volt of signal applied to the input terminals. Associated with each vertical amplifier is a control for moving the beam of light up or down in the vertical direction (which is achieved by applying a constant bias to the deflection plates, upon which the amplified signal is superimposed), so that the two beams can be positioned not to interfere with or overlap one another.

As pointed out previously, the horizontal movement of the beam results from the output of a sawtooth generator being applied to the horizontal deflection plates. For some purposes it is desirable to have the beam move slowly, but for others it is desirable to have it move quickly. The speed can be varied by changing the frequency of the generator. The controls for this usually are calibrated in terms of time per distance rather than the more usual way of specifying speed, that is, distance per time. At first this may seem confusing, but it does have advantages. In many physiological applications, the duration of a waveform or the frequency of waveforms (for example, the duration of a heartbeat or an action potential or the frequency of heartbeats or action potentials) are to be measured. If the horizontal amplifier is set at 25 msec/cm and if the waveform fills 2 cm of the screen, then the duration of the waveform is clearly and easily calculated to be 50 msec. However, if the speed were to be specified as 40 cm/sec (which is the same as 25 msec/cm), the difficulty encountered in rapid calculation of duration is obvious.

An extremely important feature of the horizontal amplifier is the triggering circuit. If the sawtooth generator is left to run freely at some frequency, the beam will continue to move repeatedly from left to right across the screen. Often, however, it is desirable to start the movement of the beam at a specific time and to have it move across the screen only once. For instance, one might wish to record visual evoked potentials (Chapter 17) in the lateral geniculate nucleus. By using the external trigger control, the sawtooth generator can be triggered by the flash of light so it becomes possible to determine the latency of evoked potential activity by measuring the distance from where the beam started to where the evoked potential first appears on the screen. Another type of triggering that can be done with most oscilloscopes allows for the close examination of a repetitive waveform. The horizontal amplifier or sawtooth generator can be connected through a triggering level control with the vertical deflection amplifier in such a way that whenever the output from the vertical deflection amplifier reaches some critical voltage, the sawtooth generator is activated and the beam moves across the screen. In examining a repetitive waveform like heartbeat, the sweep generator can be activated at the same point of each heartbeat and successive heartbeats will appear at the same place on the screen and will be superimposed one on another.

A major disadvantage of the oscilloscope for many purposes is the difficulty in obtaining a permanent record of the trace. One way is through the use of a storage oscilloscope and a camera. The trace can be "stored" on the screen by an internal electronic circuit that keeps the screen in a state of continued phosphorescence, allowing a photograph to be taken. Then the trace is "erased" and the process repeated. For many purposes, a Kymograph camera, which uses photographic paper rather than film, gives very satisfactory results at reasonable cost. The camera is focused on the screen, and the shutter is opened while the beam moves across the screen. The light intensity of the beam, but not the ambient illumination from the screen, is sufficient to expose the paper. By exposing the paper to several sweeps of a repetitive waveform, or to several successive evoked potentials, the multiple traces allow for an estimation to be made of the "stability" of the electrical activity (see the Fox and Rudell reading in Chapter 19 for an example).

An increasingly common method for storing bioelectric potentials is magnetic tape. The problem has been that many physiological potentials are made up largely of low-frequency components and most tape recorders respond poorly to low-frequency signals. Tape recorders designed to respond to such signals (frequency modulation, or FM, recorders) are extremely expensive (typically several thousands of dollars). Fortunately, it is now possible to connect the signal amplifier output to a high-frequency audio oscillator so that the output frequency of the oscillator is a function of the amplitude of the physiological signal. This audio output frequency can be recorded very well on a conventional high quality tape recorder. As will be discussed more fully in Chapter 17, the storage of signals on tape allows for long-term storage of records, the examination of records long after the recording is completed, and most important, for electronic frequency analysis of the signals.

16 LABORATORY EXERCISE VIII

THE OPERATION OF AN OSCILLOSCOPE AND THE RECORDING OF BIOELECTRICAL POTENTIALS

Chapter 15 described the oscilloscope as an electronic device that gives a visual representation of the difference in voltage between two points and that allows one to measure changes in voltage with respect to time. That chapter was largely concerned with the principles of operation of the instrument; this laboratory exercise is concerned with learning how to operate an oscilloscope. That knowledge will then be applied in recording the heart rate of an anesthetized rat before and after an injection of atropine sulfate. It is suggested that before coming to the lab, you read carefully section B of this chapter, which outlines some of the basic anatomy, physiology, and pharmacology of the autonomic nervous system so you will have some idea how atropine affects the heart.

Throughout this lab, bear in mind that despite what may be the threatening appearance of an oscilloscope, its operation is basically very straightforward. Furthermore, apart from having the intensity of the electron beam so high that it burns the phosphorescent substance on the screen, it is virtually impossible to damage an oscilloscope by turning knobs (this is not true of polygraphs). So be adventurous in turning the control knobs so you can acquire a good familiarity with the instrument.

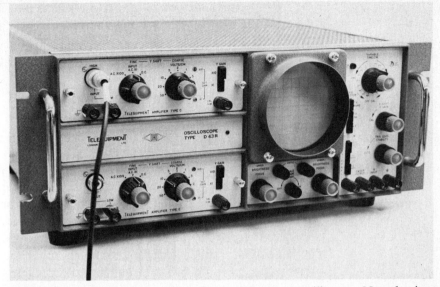

Figure 16–1. A standard type of inexpensive laboratory oscilloscope. Note that it was designed for rack mounting and so must be raised from the table surface to allow air to circulate through it to cool the tubes. The two vertical deflection amplifiers are on the left and the horizontal amplifier is on the right. The display controls are located beneath the oscilloscope screen.

A. THE OPERATION OF THE OSCILLOSCOPE [1]

Figure 16–1 shows a basic type of oscilloscope. The difference between this piece of equipment and that shown in Figure 15–12 is largely due to the fact that this one is meant to be mounted on a rack, but it can be used on a table so long as sufficient ventilation is provided. Any oscilloscope consists basically of the three parts indicated in Figure 16–1.

1. The vertical deflection amplifiers. On most models there are two amplifiers located above or beside one another, and the controls for these can be identified by their VOLTS/CM designation. These amplify the input signals being fed into the oscilloscope either directly or through a preamplifier (to be considered in Laboratory Exercise IX). It is the output from each amplifier that is projected onto the screen in the form of a spot of light deflected vertically, the amount of vertical deflection being a function of the voltage applied to the input terminals. If the oscilloscope you are using is dual beam or dual trace, there will be two beams of light or two traces, one from each amplifier, when the oscilloscope is in operation.
2. The horizontal amplifier. The controls for this can be identified by the TIME/CM designation and are concerned with the movement of the beams of light across the oscilloscope screen. This movement is cali-

---

[1] These instructions are sufficiently general to apply to the operation of most types of relatively inexpensive oscilloscopes suitable for teaching laboratory purposes, as well as many of the more sophisticated oscilloscopes encountered in research laboratories.

brated with respect to time. Closely related to this is the circuit involved in the triggering of the horizontal movement of the beams.

3. The oscilloscope tube and display controls. The brightness and the focus of the beams are controlled independently of the horizontal and vertical amplifiers. These controls are typically located in close proximity to the oscilloscope screen.

Operation

The tubes of the oscilloscope are often cooled by convection: Air enters the bottom of the case, is drawn up past the tubes and other hot components, and passes out through the slots in the top. If you are using a rack-mounted oscilloscope resting on a counter top, *under no circumstances should it be operated with the air flow obstructed*. The oscilloscope must be raised from the table with rubber stoppers or some other support. Cabinet-mounted oscilloscopes pose no problem and are designed for use resting on counter tops.

In describing the use of the oscilloscope, front panel controls and sockets will be indicated in SMALL CAPS.

Before turning on the oscilloscope, set the front panel controls as follows, keeping in mind that there are two vertical amplifiers and hence two sets of vertical amplifier controls. Note that on the model of the oscilloscope you have, many of the knobs and controls may be dual knobs that are color-coded; if so, labels of each color refer to the part of the knob similarly colored.

On each vertical amplifier:

INPUT SWITCH	Set to DC
VOLTS/CM or SENSITIVITY	0.5 volts/cm
Y GAIN (if there is one)	switch to x1
Y SHIFT or POSITION or ↕	Midposition

Display controls (one set for each amplifier if a dual-beam oscilloscope):

FOCUS	Set in midposition
ASTIG	Set in midposition
BRIGHTNESS or INTENSITY	Full anticlockwise

On the horizontal amplifier:

TIME/CM or TIME/DIV	Set to 20 MSEC
VARIABLE	Full clockwise
TRIG SELECTOR	Set to Y1 + or UPPER AC +
TRIG LEVEL	Anticlockwise position just before switch operation
STABILITY (if there is one)	Fully clockwise
X SHIFT or HORIZONTAL DISPLAY POSITION or ↔	Midposition
X GAIN or SWEEP MAGNIFICATION	Fully anticlockwise

Plug in, rotate the POWER switch to the ON position, and allow a few minutes for the instrument to warm up. (Note that further rotation of the POWER switch will increase the graticule illumination.)

Advance the BRIGHTNESS or INTENSITY control until a trace appears. If none appears after the control has been turned about halfway, use the x SHIFT (horizontal) and Y SHIFT (vertical) controls to find the beam that is aimed either too high, too low, or too much to one side or the other. Adjust the ASTIG and FOCUS controls in conjunction with one another for a well-defined trace. If you are using a dual-beam oscilloscope, be sure to focus each beam with the appropriate controls.

Now back off the STABILITY control (if there is one, otherwise the TRIG LEVEL control) until the sweep just fails to run free. This is the normal position for this control. Once set, it should not require further readjustment except at the very highest sweep speeds. The instrument is now ready for use.

Triggering

The triggering circuits of the oscilloscope are used to begin the movement of the beam across the screen at specific times. The triggering can be a function of (1) some specific input to the oscilloscope, (2) some event occurring in one or the other vertical amplifier circuit (for example, some specific voltage being exceeded), or (3) simply time.

If the TRIG LEVEL control is turned fully anticlockwise to operate the AUTO switch, the trace will reappear. In this condition the instrument is ready to accept almost any input waveform and will automatically be triggered by it. The following procedures will demonstrate the use of the remaining controls:

Return the TRIG LEVEL control anticlockwise to the position just before the switch operates. There should now be no trace visible on the screen. Take a connector wire and plug one end into the CAL or CAL OUT terminal and the other end into the INPUT socket of the upper vertical amplifier. For calibration purposes, the oscilloscope has built into it a waveform generator that produces waves which are approximately square in shape, have an amplitude of 1 volt from peak to peak, and have a frequency of 60 cycles per second.[2] The output from this is the CAL or CAL OUT terminal. Since the amplification of the oscilloscope is set at 0.5 volts/cm, the square wave will show on the screen as being 2 cm peak to peak (0.5 volts/cm $\times$ 2 cm $= 1$ volt). You should find that 6 cycles of this waveform occupy 5 cm or 5 divisions of the screen.

Using the Y SHIFT or POSITION control of the lower amplifier, either raise or lower the lower beam so it no longer appears on the screen. Using the Y SHIFT or POSITION control of the upper amplifier, roughly center the square waves on the screen.

Focus and astigmatism

By adjusting the FOCUS control for the upper channel, either the horizontal or vertical edge of the square wave can be brought into focus, but only if the

[2] Oscilloscopes differ with respect to calibration waveform characteristics, and the following comments may be modified by your instructor to suit the characteristics of your particular oscilloscope.

ASTIG control is correctly adjusted will it be possible to focus the whole of the waveform simultaneously. Once the ASTIG control is set, it should require no further adjustment, and a well-defined trace will be obtained over the whole of the screen.

Calibrated sweep speed controls

Since the square waves are being generated at 60 cycles per second, 1 cycle will take 16.66 milliseconds. The TIME/CM switch controls the speed at which the beam of light moves. With the TIME/CM switch set to 10 msec and the VARIABLE control fully clockwise, the speed is 10 msec per cm of screen, so that one cycle should occupy 1.66 cm and hence 3 cycles should occupy 5 cm.

Note: The speed calibrations apply only when the VARIABLE control is in the fully clockwise position, which is the position in which it should be left.

Sweep controls

The TRIG LEVEL control is used to set the precise part of the slope of the input waveform at which the sweep is triggered. The use of this control can be demonstrated as follows:

Set the TIME/CM switch to 5 msec; this will result in each cycle of the square wave being 3.33 cm long. Now rotate the TRIG LEVEL control. It will be found that the starting point of the trace can be moved up and down the sloping edge of the square wave (note that this square wave is not really square but is more trapezoidal). If the control is turned too far clockwise, this point rises above the top of the square wave and the sweep stops. Similarly, rotation too far anticlockwise produces the same effect.

This facility is useful for displaying complex repetitive waveforms when a normal type of sweep generator will either fail to trigger the sweep or cause double trigger action, producing a multiple pattern. Its usefulness will become evident when we record heartbeat. It may also be used as an amplitude discriminator, so that signals of small amplitude are ignored and the sweep is triggered only when the input voltage reaches a predetermined value. Positive or negative going edges may be selected by using the TRIG SELECTOR switch.

Adjust the sweep speed controls. Note that the starting point of the sweep is not affected but that the trace is expanded or contracted from the starting point. Thus, a section of the trace can be examined by setting the TRIG LEVEL control so that the sweep is triggered just in advance of the portion of interest and then expanding this portion as required by means of increasing the sweep speed.

When the TRIG LEVEL control is set to AUTO, no control over the trigger level is available and the sweep automatically adjusts itself to trigger at the mean level of the input waveform.

The Y1 and Y2 (or UPPER and LOWER) indicators of the TRIG SELECTION control which the Y amplifier will be connected to the triggering circuit and hence which of the two input signals will trigger the sweep. If it is set for Y1, signals in the upper amplifier trigger the sweep; if set for Y2, signals in the lower amplifier do the triggering. Note that if you are using the upper (Y1) channel to record, be sure the TRIG SELECTION is set for Y1 (or UPPER AC).

As mentioned in the previous laboratory exercise, we sometimes want to trigger the sweep with an external source signal, and for that the TRIG SELECTION switch is set for EXT and an input signal goes to the EXT TRIG terminal socket. If we are stimulating and recording simultaneously from the brain, we can use this facility to trigger the sweep every time we stimulate, and only when we stimulate.

X Gain (or sweep magnification) and X shift (or horizontal position)

Not all oscilloscopes have an X GAIN or SWEEP MAGNIFICATION facility, but this expands the length of the trace from one to several screen diameters. All oscilloscopes do, however, have an X SHIFT or HORIZONTAL POSITION control which is used to position the trace on the screen so that it starts at the first of the ruled lines on the screen.

If the oscilloscope you have has an X GAIN or SWEEP MAGNIFICATION control, center one of the square waves around the center vertical grid marking using the X SHIFT. Note that the actual length of the sweep and the width of the wave remain unchanged. Now, rotate the X GAIN control and the square wave will expand symmetrically around the central vertical marking. This allows one to closely examine a complex waveform. Compare this with expanding the trace using the sweep speed controls, that is, increasing the speed at which the beam moves across the screen. Now return the X SHIFT and X GAIN controls to their normal positions.

Vertical deflection amplifier

The VOLTS/CM or SENSITIVITY switch is a multiple-position switch that allows one to select the gain or amount of amplification of the amplifier. The calibrations simply indicate the number of centimeters the beam will be deflected for every volt of potential difference. If it is set for 10 volts/cm, a 5-volt potential difference would cause a beam deflection of ½ cm; if it is set for 0.1 volts/cm, a 5-volt potential difference would cause a beam deflection of 50 cm (of course the screen is only 8 or 10 cm and so the deflection would be right off the screen). Some oscilloscopes have preset controls, adjacent to the VOLTS/CM control, that enable the gain to be multiplied or divided by 10 (x10 or x1). Normally, this should be set for x1.

The DC/AC switch should normally be used in the AC position, in which a blocking capacitor removes the DC component of the input signal to the vertical deflection amplifier. The DC position is also used if it is specifically desired to include the DC component of the input waveform to be measured. In the case of the square wave input, we want the flat DC component. Turn the switch to AC and note that the calibration waveform acquires a tilt which results from the system attempting to block out this DC component.

Review the instructions at least once, making sure you know what each control does, which controls you will have to be normally switching

(VOLTS/CM, TRIG LEVEL, and TIME/CM), and which do not need any readjustment.

B. A SKETCH OF THE EFFECTS OF PHARMACOLOGICAL AGENTS ON AUTONOMIC NERVOUS SYSTEM ACTIVITY

Section C of this laboratory exercise involves using the oscilloscope to record heart contractions and to measure the heart rate in an anesthetized rat. The heart is one of the organs innervated by the autonomic nervous system and changes in heart rate can be produced by a variety of pharmacological means. One of these is the administration of atropine sulfate. After the heart rate has been recorded, atropine will be injected and changes in the rate examined. This section outlines the basic structure, function, and pharmacology of the autonomic nervous system, necessary for understanding the nature of autonomic nervous system innervation of the heart and of the effects of atropine on heart rate.

In very general terms, the autonomic nervous system regulates the activities of what have been classically regarded as nonvoluntary and vegetative functions of the body such as blood pressure, gastrointestinal secretions and motility, body temperature, urinary output, and sweating. The system is innervated from areas of the spinal cord and brainstem and those parts of the hypothalamus associated with the regulatory systems of the body governing homeostatic and emotional responses. It can be divided into two components that differ anatomically and physiologically: a sympathetic component and a parasympathetic component.

Organization of sympathetic and parasympathetic systems

The sympathetic system is composed in part of two chains of sympathetic ganglia,[3] one of which runs along each side of the spinal cord outside the vertebral column. These are innervated by sympathetic motor neurons located in the spinal gray matter whose axons pass through the spinal nerves arising from all twelve thoracic segments and from the upper two of the five lumbar segments (Figure 16–2). In contrast to the skeletal motor neurons, which go directly from the spinal cord to the neuromuscular junction of the organ of innervation, the sympathetic motor neurons synapse immediately outside the spinal cord in the sympathetic ganglia. The organs are then innervated by postganglionic fibers having their cell bodies in the ganglia. About 10 percent of the spinal nerve fibers are postganglionic fibers that return from the ganglia via the gray ramus to the spinal nerves and innervate the sweat glands and peripheral blood vessels. It is interesting to note that a few of the preganglionic fibers do not in fact leave the spinal nerve but synapse with postganglionic neurons right in the spinal nerve itself. A very important part of the sympathetic system is the medulla of the adrenal gland, to which preganglionic fibers pass directly through the splanchnic

---

[3] A ganglion in the peripheral nervous system is somewhat analogous to a nucleus in the central nervous system.

nerve. These fibers end on cells in the medulla that are analogous to post-ganglionic neurons and that, when stimulated, secrete epinephrine and norepinephrine. These substances have an excitatory effect on sympathetic effector organs, and hence sympathetic arousal can be mediated through this humoral mechanism as well as through the stimulation of sympathetic fibers.

The parasympathetic system (Figure 16–2) is composed of fibers originating in certain of the cranial nerves and in the second and third of the five sacral spinal nerves. More than 80 percent of the parasympathetic activation, though, is mediated through the Xth cranial nerve, the vagus nerve, which contains fibers innervating the heart, lungs, esophagus, stomach, small intestine, colon, liver, gall bladder, pancreas, and upper portion of the ureters. The parasympathetic component of the IIIrd cranial nerve (the oculomotor nerve) innervates the ciliary muscles and pupillary sphincter of the eye; that of the VIIth cranial nerve (the facial nerve) innervates the lacrimal, nasal, and submaxillary glands; and that of the IXth cranial nerve (the glossopharyngeal nerve) innervates the parotid gland. The sacral spinal nerve component innervates the descending colon, the rectum, the bladder, the lower portions of the ureters, and the external genitalia.

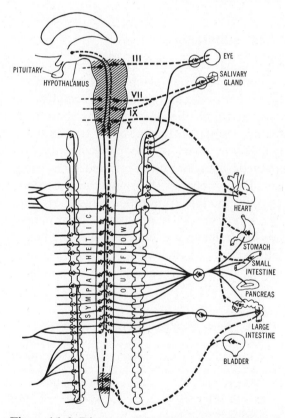

Figure 16–2. Diagram of the general organization of the autonomic nervous system. Sympathetic projections are indicated with solid lines, parasympathetic projections with broken lines. Autonomic fibers to the head and trunk are shown on the right side. Sympathetic fibers to the blood vessels, sweat glands, and smooth muscle fibers are shown on the left side. (From E. Gardner, *Fundamentals of neurology* (5th ed.). Philadelphia: Saunders, 1969, Figure 130.)

Both the sympathetic and parasympathetic systems are composed of pre- and postganglionic fibers, but there is a major anatomical difference between the systems in terms of the relative length of these fibers. In the sympathetic system the preganglionic fibers are relatively short, synapsing in the sympathetic ganglia, while the postganglionic fibers are long, having their cell bodies in the sympathetic ganglia and their terminations in distant effector organs. In contrast, the preganglionic fibers of the parasympathetic system are typically long, passing directly to the organ of innervation. The postganglionic cells and fibers are located in the wall of the organ of innervation and of course are relatively short.

Table 16–1 shows some of the effects of sympathetic and parasympathetic stimulation on various autonomic organs. Sympathetic stimulation has excitatory effects on some organs and inhibitory effects on others, as does parasympathetic stimulation. In some organs the innervation is reciprocal in that stimulation by one component is excitatory while stimulation by the other is inhibitory, although most organs are controlled dominantly by one system or the other. In the case of the heart, the organ of interest in this laboratory exercise, there is reciprocal innervation in that sympathetic stimulation increases its activity, making it a more effective pump, whereas parasympathetic stimulation decreases activity.

Transmitter substances

A major functional difference between the two components of the autonomic nervous system is in terms of chemical transmitter substances. In common with skeletal neuromuscular junctions, acetylcholine is the transmitter substance associated with the preganglionic fibers in both the sympathetic and parasympathetic systems. It is also the transmitter substance associated with the postganglionic fibers of the parasympathetic system. For this reason, parasympathetic fibers are often referred to as being *cholinergic*. In contrast, the postganglionic fibers of the sympathetic component have norepinephrine (noradrenalin) as the transmitter substance, and these fibers are often referred to as *adrenergic*. Stimulation of the parasympathetic postganglionic fibers leads to a release of acetylcholine at the neuron terminals, and this has a stimulating effect on the effector organ. Stimulation of the sympathetic postganglionic fibers leads to a release of norepinephrine, but interestingly,

Table 16–1 Effects of autonomic stimulation upon selected organs of the body

ORGAN	SYMPATHETIC STIMULATION	PARASYMPATHETIC STIMULATION
Eye (pupil)	Dilation	Constriction
Salivary and gastric glands	No important effect	Enzyme-rich secretions
Sweat glands	Copious sweating	No effect
Heart	Increased rate	Decreased rate
Lungs (bronchi)	Dilation	Constriction
Liver	Glucose released	None
Kidney	Decreased output	None
Ureter	Inhibited	Excited
Adrenal cortical secretion	Increased	None

this may be mediated through the release of a minute quantity of acetylcholine. That is, stimulation of the postganglionic fibers results in the release of a very small quantity of acetylcholine, and it is this that causes the release of the much larger quantity of norepinephrine. These transmitter substances are destroyed by enzymes, cholinesterase in the case of acetylcholine and *o*-methyl-transferase in the case of norepinephrine, although much norepinephrine is reabsorbed into the nerve endings rather than being destroyed.

Pharmacological manipulations and autonomic activation

Many pharmacological substances either mimic or block the effects of autonomic arousal. Injected into the body, norepinephrine and epinephrine act directly upon sympathetic effector organs and produce effects very similar to sympathetic arousal. In fact, during sympathetic arousal, large quantities of these substances are normally released into the blood supply from the adrenal medulla, which maintains and augments the neural sympathetic arousal. Other drugs that stimulate the sympathetic adrenergic effector organs (at A_s in Figure 16–3) are phenylephrine and methoximine. There are also substances (such as amphetamine, ephedrine, and tyramine) that have sympathetic effects not through acting on the effector organs themselves, but through causing the release of norepinephrine from the postganglionic endings (at B_s).

Conversely, there are drugs whose pharmacological action effectively blocks sympathetic activation. Reserpine is among the best known of the drugs that block both the synthesis and the storage of norepinephrine in the postganglionic nerve endings (at B_s). Another substance, guanethidine, does not block the synthesis of norepinephrine but blocks its release from the

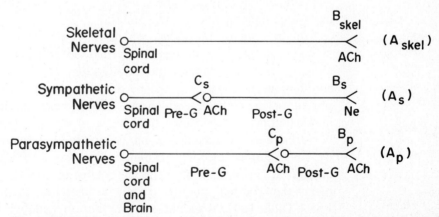

Figure 16–3. Schematic diagram of the general organization of the skeletal, sympathetic, and parasympathetic nerves indicating relative lengths of pre- and postganglionic fibers and the synaptic transmitters. *Abbreviations:* Pre-G: preganglionic fiber; Post-G: postganglionic fiber; ACh: acetylcholine transmitter; Ne: norepinephrine transmitter; A: effector organ; B: neuroeffector synapse; C: synapse between a preganglionic and a postganglionic fiber.

synaptic vesicles (B_s). Still other substances are known to have a blocking effect by acting on the adrenergic effectors themselves (at A_s), in essence making them insensitive to norepinephrine. Finally, sympathetic activation can be attenuated by blocking the transmission of activation through the autonomic ganglia (C_s) with a substance called hexamethonium. However, this substance also blocks parasympathetic activation of postganglionic fibers (at C_p).

In relation to the parasympathetic system, injection of acetylcholine does not have an effect analogous to that which norepinephrine has on the sympathetic system simply because it is destroyed too rapidly by cholinesterase. However, there are substances, called muscarinic substances (because muscarine was one of the first of these to be identified) that are not so rapidly destroyed and that have parasympathomimetic effects through their action on cholinergic effector organs (at A_p). (These also activate those few organs innervated by sympathetic cholinergic fibers.) Three of these substances are pilocarpine, methacholine, and caramylocholine. Other substances (such as neostigmine and physostigmine) inhibit the action of cholinesterase, hence increasing the effects of acetylcholine as the amount of acetylcholine (at B_p) increases with time.

Parasympathetic activation can also be inhibited by blocking the action of acetylcholine on the cholinergic effector organs (at A_p). Atropine and scopolamine act in this way, but they do not block the action of acetylcholine on the postganglionic fibers (C_s and C_p) nor on skeletal muscles (A_{skel}). It should be noted in passing that curare has a contrasting effect in that it blocks the effects of acetylcholine at the neuromuscular junction of skeletal muscles but does not block the effects of acetylcholine in the autonomic nervous system.

Finally, some substances activate both sympathetic and parasympathetic postganglionic fibers (at A_s and A_p). Acetylcholine itself is one of these for reasons discussed earlier. Another very potent substance is nicotine, from which the name of the category of nicotinic drugs is derived. And conversely, as previously described, some substances block transmission between the pre- and postganglionic fibers (at C_s and C_p).

In the case of the heart, which is reciprocally innervated by the two systems, an increase in heart rate can be effected in numerous ways by either increasing sympathetic stimulation or decreasing parasympathetic stimulation. The former could be done by, for example, injecting norepinephrine or epinephrine, which act directly on the heart, or by injecting amphetamine, which causes the release of norepinephrine from sympathetic nerve endings. A decrease in parasympathetic activation could be achieved by, for example, injecting atropine, which would block the effects of acetylcholine at the parasympathetic neuroeffector junctions. It is by this latter means that you will attempt to increase heart rate in this laboratory exercise. From Table 16–1, it should be clear that atropine has effects other than just increasing heart contractions, the most notable for purposes of the labs being that it reduces salivary gland secretion and dilates the bronchi of the lungs. Injection of atropine during animal surgery helps to prevent the respiratory congestion often associated with anesthesia.

C. RECORDING HEART RATE OF THE ANESTHETIZED RAT

Equipment and supplies for each group

Oscilloscope (raised off table with supports if designed for rack mounting)
Cables and wire
> Cable with oscilloscope connector on one end and two alligator clips on other end
> Long wire with banana plugs on both ends (for grounding Faraday cage)

Faraday cage (see Appendix B-13)
Thumb forceps
2   1-cc syringes with 26G needles
Towel
Dishpan and detergent

Equipment and supplies to be shared by groups

Nembutal anesthetic, 60 mg/cc
Atropine sulfate, 0.4 mg/cc
Wound clip applicator and clips
Wound clip remover
Animal scales
Gloves

Preparation

1. Check that all equipment and supplies are present and operating.
2. Weigh the animal and anesthetize it with 60 mg/kg of Nembutal. Do not inject any atropine.

Electrode attachment

When the animal is fully anesthetized, use your thumb forceps to lift the skin from about 1 inch behind each foreleg and firmly attach a wound clip to it (Figure 16–4). Be sure the pointed parts of the clip have in fact pierced the skin so there will be a good electrical connection. If the clips do not go in properly, remove them with the wound clip remover and start again. Imagine where the animal's heart is and try to place the clips so the heart lies right between them.

Oscilloscope settings

Set the oscilloscope controls as follows:

INPUT	AC (x100 if present)
VOLTS/CM	Maximum amplification
Y GAIN (if there is one)	x1
TRIG LEVEL	AUTO

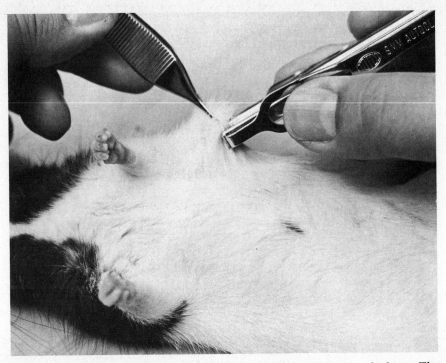

Figure 16–4. Attaching a wound clip to either side of the body across the heart. These can serve as electrodes for recording heart contractions.

TIME/CM	200 MSEC (Note: not 200 μSEC)
X GAIN (if there is one)	Full anticlockwise
VARIABLE	Fully clockwise
TRIG SELECTOR	Y1+ or UPPER AC, +

Use the cable with the oscilloscope connector on one end and the alligator clips on the other to attach the animal to the input socket of the oscilloscope. Attach the connector to the upper (Y1) channel of the oscilloscope and attach the alligator clips to the two wound clips on each side of the animal (Figure 16–5).

The oscilloscope should now be triggering itself automatically and you should be able to see blips on the screen as the beam moves across. But there will undoubtedly be a lot of electrical noise or interference generated from power lines, lights in the room, elevators, air conditioners, and so on, and for a good recording we have to use a shielded Faraday cage to block out this interference.

Place your subject into the shielded cage. This must be grounded in order to reduce the interference. Simply connect the jack on the cage to a ground terminal ($\overline{\overline{}}$) on the oscilloscope using the double banana jack lead. You should now again see the blips but the 60 cps interference will be virtually abolished. Adjust the gain (VOLTS/CM) of the oscilloscope so that the blips are about 3 to 4 cm tall.

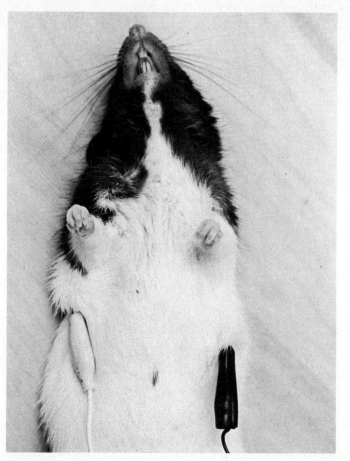

Figure 16–5. Final appearance of the animal with the alligator clips on the input leads connected to the wound clip electrodes.

Recording heart rate changes following atropine administration

Count the number of blips occurring across a given number of grid squares, and keeping in mind the speed of the beam, calculate the heart rate per minute of the rat. A second and easier way to determine heart rate is as follows: Increase the sweep speed to 20 msec/cm and use the TRIG LEVEL to trigger the sweep at some specific place through the beat. You should be able to see a second beat appearing consistently in the same place near the right side of the screen. If you cannot, slow the sweep speed to 50 msec/cm. Determine how many centimeters it is from one point on the triggering deflection to the same point on the deflection of the second beat. Convert this distance to time. This is the number of milliseconds per beat; to determine the number of beats per second, simply take the reciprocal of milliseconds per beat, multiply by 1,000 to get beats per second, and then multiply this by 60 to give the number of beats per minute. For example, if the sweep speed is set at 20 msec/cm and if the distance between deflections is 8 cm, there are 160 msec/beat. This is 1/160 beats/msec or 1/160 beats/msec × 1000 msec/sec × 60 sec/min = 375 beats/min.

   Record the heart rate, and then, without removing the electrodes, inject the animal IP with 0.4 cc of atropine sulfate. Every 30 seconds after the injection determine the heart rate. The actual heart rate does not have to be determined at this time, but determine the distance between corresponding points of consecutive beats and make a careful note of the sweep speed. The calculations can be done later. Continue these observations for about 10 minutes. You should be able to construct a graph showing the original heart rate and the changes that occur after the IP injection of atropine. If after 4 or 5 minutes you have observed no change in the heart rate, this may mean you inadvertently injected into an organ. Administer another 0.25 cc of atropine and begin your observations again. Be sure to indicate all observations on your graph.

When you are finished, disconnect your animal, remove its wound clips, and return it to its home cage. You should prepare a brief laboratory report outlining your manipulations and observations and indicating the types of conclusions you can make from your observations. Be sure to consider the types of controls and additional information you would need to make definitive statements about the effects of atropine on autonomic activity.

17

ELECTRICAL ACTIVITY OF THE BRAIN

Electrophysiology is the study of the electrical properties of living tissue and has a history stretching back to the end of the eighteenth century, when it was first suspected that the cells of the body are generators of electrical activity. The first actual recording of electrical activity from the brain was reported in a brief note in the *British Medical Journal* in 1875 by Richard Caton (1842–1926) in England. The demonstration in 1870 by Fritsch and Hitzig of an electrically excitable motor cortex led Caton to suppose it might be possible to localize sensory areas of the brain by detecting potential changes similar to those known at that time to accompany activity in peripheral nerves. In both rabbits and monkeys, he found he could detect small electric currents with a sensitive galvanometer, both with electrodes resting on the cortex and with electrodes on the scalp. Because the journal in which Caton's report was published was an obscure one (there was no English

physiology journal at the time), it was not until 1891 that these observations become widely known. And Caton's observations of recording with electrodes on the scalp were still completely overlooked and had to wait until 1929 to be rediscovered by Hans Berger (1873–1941), who succeeded in demonstrating slow-wave potentials recorded from the scalps of humans. The record of these apparently spontaneous potentials was referred to by Berger as an electroencephalogram, or EEG.[1]

Berger described two general patterns of potentials that differed with respect to their frequency and amplitude and with respect to the conditions under which they could be recorded. The first was what he called the alpha rhythm, potentials with a frequency

[1] For excellent reviews of the historical development of neurophysiology and of the history of the study of electrical activity of the brain from the time of Caton to that of Berger, the reader is referred to Brazier (1959, 1961).

215

of 8 to 13 Hz, that is, potentials that recurred 8 to 13 times per second and that could be observed when the subject was relaxed and his eyes closed. The second was what he called the beta rhythm, potentials having a frequency of greater than 13 Hz and present under conditions of attention, arousal, and mental alertness. Although the absolute amplitude of these potentials varies according to the physical characteristics of the recording system, the relative amplitude of the waveforms was observed to co-vary inversely with the frequency.

THE EEG AS A WINDOW ON THE BRAIN

The confirmation of these findings by Adrian and Mathews (1934) and the subsequent extension of them by Berger was greeted with great excitement by the neurophysiology and psychology communities, for it was assumed that these potentials were in fact summated cortical spike activity and that the EEG was therefore like a window on the brain through which one could conveniently view such activity. It was plausible to interpret low-frequency, high-amplitude waves as being summated synchronous unit activity and high-frequency, low-amplitude waves as being summated desynchronous unit activity, but as it turned out, this was a misinterpretation. Nevertheless, within this general framework of the EEG being regarded as a mirror of unit activity, considerable effort was expended during the following twenty-five years in attempting to identify new waveforms and to correlate these with various behavioral states. Given that behavior is the product of the functioning of the nervous system, given that the functioning of the nervous system can be adequately conceptualized in terms of unit spike activity, and given that the EEG reflects this spike activity, the EEG was seen as a tool with enormous potential for answering questions concerning brain-behavior relations and cerebral localization of function.

The EEG is usually recorded on a polygraph (described in Chapter 15) having multiple amplifiers and recording channels that allow recording of electrical potentials simultaneously from several points. In most human applications, the EEG is recorded through small silver disc-shaped electrodes pasted to the surface of the scalp according to a standard pattern. The potentials are presumed to reflect something of the activity in the underlying cerebrum. In most nonhuman applications, the electrodes are permanently implanted in the brain. For recordings of cortical EEG, silver ball or silver plate electrodes are placed in contact with the dura mater overlying the cortex and are held in place by having the lead wires and a headplug fastened to the skull with acrylic dental cement. In the case of recording from subcortical sites, an electrode assembly, similar to that used in Laboratory Exercise VII for electrical stimulation, is stereotaxically implanted in the brain and cemented to the skull so that the uninsulated electrode tip is located in the tissue of interest. When the animal has recovered and the recordings are to be made, it is connected to the amplifiers through flexible cables that plug into the headplug cemented to the skull.

As discussed in Chapter 15, the measurement of voltage fluctuations involves the amplification and examination of the difference between two points with respect to electrical potential. One of the two common types of electrode recording configurations, a *bipolar* arrangement, locates the two points in electrically active nervous tissue. With such an arrangement, the output of a differential amplifier is the difference in the electrical activity between the two points. Note that in this case the EEG may be a very distorted view of the actual electrical activity of the brain. Given that the patterns of electrical activity in the two parts of the brain are dissimilar, the output will not resemble either pattern, for the output of a differential amplifier is the difference in the electrical activity recorded from the two points, not the actual electrical activity at either point. All activity common to the two points is subtracted and does not appear on the record.

A second type of electrode arrangement is called *monopolar*. This is really a misnomer, for it implies that there is only one electrode, when of course there must in fact be two. One is located in electrically active tissue (and hence is called the *active* electrode), but the other, called a *reference* electrode, is located in electrically silent tissue such as the pinna of the ear or the nasal membranes. Again, it is the difference between the activity generated at the two electrode sites that is amplified and recorded. Since there is no activity generated at the reference electrode, the EEG reflects very well the electrical activity generated in the vicinity of the active monopolar electrode. When there are numerous electrodes implanted in different areas of the brain, a variation in the latter method involves the comparison of the activity generated at a particular site with the average activity at all other sites. The basic theory behind this method of an *average reference* is that at any point in time the average of the potentials recorded at a large number of sites will be zero. This of course assumes that the generators at each electrode site are independent, an assumption which should often be suspect.

There are at least two related reasons for the extensive use of bipolar rather than monopolar electrode arrangements in EEG recordings. When the EEG is used as a diagnostic tool for epilepsy, a bipolar arrangement allows for efficient identification of the locus of abnormal patterns of EEG activity. With a series of monopolar electrodes, the abnormal EEG activity appears on all or most channels and localization has to be through the rather unsatisfactory means of analyzing differences in the relative amplitude of the activity in different channels. With a standard bipolar electrode configuration, the abnormal activity will appear only on those channels for which the electrodes are located asymmetrically across the focus.

A second reason is that in both clinical and research applications, there are many fewer recording artifacts picked up with bipolar than with monopolar electrodes. These artifacts are potentials that have their origin somewhere other than in the nervous system, such as in muscle twitches or eye blinks, or that have their origin in the nervous system but are conducted to electrode sites by volume rather than neural conduction. These would appear on all or most monopolar channels but would not appear on bipolar channels, as they would produce common potential changes on both electrodes that would be canceled out. Again, with a monopolar configuration, it would be difficult to determine whether the potential was an artifact or some bizarre but potentially interesting type of cerebral activity.

In most situations, it is desirable to use both types of electrode configurations. By having the same electrode connected to both bipolar and monopolar recording channels, it is possible to determine the actual activity recorded at any site and have the advantage of being able to separate out potential changes that are just artifacts and/or due to volume conduction. Certainly if one is interested in correlating the pattern of EEG activity from some anatomical locus with some behavior, it is imperative to ensure that one is in fact looking at the voltage fluctuations of that area. Consequently, one would usually want to use a monopolar recording configuration so that the voltage fluctuations at the site of the active electrode are amplified with respect to electrically silent tissue. However, as previously pointed out, it is often desirable to use a bipolar configuration to eliminate problems of muscle artifacts and volume conduction. One problem is that if the tips of the bipolar electrode are sufficiently close together so that they pick up the same voltage fluctuations, the differential amplifier output will be flat. If the tips are far enough apart so that there is a differential amplifier output, one would want to ensure that the inputs differed only with respect to phase or amplitude, rather than frequency, for otherwise the EEG record would not reflect the actual voltage fluctuations at either active electrode site.

One of the problems central to working with EEG recordings, or in fact with any physiological recording, is data analysis. An EEG is multidimensional with nonperiodic variations in both amplitude and frequency. Probably still one of the more common methods of at least primary analysis is the eyeball method, by which a trained observer characterizes the waveform patterns in various ways. One of several conventions is to determine the proportion of a record showing activity in each of several frequency ranges that are presumed to have some psychological or clinical significance. Figure 17–1 shows EEG activity in four of the conventionally used frequency ranges designated as alpha (8 to 13 Hz), beta (13 + Hz), theta (4 to 8 Hz) and delta (less than 4 Hz),[2] but seldom does the EEG ever show "pure" activity in any of these ranges. Instead, a waveform of one frequency is often superimposed on a waveform of another frequency, making visual analysis quite difficult. But since it is theoretically possible to represent any complex waveform as the sum of a series of sine waves of different amplitudes, frequencies, and phase relations, application of spectral analysis techniques allows for breaking down complex waves into their component sine wave frequencies. Waveforms that repeat themselves exactly at regular time intervals or that repeat themselves exactly but at irregular or nonperiodic intervals can be analyzed through the use of Fourier series analysis and Fourier integral analysis techniques, respectively, and one can specify the precise component frequencies of the waveform. The EEG waveform, however, neither repeats itself exactly nor is periodic, so spectral analysis must be statistical.

The EEG is examined over some period of time, called an epoch, which might be 10 seconds or 1 minute in duration, and is analyzed for the proportion of the total waveform made up by different frequency ranges. Such a frequency analysis is usually done with the aid of electronic filters. In Chap-

---

[2] The different frequency ranges were designated with Greek alphabet letters in order of their identification rather than in an ascending order of frequency.

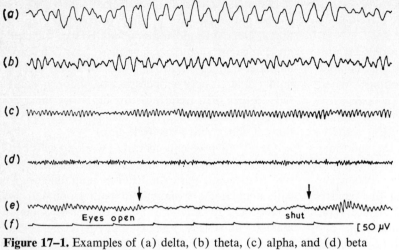

Figure 17–1. Examples of (a) delta, (b) theta, (c) alpha, and (d) beta activity. Alpha activity, recorded from the occipital region when the eyes are closed, is "blocked" when the eyes open, and trace (e) shows an example of such alpha blocking. Note the 1-second time marker shown in trace (f) and the calibration marking in the lower right showing the amount of pen deflection produced by a 50-microvolt signal. (From R. Cooper, J. W. Osselton, and J. C. Shaw, *EEG technology*. London: Butterworth and Co., 1969, Figure 6.3. Reproduced by courtesy of Butterworth, London.)

ter 15, the concept of a filter was introduced and it was pointed out that those portions of a signal above or below some frequency can be greatly reduced in amplitude or power. Through the combined use of a low-pass filter and a high-pass filter, then, it is possible to allow only those parts of a waveform falling within some specific frequency range to pass through the circuit. For example, if the capacitor and resistor of the low-pass filter are selected for 13 Hz and those for the high-pass filter are selected for 8 Hz, signals above 13 Hz and below 8 Hz would be filtered out, leaving only those parts of the signal in the alpha range. By having the recording amplifier connected to both a polygraph and a tape recorder, it is possible later to play the taped EEG through a system of electronic filters with different resistor and capacitor combinations and to measure, within each epoch, the proportion of the total power of the signal in each of the frequency ranges of interest. This is called a power spectrum and represents the proportion of the total power of the signal in each of the frequency ranges. Statistical statements can then be made as to the predominant frequency or frequencies in the original signal and how this changes with time from one epoch to the next or with the application of different treatments. As with any other form of data reduction involving summation, however, some infor-

mation is lost. For example, while a power spectrum indicates the predominant frequency of an epoch, information on the distribution of the various frequencies within the epoch is lost.

Figure 17–2 is an example of such a frequency analysis. The upper trace is the original EEG and the lower trace is the analysis of the frequency components of that EEG. The relative power in each frequency range is summated over a 10-second epoch, and at the end of the epoch each storage bank (consisting of little more than a capacitor that stores electrical charge) discharges through the analyzer pen, the magnitude of the pen deflection indicating the relative power. The writeout for the frequency analysis occurs, of course, 10 seconds after the EEG trace. Since it is convenient to have the original trace and the corresponding frequency analysis at the same position on the chart, one pen is displaced with respect to the other by a distance equal to the duration of the epoch.

The technology associated with the study of the EEG is highly sophisticated, but unfortunately conceptual thought concerning it has not kept pace with this technology and has advanced surprisingly little during the past thirty years. The original observations of Berger stimulated two related lines of research concerning the EEG. The first was based on an early

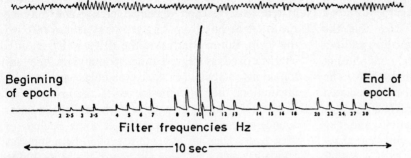

Beginning of epoch   End of epoch

Filter frequencies Hz

2 2·5 3 3·5 4 5 6 7   8 9 10 11 12 13   14 15 16 18   20 22 24 27 30

←————————— 10 sec ——————————→

Figure 17–2. A frequency analysis of a 10-second EEG trace. (From R. Cooper, J. W. Osselton, and J. C. Shaw, *EEG technology*. London: Butterworth and Co., 1969, Figure 8.12. Reproduced by courtesy of Butterworth, London.)

recognition of the utility of the EEG for the diagnosis of epilepsy, for the detection of sites whose electrical activity is abnormal but that do not spontaneously trigger seizure activity (such sites being called *loci* of abnormal activity), and for the localization of sites with abnormal activity that do spontaneously trigger seizures (such sites being called epileptogenic *foci*). Such research was largely oriented toward establishing an association between certain types of EEG activity and particular pathologies. Unfortunately, in contrast to the electrocardiogram, from which functional disorders of the heart can be detected long before they appear in acute forms, the same is not true of the EEG. While a spike and wave EEG pattern (Figure 17–3) is an indicator of *petit mal* epilepsy, by the time this appears there have been other behavioral signs of epilepsy, such as seizures. Nevertheless, the value of the EEG as a tool for confirming clinical diagnoses and for localizing epileptogenic foci cannot be overestimated.

The second line of research was more theoretical and was concerned with the EEG as an indicator of normal brain function and level of consciousness. This stemmed from Berger's observations of a striking relationship between the pattern of the EEG activity and the state of arousal or alertness of the subject. Given the assumption that the EEG reflected the degree of synchronous unit activity, it was not unreasonable to link causally the presence of low-frequency, high-amplitude waves with a somnolent, nonaroused behavioral state, and the presence of high-frequency, low-amplitude waves with an alert, aroused behavioral state. During alpha activity, the cortical neurons were seen as being relatively inactive and hence the person was mentally inactive; during beta activity the cortical neurons were seen as being

highly active and hence the person was behaviorally and mentally aroused. This line of research then revolved around the search for EEG correlates of behavioral and mental states. But, the promise of the 1930s and 1940s has not been fulfilled. The EEG

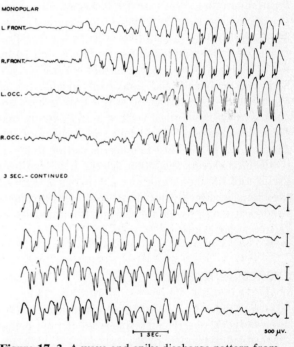

Figure 17–3. A wave-and-spike discharge pattern from a patient with *petit mal* epilepsy. Note how the seizure activity starts in the anterior cortex with later onset in the occipital cortex, and note the synchrony of activity in the two hemispheres. (From W. Penfield and H. Jasper, *Epilepsy and the functional anatomy of the human brain*. Boston: Little, Brown, 1954, Figure XV–29A.)

has not proved to be a window through which spike activity of various parts of the brain can be observed and related to behavior. It is now clear that the original correlation between EEG activation and behavioral activation was just a correlation and did not reflect a causal relationship between the two. The evidence lies in the fact that they can be dissociated in a number of ways.[3] Consistent correlations between specific patterns of electrical activity and specific behaviors are few, and the meaning and theoretical significance of those that may exist is rather uncertain.

Part of the reason for the unfulfilled early promise of the search for brain-behavior correlates is undoubtedly the fact that the basic underlying assumption, that EEG activity reflects spike activity, is not valid. Li and Jasper (1953) showed a distinct lack of correlation between the phase of the EEG and unit spike activity recorded from the same area of the cortex. The origin of the EEG is simply not known, and there is considerable doubt that it has its origin in intracellular potentials (such as dendritic postsynaptic potentials) at all, the origin perhaps being in extracellular potentials involving the neural membrane (Elul, 1967). In 1958, Jasper, Ricci, and Doane commented that, "though the electrical activity of the brain is a sensitive indicator of cerebral events, . . . interpretation of such data is limited by the inadequacy of our knowledge of the basic physiological mechanisms and functional significance of brain waves. The manner in which brain waves are generated on the cortical surface is still obscure and their true functional significance is even more uncertain" (p. 278). This statement is as true today as it was fifteen years ago. Although the EEG can be a useful tool for monitoring the physiological state of the brain, it is highly questionable as to how clear a window it may provide for viewing brain activity as related to behavior.

EVOKED POTENTIALS

A second type of slow-wave potential observed soon after Berger's observations was what is now called the evoked potential (EP). In common with the EEG, evoked potentials are recordings of voltage changes from relatively large areas of the nervous system (as opposed to single units) and may be recorded directly from the nervous system or through the scalp. But in contrast to the EEG, which is often characterized as representing spontaneous and autonomous activity, evoked potentials are voltage fluctuations that are time-locked to the presentation of some stimulus, such as a flash of light, a click sound, or electrical stimulation of some nucleus or fiber tract. They are potentials evoked by a stimulus and bear some fixed time relation to the presentation of that stimulus. Analysis of EPs is consequently in terms of the latency of various components of the fluctuations that follow the presentation of a stimulus. The epochs begin with the presentation of the stimulus and end usually within one second. Displaying EPs on an oscilloscope is one case in which use could be made of the external triggering circuit discussed in Chapter 15 and in Laboratory Exercise VIII. When the stimulus is presented, a pulse is simultaneously delivered to the external triggering circuit of the oscilloscope, which initiates the horizontal movement of the beam. The latency of the various EP components can then be measured in terms of how far the beam has moved horizontally when they appear.

Evoked potentials have been used extensively in the study of the organization of neural pathways, and in certain respects, their use has complemented histological methods for tracing connections in the nervous system. Instead of lesioning and then examining the brain for retrograde and/or anterograde degeneration, the nervous system is probed for time-locked potential changes accompanying sensory or electrical stimulation. Note that because transneuronal degeneration is very limited, evoked potentials have the great advantage over histology of allowing one to trace functional pathways across numerous synaptic links.

An example of an EP recorded from the auditory cortex of an anesthetized cat in response to a click stimulus is shown in Figure 17–4. It should be clear that, like the EEG, this record is multidimensional, having several components that bear a somewhat consistent time relationship to one another and to the stimulus. Unlike the study of the EEG, there are few conventions about data analysis and presentation, and even the direction of representation of positive and negative voltage changes is not standard. Conventions, of course, were not really necessary when the major use of EPs was in the study of the organization of neural systems in acute preparations, for the only question of concern was the latency and

[3] For example, atropine produces a sleeplike cortical EEG pattern (high-amplitude, low-frequency waves) while leaving the animal in a behaviorally alert state. One of the independent projects described in Part Five is a demonstration of this dissociation.

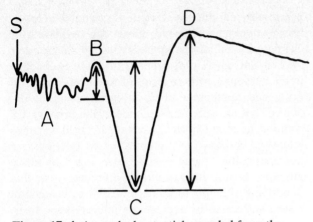

Figure 17–4. An evoked potential recorded from the auditory cortex (anterior, middle, or posterior ectosylvian cortex shown in Figure 3–9) of the anesthetized cat in response to the presentation of a click stimulus. The first small deflection, *A,* which occurs about 2 msec after the stimulus presentation (at *S*) is probably of subcortical origin, and this is followed by the negative deflection, *B,* having a latency of from 6 to 10 msec. The most characteristic response is the large positive component, *C,* which occurs some 8 to 15 msec after *S,* and the large negative component, *D,* usually follows. The actual amplitude of these different components varies as a function of the electrode locus, the stimulus intensity, and the hemisphere from which the recordings are made, as well as the type and depth of anesthetic. (Adapted from M. R. Rosenzweig, Representation of the two ears at the auditory cortex. *American Journal of Physiology,* 1951, **167,** 147–158, Figure 1.)

random time relationship to the event, and which are randomly fluctuating around some zero point (for example, the EEG or 60-cycle interference) will tend to cancel out and sum to zero.

Figure 17–5 illustrates this principle of noise reduction. Trace (a), which shows the "signal," and trace (b), which is continuous sine-wave "noise," are repeated and summated nine times. Trace (c) shows the resulting superimposition of these traces, and trace (d) is the average. Note that originally the signal and the noise were of the same amplitude, but after averaging with as few as nine repetitions, the signal-to-noise ratio is greatly enhanced. In the context of evoked potentials, this end product is referred to as an averaged evoked potential, or AEP. Examples of evoked potentials obtained through scalp

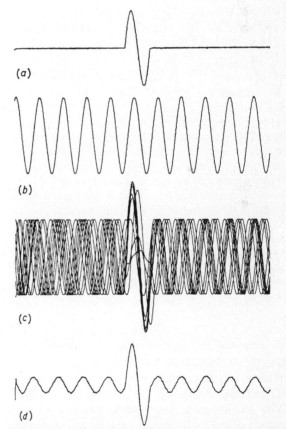

Figure 17–5. (a) An isolated sine-wave "signal" and (b) continuous sine-wave "noise" are repeated nine times. A superimposition of the nine traces is shown in (c) and their average is shown in (d). (From R. Cooper, J. W. Osselton, and J. C. Shaw. *EEG technology.* London: Butterworth and Co., 1969, Figure 7.7. Reproduced by courtesy of Butterworth, London.)

relative amplitude of the primary component of the evoked potential and not of the later components.

As much as it would have been interesting and desirable to study EPs in normal awake humans, it was not possible until very recently to detect EPs from the scalp because their amplitude is considerably less than that of the EEG (approximately 1 to 10 microvolts as compared with 10 to 100 microvolts). The development of computers of average transients (or CATS), which essentially add together a series of waveforms, has now made it possible to do so. A defining characteristic of evoked potentials, of course, is their being time-locked or bearing some consistent time relationship to some event. If that event is repeated a number of times and the resulting voltage fluctuations (which contain the evoked potential signal as well as noise) are added together or superimposed, those parts of the waveforms which are time-locked to the event will add together and be enhanced, whereas those parts of the waveforms which are not time-locked to the event, which bear a

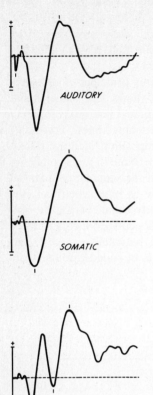

Figure 17–6. Averaged evoked responses recorded from eight adult subjects. Each tracing is the computer average of 4,800 individual responses. The amplitude calibration indicated on the left of each tracing is 10 microvolts, and the time calibration is 100 msec/div indicated at the bottom of the diagram. Negative voltages are represented by downward deflections. (From H. G. Vaughan, Jr., The relationship of brain activity to scalp recordings of event-related potentials. In E. Donchin and D. B. Lindsley (Eds.), *Average evoked potentials*. Washington, D.C.: NASA, 1969, Figure 2–1.)

electrodes and averaged in this way are shown in Figure 17–6. Note that each is an average of 4800 responses and that there is a complete absence of EEG and other "noise."

This technological development has given rise to the study of AEPs in human subjects in the context of psychophysical and signal detection situations. Attempts have been made to correlate the presence, latency, and amplitude of the various components of AEPs with reported psychophysical experience and with such processes, events, and variables as signal detection success, attention, expectancy, reward, and so on. Unfortunately, the correlations for even the

psychophysical intensity functions are not as impressive as might be expected. Given the traditional or classical model of the organization of the sensory systems and given that stimulus intensity is encoded in the nervous system in terms of frequency of neural firing and number of fibers firing, it would be expected that at least the amplitude of the primary EP component might correlate with perceived stimulus intensity. Perhaps the unimpressive correlations are not surprising, though, since the logic of these attempts is not fundamentally different from that underlying attempts to relate the EEG to behavioral states, and since the appropriate interpretation to be placed upon both the latency and the relative amplitude of most AEP components is simply unknown.

A serious problem in the use of signal averaging and in attempting to relate averaged evoked potentials to psychological events or processes is the possible interaction of the EP with ongoing neural activity. The brain, of course, is not silent until the stimulus is presented; the EP is superimposed on this ongoing activity. This ongoing activity will be random with respect to the stimulus and will sum to zero, but it is difficult to conceive of how such ongoing activity could not be of importance and significance in attempting to understand the relationship between EP components and perceptual processes. A second problem to be noted is the difficulty in inferring from averaged signals whether a change in the amplitude of an AEP component is due to an increase in the amplitude of the individual potentials or to a change in the variability of the non-time-locked potentials. A decrease in variability will, of course, enhance the amplitude of an averaged component as much as will a general increase in amplitude of the component.

SINGLE-CELL RECORDINGS

Both the EEG and evoked potentials involve recording from relatively large volumes of nervous tissue. It was suggested in the previous sections that although some of the components of these potentials undoubtedly represent the summated firing of large numbers of neurons, the actual relationship between these (especially the EEG) and single unit activity is quite uncertain. Given the assumption that behavior is the product of the pattern of firing of individual neurons, the lack of consistent and interpretable correlations between such gross potentials and behavior is therefore perhaps not surprising. During the past twenty years, however, it has become possible, and indeed quite feasible, to record the activity of single neurons in acute, and more recently in chronic, preparations; certainly some of the more exciting research during this time has involved relating various perceptual phenomena to the activity of single cells of the sensory systems.

In an acute preparation, the anesthetized animal is typically held in a stereotaxic instrument, and a recording electrode is inserted into the brain tissue so that its tip is inside or near a cell body. Such electrodes are called microelectrodes because of the extremely small tip diameter (in the order of microns), but they are basically similar to the stimulating and recording electrodes described previously in that they are simply pieces of insulated wire (pipettes similar to those described in Chapter 7 for making cortical lesions but which have been pulled so that the tip diameter is extremely small are sometimes used for intracellular recordings; the pipette is then filled with an electrically conducting solution such as KCl). It is because of the very small tip diameter that until recently it was technologically difficult or impossible to record from single cells. The difficulty was not in the construction of the electrodes but in the fact that the resistance of a conductor is inversely proportional to its diameter and, until recently, ordinary physiological amplifiers were incapable of amplifying signals through electrodes with resistance as high as that necessarily found in microelectrodes.

The electrode, of course, must be held in a micromanipulator. There is a problem because the brain pulsates in response to cardiac activity and the tip of a rigidly held electrode will not stay in the same place in the brain as the brain volume changes with blood flow. A very flexible electrode holder must therefore be used so that the electrode tip can move up and down following brain volume changes. Note that the microelectrode does not have to be located inside a cell body in order to detect activity, for the voltage fluctuations associated with the spike potentials of single cells are of sufficiently large magnitude that they can be detected some distance away. If, however, the tip is inside the cell body, only the activity of that cell will be monitored, whereas if it is outside the cell body, it may pick up the activity of several cells simultaneously.[4] The voltage fluctuations are amplified, as previously described, and are

usually displayed on an oscilloscope. As the dependent measure in most studies of interest to the physiological psychologist is the rate of firing of the cell, and in particular changes (either increases or decreases) in the rate of firing as a function of some event, recordings are typically made with a fairly slow horizontal sweep speed so that a large number of spikes appear on a single trace. A piece of equipment that greatly facilitates the detection of rate changes is an audio amplifier and loudspeaker connected to the oscilloscope amplifier, so that the blips on the screen can be heard as bips.

The key concept for understanding much of the microelectrode work on sensory system organization is the *receptive field*. This refers to that part of the receptive surface of the organism which, when stimulated, modulates the rate of firing of the neuron. Note that the receptive field is a property of the neuron, that receptive fields of different neurons greatly overlap, and that not all neurons in the nervous system have receptive fields so defined. Note also that since receptive fields are defined in terms of both increases and decreases in firing rate, the description of a receptive field must include a characterization of inhibitory as well as excitatory components.

It is not our purpose here to review the findings concerning brain organization which have been derived from single-unit recording work, but to point out that much of the work involving acute preparations has been largely, but not exclusively, concerned with questions about sensory system organization and with how environmental energy is transduced and encoded in the nervous system. This work has indicated, for instance, that many quite complex visual psychophysical phenomena can be accounted for very adequately in terms of the receptive field properties of retinal ganglion cells and that it is not necessary to invoke higher-order decision making processes to understand them (see Teitelbaum (1967) for a very readable account of this).

It has recently become possible to chronically implant microelectrodes into neural tissue and to record the activity of single cells during behavior in the waking rather than the anesthetized state. This allows, first of all, for a confirmation of findings made with acute preparations and for determining the extent to which (if any) receptive field properties are modified by the state of anesthesia. Another direction in which this work has gone is in the same tradition as that previously discussed in relation to the study of the EEG and evoked potentials and behavior—that is, toward correlating or associating certain patterns

---

[4] Discriminating the activity of one particular cell from that of several can be a problem, but it can be done on the basis of amplitude. A particular cell will always fire with the same amplitude, and the recorded amplitude will differ from cell to cell as a function of cell properties as well as the distance of the cell from the electrode tip.

of firing of single cells with the emission of certain behaviors. It is still much too early to evaluate this approach in terms of empirical outcomes, but certainly if the initial assumption of the relationship between behavior and single-cell activity is valid, this approach should produce data that are highly meaningful not only with respect to localization of function but also with respect to the study of sequencing and time relationships among responses (Bizzi, Kalil, and Tagliasco, 1971).

All this work, however, rests on two related assumptions. First, because a microelectrode can record the firing of only a very small proportion of the total number of cells in an area, one assumption must be that there is a reasonably representative sampling of these cells. As public opinion surveyors are well aware, however, when one is dealing with population sizes in the millions and sample sizes in the tens or twenties, the concept of a representative sample becomes highly suspect. In sampling, there is a bias imposed by the fact that some cells die before records can be made (is there some functional peculiarity associated with such cells?) and, probably more important, by the fact that the microelectrode is usually driven through the tissue until the spontaneous firing of a cell is detected, and it is changes in the firing of that cell which are correlated with stimulus presentation or behavioral emission. This means that there is a bias against cells with very low spontaneous firing rates. One recently developed technique (Stretton and Kravitz, 1968) does allow for histological identification of the exact cell from which records were made. An application of this method by Van Essen and Kelly (1973) has shown that cells in the striate cortex with simple receptive fields are stellate cells, whereas those with complex receptive fields are pyramidal cells (see Chapter 3). It should be noted that this inference had been made earlier by Hubel and Wiesel on the basis of the distribution of receptive field types and of cell types in the various layers of cortical cells (see Chapter 3); Van Essen and Kelly's work provided clear confirmation. The relevance of this technique for the present discussion is that it does allow for determination after the fact that the sampling of cells was random with respect to at least cytoarchitectonics.

The second assumption, which is somewhat less methodological and more conceptual, is that what happens in individual cells is behaviorally or psychologically important. There are certainly instances in which it is not the firing of a single neuron but the pattern of firing of many neurons that is important. For example, Melzack and Wall's (1965) gate control theory of pain hinges on the concept of a *balance* between the activity of the large and the small fibers of the spinal nerves. Erickson (1968) has similarly shown that in relating afferent fiber activity to taste perception it is the *pattern* of activity of many neurons, rather than the activity of any one neuron, that is important. If such interactions operate on a peripheral level, there is certainly no reason to assume they are less important centrally, despite the fact that there have been clear and striking demonstrations of relationships between psychophysical phenomena and single-unit activity in many sensory pathways.

The emphasis until recently in much of the single-unit work has been on establishing normative data in characterizing the receptive field properties of cells selected from large areas of the nervous system. There has been a recent shift toward analyzing changes in receptive field properties that accompany various treatments which produce interesting psychological or behavior effects. This work is well exemplified by the Blakemore and Cooper (1970) study reprinted in Chapter 19, which shows some of the dramatic behavioral and physiological changes that occur in the visual system following the experimental manipulation of specific parameters of the early visual environment of kittens. This plasticity, however, may not be found in all mammals. For example, Mize and Murphy (1973) replicated the Blakemore and Cooper study with both rabbits and kittens, and although they found the effect in kittens, it was not evident in rabbits. Of importance for the interpretation of this difference is the fact that the retina of the rabbit appears to be much more complex (in the sense of information apparently processed) than that of the kitten.

This experimental approach, which allows for correlating changes in brain and behavior, offers the physiological psychologist a wealth of information with which to develop hypotheses as to the organization and structure of brain-behavior relations. If, however, the fundamental assumptions underlying the work are invalid, the approach may be no more successful or fruitful than that involving the EEG.

ELECTROPHYSIOLOGICAL AND BEHAVIORAL APPROACHES TO THE STUDY OF DISCRIMINATION CAPABILITY

The preceding discussion about evoked potentials and unit recordings emphasized their use in the study of sensory and perceptual capabilities of organisms, the former having indicated a great deal about the organization of sensory projections and neural pathways and the latter a great deal about how information is transduced and encoded in the nervous system. The traditional approach of physiological psychologists to questions of discrimination capability, that is, questions of the ability of an organism to detect stimuli and to distinguish among stimuli, and questions of the neural mechanisms underlying these has been basically behavioral, involving the study of normal discriminative capabilities and the study of the effects of various neurological manipulations on these capabilities. It is appropriate, then, to consider the relationship between the electrophysiological approach and the behavioral approach, and between the types of information that can be derived from each.

To determine what stimuli and what stimulus differences an organism can detect or distinguish, the psychologist has typically used a discrimination paradigm that requires the organism to make differential responses to two or more stimuli. If the organism does make differential responses, or is able to learn to do so, the inference is that it can discriminate between or among the stimuli, although of course very little if anything can be said about the basis of the discrimination. A simple example of a discrimination paradigm involving learning to make differential responses would be a pigeon being reinforced for pecking at a light when it is red but not being reinforced when the light is green. At the beginning of training, the pigeon will probably peck at the same rate to the two stimuli, but with repeated changes in hue and corresponding changes in the availability of reinforcement, the bird will begin to show differential responses. When the light is red, the bird pecks; but when it is green, the rate of pecking decreases. The fact that the bird responds differentially means that the stimuli control the behavior of the bird and hence the bird must be able to distinguish between them. It is to be emphasized again, however, that differential responding to the stimuli in this situation indicates little or nothing about the basis on which the discrimination is made. To make the claim that the bird discriminates color or wavelength would involve extensive testing with controls for at least the dimensions of brightness (because of the spectral sensitivity function), saturation, contrast with the background, and so on.

An example of a discrimination paradigm not involving learning in the same sense would be that employed by Moffitt (1971) in his elegant study of the discrimination of speech sounds by very young infants. The study hinged on the fact that upon repeated presentation of a stimulus, there is a marked decrease in the magnitude of the orienting reaction (that complex package of autonomic and somatic responses elicited by the presentation of novel stimuli), and this reflects habituation. If a stimulus, discriminably different from the original stimulus, is then presented, there is a reappearance of the orienting reaction. Moffitt found that if after habituation of the orienting reaction to one phoneme (such as *bah*) he presented another phoneme which sounded somewhat similar (such as *gah*), the orienting reaction reappeared. This reappearance indicated that the child could detect a difference between the original phoneme and the test phoneme.

Discrimination capability is therefore judged at the end of the information processing chain, which implies that there are limits to the inferences that can be made from electrophysiological recordings. Clearly, for the organism to discriminate between two stimuli, the stimuli necessarily must give rise to different physiological responses somewhere in the nervous system, and these should be detectable with electrophysiological methods. But generally it is not sufficient evidence for the psychologist to say that because two stimuli give rise to differential electrophysiological responses somewhere in the nervous system, the organism can and does discriminate between them. The differential electrophysiological response may reflect physiological processes that are psychologically irrelevant for the organism. For example, the visual system of the cat shows very good differential responsiveness to hue or wavelength, but it is extremely difficult to demonstrate color vision in cats (Brown, Shively, LaMotte, and Sechzer, 1973). For the cat, hue is apparently a nonsalient stimulus dimension to which it pays little attention.

If there is a failure to detect differential electrophysiological responses to stimuli, then the psychologist may be in a position to argue that the organism is not capable of discriminating between those stimuli, since a necessary condition for a differential behavioral response is a differential neural response. But as Cowey (1968) has pointed out, this does require two fundamental assumptions. First, it assumes that the recording site is relatively peripheral. A lack of differential physiological response to visual stimulation recorded at the level of the retina would form the foundation of a more convincing argument than would a similar lack of differential electrophysiological response recorded at the level of the inferotemporal cortex. The more peripheral the recording site, the fewer the number of parallel information processing channels through which the information could be routed and through which a discrimination could be mediated.

A second basic assumption is that the physiological activity being recorded and analyzed is relevant activity. It is important to remember that seldom is all physiological activity detected or analyzed; instead, only slow potentials, single spike potentials, or some other potentials are analyzed. Furthermore, most amplification systems are equipped with filters to block out activity in frequency ranges judged by the experimenter to be irrelevant, and much data analysis is now done by automated equipment that examines only those aspects of the data assumed important by the experimenter. Consider, for instance, single-unit responses to the presentation of stimuli being analyzed in terms of the rate of firing calculated over a 2-second epoch. One could imagine a situation in which there would be no difference in the number of spikes evoked by the two stimuli (and hence no difference in rate of firing as calculated over 2 seconds) even when there was marked difference in the distribution of the spikes over the time period. Hence, one dependent variable, *rate of firing,* as calculated over a 2-second epoch would indicate no differential responsiveness, whereas the dependent variable, *distribution of firing,* would. Similarly, an analysis of evoked potentials in terms of the amplitude of the primary component may give different results than an analysis based on latency or on later components.

As a generalization, based more on empirical than on logical grounds, physiological data would seem to suggest more about what an organism is unable to discriminate than about what it can discriminate. That is, electrophysiological data allow one to make quite strong negative statements about discrimination capabilities. In contrast, behavioral data allow for very few negative statements to be made with confidence, for there are many reasons that an organism may be unable to perform a discrimination or display behavioral detection other than that it is unable to detect a stimulus difference. The study by Schneider (1967) discussed in Chapter 5 provides a striking illustration of how discrimination failure, as defined behaviorally, can be viewed as reflecting something other than a perceptual loss, and points to some of the logical difficulties encountered in attempting to infer the lower limits of discrimination capability from behavioral tests. Successful discrimination performance does, however, allow positive statements to be made with confidence, although, as discussed in Chapter 5, it may require extensive transfer and/or equivalence testing to determine the actual basis of the discrimination.

The electrophysiological and the behavioral approaches, then, complement each other; neither is inherently better. The behavioral approach would seem to be well suited for the study of normal discriminative capabilities, whereas the electrophysiological approach can be useful in attempting to define the lower limits of discrimination potential. The complementary use of these two approaches can be illustrated by considering the study of the effects of early monocular and binocular visual deprivation on later visual capabilities (Hubel, 1965). Such deprivation leads to apparent blindness when the deprived eye is tested behaviorally in adulthood. However, single-cell recordings from the visual cortex suggest that in the case of monocular deprivation, the loss may be permanent and unalterable because the deprived eye loses its connections with visual cortex cells. Following binocular visual deprivation, in contrast, both eyes retain their connections with the cortical cells, hence leaving open at least the possibility for the acquisition of visual capability.

18 LABORATORY EXERCISE IX

ELECTROPHYSIOLOGY

The laboratory exercise consists of two parts which, depending upon available time, could be completed in the same or in different laboratory periods. The first part involves the recording of an EEG from the exposed cortex of an anesthetized rat and the demonstration of EEG changes associated with the phenomenon of cortical spreading depression. The second part involves the recording of spike potentials from multiple cellular units (multiunit recording) and the recording of evoked potentials. The advantage of doing the two parts in the same laboratory period is that the same animal and the same exposure can be used for both. The advantage of doing the two parts in different laboratory periods is that more time will be available for the systematic exploration of the electrophysiological phenomena.

A. THE EEG AND CORTICAL SPREADING DEPRESSION

Although it is rare that the neuropsychologist would be interested in recording the cortical electroencephalogram (EEG) of an anesthetized animal, such a recording can be instructive for demonstrating the principles of EEG recording and for demonstrating the phenomenon of cortical spreading depression. This latter phenomenon was discussed in Chapter 5 as being one form of reversible functional ablation that has been used extensively in the study of hemispheric interaction. The application of potassium chloride (KCl) to the surface of the dura induces a wave of neuronal excitation, followed by long-lasting neuronal depression, that moves slowly across the cortex, propagated not electrically but by changes in ionic distribution. In this part of the lab, the EEG will be recorded from the surface of the cortex, and changes in the EEG following application of KCl will be monitored. As the EEG will be displayed on an oscilloscope, it will be difficult to make quantitative statements about the observations (for example, precise statements about a predominant EEG frequency at various points in time), but some qualitative statements should be possible. In actual research or clinical practice in which a quantitative analysis of the EEG is made, recordings would be made with a paper chart recorder and/or magnetic tape so there would be a permanent record available for subsequent frequency and/or amplitude analysis.

Equipment and supplies for each group

Rat headholder
Osteological drill
High-intensity lamp (if necessary)
Micromanipulator equipped with double electrode holder (see Appendix B–14)
Oscilloscope
Preamplifier and power supply
Cables and wires
    Cable to connect preamplifier to oscilloscope
    Input cable to preamplifier
    2 long wires with banana plugs on both ends for grounding both the shielded cage and the preamplifier to the oscilloscope
    3 8-in. wires, 1 red, 1 black, and 1 white, each with a small alligator clip on one end and a banana plug on the other end
2 silver ball electrodes (see Appendix B–15)
Multiunit recording electrode (see Appendix B–16)
6-inch piece of copper wire for positioning head
Shielded Faraday cage
Stereotaxic atlas of rat brain
Surgical instruments
    #3 scalpel handle
    #10 and #11 blade
    2 mosquito forceps
    Thumb forceps
    Rat-tooth forceps
    Lempert rongeurs
    Large scissors
    Dental probe
    Medium cutting bur (#8)
    6-in. ruler

Saline dish with saline
Bottle and eyedropper for mineral oil
Gelfoam
10   2″ × 2″ gauze sponges
Small cotton pledgets
1-cc syringe with 26G needle
Dishpan and detergent
Towels
Lab coats

Equipment and supplies to be shared by groups

Nembutal anesthetic, 60 mg/cc
25% solution of potassium chloride (KCl)
Animal clippers
Animal balance
Leather gloves
Mineral oil, extra heavy, heated slightly
Heater
Thermometer
Photostimulator for demonstration of visual evoked potentials
Audio monitor, if available, for monitoring multiunit spike potentials

Electronic equipment

Before anesthetizing your subject, all electronic equipment should be set up, turned on so the tubes have time to warm up, and adjusted so that you are set to record as soon as the exposure is prepared. If you arrive at the lab a little early, you might want to review part of the last lab to become familiar again with the operation of the oscilloscope.

If your oscilloscope and power supply are designed for rack mounting, be sure that they are raised from the table top with rubber stoppers or some other support to provide for proper ventilation. Before turning on the oscilloscope, set the front panel controls as follows:

INPUT SWITCH	AC
VOLTS/CM or SENSITIVITY	10
Y GAIN (if there is one)	x1
Y SHIFT or POSITION	Midposition
X GAIN or SWEEP MAGNIFICATION	Fully anticlockwise
TIME/CM or TIME/DIV	500 msec
VARIABLE	Fully clockwise
TRIG SELECTOR	Set to Y1+ or UPPER AC, +
TRIG LEVEL	AUTO
STABILITY (if there is one)	Fully clockwise

Turn on the oscilloscope, center the upper beam on the screen using the Y SHIFT and X SHIFT controls, make any adjustments needed for focus and astigmatism, and adjust the lower beam up or down so it is no longer on the screen.

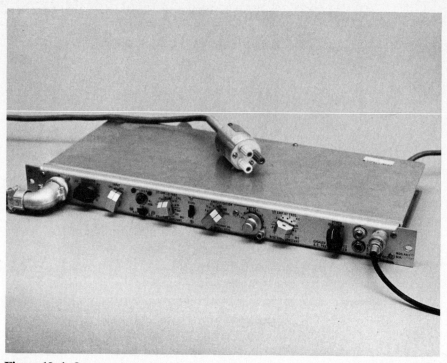

Figure 18–1. One common type of preamplifier. The power supply is not shown. As this is a differential amplifier, the input probe (resting on the top of the instrument) has three input terminals. The output, located on the right side of the front panel, goes to an oscilloscope.

Because the brain potentials are of very small magnitude, they must first be amplified before going to the input stage of the oscilloscope; the first stage of amplification is achieved with the preamplifier. These are almost always differential amplifiers which, as discussed in Chapter 15, enhance the signal-to-noise ratio by subtracting input signals common to both active leads. Besides amplifying, most preamplifiers have the facility of blocking out unwanted signals with filters, which is valuable when attempting to control electrical interference. The two knobs, ½ AMP LO FREQ and ½ AMP HI FREQ, on the Grass preamp shown in Figure 18–1 control the filtering of low- and high-frequency signals, respectively.

Turn on the power supply and connect the preamp to it, but do not turn on the preamp at this time. The controls [1] can be set as follows:

The black CALIBRATOR knob should not be touched.

INPUT	USE
½ AMP LO FREQ	0.3 cps
½ AMP HI FREQ	0.1 kc
AMPLIFICATION (toggle switch)	x1000
AMPLIFICATION (rotating knob)	100
ADJ. CAL	*Do not touch*—it will put the preamp out of calibration

[1] These particular controls are found on the Grass preamplifier shown in Figure 18–1; other makes and models should have very similar controls.

With the filters set as indicated above, signals below 0.3 cps and above 100 cps will be attenuated by at least one-half, which will still allow for the EEG, being in the frequency range of about 1 to 30 cps, to be amplified and detected.

Attach the three-terminal input unit (called an *input probe*) to the input terminal of the preamp. Connect the OUTPUT of the preamp to the INPUT socket of the upper (Y1) channel of the oscilloscope using the cable with appropriate connectors. Then use a wire with banana jacks to connect the GND socket of the preamp to a ground terminal ($\overline{\overline{}}$) on the oscilloscope. Taking the three short leads, plug the white lead into the white terminal of the input probe and the red and black leads into the yellow and blue terminals.

Initial stages

Follow the same operating procedures outlined in previous labs to expose the cortex of your subject, but in this lab it will be necessary to expose the cortex of both hemispheres. If at all possible, do not nick the dura mater or there may be problems in controlling the application of KCl.

1. Obtain and weigh your subject. Calculate the amount of anesthetic required on the basis of a dosage of 60 mg/kg. When you inject your subject with anesthetic, be sure to stretch the abdominal wall well. Do not inject any atropine, as this will affect the EEG activity.
2. Clip the fur from the head to the level of the eyes.
3. Mount the animal firmly into the headholder and adjust the angle of the head so the top is relatively flat.
4. Stretching the skin laterally with your left thumb and middle finger, and starting far anteriorly, make the initial incision using the #10 blade in the #3 handle. Scrape the periosteum from the midline to either side and retract it with the mosquito forceps. With a gauze sponge, wipe the cranium clean and identify bregma and lambda. The mosquito forceps should be positioned at about bregma.
5. Using the medium cutting bur, thin the crania overlying both hemispheres; break through the bone with the dental pick. Expand the exposure with rongeurs, going 2 or 3 mm anterior to bregma, lateral to the coronal suture, posterior almost to the lambdoidal suture, and no closer than 1 mm to the midline. Great caution must be exercised so that the thin ridge of bone that will run along the midline remains intact. Do not make it any thinner than 2 mm and be careful not to apply any twisting action when using the rongeurs.
6. *Do not cut the dura at this time.* The EEG can easily be recorded through it and by keeping it intact, the cortex will not dry out. Should the dura be nicked inadvertently, it is best to cut it and retract it completely as described in Laboratory Exercise IV, for otherwise it may be difficult to control the application, and especially the removal, of KCl.

Recording the EEG

Turn on the preamplifier. Attach the silver ball electrodes to the electrode holders of the micromanipulator and orient them at about 45°, as shown in Figure 18–2; adjust them so the tips are 5 to 8 mm apart and are about the same height. Place the animal (in the headholder) and the micromanipulator in the shielded cage. Connect the wire mesh of the cage to a ground terminal on the oscilloscope using the long wire with the banana plugs. Carefully attach the alligator clips of the red and black lead wires to the loose ends of the electrode wires and attach the clip of the white lead to the pinna of the ear. The white lead serves as the reference lead which, in a chronic recording preparation, would have to be connected to a bonescrew. Now place several drops of mineral oil onto the dura and carefully lower the two electrodes until they just rest on the surface of the dura, as shown in Figure 18–2.

You should now be able to see a fairly clear record of voltage fluctuations with respect to time. This is electrical activity generated in the central nervous system. You may want to adjust the amplification of the oscillo-

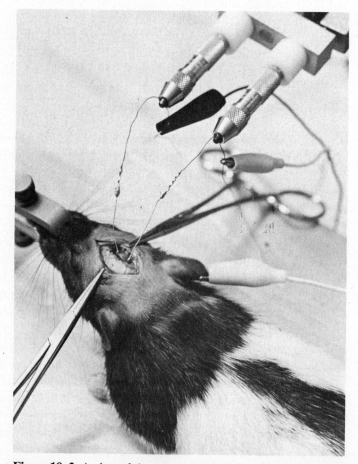

Figure 18–2. A view of the exposure. Note the angle of the electrodes with respect to the cortical surface (about 45°). The alligator clip attached to the pinna of the ear serves as the common reference electrode.

scope to get the optimal recording. Although it is very difficult to do so accurately, try to estimate the dominant frequency of the EEG by attempting to count the number of cycles of activity per unit distance and converting this to cycles per unit time. Try adjusting the speed of the beam to facilitate counting. Keep in mind that the EEG you observe is determined largely by the depth of anesthesia in your subject and what you are observing now is not, of course, what would be observed in an awake animal.

Demonstration of visual cortical evoked potentials

Figure 18–3 shows a rather common type of laboratory photostimulator. If one is available, your instructor may connect it to your oscilloscope to demonstrate visual evoked potentials in your animal. Such a stimulator consists of a light source having a very rapid rise-time and fall-time (that is, the bulb reaches its maximum and minimum light intensities almost instantly, a property not shared by incandescent lamps), the intensity of which and the frequency of flashing of which can be precisely controlled. There is a SYNCHRONOUS OUTPUT jack through which the stimulator can be connected directly with a wire to the EXTERNAL TRIGGER or TRIGGER INPUT jack of the oscilloscope. Whenever a flash of light is triggered by the stimulator, a pulse is sent to the oscilloscope which, if the TRIGGER SELECTOR control is set for EXTERNAL, will trigger the oscilloscope sweep mechanism.

Adjust the sweep speed of the oscilloscope to 10 msec/cm and reduce the amplification level somewhat. Place the light source in front of the animal and turn the stimulator on to a repetitive flashing rate of 1 or 2 flashes per second. Although it may involve some adjustment of amplification or electrode placement, it should be possible to observe a well-defined visual evoked potential provided that one, but not both, of the recording electrodes is on Area 17. Because the response characteristics of the evoked potential are different from those of the EEG, turn the ½ AMP HI FREQ switch on the preamplifier to 30 kc so that the filter is completely open. If you find inter-

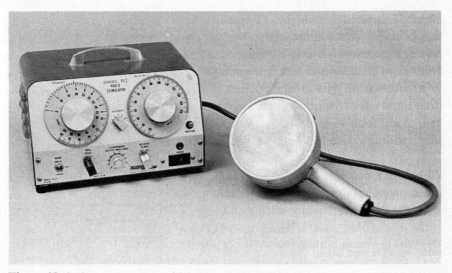

Figure 18–3. A common type of laboratory photostimulator.

ference from the EEG, you can also turn the ½ AMP LO FREQ switch to 30 cps, which will attenuate EEG signals. Note that the sweep of the oscilloscope starts when the flash occurs and that the evoked potential is time-locked to the flash, as evidenced by the fact that one evoked potential is superimposed on the preceding one. Note also that there are several components to the evoked potential, some of which may be more stable, or less variable, than others. Be sure to measure the latency of the primary component.

Induction of cortical spreading depression

Readjust the settings on the oscilloscope and preamplifier to what they were before and again record the EEG. A 25% solution of KCl will now be applied to the surface of the dura, which will induce a wave of cortical spreading depression.

Raise the electrodes from the surface of the dura and, using cotton pledgets or cotton sponges, wipe off any excess mineral oil. With your ruler, measure the approximate distance between the tips of the electrodes and then lower the electrodes to the surface of the dura. Be sure that the EEG is again being recorded.

Hold a very small piece of Gelfoam (about 1 to 2 mm square) in the tips of the thumb forceps and soak it in the KCl solution. Now lay it gently on the dura at the most anterior part of the exposure and note the time (avoid getting KCl on the entire exposure and on the electrodes). From this point on, whenever any change in the trace appears (for example, apparent change in amplitude or frequency of the waves), make a note of the time and the type of change. Knowing the distance between the electrodes, it may be possible to calculate the rate at which the spreading depression moves across the surface of the cortex by noting the time at which the first change occurs in your record (which may be seen as an increase in the EEG amplitude, which occurs when the spreading depression reaches the first electrode site) and by noting the time at which the EEG record becomes very depressed (as the wave reaches the second electrode site). Continue observations of the EEG for 10 to 15 minutes and watch for any evidence of a cycling of amplitude changes. During or after this time, raise the electrodes from the cortex, lightly clean them with a saline-soaked sponge (in case any KCl has got on them), and place them on the cortex of the opposite hemisphere. This will allow you to compare the amplitude of the EEG in the depressed hemisphere with that in the nondepressed hemisphere.

Remove the Gelfoam and any excess KCl with small cotton pledgets, moisten the dura with saline, and apply more mineral oil to it. Continue to monitor the EEG for a few minutes, noting any changes and the time of those changes.

B. MULTIUNIT RECORDINGS AND EVOKED POTENTIALS

While recording from single units is technically difficult because of the small electrode tip (see Chapter 17), recording spike potentials from several units simultaneously can be done satisfactorily using an electrode basically similar to that used in Laboratory Exercise V to make electrolytic lesions. As described in the fabrication instructions included in Appendix B, the electrode consists of a size 4 stainless steel insect pin insulated with Insl-X (an insulating substance similar to the Epoxylite used to make the lesion electrode) but *not* scraped at the tip. This electrode will also pick up evoked potentials from the interior of the brain. These electrodes must be prepared in advance, as the Insl-X requires 16 to 24 hours for drying.

Preparation of subject

Remove the animal from the shielded cage, disconnect the leads from the silver ball electrodes, and remove the electrodes from the electrode holders. Follow the instructions of previous laboratory exercises:

1. Incise and retract the dura of the hemisphere that did not receive the spreading depression (Laboratory Exercise IV). This will allow for easy penetration of the brain by the electrode with a minimum of friction being applied to the electrode insulation.
2. Position the animal's head so bregma is 2.25 mm above lambda, as it would be if the animal were in a stereotaxic instrument (Laboratory Exercises V and VII).
3. Check with the battery tester (Laboratory Exercise V) that there are no leaks in the insulation of the electrode shaft and that, even though not scraped, there is current flow through the sharp electrode tip.

Fasten the electrode into the jaws of one of the electrode holders and use a ruler as a set square to orient the electrode vertically. Return the micromanipulator and the animal in the headholder to the shielded cage. Connect one of the active leads (red or black) to the uninsulated portion of the electrode, connect the white reference lead to the pinna of the ear, and connect the second active lead to the white reference lead. This will be a monopolar recording. Input through the active electrode lead (signal plus noise) will be amplified with respect to the white reference lead. The input through the other active lead (containing just noise) will also be amplified with respect to the white reference lead, and the two amplified signals will be subtracted, leaving as the output just the signal that was in the electrode lead.

Set the oscilloscope amplification to 5 volts/cm, the sweep speed to 100 msec/cm, and set the oscilloscope to trigger itself. The filters on the preamplifier should be adjusted to block the low-frequency EEG signals but to allow through the high-frequency spike potentials.[2] Without such filtering, the spike potentials would be seen on a fluctuating rather than a stable base-

---

[2] Spike potentials are high-frequency signals not in the sense of their occurring frequently, but in the sense that the voltage changes associated with them are extremely rapid. The time it takes for the voltage to go from the resting potential of approximately -70 mv to the peak of the action potential of approximately $+40$ mv is but a fraction of a millisecond. This is so regardless of whether the frequency of spike potentials is less than 1 per second or more than 500 per second. What makes a signal a low-frequency or a high-frequency signal is, then, the rate of voltage change in the various signal components.

line. Therefore the ½ AMP LO FREQ filter should be set to 30 cps and the ½ AMP HI FREQ filter to 30 kc.

Position the electrode tip about 3 mm posterior to bregma and 2.5 to 3 mm lateral to the midline over the hemisphere with the incised dura. Now begin slowly to lower the electrode into the brain tissue. When the electrode touches the pia mater (which results in a relatively noise-free oscilloscope trace), note the vertical reading on the micromanipulator. This can be used to determine from where in the brain different recordings are being made. Now slowly lower the electrode through the hippocampus into the thalamus and constantly watch the screen for evidence of spike potentials. Once spike potentials appear, they will be seen as very distinct from the high-frequency noise in your trace; they will appear as vertical lines (at least at a sweep speed of 100 msec/cm) usually of much greater amplitude than the noise; most important, their amplitude will be distributed asymmetrically around the baseline. To confirm you are in fact recording spikes, increase the sweep speed to 1 to 2 msec/cm. Recall that the duration of a spike potential is in the order of 1 msec, and at this new sweep/speed the deflections should spread out to ½ or 1 cm on the screen.

In the region of the medial geniculate nucleus, you should be able to record clear auditory evoked potentials to hand clapping, finger snapping, and whistling, and these may be accompanied by changes in the unit activity.

If the two parts of the laboratory exercise are done in different laboratory periods, there will probably be ample time to explore systematically, with the aid of a stereotaxic atlas, some of the thalamic nuclei and various tracts such as the medial lemniscus, the optic tract, or the trigeminal nerve (about 9 or 10 mm ventral to the pia mater) with respect to evoked potentials and changes in multiunit firing rate to sensory stimulation. Figure 18–4 is a schematic diagram of the somatotopic representation of the face region on the trigeminal nerve and the Gasserian ganglion of the rat. The cross-hatching indicates those regions of the face which, when tactually stimulated, produce varying degrees of multiunit activity in the ipsilateral trigeminal nerve when using electrode penetrations having lateral and A-P coordinates as indicated on the lower horizontal and left vertical axes, respectively. This was derived from one 450-gram rat of the Holtzman strain; students might attempt to construct a similar set of somatotopic figures for rats of the particular weight and strain they are using.

If one is available, an audiomonitor greatly facilitates such systematic mapping, for it allows one to hear spike potentials as "bips," and changes in the rate of firing can be much more easily detected when heard than when seen on an oscilloscope screen.

Cleaning up

Before beginning to clean up, administer an overdose of anesthetic to your rat and expose the thoracic cavity as described in Laboratory Exercise VI. Turn off the electronic equipment so it has time to cool before being put away. Then, as in all labs, clean your equipment, wash and dry your instruments well, and leave the work area in an orderly fashion. Do not wash the electrodes; just wipe them with a damp sponge.

LEFT HEMISPHERE

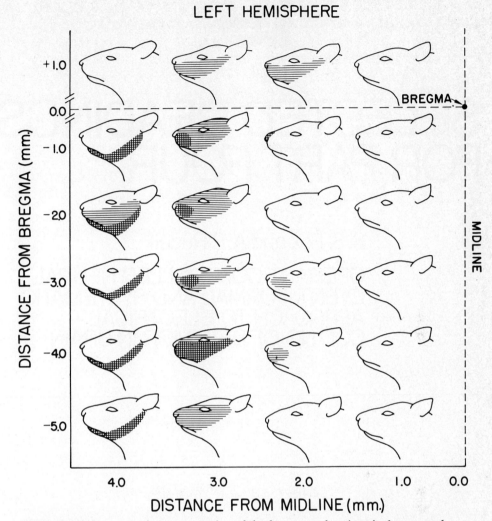

Figure 18–4. Somatotopic representation of the face upon the trigeminal nerve and Gasserian ganglion in a 450-gram Holtzman rat. Increasing amounts of cross-hatching indicate areas of maximal multiunit activity. (Courtesy of A. G. Marwine and H. P. Zeigler.)

19

SELECTED READINGS FOR PART FOUR

S. S. Fox and A. P. Rudell

OPERANT CONTROLLED NEURAL EVENT: FORMAL AND SYSTEMATIC APPROACH TO ELECTRICAL CODING OF BEHAVIOR IN BRAIN

Fox and Rudell present an interesting alternative to the traditional electrophysiological approach to the study of brain-behavior relations. They begin their paper with a critique of this approach, mentioned in Chapter 17, and some of the problems they view to be inherent in it. Their alternative is basically one of reversing the independent-dependent variable relationship, and so instead of attempting to determine what electrophysiological activity goes along with or is associated with the emission of a particular behavior, one examines what behavior goes along with or is associated with the emission of a particular electrophysiological response. They propose, and demonstrate, that the emission of an electrophysiological response can be established and controlled by operant conditioning, which involves the selection of a criterion response, the establishment of a baseline rate for that response, the reinforcement of some defined change in the response, and the recording of the changes in frequency of the chosen response.

The particular electrophysiological response chosen was the part of the visual evoked potential that occurs between 170 msec and 193 msec after the presentation of a flash of light. During repeated presentations of the flash of light, the voltage fluctuations occurring during the interval of interest were measured and the mean and standard deviations computed. This represents the baseline. When training started, the cats received reinforcement in the form of milk squirted into the mouth whenever that component of the evoked response exceeded 1.2 standard deviations below the mean of the baseline.

Note, first, that the electrical activity of the brain can be conditioned or modified. This, however, should

From *Science*, 1968, **162**, 1299–1303. Reprinted with the permission of S. S. Fox and the American Association for the Advancement of Science. Copyright © 1968 by the American Association for the Advancement of Science.

not be too surprising if one assumes that electrophysiological responses indicate something about the activity of the brain and that that activity has something to do with behavior, for if behavior can be conditioned or modified, it implies that electrophysiological activity can be conditioned or modified. This was the basic logic of the study. Note also the use of yoked controls, control animals that received the same pattern of reinforcement and the same stimulus presentations, but whose reinforcement was not contingent on the electrophysiological response to the stimulus presentation. These animals show that the results obtained with the experimental animals were not due to the reinforcement itself or to the stimulus itself, but were due to the reinforcement contingencies.

The second study was conducted simply to show that the results were not specific to reinforcing decreases in the voltage fluctuations of the EP component and that they could be obtained as well with increases in voltage.

Unfortunately, Fox and Rudell found that the behavioral measures they attempted to use and to correlate with the changes in electrophysiological response were too insensitive. The value and importance of this study lies, however, less in the actual findings than in the fact that is presents a new paradigm for the study of brain-behavior relations.

ABSTRACT: *Traditional studies of electrophysiological correlates of behavior contain inherent high variability resulting from the arbitrary choice of behaviors, brain locations, and wave parameters. The operant control of neural events is a formal and systematic approach to the study of prespecified parameters and components of brain activity as they encode behaviors. Two studies in which the electrical activity of brain was the criterion for reinforcement demonstrate the acquisition, under such operant control, of two mutually exclusive behaviors or states which selectively alter evoked potential components.*

The purpose of this report is to raise some reservations regarding traditional approaches to the study of neural correlates of behavior and to offer a strategy for investigating behaviorally relevant bioelectrical activity of brain. Electrical activity of the brain has been of continuous interest in studies of neural correlates of behavior, especially learning (1, 2), in which bioelectrical activity of brain in the form of cortical evoked potentials, single cell discharge, spontaneous electroencephalogram, d-c shifts, impedance changes, and the like has been related to changes in behavioral state accompanying learning or differential performance.

Although a variety of such changes has been described, replicability has been a recurrent problem, and the variable, transient, unreliable, and arbitrary character of such responses is well recognized (1); this character is consistent with any arbitrarily selected collateral response system (heart rate changes, galvanic skin response, and other).

We are concerned with the apparent simplicity of these studies and feel that reexamination of such correlative paradigms leads to the conclusion that the understanding and control in such experiments may be less than is believed, for a number of reasons as follows.

1. The inherent variability of spontaneous behavior contributes substantially to the variability of the bioelectric response to a so-called "neutral" stimulus, resulting in less than complete confidence in the knowledge of the conditioned stimulus.

2. The choice of a given behavior is arbitrary in reference to a chosen brain location. The fact that electric responses to stimuli can be recorded from many widely separated areas of the brain has encouraged the placement of large arrays of electrodes to compensate for the lack of specific information by force of number of placements in locating brain responses that may be relevant to the specific behavioral paradigm.

3. Transient responses may be expected, and the process of establishing a particular functional connection may at some specific time in training be considered complete. Continuation of the behavioral task may depend upon processes not necessarily occurring at the original location. Thus, the component nature of complex behavior may be both multiple and sequentially represented in brain.

4. The arbitrary choice of behavior also takes into account in acquisition or performance only one or a few end-point responses, and not the infinitely complex and unknown (possibly not parallel in time) set of collateral responses that are occurring in the conditioning paradigm (3) and that have unknown individual and conjoint influences on the bioelectric response. Most important is that behavior is rarely described accurately on a time base comparable to the base used to describe the momentary fluctuations in excitability as reflected in the bioelectric response. Correlation of momentary and discrete bioelectric events, therefore, with multiple determined molar behaviors may be in error by one or more orders of magnitude (days compared to milliseconds).

5. Bioelectric response parameters for evaluation is often not prespecified and awaits the empirical outcome of an experiment. Parameter specification for

correlation with molar behavior is necessarily arbitrary and may be unrelated to the major response system under conditioning control by the animal.

Therefore, knowledge of the effective stimulus, of the actual response being conditioned, of the relevant recording site, and of relevant parameters of the dependent variable probably contributes substantially to the variability of results in studies of bioelectric correlates of behavior.

A modified approach to the study of the behaviorally significant bioelectric events is described here. This approach provides for the formal, sequential, and systematic study of bioelectric response parameters which either separately or conjointly are relevant to or encode learned behavior. Available techniques (4, 5) are used and these methods are applied to functional bioelectric coding.

Several findings have been important for our renewed belief that the sequential stimulus information conveyed to the central nervous system may be equally well evaluated by a rigorous analysis of the evoked potential waveform or by analysis of single cell activity. We have demonstrated (6) that the evoked potential or spontaneous waveform recorded from the brain is closely related to the sequential, pulsatile activity of a single cell. The curve of probability of firing of a single cell either continuously or at intervals after a stimulus is duplicated accurately by the waveform of the evoked potential or of spontaneous slow activity. Thus the evoked potential represents, as does sequential single cell firing probability, the spontaneous or stimulus-initiated pulse code of the nervous system. Our study, therefore, is a first step in the development of an approach by which parameters of the sequential components of the evoked potential waveform which are relevant to the coding of learned behaviors may be formally specified.

The approach consists of the following phases. Instead of being made a dependent variable, the evoked potential is made the criterion for reinforcement or the independent variable, and the location and parameters of components of the evoked responses may be specified in advance. By allowing the animals a free range of behavior and by making reinforcement contingent upon the prespecified neural response, the animals are allowed to use whatever behavior is available in generating the specified response. A neural response of relatively low probability is chosen from an animal's repertoire. Reinforcement is expected to increase the probability of the occurrence of the response if it is relevant to behavior, that is, under control of reinforcement.

Our general procedure for operant conditioning is as follows. Initially, measures are taken of the mean and variance of an evoked response, from an arbitrarily chosen brain location. On this basis, a criterion response is established, and the probability of its occurrence without reinforcement is determined. This probability is determined anew each day before the training session. During training, reinforcement is presented immediately after the occurrence of a criterion response. The pattern of reinforcements generated by the experimental animal serves as the basis for reinforcement for a yoked-control animal—which in every respect is treated as the experimental animal—except that reinforcement is not contingent upon its own response, but was determined by tapes produced by the performance of the experimental animals on the same day.

Specific to these studies, four cats were implanted with (i) long-term cortical and subcortical electrodes led to a multiconnector plug fastened to the skull, and (ii) a plastic tube anchored at one end near the plug and at the other to an upper tooth, for the rapid delivery of milk reinforcement, leading respectively to the appropriate amplifiers and milk reservoir. The animals were placed in an empty shielded box with a frosted glass window and were allowed a free range of activity, except for the physical limitations of the cable and box. The entire conditioning program was under the on-line, real-time control of a computer system (PDP–8) located in another room.

At intervals of 4 seconds, the computer triggered a Grass PS2 photostimulator, delivering a 10-msec light flash to the animal through the window of the recording box. Analog brain voltage from the amplifiers, 150 msec before and 350 msec after the light flash, was digitized for the computer's operation. The digital values were displayed on a storage oscilloscope. To establish a training criterion before conditioning, the mean and standard deviation of 2000 responses from the left visual cortex (VII) were computed. In the first study, the criterion was established by requiring that the mean voltage of a selected portion of the evoked response (between 170 and 193 msec after the stimulus) be 1.2 standard deviations more negative than the mean before conditioning. In the second study, it was required that this same voltage be 1.2 standard deviations more positive than the mean before conditioning.

During conditioning, flashes were presented as above, but after each flash the incoming value of the selected points was compared with the criterion value and reinforcement was delivered if the criterion was met. Thus, the program provided reinforcement of behavioral states of the animals which altered by a criterion amount the selected parameters (voltage in this case) of the flash-evoked potential of visual cortex.

A food-deprived animal was expected to maximize those responses which led to reinforcement. However, unless the amplitude of the evoked potential at the points selected was in some way related to either behavioral or neural information, it should be impossible for the animal to generate them with a probability higher than that determined during base-line measurements. It is possible that amplitude at these points might be increased by some other means. For example, the conditioning program might be construed as classical conditioning with partial reinforcement, rather than operant conditioning, in that some part of the time a reinforcement is immediately preceded by a light flash. This and other possibilities are excluded by the yoked-control animals.

For training of behaviors related to increased negativity in the first study, 2000 trials (flashes) per day were presented to the animals for 12 days, with no reinforcement for the first 500 trials so that we could determine the base rate of responding. A response 1.2 standard deviations above the mean would be expected to occur by chance approximately 12 percent of the time. The observed mean rate of criterion responding during the 12 nonreinforcement sessions was 8.7 percent for the yoked-control animals and 16.9 percent for experimental animals. This slightly higher preconditioning rate of criterion responding found in experimental animals was anticipated since, once the behavior was conditioned, the trials on which the determinations were made for the experimental animals also functioned as extinction sessions.

The results of this initial study demonstrate the acquisition, by animals reinforced in this way for increased negativity, of responses which alter parameters (amplitude) of specific components of the evoked potential. Figure 1a contrasts the mean daily performance (12 days) of the experimental animals with their respective yoked-control animals during periods of nonreinforcement and periods of reinforcement. The sudden increase in criterion responses to a high level (37.9 percent) by the experimental animals at the onset of reinforcement is in sharp contrast to the continued, stable, low performance (6.2 percent) of the controls. Further, there was no overlap between experimentals and controls for any 50 flash block on any day for the reinforcement period.

An animal performing as high as 70 percent criterion responses for any block of 50 flashes or for any day and showing no gross motor behavior which could be related to the performance sat quite still in

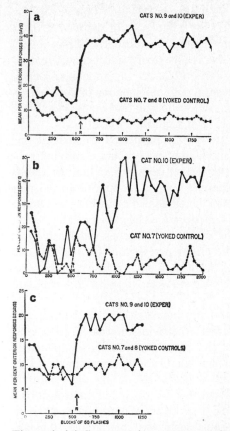

Figure 1. (a) Successes (mean percent) in meeting the criterion amplitude of a prespecified evoked potential component over 12 days. The letter *R* with the arrow indicates the end of the extinction period and beginning of reinforcement each day. Animals are reinforced for increased negativity at 170 to 193 msec after the light flash. (b) Acquisition (percentage of successes) in meeting the criterion response for the first day of extinction and training. (c) Performance (percentage of successes) in meeting the criterion amplitude of the same prespecified evoked potential components as in (a), but animals are reinforced for decreased negativity.

a variety of positions in the recording box. No differences between experimental and control animals were observed. The underlying behavioral or other events, therefore, which produce the observed alteration in brain activity are obscure.

The acquisition of such operant controlled neural events may be extremely rapid, as short as a single training session. Figure 1b shows the performance of an experimental animal and his yoked control on the first training day. Comparison of Figure 1, a and b, indicates that the performance of these animals on this first day is quite representative of that on the next 11 days. We suspect, however, that acquisition rate depends on the complexity of the formal questions asked concerning the functional utilization of specific parameters of the neural events under investigation. The use of criteria involving second-order or derivative measures, or combinations of parameters, or combinations of locations in time on the bioelectric signal will effect such acquisition functions.

A second study was conducted to indicate the lability and generality of the operant controlled neural events and to further demonstrate that the results of the first experiment were not specific to the particular response (increased negativity) chosen. States which resulted in decreased negativity at the same location on the evoked potential as previously were reinforced. The criterion responses for the first and second studies were mutually exclusive and represented a difference between them of 2.4 standard deviations.

The second study indicates that, as before, animals can generate a behavior or state which results in such neural changes. Figure 1c shows that mean daily performance for experimental animals (18.9 percent) differs dramatically during the reinforcement period from that of the yoked controls (10.4 percent), while performance during the 12 nonreinforced sessions again was comparable (9.5 percent for the experimental animals and 8.9 percent for the controls). Again, performance of the experimental animals was somewhat higher during nonreinforcement, attributable to effects of repetitive training and extinction. This conditioned decrease in negativity of the chosen evoked potential component immediately followed the training which resulted in increased negativity in the same animals. Again, no related behaviors were observed. In all cases, after the two experiments, yoked-control animals, reinforced for the same changes in bioelectric activity as experimental animals, showed similar conditioning, thus eliminating the possibility of any inherent differences between the two groups.

The specificity of changes should also be emphasized. The definition of the criterion response restricted only the amplitude of the response between 170 and 193 msec, but did not specify the manner in which the decreased negativity was to occur nor the extent to which correlated changes in other components of the evoked potential might occur. Nevertheless, it was observed that an animal may generate highly localized and specific responses which affect only the designated components of the evoked response.

The discrete nature of the change in response is suggested by the raw data (oscilloscope traces) of Figure 2, which shows 15 evoked responses from an experimental animal during a nonreinforcement period and 15 responses during reinforcement. The evoked potentials generated during reinforcement represent 8 out of 15 successes. For all of the reinforced sweeps the potential differs from the nonreinforced condition. More important is the specificity of the alteration and its restriction to the designated component (area between the parallel vertical lines).

The response of this animal represents a specific and local change in the direction of the potential and not simply an alteration of overall voltage, although such specificity was not required by the experimental paradigm. Minimally, the evoked potential in this case is not a single functional event, coding a single message throughout its extent. Such specificity of functional control suggests the relative functional independence of the individual components of the evoked potential, and implies considerable specificity, complexity, and relative independence of component behaviors.

Operant control of neural events as an approach to functional coding in bioelectric events allows systematic and formal study of prespecified parameters of bioelectric activity, singly or together as they functionally relate to behaviors. In these studies the operant controlled neural event has already indicated the relative independence of specific wave components. The approach, therefore, affords all the information concerning the functional aspects of bioelectric events available from traditional correlative methods in which some behavior is observed, but with the additional power of parameter selection and rapid resolution of sequential experimental questions. The operant controlled neural event, however, provides no more and possibly less information regarding the behaviors being coded than do correlative methods. The same problems of multiple determination and multiple representation of behaviors by brain events exist in the present system, with the exception that there is greater assurance that the relevant behaviors are in a steady state. The elucidation of specific behaviors or classes of behaviors related to specific neural events must await measurement of behaviors and brain events on the same time base with the same zero time and with the same resolution.

At present, it is difficult to think of behaviors which may be measured continuously with millisecond resolution in such an analog fashion. The major problem of brain-behavior relationship may now be in the measurement of behavior.

Finally, the operant controlled neural event has

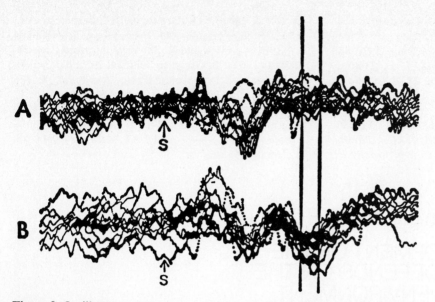

Figure 2. Oscilloscope traces from animal reinforced for behaviors producing decreased negativity. (A) Fifteen traces taken from an extinction period; (B) 15 traces taken from the reinforcement period immediately following. Eight of the responses in (B) resulted in reinforcement. The criterion component of the evoked response lies between the two parallel vertical lines. The letter S with the arrow indicates the light flash stimulus. There are specificity and localization of the change. There is also some increased variability before the stimulus in (B).

been demonstrated as being capable of experimentally separating functional implications of parameters and components of waves in brain. To the extent that electrophysiologists have developed hypotheses regarding microanatomical correlates of bioelectrogenesis in brain, in terms of cortical morphology or synaptic configuration or connectivity (7), such hypotheses should serve as a rational guide in the selection of parameters to be investigated as operant controlled neural events. To the extent that such microanatomical substrates are already understood in terms of parameters of electrical events or the reverse, the operant controlled neural event allows the determination of the relative independence of these as well as the separate and conjoint functional role of such anatomical systems in brain.

References and notes

1. E. R. John, *Ann. Rev. Physiol.* **23,** 451 (1961); F. Morrell. *Physiol. Rev.* **41,** 443 (1961).
2. H. Yoshii and N. Ogura, *Med. J. Osaka Univ.* **11,** 1 (1960); D. S. Runchkin, J. Villegas, E. R. John, *Ann. N.Y. Acad. Sci.* **115,** 799 (1964); J. Villegas, *ibid.* **122,** 362 (1964); W. R. Adey, *Progr. Physiol. Psychol.* **1,** 1 (1966).
3. K. Bykov, *The Cerebral Cortex and the Internal Organs* (Chemical Publishing, New York, 1957); E. Meurice, H. Weiner, W. Sloboda, *J. Exp. Anal. Behav.* **9,** 121 (1966); D. H. Cohen and R. G. Darkovic, *ibid.,* p. 681; R. J. Gavalas, *ibid.* **10,** 119 (1967).
4. N. E. Miller, *Ann. N.Y. Acad. Sci.* **92,** 830 (1961); *Proc. World Congr. Psychiat. Montreal* **3,** 213 (1963); ——— and A. Carmona, *J. Comp. Physiol. Psychol.* **63,** 1 (1967); N. E. Miller and L. V. DiCara, *ibid.* **63,** 12 (1967); L. V. DiCara and N. E. Miller, *Science* **159,** 1485 (1968); A. Carmona, thesis, Yale University, New Haven (1967).
5. H. D. Kimmel and F. A. Hill, *Psychol. Rep.* **7,** 555 (1960); J. Olds and M. E. Olds, in *Brain Mechanisms and Learning,* J. F. Delafresnaye, Ed. (Blackwell, Oxford, 1961), p. 153; R. L. Fowler and H. D. Kimmel, *J. Exp. Psychol.* **63,** 563, (1962); J. Olds, *Electroenceph. Clin. Neurophysiol. Suppl.* **24,** 219 (1963); E. Kimmel and H. D. Kimmel, *J. Exp. Psychol.* **65,** 212 (1963); J. V. Basmajian, *Science* **141,** 440 (1963); D. Schapiro, A. B. Crider, B. Tursky, *Psychon. Sci.* **1,** 147 (1964); W. H. Green, thesis, University of Florida, Gainesville (1964); D. C. Rice, thesis, University of Wisconsin (1964); A. B. Crider, A. Shapiro, B. Tursky, *J. Comp. Physiol. Psychol.* **61,** 20 (1966); J. Olds, *Progr.*

Brain Res. **27,** 144 (1967); R. J. Gavalas, *J. Exp. Anal. Behav.* **10,** 119 (1967).

6. S. S. Fox and J. H. O'Brien, *Science* **147,** 888 (1965); S. S. Fox, J. Liebeskind, J. H. O'Brien, H. Dingle, *Progr. Brain Res. Ser.* **27,** 254 (1967); S. S. Fox and R. J. Norman, *Science* **159,** 1257 (1968).

7. D. Purpura, *Intern. Rev. Neurobiol.* **1,** 47 (1959); ———, M. Girado, H. Grundfest, *J. Gen. Physiol.* **42,** 1037 (1959); *Electroenceph. Clin. Neurophysiol.* **12,** 95, (1960); D. Purpura and H. Grundfest, *ibid.,* p. 95; D. Purpura, *Ann. N.Y. Acad. Sci.* **94,** 604 (1961); ——— and R. Shofer, *J. Neurophysiol.* **26,** 494 (1963); B. Grafstein, *ibid.* **24,** 79 (1963); G. D. Pappas and D. Purpura, *Progr. Brain Res.* **4,** 176 (1964); D. Purpura, R. Shofer, E. Housepian, C. Noback, *ibid.,* p. 187; D. Purpura and F. S. Musgrave, *J. Neurophysiol.* **27,** 133 (1964); D. Purpura, *ibid.,* p. 117; ——— and J. G. McMurtry, *ibid.* **28,** 166 (1965).

C. Blakemore and G. F. Cooper

DEVELOPMENT OF THE BRAIN DEPENDS ON THE VISUAL ENVIRONMENT

This article demonstrates a relatively early use of single-unit recordings to study alterations in the visual system following the experimental restriction of early visual experience. The study is based empirically on the findings of Hubel and Wiesel (1963) that visual cortex cells in normal cats and in newborn kittens have receptive fields that (1) are locus-specific in that stimulation of only a specific retinal locus will drive each cell, (2) are orientation-specific in that the optimal stimulus for each cell is a line or bar of light having a specific orientation, and (3) are binocular in that most can be driven by stimulation of corresponding points of both retinae. It furthermore rests on the normative observation that in kittens raised with normal visual experience there is no preferred or predominant receptive field orientation. The study shows very elegantly that the distribution of receptive field orientation is altered following early inexperience with lines and edges of some given orientation. Of particular interest in reference to Chapter 17 is the fact that the cats show behavioral visual deficits quite consistent with the electrophysiological ones: The cat raised in a vertical visual world appeared unable to detect lines and edges that were horizontal and showed a marked absence of visual cortex cells with horizontal receptive fields.

Since this study was published, it has become questionable whether the receptive fields of completely inexperienced kittens do in fact show an orientation preference, in that visual cortex cells may respond equally to spots of light and to lines of any orientation (Barlow and Pettigrew, 1971). This, of course, is of critical importance for the interpretation to be given to the Blakemore and Cooper results—that is, whether their findings indicate a modification of an existing receptive field organization with which the kitten is endowed or a restriction in the development of the normal receptive field organization. The student is referred to a recent concise review of this controversy by Blakemore (1974).

In a normal cat, neurones of the visual cortex are selective for the orientation of lines and edges in the visual field, and the preferred orientations of different cells are distributed all around the clock.[1] Hirsch and Spinelli[2] have recently reported that early visual experience can change this organization. They reared kittens with one eye viewing vertical stripes, the other horizontal, and found that out of twenty-one neurones with elongated receptive fields all were monocularly driven, and in all but one case the orientation of the receptive field closely matched the pattern experienced by that eye.

We began a related project about a year ago and this is a preliminary report of our results. Our approach was rather different from that of the group at Stanford. We allowed our kittens normal binocular vision in an environment consisting entirely of horizontal or vertical stripes. The kittens were housed from birth in a completely dark room, but from the age of 2 weeks they were put into a special apparatus for an average of about 5 h each day. The kitten stood on a clear glass platform inside a tall cylinder

From *Nature,* 1970, **228,** 477–478. Reprinted with the permission of C. Blakemore and Macmillan Journals, Ltd., London.

Figure 1. The visual display consisted of an upright plastic tube, about 2 m high, with an internal diameter of 46 cm. The kitten, wearing a black ruff to mask its body from its eyes, stood on a glass plate supported in the middle of the cylinder. The stripes on the walls were illuminated from above by a spotlight. The luminance of the dark bars was about 10 cd. m^{-2} and of the bright stripes about 130 cd. m^{-2}; they were of several different widths. For this diagram the top cover and the spotlight have been removed from the tube.

the entire inner surface of which was covered with high-contrast black-and-white stripes, either horizontal or vertical (Fig. 1). There were no corners to its environment, no edges to its floor and the upper and lower limits to its world of stripes were a long way away. It could not even see its own body, for it wore a wide black collar [3] that restricted its visual field to a width of about 130°. The kittens did not seem upset by the monotony of their surroundings and they sat for long periods inspecting the walls of the tube.

We stopped this routine when the kittens were 5 months old, well beyond the "critical period" in which total visual deprivation causes physiological deficits.[4] From that time the cats were taken for several hours each week from their dark cage to a small, well-lit room, furnished with chairs and tables, where we watched their visual reactions.

At first they were visually extremely inept, whether they had been exposed to vertical or horizontal stripes.

Their pupillary reflexes were normal but they showed no visual placing when brought up to a table top and no startle response when an object was thrust towards them. They guided themselves mainly by touch and were frightened when they reached the edge of the surface they were standing on. But they quickly recovered from many of these deficiencies, which were probably visuomotor problems of the kind that Held and Hein described.[5] Within a total of about 10 h of normal vision they showed startle responses and visual placing, and would jump with ease from a chair to the floor.

On the other hand, some of their defects were permanent. They always followed moving objects with very clumsy, jerky head movements and they often tried to touch things moving on the other side of the room, well beyond their reach. Perhaps most telling of all, despite their active, and as time went on increasingly frenzied, visual exploration of the room, they often bumped into table legs as they scurried around.

There were, moreover, differences between cats reared in horizontal and vertical environments. They were virtually blind for contours perpendicular to the orientation they had experienced. They showed no startle response for an approaching 'Perspex' ('Plexiglas') sheet covered with black stripes, nor would they visually place on such a pattern, if the stripes were of the inappropriate orientation. The differences were most marked when two kittens, one horizontally and the other vertically experienced, were tested simultaneously with a long black or white rod. If this was held vertically and shaken, the one cat would follow it, run to it and play with it. Now if it was held horizontally the other cat was attracted and its fellow completely ignored it.

We moved on from behavioural studies to neurophysiology when the cats were 7.5 months old. They were anaesthetized with nitrous oxide and paralysed with succinyl choline while we recorded from single neurones in the primary visual cortex, using sodium chloride filled micropipettes. The refractive states of the eyes was corrected with contact lenses, spectacle lenses and 3 mm artificial pupils. There was no evidence of severe astigmatism, which might have explained our behavioural findings.

We used thin bright slits or edges to plot receptive fields on a screen 114 cm from the cat. The luminance of the background was about 5 cd. m^{-2} and of the bright target about 17 cd. m^{-2}. Our initial procedure was to make one long penetration deep into the medial edge of the post lateral gyrus, studying every single neurone encountered. We found units on

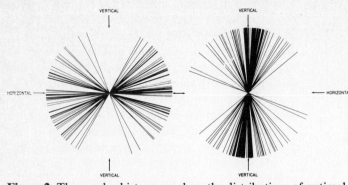

Figure 2. These polar histograms show the distributions of optimal orientations for fifty-two neurones from a horizontally experienced cat on the left, and seventy-two from a vertically experienced cat on the right. The slight torsion of the eyes, caused by the relaxant drug, was assessed by photographing the pupils before and after anesthesia and paralysis. A correction has been applied for torsion, so the polar plots are properly oriented for the cats' visual fields. Each line shows the optimal orientation for a single neurone. For each binocular cell the line is drawn at the mean of the estimates of optimal orientation in the two eyes. No units have been disregarded except for one with a concentric receptive field and hence no orientational selectivity.

the average about 80 μm apart, so presumably our electrode was not specially selective for the cells from which it recorded. After the long penetration we moved the electrode to other positions in area 17 and sampled just a few neurones at each place. Our exploration thus covered many cortical columns [1] and quite a large area of the visual field around the area centralis.

So far we have studied 125 neurones from two cats, one horizontally, the other vertically experienced. Of all these units, only one did not have distinct orientation selectivity and it had the action potential waveform and concentric, monocular receptive field of a projection fibre from the lateral geniculate body. About 75 percent of cells, in both cats, were clearly binocular and in almost every way the responses were like those in a normal animal. The distributions of preferred orientation, however, were totally abnormal (Fig. 2). Not one neurone had its optimal orientation within 20° of the inappropriate axis and there were, *in toto,* only twelve within 45° of it. This anisotropy is highly significant ($P <$ 0.00001 : chi-squared test).

Evidently the visual experience of these animals in early life has modified their brains, and there are pro-

found perceptual consequences. But we do not think that there is merely passive degeneration of certain cortical neurones because of under-activity. For we did not notice any obvious large regions of "silent" cortex, corresponding to the "missing" cortical columns. It seems instead that the visual cortex may adjust itself during maturation to the nature of its visual experience. Cells may even change their preferred orientation towards that of the commonest type of stimulus; so perhaps the nervous system adapts to match the probability of occurrence of features in its visual input.

We thank Patrick Jackson and Ian Creese for building the striped tubes and the MRC for research grants.

References

[1] Hubel, D. H., and Wiesel, T. N., *J. Physiol.,* **160,** 106 (1962).
[2] Hirsch, H. V. B., and Spinelli, D. N., *Science,* **168,** 869 (1970).
[3] Hein, A., and Held, R., *Science,* **158,** 390 (1967).
[4] Hubel, D. H., and Wiesel, T. N., *J. Physiol.,* **206,** 419 (1970).
[5] Held, R., and Hein, A., *J. Comp. Physiol. Psychol.,* **56,** 872 (1963).

part five

INDEPENDENT PROJECTS

20

SOME SUGGESTED LABORATORY PROJECTS

When most or all the laboratory exercises have been completed, students may wish to undertake independent projects that will allow them to work on their own and to use some of the skills acquired during the laboratory exercises. This section suggests various projects that might be appropriate in terms of both the level of technical sophistication necessary to carry them out and their involving effects usually evident in individual subjects. Students should be able to work on their own with only limited guidance, and each group can work on a project of its choice quite independent of other groups.

Because available equipment, supplies, and facilities vary greatly from institution to institution, the instructions have been written in a very general form. They outline certain background papers to which the student should refer, certain general considerations involved in carrying out each project, and certain procedural details, and refer the student to appropriate laboratory exercises for others. The student should read carefully the background material as well as other references provided by the instructor, and then discuss with him what might be an appropriate project, given whatever limitations there are on equipment or facilities. Students should then prepare a written proposal to be submitted to the instructor, indicating in detail the procedures to be followed and the equipment needed, and specifying precisely the independent and dependent variables and measures to be used in carrying out the project. Alternatively, for any of many reasons, the instructor may prefer a more structured approach and may prepare for each project detailed instructions written around available equipment and facilities. Either way, however, students should submit a written report when the project is completed, for writing a report does encourage organization and systematic behavior.

A. FOOD INTAKE AND WEIGHT REGULATION: CHANGES FOLLOWING VENTROMEDIAL HYPOTHALAMIC LESIONS

Rats with bilateral lesions of the lateral nucleus of the hypothalamus cease to eat or drink and will starve to death unless carefully tube fed and brought through the series of recovery stages described by Teitelbaum and Epstein (1962). Bilateral lesions of the ventromedial nucleus of the hypothalamus result in a syndrome with opposite characteristics with respect to feeding behavior—that is, the rat grossly overeats and becomes obese. It does not, however, gain weight indefinitely; eventually the weight stabilizes at a new level considerably above normal, and the rat regulates its food intake to maintain that level. The purpose of this project is to plot these weight changes associated with ventromedial hypothalamic lesions and to look at some of the variables that influence these changes.

Suggested background reading

Hetherington, A. W., & Ranson, S. W. Hypothalamic lesions and adiposity in the rat. *The Anatomical Record,* 1942, **78,** 149–172. (Reprinted in Isaacson, 1964).

Schacter, S. Some extraordinary facts about obese humans and rats. *American Psychologist,* 1971, **26,** 129–144.

Teitelbaum, P. Sensory control of hypothalamic hyperphagia. *Journal of Comparative and Physiological Psychology,* 1955, **48,** 156–163.

Teitelbaum, P. The use of operant methods in the assessment and control of motivational states. In W. K. Honig (Ed.), *Operant behavior: Areas of research and application.* New York: Appleton-Century-Crofts, 1966, pp. 565–608.

Teitelbaum, P. *Physiological psychology.* Englewood Cliffs, N.J.: Prentice-Hall, 1967, chaps. 8 and 9.

Teitelbaum, P., & Epstein, A. N. The lateral hypothalamic syndrome. *Psychological Review,* 1962, **69,** 74–90.

Subjects

Because hypothalamic obesity is a very robust effect and should be evident in individual subjects, two experimental rats and two sham-operated control rats are quite sufficient. If any within-group manipulations are to be done with, for example, diet, the number of subjects would have to be increased accordingly. Young male rats, weighing about 200 to 250 grams at the start of the project, should be used.

Lesions

Follow the procedures described in Laboratory Exercise V to make bilateral lesions of the ventromedial nucleus of the hypothalamus. As the nucleus is quite close to the midline (about 1 mm on either side), considerable care will have to be taken to ensure that the sagittal sinus is not ruptured when drilling the trephine holes or when inserting the lesion electrode. A current of 2 ma delivered for about 20 seconds should be sufficient to make a complete lesion. In performing the sham operations, follow the same procedures but do not pass any current through the electrode tip.

Recovery

Ventromedial hypothalamic lesions not only change feeding behavior but also produce a very emotional animal that may be difficult to handle. Do not attempt to handle it after surgery without heavy gloves. If the animal is particularly wild, it may be necessary to use padded tongs to pick the animal up by the base (not the tip) of the tail to move it, but be sure to check with your instructor before resorting to this measure.

Possible dependent variables

The most obvious dependent measure to record is weight change. The animals should be weighed for at least several days prior to surgery. Immediately after the operation, you will find that most animals lose some weight. The experimental animals will then show a marked increase in weight. Plan to weigh each animal at about the same time of day on every second or third day for 30 or 40 days, the time it typically takes for experimental animals to reach the static phase of hypothalamic hyperphagia. Food consumption can also be measured at the same time, and it is suggested that powdered food or meal be used rather than pellets because it is easy to measure and easy to adulterate, if desired.

Once the static phase is reached, the taste and texture of powdered food can be manipulated in ways similar to those described by Teitelbaum (1955), and again food intake and weight can be monitored in the two groups of animals to assess sensitivity to food adulteration.

If operant conditioning apparatus is available, there are many interesting dependent measures that can be examined, some of which are described by Teitelbaum (1966). For example, the animals can be shaped to press a bar for food, and the rate of bar pressing can be recorded as a function of different fixed ratio schedules. The ratio can be increased until the animals stop pressing. This will allow the two groups to be compared with respect to the terminal ratio as well as with respect to the response rate at the various intermediate ratios.

Report

Your instructor will tell you the type of report he expects, but as a minimum it should include a description of what you did, what you found, and what you think it means. If your instructor feels that a histological analysis of the lesions is necessary, the animals will be perfused and the brain prepared for you, or you will be told how to do this.

B. ACTIVITY AND EXPLORATORY BEHAVIOR: CHANGES WITH HIPPOCAMPAL LESIONS

Bilateral lesions of the hippocampus in rats produce a variety of effects, one of which seems to be to increase the level of activity of the animal when it is placed in, for example, an open-field situation. The purpose of this project is to examine these changes in activity and to consider possible reasons for it.

Suggested background reading

Douglas, R. J. The hippocampus and behavior. *Psychological Bulletin,* 1967, **67,** 416–443.

Gross, C. G. General activity. In L. Weiskrantz (Ed.), *Analysis of behavioral change.* New York: Harper & Row, 1968, pp. 91–106.

Halliday, M. S. Exploratory behavior. In L. Weiskrantz (Ed.), *Analysis of behavioral change.* New York: Harper & Row, 1968, pp. 107–126.

Kimble, D. P. Hippocampus and internal inhibition. *Psychological Bulletin,* 1968, **70,** 285–295.

The first two suggested readings are review papers that should provide the student with an overview of the basic anatomy and physiology of the hippocampus and of some behavioral research involving hippocampal lesions. It is strongly suggested that students read some of the original articles cited in these papers on activity, habituation, and exploratory behavior. The latter two readings should provide the student with an appreciation of some of the problems of measuring and interpreting activity, and of distinguishing activity from exploratory behavior.

Subjects

The effects of hippocampal damage on activity are reasonably pronounced, so that three experimental and three sham-operated control rats should be sufficient to observe effects. It is particularly important that male rats (200 to 250 grams at the start of the project) be used, as females show much more variation in activity as a function of the estrus cycle.

Preoperative activity assessment

In consultation with the instructor, and based on the readings, you should decide on some apparatus and set of procedures for assessing activity. A convenient and inexpensive apparatus to use is the open-field maze (shown in Figure 12–4), which consists simply of a 3-foot-square box (walls should be at least 12 inches high to prevent the rat from climbing out) with 6-inch squares drawn on the floor. The dependent measure can be the number of squares entered during some time period, such as 5 or 10 minutes. Note that it will be necessary to develop an operational definition of enter, such as both forelimbs over the line, the snout past the line, all four feet over the line, and so on. Be sure to define all dependent measures clearly and concisely. It is most important as well that your animals be tested in a quiet room, free from distracting noises.

Lesions

The hippocampus is a large structure, but it does not have to be completely removed to produce effects. Follow the procedures outlined in Laboratory Exercise V for making subcortical lesions, and aim the electrode tip to the posterior two-thirds of the dorsal portion of the hippocampus on each side. A 2 ma current passed through the electrode for 20 to 30 seconds will produce a good-sized lesion. If you wish to damage more of the hippocampus, it will be necessary to make two lesions on each side, one located at about the middle of the dorsal portion of the hippocampus and one located in the ventral portion. Again, use a 2 ma current delivered for about 20 seconds in making each of the four lesions.

Prepare the sham-operated animals in exactly the same way as the experimental animals, lowering the electrode into the hippocampus but not passing current through it.

Recovery

Allow the animals about two weeks to recover fully from the surgery before attempting to assess activity, and during this recovery period handle the animals regularly.

Postoperative testing

Retest all animals for activity, using the same criteria and dependent measures used preoperatively. It is suggested that the animals be tested for a number of days and that changes in activity as a function of time be plotted for the experimental and the control subjects. It is also suggested that on the basis of your reading you devise dependent measures other than activity, such as habituation of a startle response to repeated hand claps. (These measures should be taken only after the activity measures are completed.)

Report

Your instructor will tell you what type of report he expects, but as a minimum it should include a description of the intended lesion, the preoperative and postoperative activity scores for each animal, other dependent measures you used, and your interpretation of the results. If your instructor feels that histological analysis is necessary, the animals will be perfused and the brains prepared for you, or you will be shown how to do this.

C. ELECTRICAL STIMULATION OF THE BRAIN AS A DISCRIMINATIVE CUE

While electrical stimulation of the brain (ESB) has been widely used as a means of eliciting or evoking responses, it can also be used as a discriminative cue in learning situations. Virtually all this work, however, has involved classical conditioning paradigms, with the ESB serving as the CS and/or UCS. The purpose of this project is to study ESB as a discriminative cue in an instrumental learning situation.

Suggested background reading

Doty, R. W. Conditioned reflexes formed and evoked by brain stimulation. In D. E. Sheer (Ed.), *Electrical stimulation of the brain*. Austin: University of Texas Press, 1961, pp. 397–412. (Reprinted in Gross and Zeigler, 1969).

Doty, R. W. Electrical stimulation of the brain in behavioral context. *Annual Review of Psychology,* 1969, **20,** 289–320.

Sutherland, N. S., & Mackintosh, N. J. *Animal discrimination learning.* New York: Academic Press, 1971.

In order to gain an appreciation of what procedures were actually used in the classical conditioning paradigms, students should read at least one or two of the original papers cited by Doty in these review papers. Students who are unfamiliar with the animal discrimination learning literature are strongly encouraged to read portions of Sutherland and Mackintosh (1971), or at least Sutherland (1964).

Equipment

A simple and inexpensive instrumental learning apparatus is a straight runway, perhaps 6 feet long, 12 inches high and 6 inches wide, having a start box with a swinging door (as opposed to the more common guillotine door) at one end and a food cup at the other end. The dependent measures in such an apparatus could be the response latency (the time it takes the animal to leave the start box), the running time (the time it takes the animal to reach the goal box after leaving the start box), or a combination of the two. When used to study discrimination, what is of interest is the difference between the times on those trials during which the discriminative cue is present and those trials during which it is not present. Recall from Chapter 17 that evidence for discrimination is derived from differential responsiveness. In a runway situation with these dependent measures, that differential is with respect to time rather than choice behavior (running versus not running).

A mating connector plug compatible with that to be cemented to the skull (see next section) will have to be prepared as described in Appendix B–12. It may be possible to use the stimulator, wire, and connecting plug used in Laboratory Exercise VII. Phono-pickup wire, suspended from above the runway with long rubber bands, forms a light and flexible connection that allows the animal to move freely without the wires dragging behind it or pulling at the skull. The same stimulator used in Laboratory Exercises VI and VII can be used; it should be operated by a thumbswitch as described in

Laboratory Exercise VII. To test the experimental and control animals in the same way, the thumbswitch should be connected to a single-throw double-pole toggle switch (Cornsweet, 1963), so that it can be used to activate either the stimulator or a light suspended above the start box.

Subjects

It is suggested that three or four male rate (200 to 250 grams at the start of testing) be used as experimental animals and two rats be used as controls. The controls should be tested in the same way as the experimental animals, but a conventional discriminative cue, a light, is used instead of electrical stimulation of the brain.

Electrode implants

Follow the procedures described in Laboratory Exercise VII for implanting bipolar electrodes. It does not really matter in which part of the cortex you implant the electrode, but do avoid the motor area. It is very important that the shaft of the electrode be long enough that the tips completely penetrate the dura mater and are in the cortex proper. The dura mater is exquisitely sensitive and stimulation of it is most aversive.

Procedures

Several days after surgery, connect the mating plug from the stimulator to the headplug, place the animal into an open-field maze (Figure 12–4), and apply several short, low-voltage (less than 5 volts) pulses. Watch for any evidence of this being aversive for the animal. Be aware that continued stimulation, particularly at relatively high voltage levels, can produce seizure activity, so work with low voltages, pulses of short duration, and relatively long interpulse intervals (for example, no more than once every 10 or 15 seconds). Follow the same basic procedures described in Laboratory Exercise VII to determine if the stimulation is either aversive or rewarding for the animal. If it appears to be so, the animal should be discarded.

Place the animals on a 24-hour food deprivation schedule like that used in Laboratory Exercise IV. Start adaptation to the runway several days later, testing the animal just prior to giving it its daily ration. At first, place a few Noyes pellets in the start box. As soon as the animal will eat them, position them farther and farther from the start box so the animal has to run part way down the alley to eat them. As soon as the animal is shaped and will run all the way from the start box to the goal area to eat pellets from a cup, training can start.

Connect the animal to the stimulator, but do not apply any stimulation for the first four days. Instead, train it for 25 trials per day simply to run to the goal area for food whenever the start box door opens. Of course, food should be available in the goal area on all trials. Record the response latency and the running time using two stopwatches (unless the apparatus is wired with photorelays connected to clock timers). Start one watch as soon as you open the door and stop it when the animal reaches some point you have marked in the runway just outside the door. At the same time that you stop the first watch, start the second one and stop it when the animal reaches some fixed point at the end of the runway. Record these times on each trial. You should also establish some time criterion for a nonresponse (for example, staying in the start box for more than 15 seconds, not reaching the goal area within 30 seconds, etc.).

When the discrimination training actually begins, the animals should receive 24 trials of testing per day and on 12 of these trials specified by a Gellerman sequence, the animals should receive a series of 5 or 6 ½-second pulses of stimulation just as the start box door opens. For half the subjects these stimulation trials should be nonrewarded, and the trials with no stimulation should be rewarded. For the remaining subjects it should be the opposite so that stimulation comes to signal reward.

The running times for these two types of trials should quite quickly separate evidence of discrimination. You will have to decide on some criterion based on time differences for terminating testing, and the dependent measure might be trials to this criterion.

The control animals should be tested in exactly the same way except that instead of receiving pulses of brain stimulation, they should be exposed to a flashing light suspended above the runway as the discriminative cue.

Other Questions

Students who wish to pursue this might be interested in seeing whether animals can discriminate between stimulation of two different cortical sites. Certainly the considerations proposed by Corballis and Beale (1970) would suggest that the discrimination of mirror-image stimulation points (that is, points located at homolateral points of the two hemispheres) should be much more difficult than discrimination of non-mirror-image points or points on the same hemisphere. To look at this would, however, involve the use of at least twelve animals.

Report

Your instructor will tell you the type of report he expects, but as a minimum it should include a description of the stimulation sites and the voltage used for each subject, as well as a graph showing the median response latency and running time for each animal for each day during the 100 training trials and the discrimination testing sessions.

D. ELECTRICAL STIMULATION OF THE HYPOTHALAMUS: SITUATIONAL DETERMINANTS OF STIMULUS-BOUND BEHAVIOR

Laboratory Exercise VII involved a demonstration of the rewarding effects of lateral hypothalamic stimulation. As was discussed in relation to the Valenstein et al. reading (Chapter 14), stimulation of the same hypothalamic site can elicit various stimulus-bound behaviors such as feeding, drinking, gnawing, or wheel running. The purpose of this project is to demonstrate how certain of these stimulus-bound behaviors are situationally bound. It is suggested that the behaviors looked at be feeding and wheel running.

Suggested background reading

Hoebel, B. G. Feeding and self-stimulation. *Annals of the New York Academy of Sciences,* 1969, **157,** 758–778.

Hoebel, B. G., & Teitelbaum, P. Hypothalamic control of feeding and self-stimulation. *Science,* 1962, **135,** 375–377.

Rosenquist, A. C., & Hoebel, B. G. Wheel running elicited by electrical stimulation of the brain. *Physiology and Behavior,* 1968, **3,** 563–566.

Valenstein, E. S., Cox, U. C., & Kakolewski, J. W. Reexamination of the role of the hypothalamus in motivation. *Psychological Review,* 1970, **77,** 16–31.

Equipment

If the effects on feeding and wheel-running behavior of hypothalamic stimulation are examined, it will be necessary to use a running wheel that has a home cage or chamber connected directly to it to allow the animal to move from the chamber to the wheel without getting the stimulation wires entangled.

It will also be necessary to prepare a connecting plug compatible with the headplug to be cemented to the cranium of each subject. It is suggested that phono-pickup wire, which is very light and flexible, be suspended with large rubber bands from above the chamber; this will allow the animal to move freely without having the wire drag behind or pull at the skull.

Subjects

It will have been noted when reading the Valenstein et al. article that only 25 percent of their subjects showed stimulus-bound behavior, so it will be necessary to prepare six or eight male rats for this project in order to ensure enough successful animals.

Electrode implants

Follow the procedures described in Laboratory Exercise VII to implant a bipolar electrode into the lateral nucleus of the hypothalamus of each subject and to cement the headplug firmly to the skull.

Procedures

Allow each animal at least a week to recover from the surgery and then follow the procedures described in Laboratory Exercise VII to assess rewarding effects of stimulation. Use an oscilloscope to measure the voltage ultimately used to stimulate individual animals.

Place the animals on a 24-hour food deprivation schedule as described in Laboratory Exercise IV and test each one daily several hours after feeding. During each testing session, stimulate the animal with brief and regular pulses both when food pellets are available and when they are not, and record the behavior of the animal (wheel running, feeding, or anything else) during each such trial. If it is possible to connect an operant chamber to the running-wheel compartment, you could also compare the behavior of the animal when the stimulator is activated at regular intervals as opposed to being activated by bar presses.

Report

Your instructor will tell you what he expects for a laboratory report, but as a minimum it should include a description of the intended electrode placement and the procedures followed for behavioral observation. Histological analysis of the electrode placements would be desirable, especially in the case of animals not showing stimulus-bound behavior. Your animals will be perfused and the brains prepared, or your instructor will show you how to do this.

E. DISSOCIATION OF EEG AROUSAL AND BEHAVIORAL AROUSAL

It was pointed out in Chapter 17 that until quite recently there was believed to be a causal relationship between EEG arousal and behavioral arousal, but it is now quite clear that the relationship is much more complex. EEG arousal and behavioral arousal can be dissociated in a number of ways, but one of the earlier demonstrations involved the study of drug effects. Bradley (1958) found that IP injections of atropine sulfate (a cholinergic blocking agent discussed in Chapter 16) had no detectable effect on the activity of the animal but produced a sleeplike EEG pattern (low-frequency, high-amplitude waves). He also found that injections of physostigmine sulfate (a cholinergic potentiator) had the converse effect of producing an "aroused" EEG pattern (high-frequency, low-amplitude waves) while, like atropine, having no detectable effect on behavior. The purpose of this project is to replicate these most interesting findings with at least one of the two drugs.

Suggested background reading

Bradley, P. B. The central action of certain drugs in relation to the reticular formation of the brain. In H. H. Jasper (Ed.), *Reticular formation of the brain.* Boston: Little, Brown, 1958, pp. 123–149.

Thompson, R. F. *Foundations of physiological psychology.* New York: Harper & Row, 1967, chap. 14.

Subjects

If only one drug is to be used, it is suggested that it be atropine, and it should be necessary to use only two rats in order to observe the effects. However, if both atropine and physostigmine are used, then a minimum of four subjects should be tested. All subjects can receive both drugs, but the order of drug administration must of course be counterbalanced—that is, two subjects should get atropine first and physostigmine second, and two subjects should get the drugs in the reverse order.

Equipment

This project can be done using a preamp and oscilloscope to monitor the EEG, but if a polygraph or pen recorder is available, its use would greatly facilitate recording and analysis.

The observations of each animal while in the drugged and nondrugged states should be made with the animal in a plain box with a Plexiglas front, and this box should be able to be placed into a shielded cage like that used in Laboratory Exercises VIII and IX. The cage should be positioned on its end so there is room for cables to be suspended from the top. A connecting plug, compatible with the headplug to be cemented to the cranium (see next section) will have to be prepared beforehand as described in Appendix B–12. It is highly recommended that the wires used to connect the plug to the preamp be low-noise EEG cable, which is designed to produce a minimum of movement artifact. There will have to be one cable for each electrode lead and for the reference lead. At the point (inside the shielded cage) where these are connected to the input probe of the preamplifier, the shielding around all cables should be connected to the reference electrode lead and its shielding. If the cables are suspended from the top of the shielded cage using soft rubber bands, the animal can move about freely without the cable either dragging behind it or pulling excessively on the head.

When constructing the connecting plug and cable, be sure to note which plug holes are to be connected to which preamplifier input leads. The preamplifier can then be connected to the oscilloscope or pen recorder.

Electrode implants

The procedures for implanting the electrodes are a combination of those used in Laboratory Exercise VI involving the placement of a bonescrew, those used in Laboratory Exercise VII involving implanting chronic stimulating electrodes and cementing headplugs to the skull, and those used in Laboratory Exercise IX involving electrophysiological recording. Each electrode can be simply a 2 cm piece of .010-inch Diamel-insulated Nichrome wire with about 2 mm of one end bent at right angles and scraped of insulation, and with a male electrode pin soldered to the other end. The bent portion of the wire can rest on the surface of the dura. Since bipolar recordings will be made in order to reduce artifacts, two such electrodes will be needed for each subject. One reference electrode lead should also be prepared for each subject by scraping 10 or 15 mm of insulation from a 3 cm piece of .005-inch Diamel-insulated Nichrome wire and soldering an electrode pin to the other end.

Following the procedures described in Laboratory Exercise VII, one electrode should be implanted slightly anterior to, and one several millimeters posterior to, the frontoparietal bone suture. Both electrodes should be placed in the same hemisphere. Before implanting the electrodes, however, the four anchor bonescrews should be in place and the surface of the cranium roughened. The reference electrode is a fifth bonescrew, placed into the frontal sinus, several millimeters anterior to bregma. The uninsulated portion of the reference electrode wire can be wrapped tightly around the reference electrode bonescrew and fastened firmly with dental cement applied around the screw. The pins from the three leads can be inserted into the correct holes of the plug, and the wires should be aligned in an anterior-posterior plane and must not touch or cross one another. The wires and the plug can then be cemented in place as described in Laboratory Exercise VII.

Testing procedures

Allow several days for the animals to recover from the surgery and then begin adaptation to the testing situation. With the plug attached, place each animal in the box for short periods of time for several days. During these periods record the EEG [1] and attempt to develop ways to characterize it; also, watch the behavior of the animal and develop ways to code it. If you are using a polygraph or pen recorder, do not record the EEG continuously, as this just wastes paper; instead, record it for a short period every 2 or 3 minutes.

Test the animal for at least two days for a 25-minute period following the IP injection of 0.1 cc of isotonic saline. Every 2 minutes record the behavioral state of the animal and characterize the EEG. After 10 observations (after 22 minutes), clap your hands loudly and observe the startle response of the animal and record any change in the EEG arousal pattern. Repeat this 3 or 4 minutes later.

On another day the animal can be tested with the first drug. Weigh the animal, connect it to the preamp, inject it IP with atropine sulfate (3 mg/kg) or with physostigmine sulfate (0.75 mg/kg), and place it in the observation box. Repeat the same procedures described above and record the EEG and the behavior every 2 minutes and then test for a startle response and EEG blocking. Observations can be repeated every other day for several days. Before injecting an animal with the second drug, leave it for a week to ensure that all traces of the first drug are removed from the system, and then repeat all the same procedures.

Report

Your instructor will tell you what type of report he expects, but as a minimum it should include a description of the behavior of the animals and the EEG pattern observed during the adaptation phase and the saline-injection periods, how these changed with each drug injection, and whether the changes themselves seemed to change with repeated injections. If observations were made with both drugs, be sure to comment on whether the order of drug administration had any effect on the outcome.

---

[1] If you are using a polygraph with multiple recording channels, connect the cables so that one channel records bipolar and two other channels record monopolar from each active electrode. This may allow interesting comparisons to be made.

references

Adrian, E. D., & Mathews, B. H. C. The Berger rhythm: Potential changes from the occipital lobes of man. *Brain,* 1934, **57,** 355–385.

Arbib, M. A. *The Metamorphical brain.* New York: Wiley-Interscience, 1972.

Barlow, H. B., & Pettigrew, J. D. Lack of specificity of neurones in the visual cortex of young kittens. *J. Physiology (London),* 1971, **218,** 98–100.

Berger, H. Uber das Elektrenkephalogramm des Menschen. *Arch. für Psychiatrie und Nervenkrankheiten,* 1929, **87,** 527–570.

Birch, H., Cotman, C. W., & Thompson, R. F. Technique and instrumentation in physiological psychology. *American Psychologist,* 1969, **24,** 264–267.

Bizzi, E., Kalil, R. E., & Tagliasco, V. Eye-head coordination in monkeys: Evidence for centrally patterned organization. *Science,* 1971, **173,** 452–454.

Blakemore, C. Developmental factors in the formation of feature extracting neurons. In F. O. Schmitt & F. G. Worden (Eds.), *The neurosciences: Third study program.* Cambridge, Mass.: MIT Press, 1974.

Blakemore, C., & Cooper, G. F. Development of the brain depends on the visual environment. *Nature,* 1970, **228,** 477–478.

Boring, E. G. *A history of experimental psychology.* (2nd ed.) New York: Appleton-Century-Crofts, 1950.

Bradley, P. B. The central action of certain drugs in relation to the reticular formation of the brain. In H. H. Jasper (Ed.), *Reticular formation of the brain.* Boston: Little, Brown, 1958.

Brazier, M. A. B. The historical development of neurophysiology. In J. Field (Ed.), *Handbook of physiology, section I: Neurophysiology. Vol. 1.* Washington, D.C.: American Physiological Society, 1959.

Brazier, M. A. B. *A history of the electrical activity of the brain.* London: Pitman, 1961.

Brodal, A. Experimentelle Untersuchungen über

retrograde Zellveränderungen in der unteren Olive nach Lasionen des Kleinhirns. *Z. ges. Neurol. Psychiat.*, 1939, **166**, 646–704.

Brodmann, K. *Vergleichende Lokalisationslehre der Grosshirnrinde in ihren prinzipien Dargestellt auf Grund des Zellenbaues.* Leipzig: J. A. Barth, 1909.

Brown, J. L., Shively, F. D., LaMotte, R. H., & Sechzer, J. A. Color discrimination in the cat. *Journal of Comparative and Physiological Psychology,* 1973, **84**, 534–544.

Brush, E. S., Mishkin, M., & Rosvold, H. E. Effects of object preferences and aversions on discrimination learning in monkeys with frontal lesions. *Journal of Comparative and Physiological Psychology,* 1961, **54**, 319–325.

Brush, S. G. Should the history of science be rated X? *Science,* 1974, **183**, 1164–1172.

Bures, J., Petran, N., & Jachar, J. *Electrophysiological methods in biological research.* (3rd ed.) New York: Academic Press, 1967.

Butter, C. M. The effect of discrimination training on pattern equivalence in monkeys with inferotemporal and lateral striate lesions. *Neuropsychologia,* 1968, **6**, 27–40.

Corballis, M. C., & Beale, I. L. Bilateral symmetry and behavior. *Psychological Review,* 1970, **77**, 451–464.

Cornsweet, T. N. *The design of electric circuits for the behavioral sciences.* New York: Wiley, 1963.

Cowey, A. Discrimination. In L. Weiskrantz (Ed.), *Analysis of behavioral change.* New York: Harper & Row, 1968.

De Groot, J. *The rat forebrain in stereotaxic coordinates.* Amsterdam: North-Holland Publishing Company, 1959.

Diamond, I. T., & Hall, W. C. Evolution of neocortex. *Science,* 1969, **164**, 251–262.

DiCara, L. V., Weaver, L., and Wolf, G. Comparison of DC and RF for lesioning white and grey matter. *Physiology and Behavior,* 1974, **12**, 1087–1090.

Dimond, S. *The double brain.* London: Churchill Livingston, 1972.

Doty, R. W. Functional significance of the topographical aspects of the retino-cortical projection. In R. Jung & H. Kornhuber (Eds.), *The visual system: Neurophysiology and psychophysics.* Heidelberg: Springer-Verlag, 1961.

Doty, R. W. Electrical stimulation of the brain in behavioral context. *Annual Review of Psychology,* 1969, **20**, 289–320.

Doty, R. W. Survival of pattern vision after removal of striate cortex in the adult cat. *Journal of Comparative Neurology,* 1972, **143**, 341–370.

Doty, R. W., & Giurgea, C. Conditioned reflexes established by coupling electrical excitation of two cortical areas. In A. Fessard, R. W. Gerard, & J. Konorski (Eds.), *Brain mechanisms and learning.* Oxford: Blackwell, 1961.

Dusser de Barenne, J. G., & McCulloch, W. S. Suppression of motor responses obtained from area 4 by stimulation of area 4s. *Journal of Neurophysiology,* 1941, **4**, 311–323.

Elul, R. Statistical mechanisms in generation of the EEG. In L. J. Fogel & F. W. George (Eds.), *Progress in biomedical engineering.* Washington, D.C.: Spartan, 1967.

Erickson, R. P. Stimulus coding in topographic and nontopographic afferent modalities: On the significance of the activity of individual sensory neurons. *Psychological Review,* 1968, **75**, 447–465.

Fellows, B. J. Chance stimulus sequences for discrimination tasks. *Psychological Bulletin,* 1967, **67**, 87–92.

Flourens, P. *Researche expérimentales sur les propriétés et les fonctions du système nerveaux dans les animaux vertébrés.* (2nd ed.) Paris: Balliere, 1842.

Forward, E., Warren, J. M., & Hara, K. The effects of unilateral lesions in sensorimotor cortex on manipulation by cats. *Journal of Comparative and Physiological Psychology,* 1962, **55**, 1130–1135.

Fried, P. A. Septum and behavior: A review. *Psychological Bulletin,* 1972, **78**, 292–310.

Fritsch, G., & Hitzig, E. Uber die elektrische Erregbarkeit des Grosshirns. *Arch. für Anat., Physiol., und wissenschaftl. Mediz., Leipzig,* 1870, 300–332.

Gall, F. J., & Spurzhein, G. *Anatomie et physiologie du système nerveaux en général, et du cerveau en particulier.* Paris: F. Schnell, 1810, Vol. 1.

Gardner, E. *Fundamentals of neurology.* (5th ed.) Philadelphia: Saunders, 1968.

Gazzaniga, M. S., Bogen, J. E., & Sperry, R. W. Some functional effects of sectioning the cerebral commissures in man. *Proceedings of the National Academy of Sciences,* 1962, **48**, 1765–1783.

Gazzaniga, M. S., Bogen, J. E., & Sperry, R. W. Laterality effects in somesthesis following cerebral commissurotomy in man. *Neuropsychologia,* 1963, **1**, 209–215.

Gazzaniga, M. S., Bogen, J. E., & Sperry, R. W. Observations on visual perception after disconnexion of the cerebral hemispheres in man. *Brain,* 1965, **88**, 221–236.

Gellerman, L. W. Chance orders of alternating stimuli in visual discrimination experiments. *Journal of Genetic Psychology,* 1933, **42,** 207–208.

Goddard, G. V. Functions of the amygdala. *Psychological Bulletin,* 1964, **62,** 89–109.

Grafstein, B. Mechanisms of spreading cortical depression. *Journal of Neurophysiology,* 1956, **19,** 154–171.

Grant, L. E., & Jarrard, L. E. Functional dissociation within hippocampus. *Brain Research,* 1968, **10,** 392–401.

Gregory, R. L. The brain as an engineering problem. In W. H. Thorpe & O. L. Zangwill (Eds.), *Current problems in animal behaviour.* Cambridge, Eng.: Cambridge University Press, 1961.

Gross, C. G., & Zeigler, H. P. *Readings in physiological psychology: Learning and memory.* New York: Harper & Row, 1969.

Grossman, S. P. *A textbook of physiological psychology.* New York: Wiley, 1967.

Harlow, H. G. The formation of learning sets. *Psychological Review,* 1949, **56,** 51–65.

Hart, B. L. *Experimental neuropsychology: A laboratory manual.* San Francisco: Freeman, 1969.

Hebb, D. O. Drives and the C.N.S. (conceptual nervous system). *Psychological Review,* 1955, **62,** 243–254.

Hebb, D. O. Alice in Wonderland or psychology among the biological sicences. In H. F. Harlow & C. N. Woolsey (Eds.), *Biological and biochemical bases of behavior.* Madison: University of Wisconsin Press, 1958.

Herrick, C. J. *Neurological foundations of animal behavior.* New York: Henry Holt, 1922.

Hirsch, H. V. B., & Spinelli, D. N. Modification of the distribution of receptive field orientation in cats by selective visual exposure during development. *Experimental Brain Research,* 1971, **13,** 509–527.

Hoebel, B. G. Feeding and self-stimulation. *Annals of the New York Academy of Sciences,* 1969, **157,** 758–778.

Hoebel, B. G., & Teitelbaum, P. Hypothalamic control of feeding and self-stimulation. *Science,* 1962, **135,** 375–377.

Horsley, V., & Clarke, R. H. The structure and function of the cerebellum examined by a new method. *Brain,* 1908, **31,** 45–124.

Hubel, D. H. Eleventh Bowditch Lecture. Effects of distortion of sensory input in the visual system of kittens. *Physiologist,* 1965, **10,** 17–45.

Hubel, D. H., & Wiesel, T. N. Receptive fields, binocular interaction and functional architecture in the cat's visual cortex. *Journal of Physiology,* 1962, **160,** 106–154.

Hubel, D. H., & Wiesel, T. N. Receptive fields of cells in striate cortex of very young, visually inexperienced kittens. *Journal of Neurophysiology,* 1963, **26,** 994–1002.

Isaacson, R. L. (Ed.) *Basic readings in neuropsychology.* New York: Harper & Row, 1964.

Jacobsen, C. F. Studies of cerebral function in primates: I. The functions of the frontal association areas in monkeys. *Comparative Psychology Monographs,* 1936, **13,** 3–60.

Jane, J. A., Masterton, R. B., & Diamond, I. T. The function of the tectum for attention to auditory stimuli in the cat. *Journal of Comparative Neurology,* 1965, **125,** 165–191.

Jasper, H., Ricci, G. F., & Doane, B. Patterns of cortical neuronal discharge during conditioned responses in the monkey. In G. E. W. Wolstenholme & C. M. O'Connor (Eds.), *Neurological basis of behavior.* London: Churchill, 1958.

Kimble, D. P. Hippocampus and internal inhibition. *Psychological Bulletin,* 1968, **70,** 285–295.

Klüver, H., & Barrera, E. A method for the combined staining of cells and fibres in the nervous system. *Journal of Neuropathology and Experimental Neurology,* 1953, **12,** 400–403.

Klüver, H., & Bucy, P. C. Preliminary analysis of functions of the temporal lobes in monkeys. *Archives of Neurology and Psychiatry,* 1939, **42,** 979–1000.

Konig, J. F. R., & Klippel, R. A. *The rat brain: A stereotaxic atlas of the forebrain and lower parts of the brain stem.* Baltimore: Williams and Wilkins, 1963.

Krech, D. Cortical localization of function. In L. Postman (Ed.), *Psychology in the making.* New York: Knopf, 1962.

Krieg, W. J. S. Accurate placement of minute lesions in the brain of the albino rat. *Quarterly Bulletin of the Northwestern University Medical School, Chicago,* 1946, **20,** No. 2.

Lashley, K. S., & Clark, G. The cytoarchitecture of the cerebral cortex of Ateles: A critical examination of architectonic studies. *Journal of Comparative Neurology,* 1946, **85,** 223–306.

Leaõ, A. A. P. Spreading depression of activity in the cerebral cortex. *Journal of Neurophysiology,* 1944, **7,** 359–390.

Leaõ, A. A. P. Further observations on the spreading depression of activity in the cerebral cortex. *Journal of Neurophysiology,* 1947, **10,** 409–414.

Li, C.-L., & Jasper, H. H. Microelectrode studies of

the electrical activity of the cerebral cortex in the cat. *Journal of Physiology,* 1953, **121,** 117–140.

Loucks, R. B. The experimental delimination of neural structures essential for learning: The attempt to condition striped muscle responses with faradization of the sigmoid gyri. *Journal of Psychology,* 1935, **1,** 5–44.

Marshall, J. F., Turner, B. H., & Teitelbaum, P. Sensory neglect produced by lateral hypothalamic damage. *Science,* 1971, **174,** 523–525.

Massopust, L. C., Jr. Diencephalon of the rat. In D. E. Sheer (Ed.), *Electrical stimulation of the brain.* Austin: University of Texas Press, 1961.

Melzack, R., & Wall, P. D. Pain mechanisms: A new theory. *Science,* 1965, **150,** 971–979.

Meyer, D. R., Treichler, F. R., & Meyer, P. M. Discrete-trial training techniques and stimulus variables. In A. M. Schrier, H. F. Harlow, & F. Stollnitz (Eds.), *Behavior of nonhuman primates, Vol. 1.* New York: Academic Press, 1965.

Milner, B. Psychological deficits produced by temporal lobe excision. *Research Publication of the Association for Research on Nervous and Mental Diseases,* 1958, **36,** 244–257.

Milner, B. Interhemispheric differences in the localization of psychological processes in man. *British Medical Bulletin,* 1971, **27,** 272–277.

Milner, P. M. *Physiological psychology.* New York: Holt, Rinehart & Winston, 1970.

Mize, R. R., & Murphy, E. H. Selective visual experience fails to modify receptive field properties of rabbit striate cortex neurons. *Science,* 1973, **180,** 320–323.

Moffitt, A. R. Consonant cue perception by twenty- to twenty-four-week-old infants. *Child Development,* 1971, **42,** 717–731.

Molino, A., & McIntyre, D. C. Another inexpensive headplug for the electrical recording and/or stimulation of rats. *Physiology and Behavior,* 1972, **9,** 273–275.

Myers, R. D. Methods for chemical stimulation of the brain. In R. D. Myers (Ed.), *Methods in psychobiology, Vol. 1.* New York: Academic Press, 1971.

Myers, R. D. (Ed.) *Methods in psychobiology, Vol. 1.* New York: Academic Press, 1971.

Myers, R. D. (Ed.) *Methods in psychobiology, Vol. 2.* New York: Academic Press, 1972.

Nauta, W. J. H., & Karten, H. J. A general profile of the vertebrate brain, with sidelights on the ancestry of the cerebral cortex. In F. O. Schmitt (Ed.), *The neurosciences: Second study program.* New York: Rockefeller University Press, 1970.

Oatley, K. *Brain mechanisms and mind.* London: Thames and Hudson, 1972.

Olds, J. Pleasure centers in the brain. *Scientific American,* 1956, **195,** 105–116.

Olds, J. Approach-avoidance dissociation in rat brain. *American Journal of Physiology,* 1960, **199,** 965–968.

Olds, J., & Milner, P. Positive reinforcement produced by electrical stimulation of septal area and other regions of rat brain. *Journal of Comparative and Physiological Psychology,* 1954, **47,** 419–427.

Papez, J. W. *Comparative neurology.* New York: Hafner, 1961.

Peele, T. L. *The neuroanatomical basis for clinical neurology.* (2nd ed.) New York: McGraw-Hill, 1961.

Pelligrino, L. J., & Cushman, A. J. *A stereotaxic atlas of the rat brain.* New York: Appleton-Century-Crofts, 1967.

Peterson, G. M., & Fracarol, La C. The relative influence of the locus and mass of destruction upon the control of handedness by the cerebral cortex. *Journal of Comparative Neurology,* 1938, **68,** 173–190.

Pfaff, D. W. Interactions of steroid sex hormones with brain tissue: Studies of uptake and physiological effects. In S. Segal (Ed.), *The regulation of mammalian reproduction.* Springfield, Ill.: Charles C Thomas, 1972.

Pfaff, D. W., & Keiner, M. Estradid-concentrating cells in the rat amygdala as part of a limbic-hypothalamic hormone-sensitive system. In B. Eleftheriou (Ed.), *The neurobiology of the amygdala.* New York: Plenum Press, 1972.

Romer, A. S. *The vertebrate body.* (3rd ed.) Philadelphia: Saunders, 1962.

Romer, A. S. *Vertebrate paleontology.* Chicago: University of Chicago Press, 1966.

Rose, J. E., & Woolsey, C. N. Cortical connections and functional organization of the thalamic auditory system of the cat. In H. F. Harlow & C. N. Woolsey (Eds.), *Biological and biochemical bases of behavior.* Madison: University of Wisconsin Press, 1958.

Rosenquist, A. C., & Hoebel, B. G. Wheel running elicited by electrical stimulation of the brain. *Physiology and Behavior,* 1968, **3,** 563–566.

Rosensweig, M. S. Representation of the two ears at the auditory cortex. *American Journal of Physiology,* 1951, **167,** 147–158.

Russell, I. S. Neurological basis of complex learning. *British Medical Bulletin,* 1971, **27,** 278–285.

Russell, I. S., & Ochs, S. Localization of a memory trace in one cortical hemisphere and transfer to the other hemisphere. *Brain,* 1963, **86,** 37–54.

Schneider, G. E. Contrasting visuomotor functions of tectum and cortex in the golden hamster. *Psychologische Forschung,* 1967, **31,** 52–62.

Sholl, D. A. *The organization of the cerebral cortex.* New York: Hafner, 1956.

Skinner, J. E. *Neuroscience: A laboratory manual.* Philadelphia: Saunders, 1971.

Skinner, J. E., & Lindsley, D. B. Reversible cryogenic blockage of neural function in the brain of unrestrained animals. *Science,* 1968, **161,** 595–597.

Stretton, A. O. W., & Kravitz, E. A. Neuronal geometry: Determination with a technique of intracellular dye injection. *Science,* 1968, **162,** 132–134.

Sutherland, N. S. The learning of discriminations by animals. *Endeavour,* 1964, **13,** 148–152.

Sutherland, N. S., & Mackintosh, N. J. *Mechanisms of animal discrimination learning.* New York: Academic Press, 1971.

Teitelbaum, P. Sensory control of hypothalamic hyperphagia. *Journal of Comparative and Physiological Psychology,* 1955, **48,** 156–163.

Teitelbaum, P. The use of operant methods in the assessment and control of motivational states. In W. K. Honig (Ed.), *Operant behavior: Areas of research and application.* New York: Appleton-Century-Crofts, 1966.

Teitelbaum, P. *Physiological psychology.* Englewood Cliffs, N.J.: Prentice-Hall, 1967.

Teitelbaum, P., & Epstein, A. N. The lateral hypothalamic syndrome: Recovery of feeding and drinking after lateral hypothalamic lesions. *Psychological Review,* 1962, **69,** 74–90.

Teuber, H.-L. Some alterations in behavior after cerebral lesions in man. In A. D. Bass (Ed.), *Evolution of nervous control from primitive organisms to man.* Washington, D.C.: American Association for the Advancement of Science, 1959.

Teuber, H.-L., Battersby, W. S., & Bender, M. B. *Visual field defects after penetrating missile wounds of the brain.* Cambridge, Mass.: Harvard University Press, 1960.

Thompson, R. Introducing subcortical lesions by electrolytic methods. In R. D. Myers (Ed.), *Methods in psychobiology, Vol. 1.* New York: Academic Press, 1971.

Valenstein, E. S. *Brain control: A critical examination of brain stimulation and psychosurgery.* New York: Wiley-Interscience, 1973.

Van Essen, D., & Kelly, J. Correlation of cell shape and function in the visual cortex of the cat. *Nature,* 1973, **241,** 403–405.

Vogt, O., & Vogt, C. Ergebnisse unserer Hirnforschung. *Journal für Psychologie und Neurologie,* 1919, **25,** 277–462.

Walker, A. E. The development of the concept of cerebral localization in the nineteenth century. *Bulletin of the History of Medicine,* 1957, **31,** 99–121.

Warren, J. M., Abplanalp, J. M., & Warren, H. B. The development of handedness in cats and rhesus monkeys. In H. W. Stevenson (Ed.), *Early behavior: Comparative and physiological approaches.* New York: Wiley, 1967.

Warren, J. M., Cornwell, P. R., Webster, W. G., & Pubols, B. H. Unilateral cortical lesions and paw preferences in cats. *Journal of Comparative and Physiological Psychology,* 1972, **81,** 410–422.

Webster, W. G. Functional asymmetry between the cerebral hemispheres of the cat. *Neuropsychologia,* 1972, **10,** 75–87.

Webster, W. G. Assumptions, conceptualizations, and the search for the functions of the brain. *Physiological Psychology,* 1973, **1,** 346–350.

Weiskrantz, L. Memory. In L. Weiskrantz (Ed.), *Analysis of behavioral change.* New York: Harper & Row, 1968. (a).

Weiskrantz, L. Treatments, inferences, and brain function. In L. Weiskrantz (Ed.), *Analysis of behavioral change.* New York: Harper & Row, 1968. (b).

Weiskrantz, L. Some traps and pontifications. In L. Weiskrantz (Ed.), *Analysis of behavioral change.* New York: Harper & Row, 1968. (c).

Weiskrantz, L. Problems and progress in physiological psychology. *British Journal of Psychology,* 1973, **64,** 511–520.

Wolf, G. Elementary histology for neuropsychologists. In R. D. Myers (Ed.), *Methods in psychobiology, Vol. 1.* New York: Academic Press, 1971.

Woolsey, C. N. Organization of somatic sensory and motor areas of the cerebral cortex. In H. F. Harlow & C. N. Woolsey (Eds.), *Biological and biomedical bases of behavior.* Madison: University of Wisconsin Press, 1958.

Young, R. M. The functions of the brain: Gall to Ferrier (1808–1886). *Isis,* 1968, **59,** 251–268.

Young, R. M. *Mind, brain and adaptation in the nineteenth century.* London: Oxford University Press, 1970.

appendixes

APPENDIX A

DISTRIBUTORS, CATALOG NUMBERS, AND APPROXIMATE PRICES OF EQUIPMENT AND SUPPLIES USED IN LABORATORY EXERCISES

A–1 Surgical instruments and supplies required for each group

A–2 Equipment for each group

A–3 Supplies for each group

A–4 Equipment to be shared by groups

A–5 Supplies to be shared by groups

A–6 Names and addresses of distributors of equipment and supplies

Appendix A–1

Surgical Instruments and Supplies Required for Each Group

Item	Distributor [1]	Cat. no.	Approx. price [2,3]
Halstead mosquito forceps (2)	Irex	IR–303	$ 5.50
Sharp and blunt scissors, 5½ in.	Irex	IR–102	4.50
Straight iris scissors, 4½ in.	Irex	IR–105	6.75
Rat-tooth forceps, 1 × 2 teeth	Irex	IR–302	2.50
Adson thumb forceps, serrated	Irex	IR–380	4.00
#3 scalpel handle	Irex	IR–713	1.25
#4 scalpel handle [4]	Irex	IR–714	1.25
Virchow brain knife [4]	Roboz	MX34–50	15.00
#7 dental flex explorer	S. S. White		1.60
Lempert rongeurs [5]	Lawton	67L–0715	40.00
Needleholder	Irex	IR–240	10.00
Cement spatula	S. S. White	313	5.00
Stainless ruler, 6 in.	Mueller	OP–2720	1.00
Watch glass	Clay Adams	1499	2.50/25
#8 cutting bur, long shaft, friction grip	S. S. White		1.40
#½ cutting bur, long shaft, friction grip	S. S. White		2.00
Size 16 suture needle	Roboz	MS–140–16	2.10/doz
Nembutal anesthetic, 60 mg/cc [6]	Local medical supply		3.00/50 ml
Atropine sulfate, 0.4 mg/cc	Local medical supply		4.00/25 ml
Caulk NuWeld liquid and powder (dental cement) or Getz Tru-Cure dental cement	Caulk, Getz		
Bonescrews (watchmaker's screws)	Lomat	P52–10	35.00/1000
Bone wax	ASR Medical		4.50/doz
Glass pipette (see Appendix B–1)	Fisher	13–678–5A	9.00/400
#10 scalpel blades	Local medical supply		1.75/doz
#11 scalpel blades	Local medical supply		1.75/doz
#22 scalpel blades [7]	Local medical supply		1.75/doz
Wound clips	Clay Adams	132355	40.00/1000

[1] The listing of distributors and catalog numbers is principally for purposes of identification of equipment and supplies, but it can also be used for ordering. Equipment and supplies of equal or better quality and price can of course be obtained elsewhere, and the listing does not imply endorsement of specific distributors and manufacturers. Addresses of distributors and manufacturers are listed in Appendix A–6.

[2] Except where indicated, prices are unit prices assessed educational and research institutions.

[3] Prices listed are approximately those that were in effect in 1973/1974 and are intended to be only a general guide to present costs.

[4] A #4 scalpel handle is required only if a Virchow brain knife is not provided. A #22 blade in the #4 handle can be used for sectioning the cow or sheep brain in Laboratory Exercise I, but the use of a brain knife does give more satisfactory results.

[5] The rongeurs distributed by Lawton are recommended in particular, as the tip design is narrower than many and makes it easy to use.

[6] Permission from federal drug authorities will be required to purchase and use Nembutal.

[7] #22 scalpel blades are needed only if the #4 handle is used instead of a brain knife in Laboratory Exercise I (see note 4).

Item	Distributor	Cat. no.	Approx. price
1-cc syringes, disposable	Local medical supply		12.00/100
26G needles, disposable	Local medical supply		5.00/100
4″ × 4″ gauze sponges	Local medical supply		5.00/200
2″ × 2″ gauze sponges	Local medical supply		2.00/200
#2 and #3 cotton pledgets	Local medical supply		1.50/box
Gelfoam sponges (3 mm or 7 mm)	Local medical supply		2.00/4·
Size 00 surgical silk, black braided	Local medical supply		10.00/100 yd
Eyedropper	Local medical supply		.10

Appendix A–2

Equipment for Each Group

Item	Distributor [1]	Cat. no.	Approx. price [2,3]
Display tray for dissection	Stansi	17422	$ 2.75
Instrument sterilizing tray	Central Scientific	12994–1	7.50
Hand microtome and knife	Stansi	77460	41.00
Headholder [4]	Kopf	320	45.00
Universal stand [4]	Kopf	310	50.00
Osteological drill, Foredom Model F–1	Turtox	312A106	40.00
Size 602 collet for small bur	Turtox	312A182	2.50
Micromanipulator [5] (Prior) #22 #30 rectangular base	Stoelting	#22 right	225.00
Electrode holder	Stoelting	#60	6.00
Double electrode holder (see Appendix B–14)			15.00
Magnifier on stand [6]	Turtox	325A106	13.50
High-intensity lamp [7]	Local electrical supply		15.00

[1] The listing of distributors and catalog numbers is principally for purposes of identification of equipment and supplies, but it can also be used for ordering. Equipment and supplies of equal or better quality and price can of course be obtained elsewhere, and the listing does not imply endorsement of specific distributors and manufacturers. Addresses of distributors and manufacturers are listed in Appendix A–6.

[2] Except where indicated, prices are the unit prices assessed educational and research institutions.

[3] Prices listed are approximately those that were in effect in 1973/1974 and are intended to be only a general guide to present costs.

[4] The universal stand, shown in Figure 6–10, must be screwed to a wooden support platform.

[5] For the sake of economy, the micromanipulator could be omitted and in Laboratory Exercises VI and IX the electrodes could be held in a support stand and clamp arrangement. Laboratory Exercises V and VII do, however, require the use of stereotaxic coordinates and so could not be done without the micromanipulator.

[6] A magnifier is potentially useful, especially when incising the dura mater, but many students do not make use of it, and it could be omitted for the sake of economy.

[7] The necessity for a high-intensity lamp depends, of course, on laboratory illumination.

Item	*Distributor*	*Cat. no.*	*Approx. price*
Oscilloscope [8]			700.00
Preamplifier [9]	Grass	P511	350.00
Power supply	Grass	RPS106	325.00
Brain stimulator (see Appendix B–9)			
Faraday cage (see Appendix B–13)			
Lengths of wire, 1 foot long each, with a banana plug on one end and alligator clip on other end [10] (3)			
4-foot lengths of wire with banana plugs on both ends [10] (2)			
8-foot cable with alligator clips on one end and oscilloscope input connector on other end [10]			
6-foot cable with a preamplifier output connector on one end and oscilloscope input connector on other end [10]			
600-ml beaker	Fisher	2–540M	4.75/doz
Petri dish bottom, 150×20 mm	Fisher	8–748F	1.25
Specimen dish (for saline)	Turtox	320AA64, size A	11.75/doz
500-ml distillation flask	Fisher	10–182–50A	2.50
#7 rubber stopper with hole	Fisher	14–135L	2.50/lb

[8] Oscilloscopes priced well under $1000 are available and are quite satisfactory for teaching laboratory purposes, although in some cases not for research purposes. A general purpose oscilloscope, without differential amplification capability, such as the Telequipment Model T1D54 or the Advance Electronic Model OS 1000, both priced at about $700, give quite satisfactory results provided that a Faraday cage (Appendix B–13) is used. Because a preamplifier is also needed for Laboratory IX (see Note 13), consideration might be given to the Phipps and Bird PBM Scope, Cat. No. 7092–670, priced at about $700, which has a built in preamplifier (and also has differential amplification capabilities). Its disadvantages are that it is a single-beam oscilloscope, and more important, it requires constant manual calibration. Consideration should be given to the fact that if a dual-beam or dual-trace oscilloscope is used, it is possible for pairs of groups to share it, one group using the upper beam and one using the lower beam. If economy is of concern, it is suggested that pairs of groups work together. Having groups of four rather than two working in Laboratory Exercise IX does ensure that there is sufficient surgical and technical competence in each larger group that the lab can be completed with reasonable dispatch.

[9] The type of preamplification capability required will depend on the characteristics of the oscilloscope being used. The author has found that the Grass P511 preamplifier, used in conjunction with a Telequipment oscilloscope (shown in Figure 18–1) is very satisfactory and can be used to illustrate the use of differential amplification and electronic filters. Since four of these are powered from one Grass power supply, it is possible to have 16 students working in pairs on Laboratory Exercises VIII and IX with four moderately priced oscilloscopes, four preamplifiers, and one power supply. The addition of four preamplifiers and one power supply would allow the students to work in pairs if they share the beams of the oscilloscopes.

[10] Cables and wires of a length appropriate for particular laboratory settings are most economically made by the instructor or an assistant.

Item	Distributor	Cat. no.	Approx. price
6-in. glass tubing for stopper	Chemistry department		
4 feet surgical tubing, $\frac{1}{4}''$ ID $\times \frac{3}{32}''$	Mueller	HS–3338	8.50/50 ft
Three-way connectors (4)	Fisher	15–316A	8.50/doz
Utility jar for brains	Turtox	315AA625	1.20
Small dishpan	Local hardware store		
Rectal electrode (see Appendix B–5)			

Appendix A–3

Supplies for Each Group

Item	Distributor [1]	Cat. no.	Approx. price [2,3]
Cow or sheep brain	Carolina	P2320	$6.00 (cow brain)
Cow spinal cord section	Carolina	P2325	1.50
Rat brain	From a psychology department		
Microscope slide, 75×50 mm (6)	Fisher	12–550C	8.75/gross
Tissue capsules (20)	Thomas	6755–T64	4.50/100

[1] The listing of distributors and catalog numbers is principally for purposes of identification of equipment and supplies, but it can also be used for ordering. Equipment and supplies of equal or better quality and price can of course be obtained elsewhere, and the listing does not imply endorsement of specific distributors and manufacturers. Addresses of distributors and manufacturers are listed in Appendix A–6.

[2] Except where indicated, prices are the unit prices assessed educational and research institutions.

[3] Prices listed are approximately those that were in effect in 1973/1974 and are intended to be only a general guide to present costs.

Appendix A–4

Equipment To Be Shared by Groups

Item	Distributor [1]	Cat. no.	Approx. price [2,3]
Wound clip applicator [4]	Clay-Adams	B–2350	$ 45.00
Wound clip removers	Clay-Adams	B–2370	10.00

[1] The listing of distributors and catalog numbers is principally for purposes of identification of equipment and supplies, but it can also be used for ordering. Equipment and supplies of equal or better quality and price can of course be obtained elsewhere, and the listing does not imply endorsement of specific distributors and manufacturers. Addresses of distributors and manufacturers are listed in Appendix A–6.

[2] Except where indicated, prices are the unit prices assessed educational and research institutions.

[3] Prices listed are approximately those that were in effect in 1973/1974 and are intended to be only a general guide to present costs.

[4] One wound clip applicator is quite sufficient for up to six groups of students.

Item	Distributor	Cat. no.	Approx. price
Bonescrew-driver [5] (see Appendix B–10)	Roboz	MX8–48	16.00
1000 ml Erlenmeyer flask (2)	Fisher	10–090D	2.00
600 ml beakers (4)	Fisher	2–540M	4.75/doz
Petri dish bottoms, 150×20 mm (4)	Fisher	8–748F	1.14
Thermometer	Fisher	14–983–15A	4.00
Electrode tester (see Appendix B–6)			
Vacuum pump [6]	Fisher	1–094	150.00
Hot plate	Fisher	11–495–50	105.00
Animal clippers, Oster model A–2 [7]	Fisher	1–305	75.00
Oster surgical shaving head	Fisher	1–305–5	20.75
Respirator [8]	Harvard	680	400.00
Photostimulator	Grass	PS–2	400.00
Microprojector, Tri-simplex	Turtox	330AA20	200.00
Stained sections of human spinal cord	Carolina		1.50
Animal balance, Ohaus triple-beam	Fisher	2–034–25	50.00
Heating pad or heating lamp	Local medical supply		15.00
Lesion maker (see Appendix B–4)			
Avoidance box (see Appendix B–8)			
Shock source (see Appendix B–7)			
Handedness box (see Appendix B–2)			
X-ray viewers	Mueller	TF–3054	65.00
Rat cages	Hoeltge		
Heavy work gloves [9]	Local hardware store		
Towels [10]			
Lab coats			

[5] One bonescrew-driver (see Appendix B–10) is sufficient for two or three groups of students.

[6] Most vacuum pumps like the one indicated in the listing have sufficient capability for a minimum of ten to twelve groups of students. However, this depends entirely upon the size of the pipette tips.

[7] One animal clipper is sufficient for up to four groups of students if all groups are starting at the same time.

[8] A respirator is not necessary, but if one is available it is worth having during the laboratory to handle cases of congestion.

[9] One pair of gloves should be available for every two groups of students.

[10] Gauze diapers work very well as towels for drying instruments and equipment.

Appendix A–5

Supplies To Be Shared by Groups

Item	Distributor [1]	Cat. no.	Approx. price [2,3]
Physostigmine sulfate	Local medical supply		
Epoxylite insulation	Epoxylite Corp.		
Insl-X insulation	Insl-X Products Corp.		
Nichrome wire, .005-in. diameter, Diamel coated	Johnson, Matthey		
Nichrome wire, .010-in. diameter, Diamel coated	Johnson, Matthey		
Copper wire, uninsulated, 28 gauge	Fisher		
Pure silver wire (see Appendix B–15)	Fisher		
Microdot 250–3804 cable	Randall	250–3804	$ 0.80/ft
Stainless steel insect pins, no. 4	Wards	14W0155	1.00/100
Amphenol pins, male	Amphenol	220–PO2	.05
Amphenol pins, female	Amphenol	220–PO2	.12
Polyethylene gloves	Fisher	11–394–110B	7.55/100
Cheesecloth	Fisher	6–665–20A	2.00/10 yd
String	Local hardware store		
Scissors for string, wire, etc.	Local hardware store		
Rubber bands			
Label tape	Fisher	11–875A	1.85/roll
Detergent	Fisher	4–320	3.00/3¼-lb box
Paper towels			
Extra heavy mineral oil	Local drugstore		
Marker pens	Fisher	13–382–10E	12.80/doz

[1] The listing of distributors and catalog numbers is principally for purposes of identification of equipment and supplies, but it can also be used for ordering. Equipment and supplies of equal or better quality and price can of course be obtained elsewhere, and the listing does not imply endorsement of specific distributors and manufacturers. Addresses of distributors and manufacturers are listed in Appendix A–6.

[2] Except where indicated, prices are the unit prices assessed educational and research institutions.

[3] Prices listed are approximately those that were in effect in 1973/1974 and are intended to be only a general guide to present costs.

Appendix A–6

Names and Addresses of Distributors of Equipment and Supplies Listed in Appendixes

Advance Electronics Limited
Raynham Road
Bishop's Stortford, Herts.
England

    Canadian Distributor:
        Allan Crawford Associates, Ltd.
        376 Churchill Avenue
        Ottawa, Ontario

Allied Electronics
100 North Western Avenue
Chicago, Illinois 60680
U.S.A.

American Hospital Supply
1076 Lakeshore Road East
Port Credit, Ontario
Canada

Amphenol Connector Division
Controls-Operation
Bunker-Ramo Corporation
2801 South 25 Avenue
Broadview, Illinois 60153
U.S.A.

Amphenol RF. Division
Bunker-Ramo Corporation
33 East Franklin Street
Danbury, Connecticut 06810
U.S.A.

    In Canada:
        Amphenol Ltd.
        44 Metropolitan Road
        Scarborough (Toronto), Ontario

Arbor Scientific Ltd.
Box 113
Port Credit, Ontario
Canada

ASR Medical Industries
4150–60 Laclede Avenue
St. Louis, Missouri 63108

BRS/LVE   (Formerly Lehigh Valley Electronics)
5301 Holland Drive
Beltsville, Maryland 20705
U.S.A.

Canadian Laboratory Supplies Ltd.
8655 Delmeade Road
Town of Mount Royal
Montreal, Quebec
Canada

Carolina Biological Supply Company
Burlington, North Carolina 27215
U.S.A.

L. D. Caulk Company
P.O. Box 359
Milford, Delaware 19963
U.S.A.

    In Canada:
        172 John Street
        Toronto, Ontario M5T IX5

Central Scientific Company
2600 South Kostner Avenue
Chicago, Illinois 60623
U.S.A.

    In Canada:
        376 Churchill Avenue
        Ottawa, Ontario

Clay-Adams, Inc.
141 East 25 Street
New York, New York
U.S.A.

    Canadian Distributor:
        Fisher Scientific (*See*)

Epoxylite Corporation
Box 3387
South El Monte, California 91733
U.S.A.

Fisher Scientific Company
711 Forbes Avenue
Pittsburgh, Pennsylvania 15219
U.S.A.

   In Canada:
      Fisher Scientific Company Ltd.
      8555 Devonshire Road
      Montreal, Quebec

William Getz Corporation
7512 South Greenwood Avenue
Chicago, Illinois 60619
U.S.A.

Grass Instrument Company
101 Old Colony Avenue
Quincy, Massachusetts 02169
U.S.A.

   In Canada:
      Grass Instrument Company
      79 East Don Road
      Toronto, Ontario

Harvard Apparatus Company, Inc.
150 Dover Road
Millis, Massachusetts 02054
U.S.A.

Hoeltge, Inc.
5242 Crookshank Road
Cincinnati, Ohio 45238
U.S.A.

Ingram and Bell Ltd.
20 Bond Avenue
Don Mills, Ontario
Canada

Insl-X Products Corporation
115–117 Woodworth Avenue
Yonkers, New York
U.S.A.

Irex German Surgicals
Box 788, Adelaide Street Post Office
Toronto, Ontario
Canada

Johnson Matthey Metals Ltd.
608 Fifth Avenue
New York, New York 10020
U.S.A.

David Kopf Instruments
7324 Elmo Street
Tujunga, California 91042
U.S.A.

The Lawton Company
425 Fourth Avenue
New York, New York
U.S.A.

   Canadian distributor:
      Ingram and Bell

Lehigh Valley Electronics. *See* BRS/LVE

Lomat Watch Material Company
Railway Exchange Building
637 Craig Street West
Montreal, Quebec
Canada

Matheson Scientific Company
1850 Greenleaf Avenue
Elk Grove Village, Illinois 60007
U.S.A.

V. Mueller Company
6600 Touhy Avenue
Chicago, Illinois 60648
U.S.A.

   Canadian distributor:
      American Hospital Supply

Phipps and Bird, Inc.
6th and Byrd Streets
P.O. Box 2–V
Richmond, Virginia
U.S.A.

Plastic Products Company
P.O. Box 1204
Roanoke, Virginia 24006
U.S.A.

Douglas Randall Company
Division of Neeco Industries Limited
80 Galaxy Boulevard, Unit 11
Rexdale, Ontario
Canada

Roboz Surgical Instrument Company, Inc.
810 18 Street, N.W.
Washington, D.C. 20006
U.S.A.

Scientific Prototype Manufacturing Corporation
615 West 131 Street
New York, New York 10027
U.S.A.

Stansi Educational Materials Division
Fisher Scientific Company
1259 North Wood Street
Chicago, Illinois 60622
U.S.A.

   In Canada:
     Stansi Educational Division
     Fisher Scientific Company Ltd.
     P.O. Box 1099
     Montreal 101, Quebec

Stoelting Company
424 North Homan Avenue
Chicago, Illinois 60624
U.S.A.

Tektronix, Inc.
P.O. Box 500
Beaverton, Oregon 97005
U.S.A.

Telequipment U.K. Ltd. (subsidiary of
Tektronix, Inc.)

A. H. Thomas Company
Vine Street and Third
P.O. Box 779
Philadelphia, Pennsylvania 19105
U.S.A.

   Canadian distributor:
     Canadian Laboratory Supplies

Wards Natural Science Establishment, Inc.
P.O. Box 1712
Rochester, New York 14603
U.S.A.

   Canadian distributor:
     Arbor Scientific

S. S. White Company
211 South 12 Street
Philadelphia, Pennsylvania 19105
U.S.A.

   In Canada:
     S. S. White Company
     50 Paxman Road, Unit 3
     Etobicoke, Ontario

APPENDIX B

NOTES ON EQUIPMENT AND SUPPLIES

The instructor and students are referred to Skinner (1971) and to
Myers (1971, 1972) for several informative discussions concerning equipment
and supplies that might be relevant to the conduct of the laboratory exercises.
These notes are restricted to equipment and supply problems that are in
certain respects unique to the laboratory exercises as they are written.

Appendix B–1

Pipettes for Aspiration

A pipette suitable for the cortical lesions in Laboratory Exercise IV, similar to that shown in Figure 5–2, can be made by simply bending, with heat, a disposable transfer pipette (Fisher, Cat. No. 13–678–5A, $9/400 pipettes). The tips of these pipettes are approximately 1 mm in diameter, a quite satisfactory size for use in the laboratory, and the shaft is of a diameter that easily fits ¼-in. I.D. tubing. Bending the shaft does facilitate using it. To do this, roll the pipette back and forth between the fingers while heating the shaft in a medium flame. When the glass just begins to soften, bend the shaft the desired amount. If the tip is not smooth, fire polish it by quickly passing it through the flame two or three times, but be careful that the tip does not melt closed.

For some purposes other than this laboratory exercise, it is desirable to have a pipette with a smaller tip. This can be done by heating a part of the shaft near the tip end until it is very soft, and then pulling it. The pipette can be cut to the desired length and tip diameter by etching the elongated portion with a triangular file, breaking it, and fire polishing the tip. It does take some practice with this method before the pipettes are satisfactory.

To control the amount of vacuum at the tip, a small hole can also be blown in the shaft. Before bending or drawing the pipette, attach a short rubber hose to it. With a finger placed over the tip, heat the pipette at a single spot on the shaft and slowly blow through the tube. As the glass softens, a bubble will form and break, and this can be smoothed with fire polishing. To use the pipette, it is necessary to occlude the hole, and the amount of occlusion of course determines the vacuum at the tip. Pressure control holes are not recommended for the pipettes used in the laboratory exercises or whenever several people are using the same vacuum source, since unoccluded holes deplete the vacuum.

Appendix B–2

Handedness Box

The actual dimensions of the box are not very important, although a reasonable size would be about 14 in. across the front, 10 in. deep, and 12 in. high. The food wells of the box shown in Figure 7–1 are 2 cm deep and 1½ cm wide, and the holes in the Plexiglas front through which the rat has access to the food wells are 1 cm × 1½ cm. They are centered 10 cm from each wall and 10 cm above the floor. One desirable feature to incorporate is a hinged top to prevent the animal from climbing out.

Appendix B–3

Setting Up Pump and Flask

A vacuum pump like that listed in Appendix A can serve 8 to 10 groups, provided that the pipettes do not have vacuum control holes (see Appendix B–1) and that students are cautioned not to remove their pipette without first clamping the hosing. The pump can be conveniently set up in either one of two ways. First, it can be connected to a single collection flask to which all groups have access through tubing and three-way connectors. A second method is to give each group of students access to the vacuum through tubing and let each connect its own collection flask to the vacuum. The latter procedure is obviously more expensive in terms of equipment, but it does have some pedagogic value.

Appendix B–4

Lesion Makers

Commercial lesion makers can be purchased from Stoelting (Cat. No. 58040, approx. $150) or from BRS/LVE (Cat. No. 613–10, approx. $200), but Thompson (1971) has suggested a simple DC lesion maker that can be built for under $30. The circuit diagram is shown in Figure B–1. The reader is referred to Thompson (1971) for a discussion of factors influencing the choice of parameters of current, time, and electrode diameter in making subcortical lesions.

Appendix B–5

Electrodes for Subcortical Lesions

Very satisfactory lesions can be obtained using as an electrode an insect pin insulated along its length except at the tip.

Size 4 *stainless steel* insect pins (Wards, Cat. No. 14W0155, approx. $1/100) should be well cleaned and the head of each placed in an alligator clip. The pins can then be dipped almost to the alligator clip jaws in a jar of Epoxylite (Epoxylite Corp.) and then slowly withdrawn so there are no bubbles along the shaft. They should next be placed in an oven with the tips of the pins pointing up, and baked for an hour or two at 350°C or overnight at 120°C. After cooling, they should be dipped again and the baking repeated. The Epoxylite forms an excellent insulation along the pin, which can be removed from the tips by scraping with an old scalpel blade. It is recommended that the tip be viewed under a magnifier or dissecting microscope during scraping.

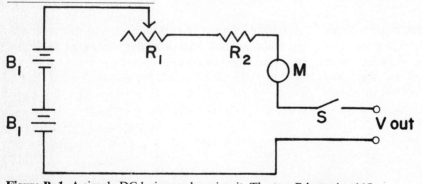

Figure B–1. A simple DC lesion-maker circuit. The two B batteries (45 volts each) are connected in series with a 1500-ohm resistor and a 50,000-ohm potentiometer. The flow of current is controlled with the ON-OFF switch and can be monitored with the ammeter (0 to 5.0 ma scale). (Adapted from R. Thompson, Introducing subcortical lesions by electrolytic methods. In R. D.Myers (Ed.), *Methods in psychobiology, Vol. 1.* New York: Academic Press, 1971, 131–153, Figure 3.)

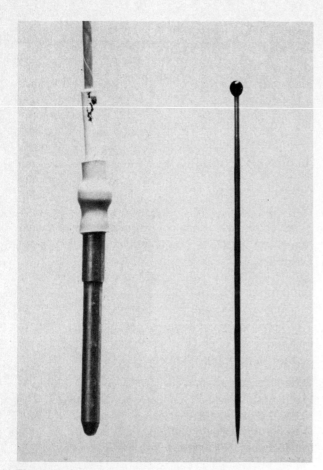

Figure B–2. An insulated electrode, made from an insect pin, suitable for subcortical electrolytic lesions, and a tip plug suitable for use as a rectal electrode.

Figure B–2 shows a lesion electrode made with an insect pin and shows a tip plug suitable for use as a rectal electrode. Such plugs can be obtained from any electronic supply company (Allied, Cat. No. 47B3986, approx. $1/10 plugs). An alternative is to make a small ball of solder connected to a wire to insert into the rectum.

Appendix B–6

Electrode Tester

Figure 8–2 is a diagram of a simple device for testing that the insulation on an electrode is intact and that there are no short circuits in bipolar stimulation or recording electrodes. It consists simply of two D-size flashlight batteries and a flashlight bulb connected together in series. To test for electrode short circuits, one lead is connected to each electrode pin; if the light goes on, there is a short circuit. To test insulation, the negative lead is connected to the electrode(s) and the positive lead to the saline solution. When the electrode is placed in the saline, bubbles should appear only at the tip(s).

Appendix B–7

Shock Sources

The reader is referred to the discussion by Cornsweet (1963) concerning the relative advantages of constant current, constant voltage, and constant wattage shock sources, and the conditions under which shock scramblers should be used in avoidance and escape learning situations. For Laboratory Exercise V, involving only a single shocked trial, a scrambler is not necessary. An AC shock source, which approximates constant current, can be inexpensively constructed using a high voltage step-up transformer and a Variac. The step-up transformer should have a primary voltage of 115 volts and a secondary voltage of about 1000 volts. Its output can be varied between 0 and 1000 volts by placing a Variac (a variable voltage transformer) between it and the power mains. By connecting this output in series with a large-valued fixed resistor (500K ohm, 5 watt), and by connecting two NE 7 neon bulbs in parallel with the output to the bars, there will be an approximately constant current output to the subject. This diagram is shown in Figure B–3. Since the contribution of the subject to the total resistance of the circuit is small, changes in the animal's resistance will produce only minimal changes in the total circuit resistance and hence will produce only minimal changes in current flow.

Appendix B–8

Passive Avoidance Box

The actual dimensions of the box are not terribly important, but that shown in Figure 8–8 is approximately 2 ft square and 18 in. deep, and has stainless steel bars centered ½ inch apart. Electrical contact is made through clips that slip onto the bars and to which the wires from the shock source are soldered. The start box is made from ½-inch lumber, and is 8 in. deep, 6 in. across the front, and 13 in. high. The door is 2½ in. wide at the base and narrows at about 3½ in. above the floor to form a slot through which a recording or stimulating cable can pass while the animal is leaving the start box.

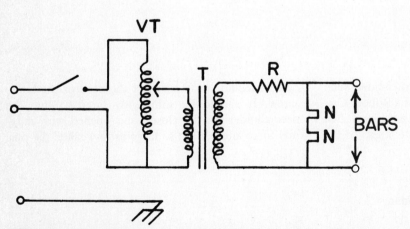

Figure B–3. Circuit diagram for an approximately constant current AC shock source. VT: variable-voltage transformer; T: step-up transformer with a primary voltage of 115 volts and a secondary voltage of 1,000 volts; R: 500,000-ohm, 5-watt resistor; N: NE 7 neon bulb. The case should be grounded.

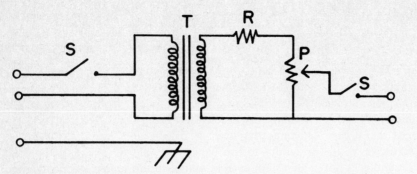

Figure B–4. Circuit diagram for brain stimulator. T: isolation transformer (primary voltage 115 volts; secondary voltage 115 volts); R: 68,000 ohm, 1-watt resistor; P: 10,000-ohm potentiometer. The case should be grounded.

Appendix B–9

Brain Stimulator

Figure B–4 shows a circuit diagram for an inexpensive AC brain stimulator that can be used in Laboratory Exercises VI and VII. The circuit is electrically isolated so that there is no danger of shock if a researcher inadvertently touches one lead and ground at the same time. It is recommended that this stimulator *not* be used for simultaneous stimulation and recording projects. If one output terminal is connected to ground (as it invariably would be in such a situation, at least indirectly through the animal), there is a real shock hazard if the researcher inadvertently touches the other output lead and ground at the same time.

The circuit diagramed in Figure B–4 makes use of an isolation transformer, and the output voltage is reduced through a fixed and a variable resistor. A step-down transformer (such as a doorbell transformer) could be used with the appropriate modifications in the resistor values, but the advantage of using the higher secondary voltage is that a somewhat more constant current is provided.

Figure 11–1 shows an outside view of the box. When constructing the stimulator, it is instructive to enclose the box with a Plexiglas bottom through which the components can be viewed.

Appendix B–10

Bonescrew-driver

This is made from a broad-tipped needleholder, such as an 8-in. Mayo-Hegar needleholder (Roboz, Cat. No. MX8–48, approx. $15). The tip must be drilled out as shown in Figure 11–3, the actual size of the hole depending on the size of the head of the bonescrew. It should be sufficiently large so that the needleholder can be closed and opened with minimal force and yet not so large as to weaken the tips.

Appendix B–11

Stimulation and Recording Electrodes

Twisted bipolar electrodes can be quickly and inexpensively constructed using .005-in.-diameter Nichrome wire covered with Diamel insulation and No. 220–PO2 Amphenol pins. Mass production of electrodes is facilitated by first constructing a pinholder, made by drilling in a block of metal a series of holes slightly larger in diameter than the pin tips. This can hold the pins while wires are soldered to them and can hold the electrodes while they are being baked.

For each electrode, start with a piece of relatively straight wire about 4 in. long, and using an old scalpel blade, scrape about 1 mm of the insulation from each end. Then, with the pins held in the pinholder, solder a pin to each end of the wire. That there is a good electrical contact should be checked at this point by using the electrode testing circuit described in Laboratory Exercise V and Appendix B–6. The wire is then simply looped in the middle and twisted on itself. A passable job can be done just by holding in one hand the ends of the wires about 1 cm from the pins and twisting the loop using the other hand. A better job can be done by (1) clamping the pins into a small laboratory vise so that each pin-wire junction is about 1 cm below the upper edge of the vise jaws, (2) inserting the small nail between the pieces of wire, (3) hooking the loop with the kind of hook available at any hardware store, (4) pulling the wire taut, and (5) twisting it. A still better job can be done by holding the pins and wire in a vise as described above, but clamping the hook into the chuck of a hand drill and operating the drill slowly while maintaining a constant upward force on the loop of the wire.

The twisted shaft of the electrode should then be dipped in Epoxylite and withdrawn slowly so there are no bubbles. It can be held upside down by one pin in the pinholder and should be baked in an oven for an hour or two at 350°C or overnight at 120°C. The Epoxylite adds one further coat of insulation and provides additional strength. Figure 12–1 shows the finished product; one electrode still has the loop and the other has been trimmed as described in Laboratory Exercise VII.

Bipolar electrodes are available commercially (see Appendix B–12), but they are quite expensive.

Appendix B–12

Construction of Headplugs

The headplug assembly highly recommended for use in the labs is that designed by Molino and McIntyre (1972); the reader is referred to their paper for complete details regarding its construction. Figure 12–2 is a photograph of the three components involved and Figure B–5 shows them in diagrammatic form. As indicated in Figure B–6, the electrode pins (Amphenol No. 220–PO2, male) are inserted into the holes of the headplug itself and make contact with pins (Amphenol No. 220–SO2, female) inserted into the holes of the connector plug and to which the connecting wires or cables have been soldered. The brass nut holds the connecting plug to the headplug and prevents disengagement during behavioral testing.

There are two points to be noted about wiring the connecting plug. First, it is suggested that the brass nut or ring screw be in place on the plug when the 220–SO2 female pins, soldered to wires, are inserted, as it may not be possible to slip the nut over all the wires and cables, especially if nine are used. Second, once the pins are all in place, it is suggested that a

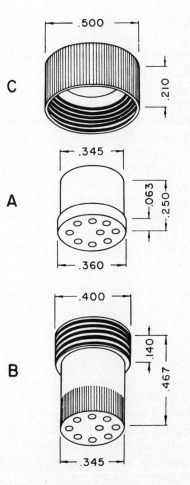

Figure B–5. Diagram of the three components of the headplug assembly. A: headplug itself; B: connecting plug; C: brass ring screw. (From A. Molino and D. McIntyre, Another inexpensive headplug for the electrical recording and/or stimulation of rats. *Physiology and Behavior,* 1972, **9,** 273–275, Figure 1(a).)

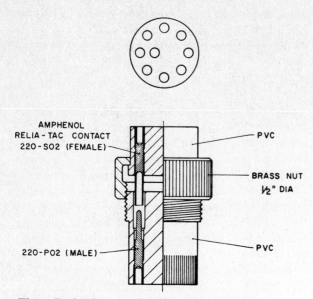

Figure B–6. Diagram of the headplug components when connected together. (From A. Molino and D. McIntyre, Another inexpensive headplug for the electrical recording and/or stimulation of rats. *Physiology and Behavior*, 1972, **9**, 273–275, Figure 1(b).)

Figure B–7. Photograph showing a connector plug wired for brain stimulation.

small amount of dental cement be built up around the wires and pins of the plug to prevent the possibility of short circuits, wire breakage, or disengagement of pins. Figure B–7 shows the final appearance of one connector plug wired for brain stimulation (and hence has only two pins).

If facilities for constructing this assembly are not available, headplugs, connector plugs, and brass rings can be obtained, at cost, through the author, at least until the assembly becomes available commercially. An alternative to the headplug assembly is to use Amphenol connector strips, which come in a 6-mm width (Amphenol No. 221–2253) and a 12-mm width

(Amphenol No. 221–2153). The former can be used as a headplug into which the male electrode pins are inserted; it is then cemented to the skull. The latter can be used as the connector plug into which the female pins are inserted after being connected to the stimulator or recording amplifier. This assembly can, however, easily become disengaged, and in the case of electrophysiological recording, does not provide as noise-free a connection as does the Molino and McIntyre (1972) assembly.

Complete bipolar and tripolar electrodes with a headplug assembly attached are available commercially (Plastic Products Company). One can also obtain cables, connecting plugs, dustcovers and cranioplastic cement. These assemblies are quite expensive but might be suitable in certain instances. Those interested should request circulars 3303–1 and 3304–1 from the company for details of construction and cost.

Appendix B–13

Faraday Cage

The cage shown in Figure B–8 is roughly 2 ft by 1 ft by 1 ft, a size that is quite adequate for Laboratory Exercises VIII and IX and independent project E. It is made from fine copper mesh and a metal frame, but there is no reason it could not be made from a much coarser mesh and a wooden frame. Note that

if a wooden frame is used, any nails or screws holding it together must be either entirely outside the mesh screen or electrically connected to it. If they project inside the screen and are not grounded, they will act as antennae and bring 60 Hz interference into the cage, which of course defeats the purpose of the

Figure B–8. A shielded cage for electrophysiological recording.

cage. Be sure that the mesh on all surfaces of the cage (including the door) is connected together electrically. Soldering a banana jack to the screen allows the cage to be conveniently connected to the recording equipment group via a wire with banana plugs.

Appendix B–14

Electrode Holders

Figure B–9 shows, at the right, the type of electrode holder that fits a Prior micromanipulator. The double electrode holder, shown at the left, is very useful in Laboratory Exercise IX, when two silver ball electrodes must rest on the cortical surface. It can be made inexpensively by a machine shop, the body of the holder being metal and the two electrode holders being held in place with nylon bushings to keep them electrically insulated. If construction facilities are not available, a simple double electrode holder can be improvised by taping the silver ball electrodes to a wooden applicator stick; the stick can be held in the micromanipulator. Just be sure that the electrodes are not touching one another.

Appendix B–15

Silver Ball Electrodes

Silver ball electrodes, as shown in Figure B–10, are best made with 28-gauge pure silver wire. When the tip of silver wire is heated, it forms a small ball that should be about ½ mm in diameter. A 2- to 3-cm length of the silver wire with the ball on one end is then soldered to a length of copper wire by which the electrode is held and to which alligator clips are connected for recording.

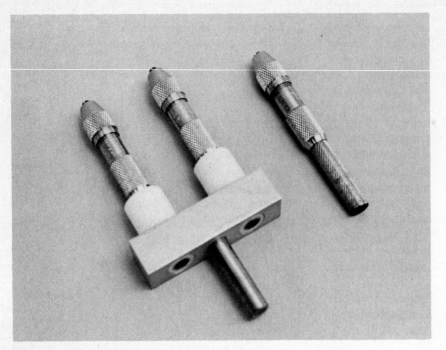

Figure B–9. A double electrode holder and a single electrode holder.

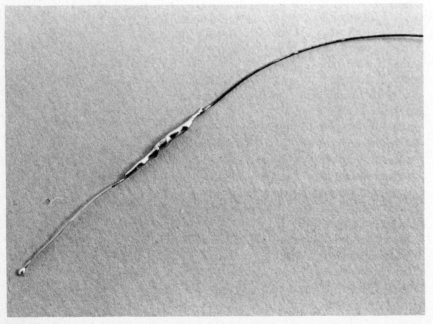

Figure B–10. A silver ball electrode soldered to a copper lead wire.

Appendix B–16

Multiunit Recording Electrodes

These can be made using the same size 4 stainless steel insect pins described in Appendix B–5 for the fabrication of electrodes for subcortical lesions. After being well cleaned, each can be held near the head in the jaws of an alligator clip and dipped into a bottle of Insl-X insulation (Insl-X Products Corp.). Each should be individually drawn from the Insl-X very slowly and at a constant rate and then just left to dry for 24 hours with the tips pointing up. In contrast to the lesion electrodes insulated with Epoxylite, no insulation need or should be scraped from the tips before using.

Appendix B–17

Solutions

0.9% Saline

Mix 9 g of NaCl (Fisher, Cat. No. S–270, approx. $5.50/5 lb) per liter of HOH. For each gallon, add 34 g of NaCl to 1 gal of HOH.

10% Formalin

For each gallon of solution, add 380 ml of formaldehyde (Fisher, Cat. No. F–78, approx. $9/gal) to either 3400 ml of saline or 3400 ml of HOH and 31 g of NaCl.

25% Potassium Chloride

To make 10 cc, sufficient for many groups of students in Laboratory Exercise IX, add 2.5 g of KCl (Fisher, Cat. No. P–215, approx. $2.50/lb) to 10 ml of HOH.

2% Ferric Chloride

Add 20 g of $FeCl_2$ (Fisher, Cat. No. I–88, approx. $4/lb) to 1 liter of HOH. This is enough for six groups of students to do Laboratory Exercise II.

1% Potassium Ferrocyanide

Add 10 g of $K_4Fe(CN)_6$ (Fisher, Cat. No. P–236, approx. $4.50/lb) to 1 liter of HOH. This is enough for six groups of students in Laboratory Exercise II.

Phenol and Copper Sulfate

Add 50 g of C_6H_5OH (Fisher, Cat. No. A–92, approx. $5.50/lb), 5 g of $CuSO_4$ (Fisher, Cat. No. C–489, approx. $3/lb), and 1.25 ml of concentrated HCl (Fisher, Cat. No. So–A–49, approx. $4/bottle) to 1 liter of HOH. This is sufficient for eight groups of students in Laboratory Exercise II.

indexes

INDEX OF NAMES

Page numbers in *italic type* refer to references.

SUBJECT INDEX

75 76 77 9 8 7 6 5 4 3 2 1